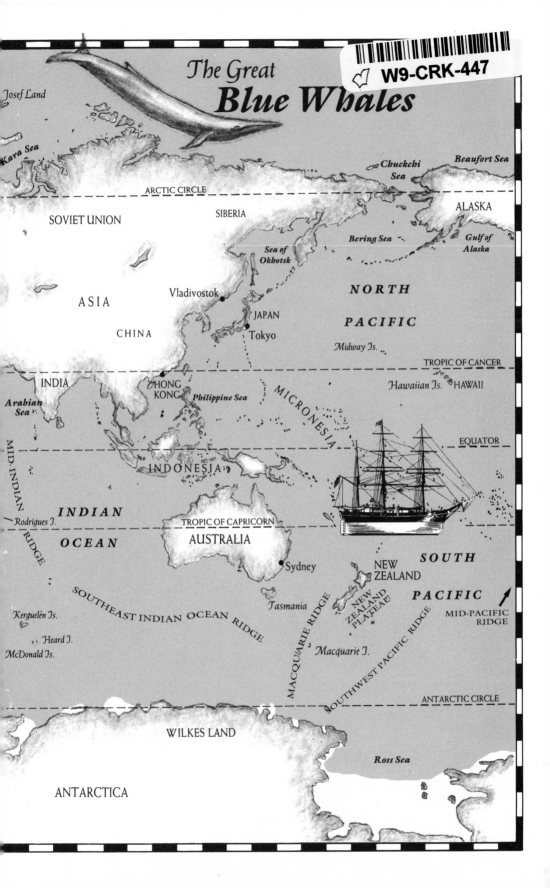

THE LAST
WHALES

THE LAST
WHALES

Lloyd Abbey

GROVE WEIDENFELD
New York

Published by Grove Weidenfeld
A division of Wheatland Corporation
841 Broadway
New York, NY 10003

Library of Congress Cataloging-in-Publication Data
Abbey, Lloyd Robert, 1943–
The last whales / Lloyd Abbey. — 1st ed.
          p.   cm.
ISBN 0-8021-1100-9 (alk. paper)
1. Whales—Fiction.   I. Title.
PR9199.3.A15L37   1990
813'.54—dc20   89-35520
                                                     CIP

Manufactured in the United States of America

Printed on acid-free paper

Designed by Sue Rose

Map by Arnold Bombay

First Edition 1989

1   3   5   7   9   10   8   6   4   2

ACKNOWLEDGMENTS

WHILE researching and writing *The Last Whales*, I consulted a very large number of sources. Many of these were technical, and I am indebted to experts who clarified concepts I couldn't grasp on my own. Among the authorities who put up with my questions were Stefani Hewlett of the Vancouver Aquarium, Michael Bigg of the Pacific Biological Station in Nanaimo, B.C., and Dale Rice of the U.S. Fisheries Service in Seattle. These three acknowledgments give no sense at all of the vast amount of help I received from scientists, field researchers, and librarians.

I am indebted also to Nancy Colbert, the literary agent whose hard work found a home for my manuscript, and to Walter Bode, my editor at Grove Weidenfeld, whose insights enabled me to make enormous improvements in the book.

The Last Whales is dedicated to the memory of my wife, Eleanor Isherwood, who helped to finance and research it and would have taken more joy in its publication than in any of her own private achievements.

The moot point is, whether Leviathan can long endure so wide a chase, so remorseless a havoc; whether he must not at last be exterminated from the waters, and the last whale, like the last man, smoke his last pipe, and then himself evaporate in the final puff.

—Herman Melville, *Moby-Dick: or the Whale*

THE LAST
WHALES

CHAPTER

1

F IVE hundred miles to the west was Rio de Janeiro and five thousand feet down was the towering Trinidad Rise. All day the Blue Whale had been swimming south for her summer home in the Antarctic. Now, well past midnight, she was tired after almost eighteen hours of nonstop flight.

September was late in the year for a rorqual to be at latitude twenty. Others already had crossed the polar front, three thousand miles south, into summer pastures where crustaceans swarmed so fat and thick they stained the water red between the ice floes. Already some factory ships were there, awaiting the start of the hunting season, awaiting the whale.

This Blue was eighty-four feet long and weighed a hundred and thirty tons, average size for the largest creature ever to have lived. When she opened her mouth to feed, the seven hundred baleen slats that extended from her upper jaw made a sieve the size of a tennis net, and when she stretched her jaws wide a diplodocus, the largest of dinosaurs, could have walked into her mouth.

Nevertheless, her hill of flesh showed evidence of shrinking. She was growing sharp and angular as her blubber thinned. Hunger was driving her south, but not just hunger. As with the Wilson's petrel and Arctic tern that were migrating far south, the hormones in her blood responded to the sun and she was lured by the lengthening daylight. But, unlike the birds', her migration was no blind drive for the pole. The slaughters she had seen in the Antarctic were vivid in her mind. Repeatedly they made her pause.

Loneliness ate her. Blue Whales mate in temperate or tropical seas, but this year she had seen no other Blues. She'd first felt the sun's pull in July, near the equator. The urge to move south had strengthened over the weeks, but, yearning to mate, she had yielded only gradually, swimming southwest instead of south to lengthen her time in warm water. Now, with the mating time for southern Blues past, unfulfilled desire kept the cow at mid-latitude.

She hung in the sea with one eye closed, wearily sculling. The full moon spread a highway clear to Trinidad, and overhead hung the domed ocean of stars. When her open eye rose clear, she saw the ghostly lights of surface plankton flicker on the sea. Not since April had she fed, though there was nourishment all around her. The surface swarmed with drift creatures—copepods, ctenophores, gastropods, larval shrimp—who hovered beneath the light by day and nightly rose for food. They had been feeding since dusk on the plants and each other. Now they formed pale clouds of protein for small fish, which in turn attracted larger feeders. Up to three feet long, voracious Spanish mackerel were hunting sardines that wheeled at the surface as they fled, flashing their six-inch sides under the moon. The turbulence created when the schools made sudden turns reached the Blue Whale's ears as dull, low-frequency thuds.

The sounds of hunting and feeding heightened her hunger. Her three stomachs, crammed with krill in previous Septembers, coiled on each other, aching. Submerging, she dreamed of Antarctic krill rising from their winter depths, lured by the plankton blooms and perpetual sun.

4

Slightly more than two inches long, they hung at an angle, heads to the surface, their constantly whirring legs making currents that carried one-celled plants into their mouths. Nervous, black-eyed, shrimplike creatures, they concentrated in swarms a thousand feet wide and many fathoms deep, and in her dream she was eating them, cutting a clean wide wake through their lawns of crackling meat. Feeding in the Antarctic, she would open her mouth till the force of the incoming water swelled the throat-pouch which ran from her lower jaw almost to her navel. At rest the pouch clung tightly against her body in a series of pleats but, when expanded, it became a giant sack, an extension of her mouth that let her ingest a hundred pounds of food at a single gulp. When totally full, the pouch held six thousand cubic feet of food, and at the height of Antarctic summer, it stretched to its maximum size each time the whale engulfed a mass of krill. Once the krill were inside, she would tighten her throat-pouch so that the water went shooting out through her baleen, leaving the krill trapped on the bristly inner edges of the baleen plates.

She touched the bristles now with her tongue, for the hunger was hurting again. Forgetting where she was, she made a feeding run on her side, her wide-spread jaws taking plankton and water together. Her pouch ballooned. She tightened it so that the water shot back out through the baleen, whirlpooling, swirling like a tide race under the moon. Her tongue moved the animals trapped inside her baleen back to her gullet, but there were very few.

This insipid spoonful did little to fill her shrunken stomachs, but she did not take any more. Her bristles, fine as they were, were too coarse to contain most of these tiny creatures, many less than a quarter inch in length, and those that hadn't escaped through her baleen felt like sand grains against her palate. A Right Whale, with its close-threaded fringe, could have feasted on this plankton, but the Blue's coarser hairs were adapted for midsize crustaceans. A Fin Whale or a Sei Whale might have feasted on the larger creatures, the shrimp and fish that shoaled about her eyes, but evolution had dangerously specialized the cow's species. Over eons the Blue Whales' blubber had grown so thick that they no longer needed to graze outside their Antarctic home, and now the southern Blues ate only euphausia superba, Antarctic krill. The habit became so strongly ingrained that it seemed encoded in their genes, and the Antarctic whaler had made their preference into their doom. The tired whale, still dreaming of food about nine feet down, turned her left eye up to the light.

Calmly she rose to breathe. First her upper jaw arched into light and disappeared, then came the long curve of her back. Four times she arched and spouted, exhaling four pear-shaped ghosts of spray, the first nine yards high, the next three successively lower. The escaping air made a *whoosh* that carried far across the ocean. Her diminutive dorsal fin appeared, then a hint of flukes as she went down.

She was well east of the continental shelf, though at five thousand feet this sea over the Trinidad Rise was shallow. A hundred yards east the flat bottom descended nonstop ten thousand feet to the ocean floor. She listened. Here at the rise's edge the ocean vibrations deflected up the underwater slope so that the pencil-point openings of her ears gathered in a cacophony of shipsound. Occasionally, from the din of traffic surrounding her, the whale picked out propeller sounds that called to mind the factory ships of the south. Always the sounds gave her pause, calling to mind the Antarctic slaughter. When she'd swum north of Ascension Island in July, the noise of passing ships had been explosive and almost unbroken. Here there were partial respites, but even in quiet times she heard the frightening clang and concussion of the enormous commercial vessels travelling to Rio or, to the south, entering the mouth of the River Plate. Though the vibrations might have deafened a man, her ears were no hollow canals of air; their channels threaded a strand of wire into her ligamentous eardrums, weakening volume while accommodating sounds above and below human hearing. The whale could send out signals at two hundred decibels without danger and simultaneously receive similar pulses. Her call was pitched deeper than an earthquake, and it raced for hundreds of miles through the sea, at five times the speed of sound above water. Too low for man, such sounds passed back and forth among the whales like underground radar, evading his iron wall of shipsound. She was always on the alert for calls, but now her ears picked up only the thunder of ships.

Lazing under the ocean, she had two sides, like the moon. A gray-blue mottle above and white-mottled gray below, she showed her deep-ocean colors to air and her daylight colors to ocean. This camouflage, with her speed and sensitive ears, helped to keep her safe, but she had to come up for breath and, when she exhaled, she raised a loud, thirty-foot signpost of gleaming spray. And in the summers she had to go south for krill.

6

Always she heard the ships. Even now there were diesel screws propelling seiners into nighttime coves beyond the western horizon, droning the same expressionless drone as the screws on the bottom trawlers. The sound of ships was disturbing, but in the seven years of her life she had never found an escape from it; it never stopped, only changed. The thunder of passenger ships gave way to the drone of seiners and trawlers; these to the steadier drone of the catchers. For those who survived, the catcher drone gave way to the thudding pulse of the cargo ships; these to the hum of the submarine, the roar and smell of the tankers, the rumble of speeding cruisers, or the subterranean tremor of the gigantic carriers launching their missiles and planes. At the moment of her birth two hundred miles off the equatorial coast of Africa, passing cruisers had been the first sound she had heard outside the womb. Not until later had she realized a whale's voice was louder and, without interference, would carry for hundreds of miles.

The noise of ships masked innumerable voices, but the whale had grown skillful at unravelling the murmurs of life under the assault of maritime traffic. Listening earlier, she had detected the desperate hiss and splash of young striped mullet fleeing bluefish down the coast, but they had grown quiet since the sunset, and what remained was almost as low pitched as the boats: the powerful, wide-spaced RRROOOPs of a croaker vibrating its air bladder and, farther east, the grunts of the open-sea myctophid fishes, lanternfishes mostly, all shorter than six inches, the teeming fodder that rose with night to the upper three hundred feet.

The sound she strained for was lower than all these, a diminished explosion too low for man's ears, though not unlike a cruiser motor's rumble. It spoke no language. Only low-frequency sound travels any length in the sea, and low-frequency sound carries little information. The best the big whales can do is to signal, "Here I am." In this first year of her sexual maturity the female yearned for a bull whale's signal. She hovered in her loneliness, her calls echoing out through the nighttime sea.

Stalled by her yearning for a mate, she spent the next two days exploring, swimming in restless circles. Ships passed constantly within sight. The sky stayed clear.

7

A third night passed. She listened, sculling lightly in her half-sleep, automatically stroking her tail, at the edge of oblivion. The sound of seiners receded, and the copepods and larvae covering the surface settled two hundred feet into the sea as the moon went down.

Toward dawn something awakened her. Under a rumble of shipsound and croaking fish she detected a sound so low that she felt it as much as heard it, as if a subterranean tremor had made the Trinidad Rise vibrate like a tuning fork. By the sound's power and frequency she could tell, even asleep, that it was the voice of a large rorqual, either a Fin or a Blue Whale. If she could hear the sound again, the time lapse would give her some sense of the whale's distance, but there was no second call from the open sea. Three freighters were booming their engines toward the east, and when they faded, the sound of the whale had faded with them.

She turned in the water, wondering, envisioning to herself the whale who had called. To answer, she contracted the muscular walls of the air sacs that catacombed her head between blowhole and bone. The air moving through them and through her larynx made a seismic low-frequency moan that shattered the calm. She paused as her answering signal moved away in two-hundred-and-fifty-foot waves that would reach sea bottom and bounce from floor to surface for hundreds of miles. She made a second explosion, then listened for a reply, but there was nothing. Distant shipsound was muffling her thunder, and she guessed that the whale had signalled from too far away to hear her at once.

She spouted and dove, leaving the rise behind, feeling again the intense passion that had kept her in the warm northern seas long after the time of mating was past and the other rorquals had undertaken the voyage to their perilous home. Her migration thus far had been hesitant and uncertain, her mind an arena where her hunger held alternate sway with her desire and her memory of the catchers, one driving her south all day at ten to fifteen knots, the others holding her back in dreams of a mate and fear of the slaughter to come. This sound made her suspect a male was finally answering her calls. Casting aside the instinctive urge to travel south and the insistent appeal of her hunger, stronger now than ever before, she defiantly changed direction, racing northeast, full speed, straining her ears for him. She felt nine weeks of tension leave her mind with the break of dawn. Yet, even as she spouted at the rise's outer rim, she could feel rolling waves from far-off storms race for the shore. They seemed to admonish her to remain here in safety.

CHAPTER

2

THE largest Blue Whale in the
northern hemisphere summered off Greenland and wintered off northern Africa. Northern hemisphere Blues were generally smaller than
those in the south, but this one measured a hundred feet from the tip of
his snout to the notch between his tailfins. His great size set him apart
from everything else that swam. Even before hunting, hundred-foot
Blues had been rare in the north, and when they occurred, such giants
were female, since cows, who carry and suckle young, require greater
blubber stores and larger abdominal cavities than their mates. The
hundred-foot Blue Whale bull was a prodigy.

It was the forty-second year in the life of the giant bull, and now, in
August, he was just beginning his southward migration from Green-

land's Cape Farewell down to the Mid-Atlantic Ridge. Long ago he and his mate had always travelled in sight of each other, or at least within an hour's swimming range, but those days were gone. Now they began their migrations at different times. This year she had preceded him by a week in late July, eager to get their sickly calf into tropical waters where it wouldn't shake from the cold.

Had it not been for the calf, she would have travelled beside her mate for the first time in years. She worried about him. For more than a month he'd been wracked with pain, though she could see no wounds on his skin. He had no way of pointing out the area of his body where the pain would come and go. In the weeks before turning south, the cow had repeatedly run her snout and her pectoral fins down the length of his back. Each time she'd reached the dorsal fin the bull had moaned, letting her know where he hurt. She had stroked him there with her pectoral fins until the increasing strength of the attacks told her that stroking was useless. At last the shivering of the calf had turned her south.

The days passed, but the bull made no move to join her, instead lingering behind to recuperate. At first he had no way of knowing what caused his pain, only that it was growing worse. Then, a few days after his mate had left, he saw parasitic worms writhe in the water where he'd urinated. Inside him, the bunching worms squeezed his urethra so hard that it hurt him to urinate, but, after an agonizing movement that left yards of living tubing in the water, the pain let up, and by the time the attack was over, he was feasting again on crustaceans. He surmised that the worms had caused the pain and that he was rid of them, yet still he delayed his journey. He lazed. Why hurry to catch up with his mate? He had lived through many births and many migrations in his forty-one years, and the northern summer was too pleasant for quick departures. The brilliant sun illuminated rafts of thysanoessa, fat, succulent crustaceans an inch long that blanketed the sea. He gorged until he floated, sharing his larder with harp and hooded seals from the late summer communes on the ice floes. Icebergs floated down from the north, miniature continents that for a while blocked out the tiring barrage of shipsound. Alone in the cold sea, he was at peace.

Nor was he truly alone: his mate sent signals to him as she journeyed south. Her ten-to-twenty-hertz soundwaves were omnidirectional: some were reflected between ocean surface and ocean floor; the rest were refracted at the depth of greatest resistance, usually the top of the coldest water layer, and were less attenuated by distance than the reflections. The sound rose to the top when it struck Cape Farewell. The bull stayed near it to hear her steady signals. In the first days after she left they came to him loud and close together, and he felt no need to follow immediately. Then there were days when he heard only waves and wind, and he began to grow restless. Low-frequency sounds from ships grew very loud, and he waited impatiently for the static to clear. Her voice always returned, but after a week, it was faint. Quite suddenly he felt that the brief Arctic night had grown long, and that the ivory gulls who ornamented the bays were flying in larger flocks for the open sea. He found himself edging south under a constant overhead thunder of wind and waves. From Greenland fjords black-and-white barnacle geese, barking like little dogs, flew off in smoky lines, southeast for Scotland. He continued south, and soon the Manhattans of ice were behind, with only occasional bergs straggling by, pillared now like cathedrals against the sun. Off Cape Farewell the North Atlantic Drift flowed southwest, but when he swam seventy miles to sea he entered the main arm of the current, which flowed north. With the coast behind he swam lower down, intermittently picking up his mate's signals two hundred to three hundred feet from the top. Once more something was wrong inside him. The pressure of urine would build for days until at last he began to grow fearful of his own body. Normally he urinated almost constantly, and the blockage brought him terrible pain. His peace of mind was gone. When he rose from the depths to breathe, the glorious blaze of the sun on the waves was black with torment.

The worms were increasing inside him. They moved their sucker mouths where his kidneys hung in clusters like bunches of grapes, the drainage tubes forming a funnel of widening slipways into his bladder. His heart was the size of a taxi, his clusters of kidneys larger. Each worm lodged its head in the soft calyx of a kidney and trailed its long tail through the drainage ducts into bladder and urethra, blocking his urine.

Rattled, the whale speeded up. Three days of nonstop travel took him south of the Gibbs Fracture Zone, a stretch of deep sea between the Mid-Atlantic Ridge and Reykjanes Ridge, which runs southwest from Iceland. After another two days of flight he was a thousand miles east of Newfoundland amid fog and storm, but here he heard his mate again.

11

At fifteen hertz her signal was easily distinguished from the higher sounds of the twenty-three-knot wind and the thundering waves, and its loudness told the bull he was gaining on her. He swam for two more days. Her pulse came loud in the mornings, continuous and clear, but on the second afternoon she passed over the Mid-Atlantic Ridge, the undersea mountain chain that runs roughly from the latitude of Labrador to that of Palmer Peninsula in the Antarctic. She had put six hundred miles between them, and in the gigantic Canaries Basin west of Morocco her sound, at first muffled by mountains and ships, disappeared altogether.

Alarmed by the total silence, he pursued in earnest at fifteen knots, swimming nonstop for ninety hours till he passed over the ridge about forty miles west of Faial in the Azores. When he heard her signals again he slowed down, feeling secure. Five more days of travel took him five hundred miles south, where rough bottom gave way to the plain at the northern rim of the Cape Verde Basin. Her voice began to grow louder, and by the time he reached the Tropic of Cancer she seemed to have stopped to wait for him. Great jets of breath in his larynx boomed his joy, and she called loudly for him to come. Worms continued to cause pain in his dorsal region, and he felt a second pain, farther up in his abdomen. He had felt it for some time, but now suddenly it became too strong to ignore. Days went by and again he neglected to join her, instead beginning to slow, then circling directionless in the quiet sea. He feared he would never be rid of the worms.

They'd invaded him long ago east of the Grand Banks where, succumbing to whim, he had swallowed a raft of nekton, most of it dead. Parasitic roundworms had inched their tubular bodies into his blood. Those in his abdomen had grown huge. The worms in his kidney—in the thousands of tiny kidneys that formed the organ—were nematodes, parasites that could either destroy him or hardly hurt him, depending on how many kidneys they touched before he expelled them or before their cycle was done. A heavy infestation could be lethal, a light one inconsequential. But smaller nematodes, lodged originally in tiny marine crustaceans he'd eaten, had entered him too. These mated and spawned in his intestines, and their larvae passed through his whole thoracic system before encysting themselves in his muscles. Free in his system, these nearly microscopic trichinella had caused the whale excruciating pain in the nostrils and the eyes. Now, with the worms in his muscles, his blood pressure fell and he suffered violent nervous disorders and problems of balance. And, like all whales, the Blue had ingested industrial poison; from time to time heavy-metal contamination unbalanced his mind.

Utterly helpless to stop the pain from the worms inside him, he thrashed and groaned as if impaled on a harpoon, then dove through the twilight region into the dark. Squid fled in all directions, showing mock-intelligent eyes behind their bundles of arms, then ink blots as their heads entered the black. His pain monstrously magnified the squid, and when one slithered across his eye, he bolted in panic. When the stinging started to fade, relief overpowered him, and for the first time in his life he even took delight in the hum of screws slicing the water. He surfaced, exhaling geysers, and his whistles resounded a mile, as if expelling all the devils that lived in his body.

He could no longer hear the signals of his mate. In his panic he had forgotten the point of his journey, and he forgot it again as the pain strengthened. Only with night did it fully stop. It left an afterglow in his stomachs, a hesitant thrill, always ready to stab again, but his mind turned anxiously back to his mate. He listened at different depths, but though there was nothing to block out her voice, all he could hear were the incessant, droning ships.

Days passed. Her signal didn't return but the pain did, and his regret that he had not pushed himself to rejoin her when he could was as strong as the pain. The sea seemed empty here, eight hundred miles off Mauritania just below the Tropic of Cancer. Tension and frustration filled the bull.

With dawn he awoke to a gale from the north, and for three days he followed the storm as it moved south-southeast across the Cape Verde Basin. The bull spent much of the second day beneath the boil of the waves, worrying. The cysts around the trichinella worms in his muscles began to calcify and his pain faded again, leaving him free to fear for his mate and youngster.

On the third morning, the gale still strong, the kidney pain came back, and at first he tried to ignore it, surfing the sky-high waves, his slim flukes synchronizing the actions of paddle and propeller, easing him in and out of the troughs and crests. Still, no matter how hard he tried, he could not shut out the pain in his back. Toward noon of the third day, when the storm broke up in a ten-mile rain, he began to choke, inexplicably losing the power to time his breath to the roll of the waves. The mercury and the worms were affecting his balance. He found himself swimming awkwardly—head down, head up—only the drag of the water telling him he was no longer horizontal. Repeatedly he sucked water into his lungs. It took much painful spouting to clear his head, and the time between breaths grew long. By midafternoon, when the gale had shattered to far-flung patches of cloud, the whale was no longer travelling. At sixteen degrees north, he was slightly west of St. Vincent in the Cape Verdes off Senegal. At half-hour intervals he rose to spout and inhale, the rest of the time hanging exhausted fifty fathoms down.

The back pain was coming in spasms roughly twenty minutes apart. It was unbearable, and after his third descent, the whale lost consciousness. Normally he had to stroke his flukes to stay buoyant, but his blubber was especially thick from feeding, and he neither rose nor sank when he hung still. Even so the blackout was dangerous, since he had to be conscious in order to rise and breathe. For half an hour he hung dazed. Eyes tightly closed, he made little clicks of recognition as images lit the insides of his lids. In his mind, he was eight months old again.

He was with his parents off eastern Newfoundland, barely weaned. It was spring, and day after day in March and April the tuglike catchers hauled the blown-up bodies of Fins into Trinity Bay. The dead whales made him anxious, but despite the horror of the sight—tuxedo bellies and the sickly, wavering grins—he didn't feel danger. He was young and strong, and aside from his instinctive fear of Orcas, the scavenging Killer Whales, he only marvelled when the mysterious dead went by. For millions of years his race had lived as lords of the sea. Only his parents or experience could teach him to fear men, and it never occurred to his parents to seek out safer seas, though they would swim away if ships approached them directly. Thousands of years had taught them the sanctity of their routine: crustaceans in summer over the Banks, crustaceans in winter off Cape Cod, where in September the calf had been born. To change their migration was as unthinkable as to change their pattern of feeding. They were raising their young near Trinity Bay where, over the years, they had heard the factory grow up: first merely a stranding site, then a gauntlet for Pilot Whales, then a full-fledged plant with two small catcher boats of its own. Humpbacks and Fins and Blues came in now. And the Pilots continued to strand.

Far from fearing men, the calf was curious about them. Each day little skiffs of seventeen feet putted their way to the outer bay in the predawn stillness, appearing just as the scattering layer went down. While his parents drowsed and nuzzled over the Banks, he would follow boats until he saw the dark seines spread down through the water and heard the grunts and heaves of the men working the nets. The muscles around his eyes enabled him to alter focus for accurate vision both above and below water, and like most cetaceans, he saw colors well. As he looked upward through the sea, the men puffed pipes and furrowed their brows. They fascinated him: the two-pronged walk, the shifting for balance, the smoking protuberances in their mouths, were amazing things. He knew from watching that the dangling nets were meant for catching fish.

Men learned of him only gradually. Timid at first, he merely passed beneath their boats and rumbled his eighty-decibel call, a subsonic quaking that made the fishermen grasp their seats and tremble. Soon they were fishing in different areas of the bay to avoid his thunder, but always he followed, finding them easily by the irregular sounds of their motors, flimsy compared with those of the whale ships. The first time he rose and showed himself, fifty-four feet long, they laughed, trying to hide their fear from one another. One ebullient younger man tried to feed him fish, but he showed no interest.

Since the Blue, unlike the Humpbacks, never blundered into the nets of the fishermen, they tolerated and even enjoyed him. His habit of surfacing in sight of their ships and dories made him well known. Soon passenger ships headed for the harbor circled to look for him. His parents began to grow nervous. The mother butted him and clicked in deep apprehension when she learned what he had been doing, and led the whole family farther offshore. But, after a month or so, when his parents were lost in their feeding, he slipped away and found the boats again.

The water had warmed in his absence. Short-finned squid were everywhere, so thick that they shut out the light. From shore to shore the Pilot Whales, twenty feet long, were in full chase, gobbling the squid. Blunt-headed animals, skinny, intelligent, and high-strung, they hunted in Vs with forty or fifty whales to a line. When they flashed by, passing over him and under him and around him as if he were no more

15

than a land rise or a dead tree, he caught their keen excitement—and their lust, their tribal abandon. These whales were plainly enjoying this close-order chase; each had a role in the herding and killing. The bull was restless and envious as he watched them. He envisioned the easy, luxurious feeding of the baleen whales. Their krill lay immobile at the surface; when they grazed, there was no herding, no tribal chase. Young and impressionable and well fed, he joined impetuously at the rear of the hunting whales and swam as fast as he could, but he was more than twice as long and ten times heavier than the largest Pilot Whale. He fell behind.

Then, to his rear, he became aware of the little skiffs he had be-friended. Their motors at full roar, they were chugging after the Pilot Whales and the squid. It seemed a wonderful game at first, a change from the uneventful feeding out at sea. But soon he heard a clattering sound, a beating of sticks and pans. The men were shouting. There were gunshots from time to time. Though he felt no fear, he was confused. When he looked past the skiffs he could see catcher boats, and beneath the din of the hunters, the twelve-hertz sound of fleeing Blue Whales reached his ears. His low-level sonar detected a rise in the rocky bottom. He stopped himself and dove to turn back, suddenly terrified of stranding. His bones could support his weight in the water but not on the land where, before starvation, dryness and overheating would end his life. One skiff raced by on either side, men hooting and banging pans. The tide was low. Suddenly shoals rose out of nowhere and he was skidding his smooth gray belly over the rock. He thrashed and turned, trying to get back into deep water. Just as he did he glimpsed a catcher boat and a breaching Blue Whale at the mouth of the bay. More boats drove by. Struggling and thrashing, he saw the beachhead out of one eye. Terrified squid were rocketing tailfirst onto rock. Once into the shoreline shallows, their blind desperation drove them higher, their jets hosing them farther and farther from sea. The blood-crazed Pilot Whales could quite easily have turned back, but they leapt into the shallows after the squid, the leaders first, at the tips of the Vs. Once these were stranded the other whales, forgetting the hunt, remained out of loyalty at the rock edge, some actually plunging ashore to help. Soon nearly a hundred of them were stranded in the heat. Propped like a statue on his offshore shoal, the bull whale paused in his struggle. He wondered helplessly as the fishing boats closed in. There were men

16

already on the rocks and others tumbled ashore with knives and short-handled hatchets. As the Pilot Whales squealed, the men bellowed, hacking and stabbing down the entire length of the beach. They cut their initials into the dead. The waves ran blood. Trapped in the sun, the handful of whales who remained alive panted and whistled, gasping white fire into their heads while out of each eye they saw the long knives peeling the blubber off their mates. The bull whale was transfixed.

When the slaughter was over, the fishermen turned back to sea. Though the water was rising, the whale was still not free of the shoal. He stared as the fishermen putted by. It would have cost the men many bullets and much spearing to kill the whale, so they merely circled a couple of times, puffing their pipes and scratching their heads. One called out to the whale incomprehensibly. Finally they left him for the hunters from the factory.

The hunters never arrived, having already taken many whales off-shore. After a time the tide came strong and lifted him free. The twilight fell. As he raced for the ocean, he paid no heed to the homing catchers with their strings of bloated whales bobbing behind. Past the rocky gates of Trinity Bay, he called and circled, without reply. Usually his parents answered his calls within minutes. The slaughter he had glimpsed at the mouth of the bay came back to him, and the strings of dead whales behind the catchers rose again behind his eyes. He filled with fear. Calling more loudly, he swam farther and farther offshore, going faster the longer he called, until by midnight he was over the middle of the Grand Banks. He sent his shattering twelve-hertz signals out to the open sea. As he listened to the sounds of fish and wind and the distant ocean traffic, he dwelt on the Blue Whale and the catcher he had barely glimpsed earlier in the day and thought of the Blue Whale calls he'd heard just before stranding. At the time he'd been too confused to comprehend their meaning. Now it was clear. His parents had come in pursuit of him, too late, but in time for the catchers.

That night the calf was lonely for the first time. Not since his birth off Cape Cod had he so sensed the vastness, the terrible emptiness of the sea. With his parents gone, he grieved, and as he grieved he reflected on himself and the pain of separation. Many Blue Whale calves were orphaned in the hunt. Those orphaned before weaning starved to death, while older ones had usually spent enough time with their parents to have the ways of their kind imprinted on their minds. The

17

bull was less than a month past weaning, and there was no companion to guide him as there might have been in the years before the hunt. Other Blue Whales lived off Newfoundland but they were scattered, their numbers sharply in decline, and they communicated only during migration when they travelled in far-flung schools. The young bull was defiant and curious by nature.

The burden of bereavement was unbearable isolation, an isolation that brought freedom from customary constraints. He watched the stars. In loneliness he followed them north, seeking the place where they seemed to touch the rim of the sea. After a month or so Newfoundland was well behind, and he was butting his way northeast through the Labrador Current. By late July he was east of Greenland, where he passed the summer in safety.

With fall he swam back south, eager for company, but off Newfoundland the passivity of the Blues and Humpbacks sickened him. They made no effort at all to change their migration route, even though their stubborn consistency only sacrificed them to the waiting men. Angrily he turned east. His rage and frustration were so great that, with his exceptional strength, he swam much farther south than instinct demanded. He was flying away from his past, his kind, as much as after the sun. Instead of wintering in temperate seas, he let his frustration and rage propel him south all the way to the latitude of Guinea. This was extremely unusual for a Blue from northern seas; in fact no other had swum so far, but the bull was driven by feelings stronger than instinct.

After a lonely, restless winter west of Guinea above the Sierra Leone Rise, he started north. Loneliness ate him. His self-consciousness isolated him from the things he heard and saw, and he despaired. He was almost ready to beach himself when, to his delight, he encountered a far-flung herd of eastern Blues who summered off Iceland. He called to them and followed.

The "herd"—a crooked nine-hundred-mile chain of solitaries and pairs—kept up a network of calls. To track the whales through their whole range would have taken a fleet, and they were so strong that even the Orcas took only the frail and infirm. Only the krill grounds gave them away. Already the hunters in the north were sharpening their knives, checking their guns, watching and waiting.

The bull whale never bothered to change his speed, to come within touching range of the others. The exchange of signals was enough. They flew north at a steady thirteen knots, and by early April he and the four whales closest to him were fifteen hundred miles east of the Grand Banks with the great ridge towering below. A few miles north they could hear other members of the herd call repeatedly without changing their position. They speeded up in pursuit.

As the bull swam north he kept on entering clouds of one-celled plants that browned the ocean. When he stopped nosing through the plants and entered an acre of euphausiids, he saw pear-shaped spouts of spray rise up on every horizon and, under the water, heard the feasting sounds: slicings, grunts, and gulps, as the jaws and throats crisscrossed the plankton, hoarding it in.

He lost himself. Not until now had he realized how much his stomachs had shrunken over the winter. A year old, he was young enough that the filtering bristles of his baleen had not yet obscured the sensitive areas of his mouth. His three-ton tongue was anchored too tightly to be of much use in cracking shells, but, with his youth, it was extremely sensitive. Though he couldn't break the hard-shelled crustaceans against his palate as he had after first being weaned, he had never eaten so many at a time, and the very feel of them pressing his tongue and the top of his mouth was an almost unbearable delight.

He found himself swimming in a trance, hardly stroking his tail except to shift ground by ten yards or so when a patch grew thin. The sense of luxury and ease never diminished and the crustaceans swarmed without end. He fed every day, eyes closed in ecstasy, always aware of the warming sun. His body had burgeoned. Before he'd swum south it had lengthened by over an inch and a half a day. During the winter fast his growth had slowed down, and now, like a tree trunk, the horny plug of his outer ear bore a thick dark ring for his summer of growth and a thinner light-colored ring for his southern winter.

After a fortnight, when the whales began swimming again and warmth spread out through the northern sea, the bull fed less frequently and listened with doubled attention. Instinct told him he had been careless, had left himself vulnerable in his delight. When he grew older and the bristles of his mouth had all filled in to lessen the pleasure of eating, he would feed with self-possession, not leaving it to the others to listen for catchers and whaling ships.

The herd swam north. They covered seven square miles of sea, a pod of a dozen following plankton blooms toward Iceland. Those who continued might go on to Jan Mayen Island or the Arctic islands beyond. As he swam, the bull could see shadows of fellow travellers on either side, and he remembered the vacant, vulnerable whales off Newfoundland. These were not frightened whales. It seemed to the bull that these Iceland whales who lived east of the guns were his proper family, and though the memory of his parents' deaths still stabbed him, he had the feeling now that all had been for the best. Even the memory of his bereavement grew tolerable.

The feeding and calling and northward flight kept up, for a day, the illusion of peace. His pod had spread out to a length of thirteen miles when the first of the cannon sounds came down to him out of the north. Before that, each whale had called at regular intervals, as predictable as a pulse. Now the rhythm of the lead whale speeded up and fluttered out like a dying heart. In an instant the rest turned back, and, as they neared, their jumbled signals were shrill and chaotic.

One after another the voices died. The bull was so startled, so dismayed to find the catchers had lain in wait that he'd hardly managed to alter course when the first of their towering foremasts cleared the horizon. It seemed huge as it drew near. He raced, uncertain if it were after him or one of the three others dodging and crossing as they retreated from its bow. The roaring catcher shifted with them, following first one whale, now another, like a lion as yet uncertain which of the antelope it will kill.

Then the puff of smoke went up, and over the chop of the sea he heard the first of the deaths: quick—merely a thrash or two. The catcher stopped to buoy it. Taking advantage of the pause, the surviving whales went bolting off to the east and west. With its catch afloat, the boat turned after the whale to the east—the older whale. The bull swam madly, drunken with joy and relief that the catcher had turned away. He raced straight west for the Labrador Basin, never pausing for rest nor breathing for more than a minute at a time, till the sound of the boat dissolved into the sea.

When it had vanished and his terror had partly subsided, he noticed the sound of the other whale who had escaped. In a matter of minutes she was beside him, sixty-eight feet long. She hovered stiff, pectorals straight out, tail treading water. She moaned to him softly. Her mother had fallen to the catcher, and just as her mother had nudged and preened her, so the bull whale preened her now.

The rest of the herd lay belly-up on the sea. It was the opening day of the hunt, and catchers from Iceland, tracking their survey plane, had gathered above the ridge. The whales they found had no chance. As the female mourned, she broke the surface with the bull swimming beneath her. A plane flew low off to the north. She caught its shadow out of the corner of her eye as she rose for air. Instantly they dove and swam forty minutes to the west, their terror returning, ears straining for the rumble of the boats. When they resurfaced, the bull was the first to break the water. He scanned the sky for a sign of the plane, then murmured lightly to the female, who came up beside him. Now, with the ocean clear again, she gave him back gratitude for compassion. The female was older than the bull, but both were yearlings. They twisted their tails around each other. His penis nudged her, and though conception was impossible, they joined, two orphans wedded by isolation. In their loss, they'd formed a bond that would endure till one or the other died.

Ice floes grew more and more frequent as they swam north. After two days they saw the cliffs of eastern Greenland break the water. Still alone, they hung in the surface waves to savor their freedom. Soon they heard catcher boats to the south. The bull whale sounded, led her north, passed Cape Farewell. After a day they were over the shelf in the Denmark Strait, off uninhabited, shipless coast.

Now it was June. Rafts of crustaceans patched the water all over the shelf, and, aside from seals and flashing herring, there were only the whales to take them. They fed to bursting, plowing the calm sea where a year before the male had swum dazed and alone.

So the summer passed, sun towering high as in the south, but here a friendly, welcoming sun. The female grieved for her dead mother, and the bull was sad at first, but after two months the scars inside him healed. He glowed inside and, for the first time since leaving Newfoundland, felt fully content.

For again all seemed to have worked out for the best, or at least as well as it could have—his parents' deaths, the deaths of the Iceland whales, his time in the southern seas. Here he was safe, it seemed, from catchers. Shipping of any kind was sparse. When they swam south past Cape Farewell or made exploratory sallies up the western coast of

21

Greenland, they saw fishing ships, and the bull remembered his time in Trinity Bay. There were settlements and plants for canning and packing, as in Newfoundland. He and the female kept to the east, but after a week when catchers came close, the two headed north along the coast. Soon icebergs grew so thick that commercial shipping of any kind was impossible. They rested well north of Angmagssalik, past sixty-five degrees. The pack ice here had only partially melted down, though it was June. Food stayed thick, and the air above them came alive with the wings of migratory birds at their summer nesting. Ivory gulls, small pretty birds, billowed and fell like summer snowstorms over the bays. The water was blue and clear and loud with sounds of shoaling fish and seals. They explored the fjords, nosing their way between the bergs in total safety. Coastline cliffs towered straight up, as sheer and high as Antarctic ice. Shipsound grew distant. It was as close as the female would come to a life without ships.

After two months they were almost tired out with feeding. They hung floating in the fjords, nudging and slapping one another. Little continents of blue, contented skin, they sent up geysers of white spray thirty feet high. It was as if two tropical islands with underground springs had somehow unanchored themselves and drifted into the ice of the northern sea.

By August the declining sun had almost left the sky. They followed it south past Cape Farewell. Again there were catchers off Newfoundland and little herds of western whales that moved their few hundred miles down the coast. He turned her east. Over the ridge they encountered whales from the Iceland waters. The pair called out. It was reassuring to be answered, to be part of a far-strung herd.

But they stayed with no group. Instead, like a pair of mated birds, they travelled privately, close together, the bull ahead most of the time. After a summer's growth the cow was almost seventy-three feet long. Like most cows, who ferry and suckle calves, she was the larger of the two.

After her winter over the northern part of the Mid-Atlantic Ridge, the cow was confused when he pressed on for the Cape Verde Basin, over three thousand miles south of Greenland, and the Sierra Leone Rise, less than five hundred miles from the equator. The bull was calm and content. As he travelled the route he had made, he felt no uncertainty, no wish to be part of one of the groups they passed. Whales on

22

their ranges appeared ahead and receded behind, short-swimming whales, cocksure of their way.

They passed many herds, but not many rorquals. When they did, he would signal the old ones with an arrogant self-possession, flying past from the distant north to the distant south, never slowing down to rest or to travel beside them. But old ones were rarer now, nearly all they encountered were young. When the sun neared its southern limit in mid-December, they were off the African coast, contentedly idling, both he and the cow completely oblivious to sounds out of the north. Like him she had grown to love the sun. His break with tradition had made him almost worship the light. As if the sun had taken the place of mother and father, he timed his flight by its changing positions in the sky. Before the solstice he allowed himself occasional sallies toward the equator but after the solstice he migrated north in a leisurely way, taking care not to let the sun fall too far behind. There were many stops along the Mid-Atlantic Ridge as the pair returned to their summer home.

When the whale awoke from his vision, the pain had become barely tolerable, just slightly below his threshold of endurance. The memories of his first year made him more eager to join his mate. He was three hundred feet from the surface, just starting to rise for breath, when two whale calls reached his ears simultaneously, both refracted from the top of the coldest water layer between three and four thousand feet down. The stronger voice was pitched below twenty hertz and the fainter voice was slightly higher. Both were attenuated by distance, over a thousand miles southeast, but their frequency showed they were Blue Whale voices, and they were coming from the region of the Sierra Leone Rise. The bull rejoiced, for there could be little doubt he was hearing his mate and calf. He answered immediately, surfaced for breath, then swam southeast at sixteen knots. He raced for the Sierra Leone Rise, constantly calling at a depth of three hundred feet. The pain intensified after an hour, but the bull tried to ignore it, to push himself on. Evening fell. He swam all night but the signals never came again.

23

CHAPTER

3

IN the southern hemisphere the Blue Whale cow dove to twenty feet and swam northeast. She was a hundred miles west of Trinidad and five hundred miles east of Brazil, leaving the undersea mountains of the Trinidad Rise. When she rose and inhaled, the young cow could feel an increasing buoyancy from beneath. The rise was just behind, and, far below, its underwater slope was cutting the ocean floor out from underneath her. Listening for whalesound, the female let herself fall toward deep water while the dawn spread a film of light over her head.

Her yearning mind spun sights of the rorqual she had heard, visions treasured from her juvenile years when sexual fantasy had filled her austral winters. Though she'd enjoyed sexual play from the beginning, it had been less than a year since her body had first triggered reproductive hormones into her blood. For her first six years she had spent the austral winters just north of the polar front. Like all whales, she had been curious and sensual. Once she had played with a five-year-old male in the storming midwinter. At five years of age, what began as exploration often ended in sexual play. She had enjoyed the nudging and calling, the slapping of flukes. She could remember his upright postures and his erections, the rush of his sperm when she'd balked at the coupling. With spring he had disappeared into the twelve-million-square-mile feeding ground around Antarctica. She never saw him again.

Before that there had been sexual play with females and with males of other species. With penis and nose replacing hands and fingers, the sensation of sex became an integral part of communication. Even at birth she had thrilled to the touch of her mother raising her into the light. In every later touch there had been something of that first gentleness, a swelling inside her stomachs that hung her pacified and still in the buoying sea.

And now, as she remembered that softness, her gray-blue skin grew sensitive. The Brazil Current, blue water that tantalized, flowed south. She gleamed. This was the full sweetness of swimming. Her skin, silken light over her blubber, took up the push and pull of the sea, making her feel each eddy and swell as if it were part of her. As she imagined the calling whale in her mind, she felt the flow of the sea awaken her body, and she swam faster toward the equator.

Her primary thrust came from sculling—the tail's upward motion—but this in itself was only part of her extraordinary strength. Loose over her muscles, her blubber could move to some extent with the water. And the skin above the blubber had a series of dermal ridges, like the ridges on the palms of human hands, which ribbed up or dimpled in, depending on whether the pressure was high or low. With the tail's flexible motion and the whale's ability to slough surface skin in flight, this reduced drag to a point no manufactured vessel could match.

To the Blue Whale motion was joy. The lifeless metal ships might move faster but none could match her grace. A submarine couldn't travel with one-tenth her economy. Only living muscles could move with such pleasure and ease.

Yet even this pleasure was nothing compared with the pleasure that she envisioned: to open herself to a male, to hold him inside her. She imagined the spent bull falling away as his life and warmth entered her, and she dreamed that the two of them swam in a sea without ships.

The sun approached its zenith. Still there was no whalesound. She was swimming at full speed in the warmth, and her mind began to drift. She was leaving the region of southeast trades and entering the doldrums, a low-pressure zone of extended calms and occasional violent storms. In the northern hemisphere summer it stretched north between three and four hundred miles from the equator. With fall, it receded south. The north-blowing trades from the permanent mid-Atlantic high at the Tropic of Capricorn were weakening and turning west. Where the whale swam, six hundred miles out from Brazil on the eighteenth parallel, the transition was just beginning. Sometimes the wind blew west and sometimes there would be calm, the sea so still that she could hear the creaking wings of the sooty shearwaters or catch brilliant reflections of sunlight from the membranous sail of a drifting man-o'-war.

It became especially calm at noon. The Blue Whale spouted and inhaled: a slow, almost deathly sigh. The ocean was blank to the eye, but she could hear a liner's coarse, overpowering drone from the eastern horizon. It troubled her. When she resubmerged, the water thrummed with the sounds of racing fish. Albacore with inflexible, driving tails were squadroning south as spring heated the ocean.

The din of the ocean liner peaked and dwindled. Here beyond shelf and slope the sea was more stratified by temperature. Diving to six hundred feet, far into the dark, the whale detected the grumbling race where Antarctic water ran northward over red clay and above it the Atlantic Deepwater Current drifted south. Far below she could hear them wrestle and she felt small in the echoing dark.

She rose back to the surface. The current's magic continued as she swam northeast to seventeen degrees. She felt the weakening of the current when she dove a second time. Again she heard other currents below, denser and louder in the dark.

Just as the atmospheric highs flowed into lows, so the denser water followed the lighter. The densest sea was in the Antarctic where the ocean froze to the bottom and the frozen sea left most of its salt behind, thickening the water. This denser water sought the thinner sea to the north. Antarctic sea poured over the floor all the way to the Arctic. Above this base, the deepwater currents of the Atlantic, most of them from the Norwegian Sea, flowed south, and, higher still, where currents met, were convergences: parallel walls of descending water spreading out into midlevel streams. Where currents parted, streams from below filled in the void. At roughly forty, fifty, and sixty degrees this mixing went on all year, and where there was mixing, there were enormous explosions of plankton in the spring, the greatest of all at sixty degrees: the polar front, outer limit of Antarctic krill.

By midafternoon the intoxication of fast flight was wearing thin. Hollow from loneliness and hunger, she no longer noticed the flow of water over her skin, dwelling instead on her growing thinness. Her blubber storehouse of fuel was also a dike against cold. She remembered how as a calf she had winced at the ice.

She was swimming gloomily at a depth of three hundred and fifty feet when she heard a rorqual call from thousands of miles to the northeast. It was so far away its reflections from floor and surface had faded out, and even the longer-lived refraction the cow picked up was very faint. At a little below twenty hertz it was lower than ocean traffic, and it seemed to the cow that an overtone came with it, an almost inaudible higher voice, as if two distant whales, perhaps a mother and calf, called out together. This attenuated call was clearly not from the rorqual she'd heard last night. She called back and swam faster, but the voice never came again and she realized almost as soon as she answered it that it was too distant to overtake. The realization made her loneliness worse than before. Seeing a cow and calf in her mind, the Blue Whale's thoughts turned to her mother.

She could hear the old whale inside her head. Seven years ago they had lingered near the equator till her mother's back had grown almost as thin as her own was now. For her it had been an ecstatic time. She had fattened on cheesy milk, letting her blanket of blubber grow shiny and thick. Even so, after their flight to the south, the Antarctic water had stung her with intimations of its lethal cold, and those hints remained in her mind like a child's first terror of falling.

She rose and kept to the surface, pointed northeast toward the towering peak that broke the tropical sea as Ascension Island. The sun was red. Cumulus clouds crossed the evening sky and the ocean rocked and shifted under a rising wind out of the west. She moved just under the surface, far enough down that the jostling waves were a roof of hisses and murmurs over her calm. And she pondered.

Before her birth, her mother would have overstayed her time in the Antarctic, converting krill into blood and blubber. After her birth in the tropics, when the others had joined the springtime rush for Antarctica, her mother had stayed behind, lingering late to fatten her calf against the cold, herself growing thin in that stratified blue sea with its sterile calm. Not till the end of spring had they crossed the polar front into the krill grounds. From spring to summer she had fed from her mother's teat and, at the last, as her whalebone lengthened, had attempted to eat the Antarctic krill. They had been grazing on euphausiids together when the catcher's undersea radar, only a curiosity to her, had struck terror into her mother. Even now she trembled inside, recalling her mother's fear of that sound. Where before the huge body had helped her to rise, now it had driven her down, obscuring the path of her flight with a screen of bubbles. Realizing that her calf would panic after a short time by herself, her mother had breached to catch the boat's attention. The radar had stopped and the calf had heard a thud above the water, had risen to see her mother racing hard a half mile off. The voice that vibrated mountains came out of her mother's head in a desperate rasp, and when the catcher's grenade exploded, the mound of her body fountained red and the boat-tugging race gave way to a terrible, spastic dance, her mother ascending twenty feet into the sky and scattering blood over twice that distance, rising and falling a dozen times until the catcher bobbed like a cork in the reddening sea. Despite her terror and shock, the calf swam after her mother.

She was gaining on the cow when muffled noises that had been constant since the spring grew suddenly loud. Explosive thumps between one and two hundred hertz, each less than a second in duration, were coming in trains of several hundred at a time. The calf could tell that these were whale calls, but they were clearly not from Blues, since Blue Whale calls were all the same, while these varied in length and frequency from one source to another. The calf still raced for the boat. Five Minkes came into sight. None of them longer than twenty-four feet, they surrounded the fifty-five-foot calf and poked their heads out

28

where her eyes had cleared the surface to look at the catcher. Now the mother whale was bloated, buoyed up with an air hose like a grotesque, floating balloon. The calf slowed down. The boat was turning south in pursuit of her and the five who'd surfaced beside her. Still in shock, the youngster could feel the pointed snouts of the Minke Whales prod her behind the flippers as the thumps gave way to trains of hundred-kilohertz clicks, four to six per second. The calf was unused to complex sequences of sound but she caught the urgency in these. Carried along by their emotion, she hurried south at fifteen knots with the Minkes surrounding her like an escort and the catcher roaring behind. Their snouts never moved from behind her fins as again and again she found herself guided under ice floes whose keels deepened the farther she swam, the catcher losing more and more time as it veered to circumvent the ice. Still it kept on. After three hours the Minkes were leading the Blue through ice cakes crowded so closely that they almost formed a solid mass on the sea. This was the pack ice. Constant near shore, farther out it advanced and retreated with the seasons and now, in the January summer, it stopped just below the sixtieth parallel.

Despite the pack ice the catcher persisted, but after twenty minutes the ice became so thick it was forced to turn. Hanging suspended just under the surface, the Blue roared loudly, expressing her grief. The Minke Whales moved off a bit, slightly frightened by the sound. Females whose calves had been born above the polar front in early June, these Minkes had suckled for four months, yet, even while nursing, all had been carrying next year's calves. Now, in high summer, they were swimming toward the ice shelf, gorging on krill to feed the fetuses inside them. The Blue Whale moaned. After an hour they pressed their snouts to her again, less urgent now. Broken, she followed them straight south.

Two days went by. They came to the limit of permanent pack ice, crossed the strait of open water between the pack ice and the shelf, then dove beneath the coastal ice. Of all the whales, only Blues and Minkes swam this far into shore, and Minkes did it more often than Blues. In the pack ice they had breathed between the floes, but under the shelf they were constantly busy clearing and widening breathing spaces Weddell seals had chewed in the ice. The Blue had trouble learning to breathe at these narrow holes. She couldn't protrude her head all the way and had to position her nostrils directly beneath the holes to spout and inhale.

Still, she caught on, learning to rise behind the chinks where light poured in and run her head along the underside of the ice until her blowholes reached the opening. Here in the ice world euphausia superba were very thick, and the Blue could see the Minkes take myctophid fish as well. Less abundant were the smaller krill, euphausia spinifera and euphausia crystallorphias, which the Minkes ate with relish. The Blue realized that these whales were versatile and strong. Grouped by sex, they had no use for long-term attachments, meeting with males only to mate.

Weeks passed. She stayed with the Minkes, feeding sometimes under ice and sometimes in open sea. Lither than big whales such as Blues or Fins or Seis, they breached completely out of the sea where the water was clear, as graceful as dolphins despite their size, although the sound of their splashes carried for miles. In open water the Blue watched the Minkes force the myctophid fish to the surface. Each time they fed on the swarming shoals, great flocks of skuas, black-backed gulls, and silver fulmars came from nowhere to dive noisily and feast. Taking no part, the Blue would hang quietly off to one side. She was storing up memories. These whales had saved her. They were her parents in a way. The Blue Whale felt she was part of their family.

The cow continued to swim for the northeast. The wind died down and she still saw the Minkes in her mind. Most southern Minkes were drab compared to those in the north, but hers had had shoulder patches of white and almost incandescent stripes on their pectorals. By the end of summer she had been able to identify each whale not only by thumps and clicks but also by trains of whistles and trains that sounded like clanging bells. She'd distinguished as well the scraping ratchets of eight hundred hertz and higher, as well as the pings that sounded like radar, their frequency anywhere from three thousand to twenty thousand hertz.

The Blue Whale warmed inside as she remembered. Once, when a submarine had neared, the Minkes had echoed the vessel's pulse with high-frequency pings, making it follow and maneuver for over four hours as it tried to locate the source and make sense of the sounds. Sometimes, hearing the Minkes answer each other over distances of miles, the Blue Whale calf had felt left out. She knew they communi-

30

cated in detail and at length, but such exchanges were impossible for Blues with their narrower repertoire of calls. She tried in vain to vary her calls, to imitate them. At last, unable to "converse," she compensated by caressing the whales with heightened tenderness, and by summer's end she knew each Minke's body as well as her own. Most of this touching was sexual, but some was for grooming. Over and over she'd run her snout down the Minkes' throats, crushing the parasitic whale lice that hid themselves in the ventral pleats. Eyes close to the Minkes' skin, the Blue could see how these sixty to seventy pleats, unlike her ninety, stopped near the flippers instead of reaching down toward the umbilicus. This difference intrigued her, as did the greater prominence of the dorsal fin, unlike her own, located high on the back toward the head. Whenever they weren't feeding or asleep, the Blue and the Minkes swam together. For hours on end they would stroke and caress one another.

The summer passed. The Blue Whale's love for the Minkes strengthened but her grief for her mother remained, and when in the fall the Minkes swam north to temperate seas, the Blue stayed a little north of the front where she hoped to find male companions but instead endured a lonely austral winter. She looked for the Minkes the following spring but they never came. Over the six ensuing years she saw many Minkes and many deaths but never encountered *her* whales again.

The Blue awoke from her memory. Now tropical dusk was staining the low-flying clouds. Usually centered on the present, she started turning over the circumstances of her life. With her natural cycle broken, her memory became especially active, looking for clues to what was happening to her. She slowed and pondered why the Minkes had disappeared and where her migration was taking her. Those strange vessels that fouled the polar sea with their noise and their death were equal mysteries. Mainly, however, she thought of the whale to whom she was calling. Why could it not respond to her passion? Where was its sound? She thought of the way a dying rorqual will slowly sink into the sea. It was so easy to let it go, the continual swimming, to let herself fall. She slowed to a stop. A great depression filled her mind. And yet the previous night she had heard the voice of a rorqual, surely a male. She cried out to him in her hope, then peeled her ears for a reply, but heard

31

only the chatter of plankton over the seamounts and the ubiquitous noise of the ships. The yearning for answers was a torture. She moaned to herself. Her bubbles spiralled through the darkness as she hovered, lamenting the death of her mother. She let her flukes go totally limp until, snout-first, she slowly sank. Then, from less than thirty miles off, the call she had heard last night rang out again.

CHAPTER

4

As the bull pursued his mate and calf twelve hundred miles north of the equator and the Blue Whale cow picked up their calls the same distance south of it, four dolphins were swimming northwest toward the Sierra Leone Rise off Africa. There were a male and two female Common Dolphins—brother, sister, and cousin. A Striped Dolphin cow swam with them. They had left captivity only lately and they travelled constantly, freakishly restless. Once in a while the dark-backed male would lead the females in aerial arches over the water, and when they turned on their sides in midflight, the male and two females flashed an elongated hourglass pattern, buff in front and gray at the rear, while the third female showed dark stripes, eye to flipper and eye to anus, between her steel-blue back and snowy abdomen.

33

The young male usually led. As he swam on against the one-knot Guinea Current, he could hear increasing noise from the blackness five thousand feet down, where the Sierra Leone Rise reared its peaks ten thousand feet from the ocean floor. Those peaks reflected much more noise than did the deeper surrounding sea, and last night's feeding told the male that the distant animals and fish who made the noise—the diurnal migrants of the deep scattering layer—would surface at night. It all recalled a precaptivity time when he'd hunted with his mother well offshore, but the memory was distant, barely formed, and it quickly passed.

Sometimes louder sounds came from the rise. The male had heard low-frequency calls like his own long-distance signals, but while the calls were more powerful, they were muffled, as if from far away. He'd only heard them a couple of times and couldn't imagine what creature made them, but, though he peeled his ears through the latter part of the morning, he heard only the scattering layer and distant ships.

Near noon he started to pick up louder noises to his east, but they were familiar: the wearisome drone of the navy cruiser that had just recently passed. His cousin had been terrified when he'd coasted in the pressure wave at the bow of the navy ship, but over the weeks at sea the others had grown used to seeing ships draw near and pass without event, and though there had been explosions on the deck, nothing resulted except an undefined fear that had made them flee. The fear had passed though, and now the male ignored the ship.

Soon another, deeper sound that came as an echo deflected upward from the rise, made him go still, for he had never heard such powerful vibrations. The others cringed. When the voice came again it wasn't an echo. The echo had had a source, but it seemed to the dolphins that this second sound came from everywhere at once. Its deep vibrations entered their bodies and made them shake. The frightened sister turned back for the continental shelf, but the male remained, hanging silently. This voice was the deepest he'd ever heard. The sea went still. The sister stopped and the male hung waiting for the voice to come again.

After a second he started at a partly hidden shape just underneath him where the light of the upper ocean started to fade. It seemed that half of the shape was in shadow and half in the light, and it swam with a bobbing motion, his body making a shadow on the snout. The snout grew clear, then the rest of the tapered head, three times his length. A

34

second passed and it dropped into shadow, but when he saw it again a train of blue flesh rose behind it. The dolphin stared, for the curving back filled over half his field of vision. Looking closer, he discerned another shape, smaller by far, though also huge, swimming beside the first.

The first shape dropped from the light but let its shadowy tail, over five yards wide, rise into sight for just a second. The dolphin was diving when the creature wheeled and rose, by now well past him, enormous and streamlined, its eighty-foot length blocking the light. By the time the tip of its head was touching the air its tail had yet to leave the dark and, just as its voice had made the young male dolphin shake, so now the force of its wake made him stroke with his flukes to keep himself erect.

It arched at the top, barely breaking the sea, wheeled its blowholes into the air, let out an explosive jet of breath, and then inhaled with a sound like a high-speed surface wind. The dolphin warmed, as he saw that the shape, despite its vastness, was like him. It rose to breathe. It swam with horizontal fins.

A calf when captured, the dolphin had never before seen a whale, and the sight so absorbed him that, though the sound of the cruiser was louder now, he paid it little mind. Ignoring the females, he rushed ahead until he was swimming beside the shape. His pulse was racing. He passed the pectoral fin, reached the head, and then looked up from under the eye.

It was oval, like an enormous dolphin eye, and the mucous that covered it, like that which covered his own eye, made blinking unnecessary. Even so, the huge eye blinked at him, as if in recognition, and he heard clicking deep in the cavern of the head. He clicked in reply and passed beneath to rise beside the sixty-foot calf, which clicked as well and blinked its paler eye. His pulse still fast, the dolphin synchronized his motion to the motion of the calf, swimming a steady eleven knots. When his heart slowed down, he saw the females swimming beside and beneath him. They signalled one another in the shadows, whistling and clicking in excitement, partly afraid. The mother whale emitted a sound like a loud belch, which the dolphins imitated at once. The mother whale made the sound again, then speeded up, as if she meant to leave them behind.

The male pursued the whale and rose over her back, unwilling to let

35

her swim away. She moved and breathed like him and had exchanged rudimentary signals, but he wanted to know so much more that the thought of having her simply disappear, perhaps the only one of her kind he would ever see, made him hurt inside. He watched the bubbles rise from her blowholes, then touched his head to her back and sent ultrasonic waves into her body to scan her insides, so absorbed in his perceptions that he forgot about everything else, and only stopped scanning when the whale began to rise.

He veered to one side as she broke the surface with the calf, and when he heard the cruiser roar, he rose to the top and looked to the east where it had closed to twenty yards. Six hundred feet long, it was passing the cow and calf when explosions from a tower thirty feet high on the side of the ship boomed out. As the dolphin wheeled aside, red wounds opened up in the whales' heads. Both started to sink. The young male dove. As he did he saw a row of bleeding holes open up along the mother whale's left side. Blood was rising out of their heads. Completely confused, the young male soared back for the top. The rattling explosions came again, but now the whales had already entered the dark below, sinking together. All four dolphins dove to touch them amid the blood. When the dolphins rose to breathe, just barely breaking the surface in their fear, the cruiser was racing southwest at high speed.

After the ship passed out of sight, the dolphins hung on the top for a while, stunned and confused. The Striped Dolphin vibrated her blowhole to emit a sound of fright. The other three took up the sound as they heard the ship fade away. The sea grew so calm and the air so still that it almost seemed the ship and the whales had been part of a dream. Still it took hours before the shock began to subside. In late afternoon the male once more started to swim for the northwest, more slowly now, and the females followed.

Seven hundred miles to the north, about a hundred miles below the Tropic of Cancer, the northern Blue Whale bull pursued the calls he had heard from the southeast. He swam from afternoon till dawn. The constant pain in his back distracted him so much that he stopped to rest as the sky paled. By early morning the stabbing pain drove everything else from his mind. He tried to end it by breaching and diving, but after

36

three hours he saw there was no remedy. The pain stopped late in the morning but returned in midafternoon, and for the six following days the attacks grew longer, separated by intervals of less than two hours. Enduring the pain was using up so much of his strength that in times of peace he hung vacantly at the top. Once during an especially long attack in early morning, he went temporarily mad. In desperation he boiled the surface where a congregation of petrels flashed white rumps and danced the waves with yellow feet.

The four restless dolphins travelled northwest after the death of the cow and calf until the bull's commotion lured the brother and sister from the bow of a liner they were following. As they left the ship, they were joined by the subdued Striped Dolphin cow and the cautious cousin. While the Blue Whale rolled and breached, driven mad by the pain in his back, the dolphins closed and circled, travelling with ease at almost twice his speed. When the bull dove from sight they followed him down to find him lost in his private hell, hovering off-balance.

The heart of the young male dolphin raced as fast as it had when the two other whales had appeared. The bull was still now. When clicks and whistles failed to draw replies, the dolphin swam over the bull whale's back, bent sideways just to the left of his dorsal fin and lightly touched him with the top of his head to send ultrasonic pulses into his body.

He made the sounds just under his nostrils and focussed them outward through his melon, the part of his head above his eyes and back of his beak. While the everyday sounds he sent into the sea returned as echoes into his oil-filled lower jaw, these more narrowly focussed sounds came back through his skull. If a dolphin were ill, the male could scan it for worms or infection. Everything, solid or liquid, affected sound velocity, and the male could "read" the changes, except in the lungs or the bones. The bones gave back no reflection to speak of, while the broadly outlined lungs reflected sound too uniformly and too well. For these reasons both were almost featureless, although the male picked up sharp detail from most other parts of the body.

He tilted his head to avoid the spine and focussed pulses through the blubber and muscle walls, instinctively adjusting period, intensity, and other variables. To his surprise, avoiding the ribs was easy, since all but

37

the first pair floated free of the whale's spine. Seconds later, as the reflected sound formed several shades of gray behind his eyes, the dolphin saw that the whale had two organs on the inner wall of his back. He didn't know that these organs were made of lobes, or that every lobe was a tiny kidney. But he could see worms in the whale's kidneys, just as he'd seen them earlier in the kidneys of the sick Striped Dolphin hovering behind him.

The sister and cousin also scanned the whale, though they'd been too frightened to examine his luckless mate. The Striped Dolphin surfaced and kept to herself, more ill each day and afraid that the three Common Dolphins would scan her too, as they'd already done many times. But they stayed below. The male's pulse speeded up from a hundred and thirty strokes per minute to a hundred and sixty as he dropped beneath the whale and beamed his soundwaves into the area behind the pectoral fins. Modifying his signals, the dolphin half discerned the heart. After a minute or two of moving up and down, he surmised it was almost as wide as his body was long. As before with the cow and calf, he became lost in his perceptions until the suffering bull began to rise. The dolphins followed, worrying over the whale, and, in their inscrutable way, seemed almost to confer, squeaking and clicking, chattering and nudging.

The bull rose listlessly. Night was well advanced. When the dolphins came close, they saw no movement in the glazed stare of his eyes. He could make no sense of the dolphins' squeals, and their constant clicking only reminded him of Orcas. Lost in his pain, he sounded for over three thousand feet and left the dolphins alone to marvel at what they had found.

He hung still in his lethargy. His helplessness focussed him on his pain as it had when he'd felt the cruisers defecate into his bed or when the hunters had butchered at will, reddening the Banks. He could not understand the purpose of these things, any more than he could understand why his strength and his balance of body and mind were being taken away.

He gave a low call. The black sea hummed outside him. Not far down, grenadiers, thin fish with narrow ratlike tails, fled from his sound. Deep-sea bacteria on the bottom made nitrogen out of radiolarian shells. Ooze on the ocean floor sent gases twelve thousand feet to the surface plankton. The sea turned waste into food and death into

38

life, and the whale was a cell in its bloodstream. Hanging head down, he became the blackness, the mindless currents humming about his ears. Time passed. His pain subsided. After many minutes, his blood grew quiet again.

This time, however, his relief was troubled. When he spouted, thirty-foot rollers roared from the west without any wind. The sun had cleared the horizon, and cirrus clouds in front of the sun made a red celestial wheel of its rays. The air hung heavy, still. Far to the west he could hear the rumbling of waves, and the clouds formed high-ribbed ramparts against the sky. A great storm was coming. Everywhere birds and fish scattered in fear, but he did not dive.

When it struck, he rode it out, soaring and surfing for most of the day until the hurricane winds were behind him. The pain didn't return and the air grew calm. Expecting another attack at any second, he watched strange flocks materialize in the vacant sky. With others, the hurricane storm had disrupted bird migrations. Red-necked phalaropes searched and scanned, blown hundreds of miles from their western flyways. He caught the lisping pipes of a warbler flock, driven two thousand miles off its course. They came close, then disappeared over his head—a swarm of insects, panting, desperate for calm and land. Gold sky. He thought of his mate. The pain still hadn't returned and the four dolphins were hovering close at his side. He started to swim. Now, still crossing the Cape Verde Basin, he was five hundred miles from the Sierra Leone Rise, where his mate would have stopped her journey south.

CHAPTER

5

Six hundred miles out from Brazil the Blue Whale cow was once more hearing the voice of the previous night. It came halfway toward dawn, a tremor deeper than shipsound from the east. Twelve seconds passed and it came again, then again, at twenty cycles a second. As it moved southwest she dove and followed, but soon the sound was muffled in thunder and she surfaced under a brilliantly clear night sky to see a cruiser's derrick against the horizon. The sound veered west toward the shelf as the enormous cruiser went past, its noise thinning out but never entirely fading into the dark.

The whale caught up with the stranger when the ship had completely gone. Looming out of the shadows, the stout, eighty-foot whale lowered its head and slanted its body toward the sky in anger. The Blue Whale paused, then circled. She danced, as if for a male of her own species, festoons of bubbles bursting out of her head.

As the stranger watched, the Blue Whale swam like a huge blue rocking horse through the shadows, coming close, then orbiting off like a planet through the dark. Glittering plankton illuminated her body, and she faded and reappeared in her dance of excitement. She glowed inside at the prospect of mating, bowed ever more steeply till she was describing a ring of headstands and tailstands. Finally she turned and presented the gray of her ventral surface, standing straight up with outstretched pectorals, her bubbles rising around her.

But her vision of mating had blinded her to reality. The twenty-cycle call had come from a proud, aging Fin Whale, who now rose to a horizontal position. She was tired. The voice bouncing up from seamounts earlier that day had not interested her. Toward noon she had been forced in its direction when a cruiser on a training run had caught the Blue Whale's vibrations in its sonar. Mistaking the voice for the sound of another ship, the cruiser had emitted its own sonar, humiliating and harrying the Fin with its constant signals, impossible to outswim. Once, when she'd turned to the west and breached, they had fired at her. Now, anxious and tired, she had escaped to find this female of another species, in estrus, dancing about her in the dark.

After coming to a stop, the Blue Whale recognized the more angular head and shorter, stouter body of a Fin. She was deflated. Even so, she had been alone for so long that the possibility of contact, even with one of another species, excited her. She lowered herself to a level line, and the Fin Whale, old, done now with mating and calving, managed a gesture of tolerant greeting, running her pectorals down the length of the Blue Whale's back. As she did, she noticed the sharp-angle slope of the youngster's sides and felt a stab of sympathy. When they rose and spouted together, pheromones from the sexually hungry Blue ran like honey over the nerves in the Fin Whale's blowholes, and the fragrance entered her head, raising emotions out of the past. Arching out of the sea, the Fin remembered her mate and her calves, lost years ago to the gunners in the Antarctic.

Under blue light from the clear night sky the two hung near the surface side by side, watching each other. The Fin Whale passed her pectorals down the Blue Whale's back a second time, then slid her slim flippers over the vast, sensitive skin of the Blue Whale's face. She

41

touched the vibrissae, long, whiskerlike hairs rooted in clusters of nerve endings where the skin was especially tender. The Blue Whale grunted and rolled, looking up at the sky of white skin passing over her. She noted the tapering **V** of the old whale's upper jaw, so different from her own round dish; the darker back and lighter stomach; the stouter, less gradual lines. Her loneliness disappeared in the thrill of this touching. The Fin Whale, too, forgot the threatening sound of the cruiser. She watched the Blue Whale roll on her back and felt her own stomach caressed down its length till she bubbled with pleasure.

They continued this way for some time, the Blue Whale nosing the newcomer's genital slit and nuzzling the points where the old whale's breasts had once protruded for her calves. Both had been isolated for months. Thoughtful, imaginative creatures, their touch communicated their memories and desires. When the Blue nuzzled her breast region, the Fin Whale envisioned her calves and imagined the touch of the Blue as the bunt of her own calf nuzzling against her. Isolated together in blackness and warmth, the whales grew more and more intimate.

When finally they fell into silence, resting side by side, both whales were dreaming. The Blue could hear the equatorial waters to the north where she had overstayed her winter. She dreamed of meeting a bull in those empty seas.

Even while sleeping, the Blue Whale swam. She was too lean simply to float. The Fin had feasted on fish for months and her blubber contained so much fat that she was buoyant. Her head just under the surface, she dreamed many dreams. As with the Blue, her unnatural life with its string of traumas had made her mind restless. Nearly a hundred years old, she recalled when Antarctic spring had brought hundreds of thousands of Blues and Fins to the feeding grounds; when the south Atlantic had been alive with rorquals, whales who swam miles apart, the sound of their voices like an approaching storm. They had made their voices pass through spaces they could not cross in a month, homing into perpetual light according to tribe, the Blue Whales arriving first, occupying the edge of the ice, then the Fin Whales, who harvested krill in far-flung herds of separate feeders out at sea. She recalled the reunions. A female who had given birth in the winter would present a calf to her family—she herself, both as mother and calf, had commanded much attention. She could see the juvenile whales she

42

had led through their summers in the red krill. Sometimes she heard the five-year-old adolescents signal each other through the feeding din, in pledges that would be fulfilled on the northern journeys. She warmed as she remembered. Matings occurred in tropical isolation, but marriages were always made on the krill grounds.

She heard the far-off summers in her head. Sometimes those early congregations, covering the sea in well-spaced feeding groups that stretched for hundreds of miles, would grow unexpectedly silent. Then out of the distance would come the din of some latecomer. In her memory she could hear the whales who came in when the rest were assembled, whales well known for their long lives and many children. Suspended amid their feast, the Fins would listen to the calls of the new arrivals echo around them. The echoes would last for a second and then the answering babble would fill the sea: grunts, roars, clicks, grates, and the smacking and swallowing sounds of fat whales feeding.

She relished that, but also remembered the later times: the factory ships, the death of her last calf, the herds that had gone. It was puzzling. Things had changed slowly at first. Her mate had been one of the last to be killed. For years, until the deaths of her calves, both she and her mate had ignored the warning signals: the South Georgia factory, the gradual decrease in populations. The number of Humpbacks had declined until it was rare to encounter even one on the krill grounds. Most rorquals had ignored this, though the slaughter was far from remote. A few of the Fins had even observed it: huge crowds of Humpbacks butchered in shallows and processed in factories on South Georgia's Cumberland Bay. Still, the rorquals had believed that their great speed would keep them secure. Even later, when the factory ships with their brood of catchers invaded the sea, it was the Blue Whales next to the ice who were killed—most of the Fins had been spared. And, later still, when the Blues had become so scarce that some Fin Whales lived out their lives without ever seeing one, it was still the other feeding groups that were slaughtered. Somehow her family had always survived. She had dreamed at one time that they were immune to the catchers; that, despite the catchers' terrible speed, her brood could somehow outwit them. But, when they had come, she had escaped only by swimming away from the rest of her family, all of whom had died, as her last calf had died inside her, six decades ago.

She saw the krill grounds now as a waste where a relict population fed

43

in fearful silence under the guns. She stayed away, gorging herself with fish in the south Atlantic, feeding her mind on memories. Over the years she had learned to ignore the shipsounds. Instead she heard the remembered summers, the ghostly chorus of Fins and Blues and Seis that once had knit the south Atlantic together. She kept these things alive in her mind, and when she heard the sound of a displaced cow, she was glad that her time for mating and calving was over with. She seldom greeted a passing stranger, but when she did, she paid no heed whether it was a Blue, Fin, Humpback, or Sei.

The sea grew ever calmer as night wore on, and the Blue Whale continued to scull, rising every twenty minutes to spout. Her sound carried far through the dark. A disembodied, laborious *huff,* it came out of nowhere, as if there were troubled spirits of whales under the waves. Hearing it, the Fin awoke. The sky was shining like glass. She had totally stopped swimming but, beside her, the Blue Whale was idling in great wide circles, having awakened from her dreams. The Fin Whale watched her, and felt another stab. She had not meant to let the Blue Whale affect her this way. She had seen so many young whales die, all because of their hunger for life. Only by avoiding life—the Antarctic meetings, the ecstasies—could whales hope to endure. This Blue Whale was obviously eager to mate and calve, but the Fin saw only a rush to death. With a mind that had long since lost its passivity, the Fin Whale thought and thought of this, but it was too hard for her. She fell asleep again. How could a whale who lived in the old way survive?

All night the Blue Whale dreamed of finding a mate. Her dream repeated itself again and again, always the same. Inside her head she would hear his call, then see him spouting to her north. She would pursue him, only to have him fade away when she drew close, to be replaced by the Fin Whale. Then the Blue would pursue the Fin and, upon overtaking the older whale, wake up to see the actual Fin Whale floating under the moon, lost in dreams of her own. The Blue would go back to sleep and dream of the bull again, but each repetition of the dream made the bull seem smaller, harder to overtake. At last, with dawn, when the bull of her dreams was no more than a speck on a distant sea, she awoke in anger. The Fin Whale had usurped his place. She circled the old whale, nudging, prodding with her rostrum. Begrudgingly the Fin shuddered awake, leaving her dreams of the past behind, but still she seemed entranced, eyes fixed, vast body floating

44

motionless. With the passage of time the Fin was finding it harder to leave the shadow world she entered in her sleep.

When the butting of the Blue stung her awake, the Fin Whale butted back in anger. Then, as though fearing she'd hurt her friend, she ran her fins once more down the Blue Whale's back, maternally caressing. But now the Blue, who had seemed starved for the old whale's touch last night, turned away and kept to herself, swimming farther north each time the Fin approached. At last, with the sun well past the eastern horizon, the Blue reversed herself and swam south. She swam for a long time at a painfully fast speed, and the Fin Whale felt her heart race with compassion as she followed. She swam hard, trying to catch up with the Blue, afraid this southward flight meant the young female had begun her spring migration and was racing toward her death. She swam as fast as she could to overtake the Blue, but it was no use. The younger cow was as fast as she was. After an hour the discouraged Fin began to slow down.

She turned back north, back to her solitary life of feasting and dreaming, and as she swam, she moaned a little, for the solitary life was only sweet when she shut out the world around her. She was angry. It was the Blue, not she, who'd demanded intimacy and broken the solitude she had so carefully guarded over the years. She closed her eyes, swimming in circles, trying to expel the thought of the Blue Whale from her mind.

As her northward flight resumed, the sound of a rorqual passed through the sea: once, twice—far off—to the northeast. The sound meant nothing to the Fin, but loud answering calls told her the Blue Whale cow had reversed direction again: she was calling out and swimming fast for the northeast. In a final attempt at communication, the Fin turned east, directly blocking the Blue Whale's path. When she drew close, the youngster paused and caressed her. They began to embrace each other, touching and nudging as they had the night before, until their pleasure made the old whale's memories dim. Then, after half an hour or so, the sequence from the northeast passed through the sea a second time. Ablaze, the Blue called back and raced for the voice with the Fin Whale behind her.

CHAPTER

6

THE bull whale from the Greenland seas was tired. After riding hurricane winds through the Cape Verde Basin, he was resting above the Gambia Plain off Africa, five hundred miles northwest of the Sierra Leone Rise. His four dolphins were still with him, although they used him more as a home base for their fifteen-knot hunting forays than as a companion.

It was night. Tired out from his pain, he slept, awakening once in a while to the sound of a passing freighter. Once, when he woke, he vibrated air through his larynx, calling out for his mate and listening. But under the cloudless sky only a cargo ship answered, accordion sounds from where sheet-metal bundles and piles of coal made a black silhouette on the moon. He slept again.

With dawn, his nerves stayed silent and some of his confidence came back. Then, swimming south, he encountered a wide white line. For hundreds of miles two parallel currents erected a highway of spray. The twin upwellings lifted rafts of detritus and eggs. Sucked up from middle depth, minerals made the foaming track a garden of plants, bacteria, and plankton.

This open-sea rip, roughly parallel to the coast, was composed of two warmwater currents of differing densities, both flowing south between the inshore Guinea Current and the Equatorial Countercurrent farther out. The rip descended to the thermocline where the warmer, upper water gave way to denser, colder sea.

Intrigued, the whale turned onto the highway. He followed the trough toward the doldrums, straining his ears for some trace of whale-sound but, instead, hearing flurries of dolphin clicks and the croaking of weakfish. The farther south he swam the smoother the sun paved the water beside the trough. There were furrows opening up all over the sea. Worms from inshore communities protruded from rotten wood, round annelid worms, the long red nerves of the oceans. Here and there pelagic crabs skated the currents. They fastened themselves to living anchors: hydroids and tunicates that were themselves anchored to flotsam from which they sifted food particles out of the waves. Birds swarmed from coastal and open water. When the whale rose, he heard wings crowding the air: spiralling bos'n birds a foot long with exotic scissored tails; darters, well out from their native marshes, stabbing fish with their sharp bills and tossing them up in the air to gulp them as they came down; open-sea jaegers wheeling and swooping, forcing terns to drop their fish; enormous rafts of inshore pelicans dotting the sea.

As he swam he looked around him. The water foamed in the trough. Though on either side it was tranquil, there were momentary rufflings when a breeze rose. Capillary action pulled the water as smooth as glass when the breeze had passed. The ocean was calm, yet still there were waves. Just off the African coast, a storm was raging, and from time to time tall, rounded waves passed over the sea like ghosts. They moved without wind, for, over the shallow inshore shelf, they had been deeper than the sea, and their excess length, translated to energy, kept them alive for hundreds, sometimes thousands, of miles. The whale watched, vaguely curious for a moment. They would die eventually, for this sea was deeper than the waves.

47

Refreshed, he swam at full speed for the south, and once more the dolphins swam rings around him and rode his bow, their remarkable speed letting them leap and do acrobatics while keeping up. They chirped and clicked to each other, and, because he could not understand them, the whale felt even lonelier than before. Then, diving for fifty feet, he heard a strange new sound in the water. Something enormous was thundering its way toward him.

Thunder was common to the whale: the rhythmic thudding caused by the swimming motion of shoals. But this noise was different. Something quite large seemed to be swimming near the surface. Giddy from sickness, he imagined his mate was coming. The dolphins, shooting off to east and west, squealed as he roared his desperate greeting. They seemed amazed that giant dolphins could utter such sounds. But, as usual, there was no answer. Then, when the whale broke the surface, his heart sank. Far to the south a small black ripple skated the sea. It grew and grew, became a triangular fin three feet high and a foot wide at the base, the steady bow wave sparkling like jewels. The Blue imagined a Killer Whale, but when he dove, his pulses picked up a shape over forty feet long—a mindless, lethargic thing. He rose. A second fin, stroking from side to side, came up twenty feet back of the first. Now he heard roaring. It was a whale shark, its teeth combing plankton from the flood that roared into its mouth and out through its gills.

The shark approached him head-on, doing little more than two knots. When he turned and looked out of one eye, the whale saw a thin, straight mouth at the very front of the head, not underslung as in other sharks he had seen. The head itself was broad and flat and there were bulbous spots all over it. Long fringes hung from the corners of the mouth, but there were no eyes, only a nostril at each tip of the six-foot slit. The whale could have killed it had he battered it head-on, and yet it made no move to turn out of his way. It would likely not even have veered for a passenger ship. At the final moment the whale made an arching turn and detected two tiny vacant eyes.

They passed each other length to length with the dolphins splashing about them. When the left eye of the Blue Whale caught the right eye of the shark, it was like sun meeting dead stone, and as always at such times, the bull whale wondered. He could never get used to the coldness of these swimming deaths, whalelike in size and their way of feeding. When the giant shark was well behind, the male dolphin skated the

48

bow where the Blue's great head was barely rippling the water, but the females hung back with the Striped Dolphin, who felt pain again and grew suddenly subdued. Smaller basking sharks rose and faded from south to north, their mouths open—great red holes—but, as the afternoon wore on, the Blue ignored them, losing concern for everything but his partner's silence.

When the sun had passed its zenith, a school of Spinner Dolphins came in. They were trim little beasts, blue-gray on the back and grayish white on the belly. There were hundreds, a field of steely gray, dominant dolphins flanking juveniles, the small calves at the center, away from sharks.

Over and over they dove for squid, almost in concert. During one dive, a six-foot bull shark headed straight at the school. Though a female dealt it a chest stab with her beak, it sheared the tail off her four-foot calf. The thrashing motion soon brought others.

The whale grew impatient and anxious. He worried about his mate. It would be folly to lead their calf through such populous waters. Yet perhaps his mate had left this channel behind. How else explain her interminable silence? The blood of the unlucky dolphin calf might lure huge sharks, and possibly Killer Whales. He turned and swam due west, avoiding the blood trough. This attack from out of the blue by a solitary was unusual, and bull sharks were usually shoreline fish, but the trough had lured him out and excited him.

The calf soon died. The mother bore it up for a while. With late afternoon, the Spinner Dolphins turned as one, two hundred and fifty or so, heading coastward, the dead calf catching the fading light as it rode on the mother's head.

The dolphins remaining behind called to the mother, and those who swam off responded with rapid clicks and sounds like hinges opening in wind. Although the sounds seemed friendly, the four dolphins who stayed behind—the Blue's companions—were unwelcome in the herd. The bull and three cows, all immature, had been raised in captivity and did not get along with the herds they met in the wild. So they stayed with the whale.

He was ill again that night, enduring another attack of pain from the worms in his kidneys. He thrashed and bellowed from evening to dark, then wandered exhausted, as if he dragged an invisible whale ship in crazy circles under the stars. Shaken, the dolphins followed him, know-

49

ing better than the whale himself what hurt him and yet unable to offer help. The Striped Dolphin female hurt as well, though her attacks were much farther apart. Six hours went by and the bull still thrashed and breached when the pain became especially sharp. As night declined, he found himself edging for shore as if magnetized. His memories of whales burning up in midday heat no longer disturbed him.

Dawn found him hanging fifty miles from the continental shelf, no farther north or south after a wild night of circling. The dolphins were exhausted. He was hanging just ahead of them in the dawn, numbed and silent, as if the night's terrible dance had thrashed the pain out of his body. They drifted close. The young male opened his eyes and spouted little umbrella jets, no more than ten feet off. The tired whale hovered and watched. They were grouped about him like calves and for a moment he had the fancy he was watching his own family.

As he rested he saw visions from his past and he burned with worry. Surely his mate would soon answer his calls. He envisioned her in his mind until he started to relive their first year together, their first migration, their first spring and summer off Greenland. The visions made him feel warm. After a minute he dozed and clicked to himself.

The first of their Greenland summers passed in peace, then the second, then years went by. Their strange migration helped them survive. Reluctant at first to travel so far from the usual route, the cow became the more eager of the two once she had learned. Most of the time she kept to the route, but catchers spotted her over the Grand Banks more than once. She was too eager, travelled too fast, left the sun too far behind. Sometimes there were quarrels with the bull. But he couldn't slow her down. One year she hit the northern edge of the Gulf Stream six weeks early, where she halted over the Mid-Atlantic Ridge, awaiting the sun, with the docile bull trailing behind. After some hours she started west in pursuit of plankton.

The first catcher she encountered, from Trinity Bay, was dragging a string of buoyed-up Fins and had no factory. Calmly the bull interposed himself between the boat and his mate. The shot went wide but the harpoon lance grazed his skin. As he led her off, trailing warm blood into the sea, spiny dogfish, a hunting pack, snapped small pieces out of his sides.

After that the cow had no wish to turn for Newfoundland. But, two years later, the traffic of catchers, or boats that sounded exactly the same, was so intense north of the ridge that the scarred-over memory of her mother's death came back with a frightening clarity, making her balk when the bull left the ridge on his way to Greenland. After an hour of seesaw struggle, she turned him south. Once more they crossed the Newfoundland shelf, this time due east of the Northern Peninsula. And here a catcher boat came putting after them. When they fled, the bull kept well to the rear of the female, falling deliberately into range. He took the light-lined harpoon on his side. It didn't explode. As his mate curved back, he sounded directly behind the boat so that the foreline caught in the screws. Before the men could cut the engines, the tug of the screws hauled the harpoon head out of his flesh and snapped the line. He joined his mate and swam out of range before the men reloaded the gun. Again he bled. They swam nonstop till they came to the shelter of Greenland's coast. Sharks took more pieces. By his eighth year he was scored with furrows and scars.

But he lived well, swam in rich waters. And there were young: at the end of his seventh year, a female; at the end of his tenth, a male. After that the cow bore a calf every other year. The young who stayed with them summered off Greenland, wintered off Africa. Every other year on the spring migration up to Greenland he delighted in showing his newest calf the route he had discovered into the north. At first, when the family comprised just the two of them and a calf, they travelled together, but after a score of years, when the family had turned to a tribe that signalled each other over hundreds of square miles, the bull felt sad to see his bolder calves seek feeding grounds west of Greenland. He grieved for a time. But then his sadness gave way to surprise. None of them died. Overfishing continued, but now the sea was free to whales. The catchers had gone.

The bull and his mate fed farther and farther west during the summer. First they joined their family out in the Denmark Strait and, later, swam with the older, more venturesome calves who summered with offspring of their own off Cape Farewell in the Labrador Basin. Twenty-six years old, the bull was almost ninety feet long and still hadn't stopped growing. His mate had almost stopped at a little less than eighty. None of their young were more than seventy-six feet long. But the bull, with his toothmarks and scars, grew prodigiously and in this,

51

as in so much else, seemed to transcend the way of things. For many years northern whales had generally died with no more than one or two calves to survive them. The guns had assured this, or if not, their fearful, far-scattered life *beneath* the guns had reduced the number of matings and births. Yet the bull had lived and given life to a dozen others. By the time the plates of his backbone fused, at thirty-two years of age, he measured one hundred feet from the notch of his tail to the tip of his upper jaw. When he and his mate swam out of the north, a network of children preceded and followed them over hundreds of square miles. They almost forgot the early years. The crystal ice and perpetual sun of the northern seas had become their kingdom. The guns were gone. They lived a happy, satisfied life.

Then, on their thirty-third migration to the Sierra Leone Rise, they heard sounds of butchery for the first time in over a decade. As they crossed the Tropic of Cancer on the westernmost arm of the Mid-Atlantic Ridge, they heard a factory ship several miles to their west. Though by now the whaling nations had agreed not to hunt Blue Whales in the northern hemisphere, this ship was killing whales out of season, without regard to species or size. It brought down the oldest male, one of the only two who'd been able to find a mate. It killed him, his cow, and his two calves, thirty-five feet and sixty-six feet. When the hundred-foot bull arrived on the scene, he found nothing. Unlike the factory ships in the Antarctic, this ship, hunting illegally, had cooked every portion of the whales, even the entrails, in order to leave behind no trace of its crime.

That winter the thirty-four-year-old bull found the glare of the sun very harsh. The cow hung listlessly in ocean clear as glass, remembering her oldest. The world was desolate. Barely conscious, they left early. A year after the loss of the oldest bull, two other calves went down to a ship out of Argentina. Others followed. It seemed to the old bull whale that it always happened the same way, just at the outer edge of his hearing, over the eastern or western horizon, just far enough off that, when his anger and frustration had conquered his terror and propelled him to the place, there was nothing to see or hear but clear blue sea and silence. A sense of helplessness, the very thing that had turned him his own way when he was a calf, came back to him now. He grew to loathe the clear blue waters near the equator. Now, when the light of eastern

Greenland shrank to blackness, he did not hurry into the south as he had in the past. Instead, he lingered as long as possible off Cape Farewell or over the Grand Banks. It was his mate, the creature of habit, who raced for the south along the route he had discovered, for, though its use was gone, it had taken on a sanctity in her mind. No matter how great her grief for her young, she feared to try a different migration. She wanted to bear her calves in the tropical sea.

They swam apart more and more often, keeping in eye range only off Greenland in the summer. Usually she preceded him into the south, against his will. Lingering late outside the fjords, he would watch the ivory gulls flock out for warmer waters, keeping in touch with her only by calls. Since by now he'd ceased to remember the different ranges his calves had claimed, their sounds meant nothing. He assumed he was hearing strangers when voices of other whales came through the ice, and, far from answering, he shut them out of mind. The pain of loss and disillusion, at first only blackness in his mind, seemed to spread out to the rest of his body. Petty diseases, which had conquered the old whales of ninety-five to a hundred and five when nothing else could, came to him now before his time. It was as if the vulnerability of his strongholds had made his enormous body vulnerable as well. Flukes and nematodes clung to his organs, clung to the nerve cords that ran from his brain. Each fall he swam farther and farther west, to pass off Newfoundland. In moments of pain he grew erratic. Once in Bonavista Bay he followed Pilot Whales so close to shore that he almost beached himself. Outside the harbor he would race for fishing vessels, scaring the men, or, like an inexperienced juvenile, shadow ships.

The bull whale's journeys into the south grew slower and later. By his forty-second year he had fathered sixteen calves, most of them dead or far away. He had lost track.

His parasites began to sap his strength, but, even when healthy, he was listless, lazy, waiting out his time. For days on end he would hang stationary off Greenland, a spouting land rise, ridged and faulted and lined with scars. Sometimes puffins from island rookeries paused in their flight to stand on his back and look into the depths, as if unaware that he was alive. All of his movements were gradual now. Even submerging, he seemed no more than a rise of land, a minor ridge caught in the tide.

And he was an island inside, as well—drifting, aimless, with perching birds. He lived for the past. An island inside. Kingdom and continent no longer.

Having seen himself broken and defeated in his mind, the Blue awoke in a bleak mood, despite the death of his pain. When he noticed the dolphins sleeping at his side, it took some time for him to remember where and when he had seen them before. When he did remember, he ignored them.

Shipsound was strangely sparse in this morning's sea. Only skimmers and petrels called above the water, circling the feeding trough a few miles to his east. The constant chatter of eaters and prey surrounded the trough like blood. It lured in fishes, then sharks, and, at last, the Killer Whales.

They were distant as yet. The Blue Whale could hear their squadron far to the south and he imagined their towering dorsals. They travelled at twenty knots through the tropical water. Memories of death came with them. Two of the dolphins still slept but the young male and his cousin were awake, and the bull, seeing the pair as if for the first time, watched them calmly, his interest slowly increasing. Quickly the pair awakened the other two and turned them northwest to safety. Then the two dolphins listened again. The Orcas sent piercing screams in all directions to panic their prey. There was little time. The young male and his cousin stood up in the water, and the sun caught their dark backs and white bellies. The whale scrutinized them. They were muscular, handsome dolphins. Before they swam, they watched the whale, the young male's sparkling eye wide and intelligent in its coal-black ring, and the whale saw the curiosity he himself had so often felt, seeking mind and emotion in an indifferent sea. He clicked. The male and his cousin made affectionate sounds, then plummeted after the others.

All four were gone in an instant, arcing and arcing into the north until there was nothing—no urine, no sonar, not a trace to give them away. The Orcas continued due north but the whale made no move to avoid them. He hardly thought of them. For the first time in his life he felt a kinship with the dolphins. Their complex sonar meant nothing to him, but he saw that they understood one another, that they communi-

54

cated more clearly than any rorqual. His own species travelled miles apart and, despite their love ties, were sluggish and unsocial compared with the dolphins, only interested in closely related species, while the dolphins' intense concern with creatures so different from their own kind made them unique. In his sickness, the Blue Whale transcended his limitations and reciprocated the interest of the dolphins.

Hovering almost entranced in the calm aftermath of his pain, he listened to the sounds of the Killer Whales grow louder and nearer. Not far to the south, the feeding trough ended, and he could tell that the Orcas were homing in on the trough. They would follow it north, hoping for dolphins or schooling fish, and find him here. The thought of escape crossed his mind but he put it aside. The Orcas were welcome. At the last he even signalled to guide them in.

It was late in the morning when he saw the first black dorsal break the water. There had been times in his life when the sight might have paralyzed him. He had seen Belugas actually roll on their backs, "playing possum" or simply immobilized in terror of these whales. But he stood his ground and the petrels, anticipating, fluttered around him.

Fifteen fins followed the first. In only seconds they swept in from the horizon until he could see the white patches that shattered their ebony lines. They were large, each well over twenty-three feet, and they didn't attack right away. Instead they circled again and again, taking their time. Like the dolphins, these clicked, a cryptic, unsettling sound of five hundred hertz. Finally one screamed. It was like the noise the whale heard in his head in the throes of his sickness. With the scream his courage broke and he wheeled in a cloud of urine and faeces, moaning his terror. There was no easy way to die.

The Orcas forked from a straight line into a box. Six flanked each side and four dropped under. Fear paralyzed him and he defecated again, the taste of his sickness filling the sea. He closed his eyes in terror.

They watched him for ten minutes, as curious and intelligent as the dolphins, clicking back and forth to each other and sending ultrasonic waves into his skin. They could have killed him if they'd wished, and with such a large animal death would be slow, but after investigating the whale, fifteen turned away to pursue the sounds from the open-sea rip. It seemed to the whale his ordeal was over, but seven new Orcas homed in on his calls. He wheeled to take them in and to his dismay saw that the whale who remained from the original sixteen still watched him with interest. When the seven whales drew near, all eight Orcas started herding the bull whale east toward the other fifteen, two on each side and four beneath to rip him open if he dove. If they were to feed on a hundred-foot animal, they would need at least ten attackers, eight or nine to keep him from diving or bolting away while one sliced pieces out of his sides, each whale in the pack taking a turn. They wanted the fifteen other Orcas with them.

Shaking in terror, the bull stroked east with his silent escort, watching with either eye each time one of them glided up to his head. These Orcas never breached or slapped the water—never travelled at more than three knots. The bull felt perplexity mix with his fear. After two minutes, he picked up the swimming sounds of the whale shark which was now feeding in the trough. A minute later, from close range, he heard the tumultuous clicking and splashing of Spotted Dolphins feeding on flying fish, completely distracted by their feast.

By now the Killer Whales were seventy yards from the trough, keeping so low that their tall black dorsals didn't show above the water and so silent that the feeding din in the trough drowned out their sounds. The bull was looking toward the trough where twelve Spotted Dolphins were resting when the fifteen Orcas he'd seen before rose out of the water ahead of him and raced for the trough at well over thirty knots, circling the twelve Spotted Dolphins in seconds and, once they had fenced them, feeding in turns so that the circle never broke. Fifty other Spotted Dolphins, hunting separately from the twelve, hurried away. The twelve dolphins were large, but each time an Orca took a victim it sank its teeth into the underside and held the six-foot animal inside the ring where, in minutes, it was butchered and consumed. They fed one or two at a time, each idle Orca keeping an eye on the other dolphins in the ring in case they tried to dive or sprint. The water was crimson with blood and loud with the squeaks of the dolphins, but the whale shark, eating plankton at the surface, didn't leave. The Orcas only killed three out of the twelve, having already fed many times since the break of dawn. After a moment the eight Orcas guarding the whale swam ahead to join the feast, leaving him free as three more dolphins were slaughtered. The Blue started south. When a few minutes later the dolphin survivors swam away, six of the Orcas who'd watched the whale before raced after him again while the seventeen others rested, gliding idly beside the shark.

The bull whale vaguely considered fighting the Orcas as they drew up on either side, but when they opened their mouths their sharp teeth daunted him. They could maneuver with lightning speed and nothing deterred them except men with ships and guns. These six were especially attracted to the whale, but there was a surplus of prey, with the dolphins, the shark, and the fish who thronged the rip. Even the ravenous Killer Whales couldn't eat everything and they seldom left half-eaten kills behind.

The bull didn't know he'd already been saved by a surplus of victims. His blue skin shivered with fear as the six sated Orcas clicked to each other, playing along his sides. He dove at full speed to get away and for the first twenty-five feet they dove beside him, but then they curved up again and swam back to the seventeen others who circled the shark. The bull raced south. When, after a minute, he heard no Orca sounds, he slowed but didn't relax. Aside from catchers, there was nothing else in the sea he needed to fear besides the Orcas. They were capable of striking at any time, though they'd been indifferent more often than not when he and his mate had crossed their path. He felt dimly amazed as he half remembered encounters where he'd turned one or two of them away by slapping his flukes. He kept fleeing south, too frightened to stop, and the pressure of fear expelled whole barrels of nematodes. After two hours he finally realized he was safe.

The nightmare was past but the bull was alone. He envisioned his mate, realizing that in his terror he had forgotten her again. He moaned to himself. Surely his mate and calf were near now. This was just north of the rise where they'd wintered every year for forty years.

He called many times, his signals minutes apart. But there was no answer. He paused. She couldn't be out of hearing or calling range. That was impossible. She had never wintered south of the Sierra Leone Rise. For a fleeting moment he felt a sense of guilt for the hours he had wasted, staying behind. He signalled again, calling out all afternoon without reply.

At last, in the hope she had actually overshot their wintering ground, he turned southeast and swam at full speed night and day till he was over the Sierra Leone Rise. Still there was no answer to his calls. He swam straight south for another day. Soon the sun, at noon, seemed to blaze directly above him.

The sun made him stop. He had neared the equator, and no matter how great his need for his mate, the southern hemisphere's foreign stars and the towering trajectory of its sun created instinctive fear in the northern whale, an ancient fear deeper than reason that the bull would never be able to overcome, any more than a mammal on land could overcome its fear of fire. Four ice ages had reinforced this behavior over the last half million years. After each ice age, when the glaciers had retreated to the poles, certain whales had followed the cold and its attendant food to the north, while others had followed it to the south. Now there were northern and southern blood groups, two separate tribes with distinct biological cycles. With its northern and southern solstices, the sun dictated the movements of the two groups.

He stared, growing certain his mate was dead. He turned back north, then west, then north again, like a compass needle seeking the right direction. But she was gone. What did it matter now where he swam?

He began to grieve to himself, admitting the loss more deeply into his mind—then suddenly stopped. Out of the south he thought he could hear a rorqual voice. A dream? He waited, heard it again. Surely his mate. He roared his reply, defying the sun. The petrels and shearwaters wheeled around him as he hurried for the unknown universe below the equator.

CHAPTER

7

As the Fin Whale followed the Blue Whale, the youngster revived emotions inside her that had been buried since the death of her last calf. The young female was on fire at the prospect of uniting with a bull, but, to the Fin, sexual yearning for a bull seemed almost as dangerous as the migratory urge that led the other rorquals south to the hunters' guns. Pregnancy would heighten the lure of the Antarctic and necessitate a longer feeding time, since the cow would have to nourish both herself and the new life she carried inside.

The pair swam northward for six days. The Blue had been warm when meeting the Fin the second time, after reversing her flight to pursue the calls from the north, but now her obsession with the calls blocked out everything else. Her eyes no longer watched the Fin when she drew up on either side. Rather, each eye stared into the distance, into nothing. After a week, the Fin had fallen over a day's journey behind. The stroke of her flukes slowed. She considered leaving the Blue Whale altogether. One time she turned away, swam south. But, after twelve hours, strange emotions, yearning partly, compassion as well, turned her north again. As she continued, two days' journey behind, she felt compelled for the first time in sixty-one years of solitude. It occurred to her vaguely that her days of freedom were over, an intuition she discarded immediately.

The Fin Whale's signal reached the Blue Whale's ears, and this time she answered but had no intention of stopping her search for a mate. The fire of her need was huge, and damming up her passion was impossible. The Fin's ovaries had shrunken, withered up, but the Blue Whale's organs had exploded into ponderous bunches of eggs, fifteen inches long. One had detached itself from its follicle while her bicornu-ate womb had been lined with a matrix of blood. Sex hormones flooded her blood as never before. She searched and called, burning her blub-ber down with the heat of her overrunning metabolism. Disturbed by the calls, the Fin Whale raced to get back into eye range, but after the youngster went silent, the northward-swimming Fin lost track of her.

After eight days the young whale slowed. The voice that she'd hoped was a bull's had gone silent, and with its silence, other things, ignored before, came into mind. The farther north she swam the shorter the days, yet her instinct demanded the steady lengthening of the days that only a southward flight could bring. The sudden silence moved her attention from her ears to her eyes, and the sun's towering ecliptic told her to turn.

For a day she stayed still, feeling the strengthening pull of the south. The hours passed without event except when a convoy of destroyers and aircraft carriers mounted some sort of watch two hundred miles south-west of Ascension Island. She listened for the voice she had followed before but heard only ships. Relentlessly the white sun urged her into the south. Her loneliness in an ocean of dead sound made her regret the desperate yearning that had drawn her so far away from the austral playgrounds where for six previous winters she'd enjoyed flirtations and games in a drunken topography of thunder and spray, the matchstick catchers with their murderous factory ships banished until spring. With

60

afternoon her migratory urge almost overpowered her. There was no mate. It was time to turn.

With a great effort of will she delayed till evening. The struggle exhausted her and she slept, waiting till dawn to swim south. She was resting six hundred miles below the equator when the pulse of the bull reached her. She was as asleep as her hunger allowed when his signal awakened her to a star-filled sky, while the southeast trades and the equatorial current drifted her west. Then, in forty minutes, a second signal came, a three-pulse sequence. He was south of the Sierra Leone Rise, calling lustily in his newfound health, and she sensed the vitality of his rolling thunder. The air sacs in his head emitted sound in all directions, and where she listened, southwest of Ascension Island, she caught a triple signal: first the reflection from the ocean floor; then the refraction from the channel of deepwater cold; at last the muffled, diminished bass from the Mid-Atlantic Ridge several hundred miles to the west of him. The Ridge, or at least its crest and its higher peaks, stopped near the equator and started again below it to her east, carried for half a thousand miles by a widening seafloor that, over millennia, had rafted the continents far apart. She answered him, elated, and, when his signal returned all the clearer, she was beside herself with passion.

She soared in pursuit of the bull whale, rumbling her calls through the upper layers of the bowl-shaped, thousand-mile basin. She travelled swiftly. Soon it took barely twenty minutes for her signals to reach the male. He answered immediately and she raced even faster toward him.

They swam nonstop at fifteen knots for a day and two nights and the time lapse between their pulses lessened and lessened. Then, on the second dawn, she caught the white plume of his spray on the northern horizon, over five hundred miles due south of the Sierra Leone Rise. His pulses continued to come but they were drowned now, not by ship-sound, but by the accelerated contractions of her own heart. With a final call he sounded. She overtook him two hundred feet below the surface, well under the dwindling shadows of dawn.

The two of them rose into twilight. As she approached him his hugeness amazed her. She had envisioned a slim, hungry bull with narrow sides, but he was vast; he loomed like a mountain, rearing his rostrum into the light, his abdomen passing interminably before her. He rose like a pale cliff out of the dark and surfaced directly above her, the crash of him like a partial collapse of sky. She studied him as he dove and hovered before her—he seemed like some prodigy out of her mind. So many times she had envisioned the mate, rehearsed the course of their meeting: the acrobatics, the delicious, slow crescendo of courtly play. But now the sheer bulk of his body eclipsed her dreams. She was at a loss. In her distraction she noticed a long brown lamprey wavering along the line where the mottled blue of his back met the mottled gray of his abdomen. With a single swipe of her pectoral she cuffed it off, and it slithered down into the shadows. Taken aback, he retreated. The slap surprised him. He had not felt the lamprey. After a moment he moved toward the female and cuffed *her*. As she veered away, he detected the roundness of her underside, a contrast to the sharp jut of her back. He had spent two days in pursuit of his mate. The sight of this new whale puzzled him.

They turned in the water together, head to tail, the rush of his body spinning her round. She rolled on her back and felt the electrifying touch of his flukes and pectorals against her; they caught her genital slit, her umbilicus, and the long, accordion folds of her sensitive throat. She thought the courtship had started. Forgetting her fantasies, she pre-sented her vagina again and again, and a novel sound came out of the labyrinth inside her head: a series of joyful modulations, high-frequency grunts, not unlike the mating songs of the Humpbacks. There was no language in the sound. It was music and marriage play. Only in child-hood had she used her voice in this way—when she had been playing at love with the eager Antarctic males.

The bull had been overjoyed by the illusion of finding his mate, but now that the cow had come into sight he was disappointed. As in her earlier meeting with the Fin, the cow saw only what she wished to see. When the bull drew back and went silent, she called to him even more loudly and swam around him in dizzying rings. His sense of a loneliness as deep as his own made him answer and swim beside her until he was carried along by her passion. For forty minutes he answered her song, and they circled and circled, their bodies whirlpooling the sea, the water's roar barely matching the roar of hot blood in her ears. Deaf to shipsound, they rose and exploded, two steel-blue hills spouting spray. Then, exhausted, they hung together in the faint light.

She was reborn. The months of waiting were forgotten. Now, even the cruel, macabre roulette of summer feeding among whale boats seemed distant, and she barely remembered the many nights she had passed dreaming of a mate, only to waken with the sight of her harpooned mother climbing the ramp.

Soon even that was forgotten. Her hunger was gone. She let her head sink under the surface and, like a baby, boiled the water with bubble festoons, vaguely abashed at the flagrant intensity of her first greeting. As she followed the male, she saw the gleaming underside of his body, sleek, thick-muscled, round, elastic, and strong. Another hunger filled her. She rose and spouted, and she remembered the lightning touch of one young male from long ago in the Southern Ocean. The bull breathed deeply, inhaling her pheromones, the scent of them rich in the air. She turned away through screens of her own bubbles, flashing the white and gray of her ventral skin under his eye. He paused, gathering his strength, preparing to follow. Her bugling ceased and she hovered, waiting.

He turned on his side at the surface and observed the shape of her, fifteen feet under. The lengthening daylight, the death of his pain, and, more than all else, his loneliness, had made him more than ready for the mating. To the rear of his worm-ravaged kidneys his eighteen-inch testes swelled with their two hundred pounds of sperm. Even now they were channelling rivers into the funnel-shaped mouth of the hollow pelvic bone that anchored his penis. He had been so overwhelmed by her greeting he almost forgot his sadness at discovering that her close-range call was not the voice of his own mate. For two days he had pursued that pulse, feverish at the prospect of reunion with his family after the agony of disease and the inexplicable flight of the Killer Whales. But his drawn-out isolation and his nonstop flight for her voice had muddled his reason, and for a moment, hovering over the Blue Whale cow, he saw his mate in her body. She had grown thin, just as his mate had thinned each year she'd suckled a calf. As the cow inverted herself and looked up toward the bull, he scrutinized her, drawing close—then suddenly paused, greatly surprised, for he saw that her ventral pleats, like his mate's, were more clearly scored than in other whales he had seen. When she turned, it seemed that her angular back was familiar too. As his mate's blubber had thinned, he'd noticed indentations like the cow's, harrowing signs that the bones were nearing light. He stroked her. His nine-foot penis unfolded straight out from his abdomen, protruding eight feet from the slit behind his navel. He

63

nuzzled her. She *was* his mate. Boiling the surface, he touched his penis to her vagina. They clasped their pectorals, hovering as one for several seconds, waving their flukes, no longer calling to each other, and, though their union was sweet to her, there was no play in it. From the moment he entered her till the moment they broke apart his sperm was a nonstop stream into her body. At last she fell away, happy and drunk, zigzagging headfirst into blackness, her abdomen glowing and satisfied.

When she surfaced—languid this time—she nudged his stomach with calflike, whimsical bunts, and her network of nerves hummed with well-being and pleasure. Although she had never witnessed a mating of her own species, she knew that ten minutes or so would pass and then he would enter again, and that this would continue, perhaps for an hour, perhaps for the better part of the day. In any event, there were many days to spend, both here and in the Antarctic. The tropics were limitless and her happiness made all danger unthinkable. She felt she was wed to him. She had not felt such security since the weaning days with her mother long ago.

Now she swam round and about him, taking in details, catching the wrinkles behind his dorsal fin, thin lines unnoticed before. With her snout she nursed and preened him there, sensing a trace of disease and intuiting the trouble in his history. As she swam, the dozen funnels inside her vagina contracted fold upon fold, locking his precious seed inside her body. She consciously strained to tighten the folds, and her pleasure flashed from the lips up the coils of tissue, making her abdomen shiver. She bunted his belly again, closing her eyes, and felt she was truly reborn; that she was starting another life, all her trouble gone.

They joined repeatedly, but by the time the sun was high, the male had grown restless. She could absorb him in their pleasure for hours on end, but only the pleasure kept him near, and when he finally grew exhausted, she could see he did not share her sense of a blood bond. Also she sensed his age, his preoccupation. She suspected he was grieving, but he did not share his pain with her, despite her repeated thrusts and encouragements. Instead, he gently stroked her, almost cajoling. He seemed like a father now. No matter. She would remain with him; she would not go back to her lonely life. But their marriage was different, less than she first had thought.

Later the full light of midday brought more revelations. He seemed afraid when he looked up at the noon sun, but she was unable to comprehend his uneasiness at being a hundred miles below the equator. In the yellow drench of noon the gleaming mount of him, vast as it was, showed many flaws. Over the arching bones the blubber bore a tattoo of pocks and scars—not merely the circular marks of isistius sharks, but concave gashes where, she imagined, Killer Whales had sliced long strips out of his flesh. And there were other, more curious welts—quite hard to come by—as if, in some frenzy, he had rammed himself against jagged reefs or knives. Also new were the parasites, invisible by night. They were swarming now: their scuttling legs crammed his vent and penis slit, and tasting his urine, she caught acrid traces of blood. She preened him with her snout, not caring whether the parasites from his body swam onto hers.

Whole and unblemished herself, she suffered for him. She ran her body down his sides, crushing penellas, and fanned his rostrum; preened his forehead and his sides with her snout and pectoral fins until, for some moments, he felt again the wholehearted passion of their first hours together. In his gratitude he emitted the high-frequency bugles of their courtship, and they caressed each other with infinite tenderness.

The sun hung almost straight overhead at midday. Conscious only of the welts and scars on the bull's enormous body, the cow kept circling him and caressing him with her pectorals, the stroke of her flukes just strong enough to buoy her up and edge her forward. The bull swam too, returning her love, his glide as graceful as her own, his fins as gentle. The dazzling brilliance of the day and the soft reciprocal stroking seemed to stun them. At one point the cow inverted herself and passed beneath his body virtually in slow motion. Then he imitated the cow, caressed the length of her, belly-up. The two continued in this way, descending farther into the ocean with each glide till they crossed the line where dusk gives way to dark. The cow looked up to see the brilliant glow of the ocean top: blue glass. They hung below the limit of light. He took her there, and as they joined, the cow stopped swimming, dropping into the blackness with him above, as if their union were everything. The cow felt vertigo swell her stomachs and her head. They went down together as if the purpose of their lives were now fulfilled and there were no reason to rise for air and light.

They shared a sense of total peace, total abandon. In the darkness it was easy for the bull to tell himself this eager youngster was his mate. But then a voice he had heard for two days now passed through the sea. The bull turned upright and swam for the light, leaving the young cow to herself. He had heard this new voice many times as he'd pursued the young whale's calls. It was easier for the bull to hear his mate's voice in this unknown, uninflected sound than to see her likeness in the youngster. Back at the surface he called out loudly and for some minutes followed the voice into the south. It was just past noon. The sun still seemed to hover directly over his head, and, as he swam farther, he had a sense of it blazing behind him. After a quarter hour he stopped. The voice he fancied was his mate's had quieted, and with its silence, his awareness of the sun's dizzy trajectory was past bearing. He turned back, the young whale following. When he heard the voice again, he answered it but didn't turn due south as before. Instead, in a compromise between the pull of the sun and the power of the voice, he swam due east. The young cow stopped him after an hour, and when they coupled and the sounds of their coupling carried far through the sea, the voice from the south went silent.

They stayed together through the midday. With afternoon he swam off alone, his love calls replaced by desperate, two-hundred-decibel vibrations. She grew fearful now lest his signals attract a ship. Where before their consummations had made her invincible, now she was overwhelmed by the fear of losing completely her already tenuous bond.

He swam in straight lines all afternoon, calling constantly for his mate, and she knew he would have left her alone again had she not followed. Unpredictably he would thrash across the surface, remembering the times when his mate and calf had been within range and he had not joined them. Following him at ten knots, she grew weak, not so much from hunger as from distress, and her lust for the south returned. She yearned to turn him southward. She could not know he was a northern whale only starting his winter fast, while her fasting time had already stretched into spring. When night fell they had swum a hundred miles toward Africa. His calling ceased with the sunset. Though she nuzzled and clicked, he was deaf to her. He went down through the blackening shadows until he brushed a fleshy alcyonarian bed: flower creatures had spread their carpet over a square-shaped calcium peak. Exhausted and close to despair, she descended beside him and they rested just over the peak, two dark blue-mottled wrecks scraping the rocks.

She kept herself parallel to him, always touching one pectoral. Her three-month wait seemed as nothing compared with the lifetime since they had met. His strange behavior bewildered her and she burned with worry. What if one of his rages should madden him? What if he left her alone? Why, at this hungry time of year, when the other whales had long since left for the south, should he swim due east all day? And why did he give no sign of sharing her ravenous hunger? Not merely his hugeness singled him out. He seemed beyond hunger as well. The southern light's magnetic pull that flickered and teased like a drug in her veins was as nothing to him and, although he suffered, he suffered a singular, inaccessible pain. She feared for him. He moved through the ocean intent on inscrutable things, his unparalleled body covered with scars. She nudged him and, though he answered her strokes and calls, he felt no bond, no consanguinity; he dreamed of his calf and his mate. He was a father to her now, or a god.

They rose for breath after fifteen minutes, then rested just under the surface. After an hour, she lifted herself due south and called after him to follow, but he remained over the peak. It was an outrider from the Mid-Atlantic range. Around it the sea was bottomless and black, but over its roof the moon caught shadows of cruel gardens: soft gorgonians and hydroids erected their tentacles and fanned for prey. She took off and returned a score of times, urging him south, but he stayed where he was. After two hours she rested beside him, hearing the drumming of tripod fish echo up from the depths. Sharks passed. Off and on through-out the latter part of the night the bull emitted pulses from his sleep. At first the cow answered, thinking he called to her. When he woke up only briefly and then continued to call in his sleep, oblivious to her, she started swimming in wide circles, puffing loudly every few minutes, hurt and confused. Well before dawn, he had sent four hours of signals into the sea. When a sawfish rose from the darkness and zigzagged its teeth through shoals of fish that fed over the peak, the bull didn't move and, when the saw cut a shallow strip down his back, he woke up only briefly. In fear she remembered the circling requiem sharks from earlier that night. His inky cloud of blood rose and dispersed.

She sensed loneliness in his obsessive signalling, and she could tell from his indifference it wasn't for her. She stopped circling and rested once more beside him. His voice made her remember the two other Blue Whale voices she'd heard from the north. All through the southern hemisphere winter she'd listened for Blue Whale calls and heard none. Then, in these last two weeks before starting south again, three voices had come, within days of each other. Two had gone silent when she pursued them, and she'd never heard them again. Now a third Blue Whale was calling in loneliness. The cow felt a rush of tenderness as she remembered those earlier signals that had died. Vaguely she wished she could tell the bull what she had heard. But there is no language among Blue Whales—only the calls of immediate emotion.

Toward dawn he grew alert and swam up from the peak, making a playful sharklike run, streaking his dorsal fin down her chest. As the water began to lighten she forgot her alarm, forgot everything in her hunger for more lovemaking. When her strenuous flirtations finally coaxed an erection from him, he took her vertically, belly to belly, moving far away from the peak. His pectoral fins pressed tight on her sides, but she knew their union had changed from yesterday. Physically part of her, he was far away in his mind. She studied the strip on his back, pinkish white among a welter of tight-knit scars grown tough and silvery with time. As they broke away she detected the slither of whale lice inside the tender furrow of skin where the blundering sawfish had opened him.

With the waning of their passion the lure of the south possessed her again. The Antarctic sky blazed in her mind, a perpetual light over pastures that teemed with food. She ran ahead repeatedly, but when he remained, it was as if she could feel a cable lengthen and strain between them. Her ventral lips still glowed where his sperm had entered her and she seethed with love of him, but he seemed senseless, hanging wistful and self-absorbed on the northern horizon while everything—sun, hunger, the restlessness in her blood—urged her south.

Not long after sunrise the calls from the south resumed. The bull answered excitedly and this time followed them without hesitation. The other whale was so close he could overtake it in minutes, travelling hardly more than two miles farther south. The young cow roared for joy and followed him, pretending the migration had begun. She warmed with excitement. As she swam she nosed his flukes and behind her eyes she saw a vision of the two of them crossing the polar front in this way: him slightly ahead, her nosing his flukes in encouragement.

When the spout of the whale he pursued came into sight, the bull dove, calling exactly the way he had called when the spout of the young Blue Whale had first cleared the horizon. He imagined his mate. While he rushed to overtake her, he looked for the shadow she would present: at first the pinpoint tip of her snout, then the great rostrum, bobbing lightly in the characteristic way the bull remembered, at last the smaller shape of his young calf at her side. As he envisioned this in his mind, he turned himself west, then, with a stroke or two, drew close enough that his vision seemed to grow real.

The bull pursued the Fin until the old whale finally turned, head low in the water, and rumbled a warning. The bull whale immediately recognized his mistake. After a moment he moaned. The Fin Whale butted at him and rumbled again, not as hotly as before. He hovered some distance off, between the cow and the Fin.

The Fin grew sad. As the cow had, the bull brought back unsettling memories. So many times she had seen the widowed Antarctic whales become obsessed with incoming migrants. They would pass eagerly from newcomer to newcomer in the hope of rediscovering a friend, a calf, a mate. It was the immensity of the loss, the harrowing weight of it, that drove them to this folly. She tensed, remembering the days after the slaughter of her own mate and her last calf. A maternal feeling slowly dissolved her initial pique. As with the cow thirteen days before, her memories made her compassionate.

The bull was a few feet off. To distract herself she swam toward him a dozen yards down, glided above him, and passed her pectorals down his length from snout to tail. The bull stayed still and she saw that he welcomed her attentions. She swam over him several times until she could hear a faint rumble inside him. Now the cow approached as well, and for twenty minutes or so the three of them were together, just under the light, so close that each could touch the other two—the two Blue Whales unmoving, side by side, and, overhead, the Fin Whale gliding back and forth, preening both with her fins.

As she caressed the long dark backs, the Fin Whale focussed her attention on the cow, for now the problem of thirteen nights ago was troubling her again. With pregnancy the cow's yearning for the south would be stronger than ever, and she would remain in the Antarctic hunting area at least an extra month as she stored up nourishment for the calf. Envisioning the catchers in the Antarctic, the Fin stopped preening, swam slightly away.

The bull called to her and swam under her, buoying her up until her maternal stroking started again. This time she swam even more slowly than before, running her sides down his and taking in details with either eye. Over and over she paused in surprise at the circular, jaw-shaped scars and scarred-over lesions. She was fairly sure his family had been killed in the Antarctic and that he hovered near the equator in fear of the guns. She knew a natural death would claim her soon, knew this as surely as she knew that the Blue Whale bull was half her age and that the Blue Whale cow was only starting her life. She kept herself close to him, reading his scars. She was confused. How had he lived so long in these oceans without her knowing it? Perhaps this whale, alone like herself, had broken the bondage of migration; had learned, like her, to feed north of the polar front. How else explain his ample girth at these latitudes, at this time of year? It seemed to come to her now, the meaning of his presence. More and more things seemed to make sense. He lived as she did, shunning the ice. He'd found the way. Perhaps this young bull whale, wise as herself, could dissuade the cow from her southward journey.

She felt great joy as she thought of the three of them together, like two parents and a calf. The bull whale rumbled his pleasure at her stroking and started to think of his earliest days: his birth off Cape Cod, the months with his parents over the Grand Banks of Newfoundland. Some distance away, the Blue Whale cow could hear the rumbling. It made her jealous. She dove and rose at full speed, soaring up between the two whales and tipping them over sideways.

The spell broken, the bull began sculling east, his rumbles of gratitude replaced by the two-hundred-decibel vibrations with which he called his mate and calf. The young cow turned and swam after, careful to keep herself between him and the Fin. The old whale followed for a while. Hours passed, and each time the Fin approached the pair, the cow drove her off.

After a while the Fin gave up. When she called in farewell and swam away with no further signals, the young Blue Whale didn't even notice. The bull was still swimming due east and calling out for his lost family.

70

The cow grew frantic. She tried to make love with him again, and when that failed, she swam straight south for several minutes, hoping that loneliness would make him follow her.

This struggle continued all afternoon. She would swim almost out of sight, then turn back when the sounds of his breath faded behind her. He made no call, content to have her venture off by herself, greeting her return with an amused, tolerant affection, as if she were playing some youthful game. At last, in a desperate attempt to show her intention, she left him far to the north, racing headlong toward the pole until his spout became only a feathery wisp behind her, then disappeared. She headed straight south. Hours passed and she listened for him, for some sign of distress or passion. Not only hunger consumed her. She ached as well for him to desire her; to call out for her as he'd called out for his mate.

Her calls again alerted the Fin, who stayed nearby during the long afternoon, ready to block the cow's migration if she could. Now she flung herself across the cow's path. The two whales clashed, then, racing full speed, the Blue broke away south, still calling the bull.

But the sun arched to the west; its decline darkened the depths, and, spouting, the cow heard only the *wide-a-waaks* of the sooty terns, explorers from the flock on Ascension Island. Here the faint rumbles of Right Whales off the coast of Tristan da Cunha caught her ear, just for an instant. Uncertain, alone, she turned north.

The Fin Whale had stopped chasing, yet she was encouraged. She could tell that the bull was holding the young cow back from her migration. Now all that was needed was for the youngster to learn to eat fish and midlatitude plankton. She swam off, avoiding the anger of the returning cow, certain the bull would keep the youngster from the ice. Soon in her dreams the Fin could see them. She would join them as they travelled safe water together. Falling asleep, she awaited the cow and her mate with self-satisfaction. Next day or the day after that the youngster would give in, and the three of them would feed in shoals of smelt.

The bull whale gave no answer to her calls, and so the cow continued toward him, sick at heart, stroking listlessly into darkness. Her back was growing raw. Since he had come she had burned more body fuel than in many previous days. Hunger had been a hollow before, a goad, but now her stomachs stabbed her with pain. Tomorrow or the next day she

71

would have to turn him south. Whatever his grief, she could not indulge him forever.

There had been stars two hundred miles below the equator, three hundred miles north of Ascension where she'd stopped her southward flight, but she swam back north under overcast sky, calling out till at last he answered, only a mile from where she had left him. Pellets the size of golf balls had filled the sea: the tankers' concentrated dung which sometimes drifted for thousands of miles. They bumped and clung as she nosed toward him through the dark. His plume of spray loomed white, and when she dove, she could hear sonar: the clicks of dolphins. Their signalling loudened as she approached until she could see them: an archipelago of gleaming, moonlit skin.

She hovered a hundred feet or so from where his huge blue mound formed a hub for the three Common Dolphins he'd met before. For a week they'd swum south, homing in on his signals. She watched, incredulous, not at the dolphins but at the bull. Dolphins were common enough to her. Even Antarctica had its various cold-water species: black and white racers that were food for Killer Whales. She saw them as chattery, alien creatures. And yet there he was, calling out to them as if they were his peers.

His moans and clicks were completely different from the sound that had answered her call on their first meeting. As she listened, watching his round, indifferent flesh reflect the light, she knew his song had nothing whatever to do with her, yet its passion stabbed her. From time to time the dolphins swam close to him and touched him with their heads. When they'd arrived hours earlier, they'd been dismayed to see worms still in his kidneys, though there were fewer than before. Soon after they'd fled the Killer Whales, the Striped Dolphin female had died from her parasites while her three companions had been able only to watch. Now the young male's fascination with whales had brought the three survivors back to the bull. But the whale appeared even sadder than when they had first encountered him, and they didn't understand why. Before this second meeting the persistence of his long-range calls had told them he'd been lonely, and when they'd picked up the sounds of a new whale swimming beside him they had been glad. Yet now, as the young cow returned from the south and the bull didn't even turn to acknowledge her, his indifference puzzled them. The memory of the cow and calf who'd fallen to the cruiser returned to their minds.

72

Though they lacked a language, the patterns of their clicks could evoke isolated perceptions such as "ship" and "wound" and "calf," and as they looked at the bull in his sadness, they signalled these patterns over and over again. From time to time the young male dolphin would swim close to the bull and click, trying to communicate his memory of the whales who had been slaughtered, but each time he did the bull would merely keep on repeating the same mournful sequence of grunts and moans. The dolphin clicked to the cow as well, but she ignored him. After an hour he turned away, growing preoccupied with his sister and his cousin. There had been mourning for the Striped Dolphin female just after she died, and now the sadness of the bull was making the females grieve again. They swam a good way off, opening blue lanes through the alleys of black oil, the sound of their passage like a jostle of ball bearings.

The cousin was the more distressed of the two. She slashed at the young male with her teeth when he tried to console her. More vicious than a natural show of anger, her behavior had been learned during the time of captivity. Twelve dolphins had been captured altogether: one mother dolphin with her three older sons, one older daughter, and male and female calves; the mother's sister with her two young cows; and two Striped Dolphins. Over the first few weeks of capture the navy had tested them to determine which were likely to follow commands in open sea. The brother and sister, both younger than their cousin and unweaned at the time of capture, had exhibited little talent for taking commands, but as long as their families were safe, both mother and aunt had responded well, as had the cousin. The trainers made few demands on the mother dolphin before her calves were weaned. Six months after capture the twelve had been placed in an open-sea pen in a secluded, fenced-off part of Lagos Harbor. Here they had learned to take metal disks down to targets that gave off nine-kilohertz pings, the same sound the trainers used to call them. The cousin had loved this game, but the game at which she'd excelled had been slicing a man-shaped dummy with a bayonetlike appendage attached to her snout. Her mother and sister couldn't perform this feat no matter how great the reward in fish and praise, but the cousin was more aggressive. Now, as she mourned the loss of the sick Striped Dolphin female and the young male tried to commiserate, her aggressiveness flared up. Each time he approached she opened a new wound in his back. Soon the brother and sister ganged up

73

to give her a thorough going over, leaving her back as bloody as theirs but cooling her temper down a bit. When the Blue Whale cow joined the bull, the brother and sister had moved about ninety yards away to attend to the cousin. Soon, begrudgingly, she let them stroke her back while the young male dolphin twined his flukes around her tail. For the better part of the night the three hung still.

The bull whale was quiet that night, though he hardly slept. The cow dozed a yard under the sea, only rising to spout, the bull hovering beside her with open eyes. His hope that his family survived had dimmed with each unanswered call, and now he had grown certain they were dead. He could see his mate in his mind and he remembered their life together: escapes from whalers, shark and Killer Whale attacks, mating, travelling, near-disasters at low tide. When the cow awoke, well before dawn, he was docile with shock.

She thrust him forcibly upright and excited him into erection. By midmorning he had entered her several times. The three Common Dolphins, recovered now, imitated the whales, the females squeaking with joy as the male pursued them. He was glad to see his cousin join the game.

Late morning came and the Blue Whale cow once more turned south. This time, at her urging, the dazed bull followed. The Common Dolphins followed her too. They clicked and chattered under the high sun, and though the female thought them a nuisance, the bull was soon chattering back in his primitive rorqual sonar. The dolphins' voices had no meaning for the whale, but all morning they kept up a token communication, as captive dolphins will do with a man.

While this went on behind her, the spirits of the cow soared with relief. Swimming yesterday had been like dragging an iron chain, but today her flukes were wings and the very waves seemed to spread themselves for her passage. After some hours the Fin appeared. She had homed in on the cow's signals. All anger forgotten, the young cow stroked her when she drew close, then the six of them continued south together. The Fin felt a sense of belonging she had not known for sixty-one years, and the cow, too, seemed satisfied and happy. Behind her the bull seemed happy, as well, in his way. Blind to the rear, she could feel him alternate from right to left, zigzagging in her slipstream, with the dolphins jumping his back or riding his bow wave mile after mile. The weight of him in her waves should have slowed her down, yet despite the burden, she swam faster. When they stopped it was after midnight. Her hunger had died. The warmth of his presence and the thought of the feast to come were enough for her now. The old Fin Whale, remembering last time, swam off and kept to herself. Again the cow and bull slept with pectorals touching, while in the starlight, the ravenous dolphins squeaked and dove, the ruthless accuracy of their sonar picking out squid at nine-fathom depths. The night was warm and the troublesome pellets of oil had disappeared. The dolphins fed till their snow-white bellies swelled like new bread under the moon. Then, toward dawn, the three of them hovered beside the whales. The bull awoke and made clicking sounds, then slid back into sleep. The cow indulged his followers, glad at least that they had grown quiet. For the moment they could remain. It was enough for her now that the bull followed her south. She glowed with joy when the early morning sun caught his steel-blue skin.

The old Fin Whale approached, worried once more. Joy like the cow's was all too often followed by death in the polar sea. Still, this southward journey was slow, lacking the urgency that generally marked southern migration. And the bull was not in bondage to the sun. He had broken free, like the Fin herself. As she thought these things, the Fin grew relieved.

They swam nonstop through the next day and the next night, and on the following dawn the surface waves reverberated the sound of distant rollers pounding land. Green Mountain broke the skyline to the south. As the restless waters assumed direction, the talkative dolphins springboarded off the waves. Four hundred and ninety miles below the equator, Ascension Island, an unremarkable lava lump on the Challenger Rise of the Mid-Atlantic Ridge, enraged the ocean. For thousands of miles to north and south the waves passed easily over the Mid-Atlantic Ridge, but here they were blocked and seemed determined to obliterate this mote that stood in their way. The cow continued south, but to her dismay the dolphins veered toward the east, riding the rollers in for the island. The bull whale hesitated between them and the cow, finally following them in. The frustrated cow hung off at the edge of the shelf and called for him, but he didn't return. The Fin continued south to feed in the open sea. At last the young cow joined the bull. For the rest

75

of the day the two whales watched the dolphins surf the crumbling waves on the island's western side.

The lengthening daylight tantalized her more than ever, pulling her, mothlike, toward the Antarctic blaze. Sensing her eagerness, the bull hung back with the dolphins, as if in play, seizing on any excuse to lag behind. His circadian clock, ticking to an opposite time from hers, made her frenetic rush seem unnatural, dangerous. Already they were seven degrees past the equator, midway between Africa and South America. Never before had the bull been so far south of his mating ground. The equinox had passed. September was ending. If they continued, the nights would shrink, and the clock in his body demanded the longer, tropical nights for his winter rest. At the back of his mind he feared the female. At first he had followed to humor her, but the southern furnaces gaped wider with every dawn, and he could see she would not be satisfied; she wanted to swim with him in perpetual light. He followed more slowly now, dismayed, imagining himself at the end of the world, barred forever from return to his summer home in the Denmark Strait.

All day the sooty terns from the island colony zigzagged swallowlike over their heads, their nasal calls filling the air as they darted for fish. Pairs pursued each other along the shore as the lengthening daylight heated their blood and ripened the eggs inside them. Their black-and-white wings filled the day. Far to the west, the few green turtles that remained were leaving the South American waters. With March they would scuffle in frenzy over the cinder beach, to lay their eggs well inland.

The dolphins surfed all day and well into night, but the whales, growing bored, finally left the tumultuous west behind and hovered in the comparative calm of the east side over bryozoan beds and ink-black urchins. From time to time they heard the signals of the Fin, who was feeding a few miles southeast of the island. The female incessantly urged the bull whale out to sea. He was sad for her but he would not follow. One time he mounted her like a cock mounting a hen, pressing his pectorals over the pitiful ridge of her back and rocking her back and forth in the predawn tide, her abdomen brushing a ridge. He tupped her roughly, expressing his rage and confusion that her sides were hollow with hunger. If she were a strange species of whale—a foreign species that fed in the south—then where was the mate of her own kind to

76

accompany her on her crazy migration? By day she continued to urge him south, but by now even she felt that they came from different worlds.

With midmorning the dolphins came in from the west, their bellies bulging with squid. The two whales turned to watch them, sensing their freedom. Though they followed the sun on their daily feeds, the dolphins had not sold themselves to the sun. Overspecialized, over-sized, the Blues could sense their difference each time they watched the dolphins' careless play, and the female resented them more than ever. She spent the day near the bull, swimming aimlessly here and there in the twenty-foot waves. With night her restlessness intensified to frenzy and she swam south for several hours. The Fin Whale tried to block her, but she evaded the Fin and swam on. The bull whale followed her part of the way, but he saw she would not turn. His heart sickened at her flight and he called out, pleading with her to delay. At last she turned, letting him enter her several times as she followed him north. Dawn found them hovering side by side within sight of the island.

This continued for half a week, the female heading south with the male swimming her slipstream, both of them playacting at migration. Every dawn she hoped that today would be the turning point, that the male would not circle back in the late afternoon as he had before, cajoling her till she finally followed. Her hope alone held her back till after three days he fell ill. The worms in his kidneys had multiplied and turned his urine red. She could scrape the penellas off his sides, could even fan the whale lice out of his wound with her pectoral fins, but this new sickness was inaccessible. She stopped travelling and attended him all one day and night while the dolphins hovered in sympathy, scanning his insides with their sonar, subdued, no longer riding the waves.

She suffered for him, and they grew closer than ever before, but with dawn the magnet inside her doubled its force. In early morning her hunger prevailed. She left him hanging half awake, lost in his sickness, on the lee side of the island. She swam for the south without making a sound.

The last tern vanished behind her, then the cloudcap over the island fell away. The cow swam hard. But at noon the sound of his dolphins came to her. Had she known how, she would have cursed them. Why did they not remain with the bull? She was butting the waves in her anger, speeding up, when a second sound reached her: the deep-level pulse of him, lost in his loneliness, calling her back.

The water cleared where she left the sea shelf's cloud of phytoplankton. When he called to her again, something inside her swelled and broke. The dolphins leaped about her, as if urging her to return. They flashed their backs at her. Now, louder, the bull whale called again. The young cow signalled once in farewell, then plowed for the southern sky.

CHAPTER

8

D ISTURBED that the cow was mi-
grating south, the Fin swam hard in pursuit and in no time at all saw the
distant, pear-shaped spout she knew so well. When she closed in, she
discovered the dolphins swimming some distance back of the youngster.
She drew up on her, cautious at first, for after her bruisings, she feared
the aching cow would be ready for a fight. She came up on her very
slowly; then, beside her, eye to eye, edged gradually nearer, her rumbles
signalling goodwill. In a quarter hour they began to relax.

They paused for a moment after three hours of leisurely swimming,
and the Fin Whale ran her pectorals down the Blue Whale's jutting
sides. As at their first meeting, it hurt her to feel the vertebrae jut like
sticks. Pitifully thin, completely in thrall to her emotions, the Blue

Whale wouldn't stand a chance against the ships in the Antarctic. As if trying to blanket the bare bones, she pressed her fat against the youngster's ribs. Soon, where her flipper touched the old whale's pectoral fin, the young whale throbbed with sensual pleasure. With the bull whale far behind, her love for her friend returned as strongly as on the night of their first meeting; she didn't want to lose the Fin, as well. Sensing her power, the Fin kept trying to turn the Blue Whale north and after four hours the cow was vacillating between due south and southwest. This kept on for the better part of the day, and their speed repeatedly slowed. Whenever plankton or smelt grew thick, the Fin hung back, still hoping to teach the Blue to feed in temperate seas. By day, though the Blue often slowed for the Fin, she was always quick to resume her flight. Yet with nightfall her resolution slackened. Again and again there would be fifteen-minute sprints straight for the south and, after each, slow southwest swims of an hour or more. The Fin wanted to stop completely, but for now she settled for this. At least the Blue Whale didn't swim in blind obedience to the sun, and this independent course could save her life.

With dawn the bull whale's signal reached them from a hundred and twenty miles to the northeast. Twenty miles west of Ascension Island, he had turned north for home and was calling the cow to follow. The Fin could see he was tantalizing the cow and hoped she would turn.

His calls were constant, but, swimming on the surface, the cow and Fin heard only the fainter signals reflected up from the ocean floor. In her race for the north, the cow had been unable to resist the bull whale's calls, whatever their volume, but now she tried to shut them out. Yet her loneliness kept her close to the Fin. In midmorning the old whale dove for two hundred feet and the youngster followed. Here his voice, refracted through the layer of greatest resistance at four thousand feet, sounded so clear that it seemed for a moment he was close by. The cow slowed down and answered him. The Fin called as well, then started leading the youngster north, but the bull whale's signals evaded them for over two hours, since the path of his soundwaves failed to cross their own. The cow turned southwest with the Fin Whale trailing in disappointment.

Almost three hours passed before they heard him again. He was thirty miles farther north, about four hundred and forty miles below the equator, his sickness past. The young cow vacillated between the west and north, her reception sporadic. After fifty hours the bull crossed the equator. The cow and Fin heard his voice less often once he'd left the equator behind, but each time it came he seemed to have moved even farther north. Even while trying to shut him out, the cow had been hoping for him to turn and swim toward her with passionate calls as he had at the first. Feeling again the frustration she'd felt off Ascension Island, she turned back south.

Her reversals had slowed her migration and after two days she was less than two hundred miles southwest of Ascension. His calls were steadier now, coming every two to three hours from well above the equator, and the Fin Whale warmed inside, feeling hopeful the cow would turn north a second time. His voice intrigued her. When she'd heard rorqual calls from the northern seas before, she'd assumed they'd come from Antarctic whales who'd grown bored waiting out their wintering time and were seeking adventure beyond the equator. Now his calls raised a new vision in her mind. She saw him basking among vast herds in the outer reaches beyond the equator, northern boundary of the world, where the whaling ships and cruisers would fear to follow. In another vision she saw an empty sea and, in it, the first Blue Whale in ten decades to live and grow without facing the guns. Despite her lack of language, the elation the vision brought was so infectious that by dawn the Blue was swimming north again.

The Fin swam fast, hour after hour, her vision so clear that she was surprised when the cow slowed down, but the morning grew long and in her excitement she hadn't noticed the bull whale's calls had all but died. With noon the ravenous youngster changed her direction from north to southwest. The Fin's euphoria disappeared as she trailed behind.

Now the voice had stopped completely. As the cow continued south, the Fin slowed down. Watching the youngster's stubborn flight, she started to feel resigned, despite her love, while the dolphins beside her, apparently carefree in their easy, graceful arcs, were actually terrified of being left alone. They'd been distressed when the two cows had left the bull and now it appeared that *they* were splitting up as well. Trembling, the dolphins swam back and forth between the pair.

This growing desperation focussed the great difference between the whales and dolphins. The intimacy of the Fin with the Blues had

81

resulted from the ruthless decimation of both species. When not desperate from the trials of near extinction, Fins and Blues felt no deep need for social life. The old Antarctic congregations had sprung from hunger, not social instinct, and, though marriages were made in the Antarctic where the young whales met their peers, actual mating and family life occurred in northern isolation. By contrast, all species of dolphins were naturally social, incapable of living alone. Life in schools not only made easier the nightly search for prey but also nurtured the social groupings through which each dolphin found a role and place. In the largest inshore schools there were mating groups, adolescent groups, females with lovers, mothers with suckling calves, mature males who acted as sentries and guards, herd elders whose signal repertoire preserved and passed on for the others a tradition of songs and memories.

Whales sought food and one or two chosen companions, while the young dolphins who swam with the whales had been cast out by their own kind and didn't know what they were seeking. Almost killed in a tuna seine, captured and trained by the navy, they'd had no chance to find their place in a school. Without this, they'd be restless and discontented all their lives.

Dimly they could sense this inadequacy. The need for a group had made them especially vulnerable to their trainers, and their travel with the whales created, at best, an artificial camaraderie, since there was no communication. Still five years away from sexual maturity, the three would either have to return to their school on the African shelf or seek fellowship among open-sea Common Dolphins. The older they grew, the stronger they felt the need to belong, and though their dissatisfaction was different from that of the solitary whales, it was fully as strong.

The dolphins needed a home. Of all communities in the sea, the settled schools of inshore dolphins represented the closest approach to civilization, not as defined in terms of machines or technology but as realized among all intelligent beings, cetacean or human, where communication and social bond transcended the mere exigencies of life. Among the settled inshore schools the exchanges and recitations were more precise and particularized than in any animal except man. Such vocalization was subtlest and richest among the old, but old dolphins could only survive in rooted communities, whose concern for the weak and infirm in itself showed their high level of civilization. Polar krill, a mate, and a calf would have contented the Blue Whale cow, but the

82

three dolphins sensed needs inside them that only a school could satisfy. The history of the Blue Whales, living in groups of two or three as their numbers declined, was a story of scattered individuals struggling to survive. The dolphins, however, were a rich and ancient culture in its twilight. Catchers took the whales one at a time but dolphins generally died in groups: gill nets, tuna seines, drive fisheries, and pollution were lessening their numbers every year.

As the gap between Blue and Fin steadily widened, the dolphins began to feel as rootless as in their first few days of freedom. Less than four months had passed since they had left Lagos. It hadn't really been an escape. After six months of indoor experiments during which all except the young brother and sister had proven their sonar could distinguish among different kinds of metal and that they could find, retrieve, or mark targeted objects on command, they'd been flown to a section of Lagos Harbor where an area roughly fifty by a thousand feet had been netted off. Here they'd learned to mark and retrieve at greater distances and depths.

At least the older dolphins had. The young brother and sister, unweaned when captured, hadn't been as intensively trained as the others and were present mainly for their mother's peace of mind. Soon the mother, aunt, cousins, and older siblings started working outside the pen. Here they adapted to harnesses, learned to mark metal targets at six- to nine-hundred-foot depths and to bear objects into areas marked off by pinging buoys. Common Dolphins are not noted for stability as captives, but these dolphins were a family, and this, as well as the gentleness and skill with which they'd been captured and introduced to their new life, had rendered them calm and secure. There was little fear of having the dolphins flee. Most came back promptly to the boat when the whistle or buzzer summoned them. Like all dolphins, they feared to leap surface barriers, and once back in their open-sea pen (its boundaries marked by fifty-gallon drums), not one made the two-foot jump to freedom.

When, after a year, the brother, sister, and cousin at last "escaped" with two Striped Dolphins, it was really accidental. They had simply been lofted over the drums in a storming sea. Even then the three Common Dolphins had stayed by their mothers, nudging and calling

83

back and forth at the edge of the pen. When they'd decided to swim away with the two Striped Dolphins, the penned relatives, content with their routine, had expected the five to return after play and exploration. But the exploration had lasted all that day and they hadn't returned. Next day, in calmer weather, the five had kept on exploring. The three Common Dolphins had meant to turn back for the pen, but, what with racing motorboats, buzzing planes, swooping helicopters, sportsmen shooting from hydrofoils, and a dozen other distractions, they'd gotten lost. Lagos Harbor, a maze of jetties, emptying creeks, and blind-alley channels, had dizzied them. By afternoon the five were approaching the open sea.

The farther they swam the more reluctance gave way to exhilaration. Two walls at the harbor entry protected incoming ships against the punishing and virtually perpetual southwest swell, and as the dolphins moved down the eastern wall, they could feel sediment prickle their skin as the irresistible ocean drift eroded the concrete. Though they didn't know why, the feeling pleased them. Despite their love for their captive families, the three Common Dolphins felt euphoria when they finally swam out to the offshore sea.

Their wandering was born of the restlessness captivity had caused, but hunger limited how long they could live this way. Food was most abundant over the shelves that edged the land. After the older Striped Dolphin had joined a school of her own kind and the other four dolphins had turned west to the open Atlantic, they'd looked for rises to deflect the currents up and raise the nutrients for animals and fish. Now, with the whales leaving the Mid-Atlantic Ridge to enter deep, unbroken sea, the food grew sparse. It was the southern hemisphere spring, and despite their immaturity, all three survivors could feel a burgeoning sexual drive.

The Fin slowed down even more when the cow continued stubbornly southwest for another day. The fast-swimming Blue called out as the gap widened between them, but the Fin moved listlessly at a wavering speed. The dolphins had left the bull because they couldn't bear to watch his growing sickness after the Striped female had died. Faced now with a choice between the rapidly thinning cow and the fat Fin, they stayed behind with the Fin. Three days had passed since the cow had disappeared on the southwest horizon.

In late afternoon the dolphins left the Fin to hunt, but the sea yielded nothing, not even sounds of crustaceans in the depths. The sky was blank and they could hear no feeding birds. The richest waters were always over the shelves along the coasts, and the dolphins, alarmed by the emptiness of the sea and the growing ache of hunger, knew they must leave the whales and swim for a coast to survive. The dawdling Fin was a hundred miles south of Ascension Island. The dolphins had turned back for Ascension and the African shelf beyond, when a distant din of clicks and whistles made them stop.

They turned to the west. The noises loudened very quickly, coming first from the water alone and then from both the water and air. The horizon churned with spray as arching backs and blue-black dorsals filled the entire length of the western sky. The wide spacing of the subgroups in this school of Common Dolphins showed that the members felt secure. No species raised more spray or made more noise than Common Dolphins. The three youngsters were tense with anticipation as the five hundred drew near, swimming west for the fertile waters over the Mid-Atlantic Ridge.

As the dolphins drew close it was clear that they were different from the brother, sister, and cousin, whose long snouts identified them as shallow-water creatures who normally lived on the coastal shelves. The five hundred open-sea dolphins were slightly smaller, with shorter snouts. The southern spring had excited them, and as soon as the sister and cousin approached, young males raced ahead and danced and leaped for them, showing off. The sister enjoyed this new attention, but after some minutes, the cousin, unbalanced by captivity, butted a bachelor and, when he persisted, thrust with her beak. He was daunted but others were not. After a moment, the male attacked his cousin's aggressors, then pursued her as she swam off after the Fin. She stopped for him and for a moment the two of them hovered apart from the school. He felt certain that he could soothe her, turn her back, have his own way. It made no sense to remain alone or return to the Fin. But the cousin was in the grip of the strange rage that had sporadically troubled her ever since she'd been taught how to use the bayonet. The male cajoled but when she turned and swam on, he wavered, uncertain whether to follow her or remain with the others. He called to his sister, but her attention was all for the males who surrounded her. Had she followed, he would have swum in pursuit of the Fin. His cousin faded from his sight. Angrily, grudgingly, he turned to the school again. Once he was gone, the cousin hesitated, swimming in circles and sometimes going still.

Next morning the sea seemed empty to the Fin, who, over the days away from the cow, had come to expect the dolphins' arcing approach. They came from the emptiness like children, rejoining her when the sun rose high. Now, with the horizon blank and the bull and cow both silent, she was disconsolate, fronting the black Brazilian Basin. This sense of desolation at being alone was new to her, since over the decades after her family's death she had ceased to fear isolation or to worry about other whales. Yet a vision of the young cow being slaughtered by the ice had become vivid during the night and was hard to dispel. She clenched her lids as she tried to shut it out of her mind. When she reopened them, she lost herself for a while in waking dreams. Reveries filled so much of her life that what had actually happened often appeared unreal—not only her time with the Blues but also her earlier life: mating, calving, fleeing the guns. As with most of her unsettling intuitions, she shook this feeling aside and tried to divert herself by turning to present things. The day was calm, the sea a rich, continuous blue outside her eyes. Past flowed into future imperceptibly until the Fin could feel the margins between herself and the outside world blur, then disappear. The Blue Whale cow was completely forgotten. For a moment she knew what death was. Her mind went blank.

Then, in the distance, she saw a single arcing shape. She signalled twice. The cousin raced to rejoin her, but then slowed down in alarm. Something appeared to be wrong with the whale. She breached and rumbled, falling in thunder to one side. The cousin couldn't tell that the old Fin's call was a sound of joy.

When the cousin came within touching range, the Fin, still on her side, arched one huge pectoral over the dolphin and brought it down lightly on her head. The image of the Blue Whale cow was bright in her mind again. She remembered their first meeting, the sweetness of stroking after her many years alone. Her tremulous fin moved back and

86

forth over the dolphin while she called with low-intensity sounds that gently vibrated the cousin from snout to tail. After three minutes she righted herself and the quivering cousin rode her bow wave, glowing with pleasure as the Fin speeded up, pursuing the cow in earnest once again.

Six hundred miles north the Blue Whale bull was seeking the cow as well. When she had left him behind at Ascension Island, his infestation of nematodes had immobilized him, but within hours after she left, he had expelled them, just as he had before, when escaping the Killer Whales. In sudden relief he had pursued her, only to flee. He was bewildered by the conflict between his desire for the cow and his terror of the southern sun's elevation, drives that held alternate sway depending on his position. Once the stop sign of the sun's noon elevation at the equator was taken away, his loneliness slowly outweighed his fear. Sixty miles north of the equator, his isolation overwhelmed him and he marvelled that his fear of the southern sun could have been so strong as to turn him north. The heightened loneliness grew so much stronger than the fear that after a day he found himself swimming south again, and even now he was closing in on the equator a second time. The better part of a week had passed since the cow had left him and she was south of him by over a thousand miles, but he was driven by isolation, not reflection, and he felt certain he could win her back again.

It was early October. This was the fifth day to dawn since the Fin had let the cow swim on alone. She was fifteen hundred miles east by north of the city of Salvador on the north coast of Brazil. Moving southwest, she would swim for hours at the surface and hear neither the bull nor cow, but when she swam three hundred feet down the arcing soundwaves of both whales occasionally reached her. She could tell that the cow, more than three hundred miles away, was swimming southwest but had slowed down. The sounds of the bull whale told the Fin he was no longer moving north. She could hear the bull and cow signal each other repeatedly, and she hoped even now that the cow would turn back. She hadn't expected her to slow. Calling loudly, she kept to a steady thirteen knots in pursuit of the youngster, while the cousin followed behind.

The pulses of the bull told the Fin that his flight paralleled hers as he moved southwest toward the equator. She answered his calls. If she continued swimming her present course and the young cow didn't speed up, she could overtake her before she crossed the polar front. So the Fin was calm. The youngster's voice showed she was still in swimming range.

The three whales swam all day. Late in the evening a change in the intervals of the calls of the young cow alarmed the Fin. The youngster, travelling faster, was swimming more and more to the south, less and less to the west. At the same time the bull had reached the equator.

The Fin speeded up. Now every time the bull whale's voice came down from the north she sent back sounds of shattering volume. She wished he would hurry, for, with the youngster swimming farther and farther south, she wanted the lure of his sex to complement her calls.

It was night when he passed below the equator the second time. He glanced at the sky furtively, then defiantly, certain the stars wouldn't turn him back. He swam with resolution for ten hours, constantly calling, then looked up again, still confident. The signals of the cow were far apart. When he failed to hear her for four and a half hours, he slowed down to spout and breathe for several minutes. The night was calm and he felt expansive. Before resubmerging, he nonchalantly rolled on one side to glance up at the sky.

The glance turned into a stare. Pisces, which should have been south or overhead, had inched its way into the north, while Fomalhaut, the mouth of the Fish, had actually left the equator behind. Its first-magnitude brightness dominated the night. Not far from it, Menkar, a fainter star, lay just a little to his north while, to his south, strange constellations drifted clockwise, not counterclockwise, in mirroring parodies of the northern sky. The movement, indiscernible moment by moment, troubled him now on this third sighting of the night, yet he didn't turn north again. Instead he levelled out in the water, undecided, and stayed still for half an hour. New constellations, hardly noticed in earlier years, had drawn strangely near.

He started to circle. With his family dead and the entire northern hemisphere empty of friends, little remained for him there. Yet the sight of the stars eventually made his fear outweigh his love. He grunted and puffed, feeling his sickness begin to trouble him again. When he turned his head, his urine was dark and a six-foot nematode protruded from his vent. He groaned as he passed it, then looked again at the shining sky. His muscles shivered. Trying to subdue his fear, he kept turning with his head out of the water, taking in the entire sky so that he saw familiar northern stars as well as the strange ones to the south. But his frustration continued to grow, his rotations making the stars spin at great speed until he felt dizzy.

It was too much. He turned himself north. The call of the cow came again, fainter and farther. He raced away from it. By noon he was eighty miles above the equator.

Here he broke silence, not with a thump or a blast of anger or a subterranean pulse to a Blue Whale in another part of the sea. This sound left his head in a continuous roar like the din of a low-flying storm, and after it ended, there was the swish of him rising out on the ocean surface, the gasp as he sucked air into the hollows of his head, then the swish of descent, not as far this time, once more the roar, and then, again, the rise, the gasp. The pattern continued for several hours that afternoon and, after a pause, resumed again at night. He knew that, except for the loudest roars, such noises couldn't carry very far, but in his anguish he was unable to keep silent. When at last his outbursts stopped, his eyes were as blank as the mind behind. Yet even now his loudest sounds were bouncing from Africa to America and back again in the bottomless Brazilian and Cape Verde basins.

Far to the south the Fin Whale heard them. She paused a moment. The low-frequency noises went on and on, all from the same point in the ocean, with no intervals for the caller to catch replies. The exhausted Fin sank low in the water, the cousin at her side. The dolphin knew she'd never see the bull again.

In her eagerness to catch the young Blue Whale and turn her back, the Fin hurried nonstop for another three nights and three days. The dolphin stayed with her at first. Sometimes she played, riding her bow wave, jumping her back. More often she swam in mindless silence.

The Fin was mute most of the time, mute and withdrawn. She understood that the bull's recollection of the Antarctic might keep him north of the polar front, but she was bewildered by his failure to follow

89

the cow in these safer seas. His strange explosive roars had troubled her. When they came again, she tried to ignore them.

Between her two troubles—the bull to the north, the cow to the south—she was swimming in a beeline, as if suspended from a wire that joined the two. At times, surmising how much the Blue Whales had possessed her, she would hold back for an hour or so with the dolphin. Yet she never escaped her obsession for very long. She felt a sense of entrapment and growing fear, for the cow was speeding south to the ice. Or almost south: her one concession to the bull was a westward drift that slowed her. The young cow swam in jerks—straight south, south-west, straight west, straight south—and the steadier flight of the Fin could still overtake her. And yet, once the cow was overtaken, what then? The Fin Whale lifted her eyes out of the water to distract herself from the fears that filled her head.

She looked about. The Common Dolphin was still coasting at her bow. She closed her eyes and heard her splash, and, after a while, association opened a vision of rorquals homing in on the ice: at first a few, but soon in her mind there were many thousands. They swam beside her into the south's perpetual sun, their flukes and fins brushing her sides.

Now the cow was calling out just to the north of the Rio Grande Rise. The Fin Whale listened just south of the Trinidad Rise. When the cow's voice came again, the Fin was nine miles farther south. She roared her answer, more anxious now, for she feared the cow was speeding up as she headed toward Tierra del Fuego and the island chain beyond.

Those islands led to the ice. The Fin slowed down for a moment or two and recalled the whaling stations at South Georgia just below the polar front. She envisioned the terrible factory on Cumberland Bay. The cousin sensed her fear and urged her west, since by now she was only a hundred miles from the South American shelf. The cousin had never swum off South America, but the drumming of croakers was so loud that she knew a westward flight would lead her to land. Croakers were always shoreline fish. Soon she swam off, arcing and calling, trying to turn the Fin for shore.

But the Fin swam on, straight south, and the cousin soon came back. When, after three days, she was over the Argentine Basin off northern Uruguay, the cousin slowed again. She could bear the temperatures here, but she knew she couldn't stand the cold farther on. The croaker calls from the west had faded out for over two days, but now, louder than ever, they seemed to be calling the dolphin west. The cousin instinctively feared the Fin Whale's drive for the south, for food was sparse this far offshore and she was no subpolar dolphin. Yet the Fin had been like a shoreline to the cousin, partly answering her need for companionship, her desperate desire for affection. As she turned for coastal Uruguay her stomachs, thin already, tensed and tightened with new fear. Lone dolphins were ill equipped to cope with schools of sharks or pods of Killer Whales. But there was no choice. She called to the Fin as she swam away. In her worry, the Fin Whale hardly noticed that her "family," two rorquals and three dolphins once united in the equatorial seas, had come apart. As the dolphin called from the west, the Fin made a curious noise with her baleen, a sound like a chuckle, and, as she did, she heard her mother and her father in her mind. She closed her eyes and re-envisioned the laggard whales known for long lives and many children, the latecoming rorquals who, in their pride of speed, had swum high, as though the factories did not exist. A white destroyer neared, veered by. With the cousin arcing sadly for the croaker calls to the west, the old Fin Whale drove on, lost in her dreaming.

CHAPTER

9

Despite initial quarrels, well before the middle of October the young male dolphin was as at home and as accepted as his sister in the open-sea school of five hundred. The school stopped travelling as soon as they found food, then kept to the one feeding ground roughly three hundred miles south-southwest of Ascension Island. But, after three days, the well ran dry. No matter how far the dolphins ranged on their nightly hunts, they found no squid. Then, one morning, they did not form the usual subgroups but instead swam west in deliberate ranks. They swam all day, and the male could tell by their spacing that this was no random search, no whimsical excursion. They were headed deliberately for another feeding ground. At first he followed passively. When sounds of shoals came from close by and the school ignored them, he grew impatient. It seemed pointless to him to swim in tight formation, minimizing the chance of finding food. Why ignore fish swimming nearby? Why not turn back toward the axis of the Mid-Atlantic Ridge? Over that height the water was rich. As if he could smell it, the male kept veering out of line. But none of the others would follow him. The longer snout that distinguished him and his sister as inshore dolphins appeared more prominent to the rest.

For both the brother and sister the coming of spring had begun to evoke a homing instinct, but their home was far to the east, on the African shelf. Since they remembered the time they'd lived there only dimly, they didn't fully understand why this westward swim made them so uneasy. Attached to the open-sea school, the sister kept her restlessness to herself, and after the first few miles the male also fell into line. Only with late afternoon did he waver, suddenly stirred. A sound was coming from the southwest. Above the lower peaks it became a seismic roar, like canyons crumbling. Most dolphins swam faster, but the male hung behind, delaying his file. For a moment he felt an impulse to swim off and leave them all. Far off he could see that his sister was also stirred by the rorqual sound. She had swum some distance away from her ardent bachelors.

The male was struck by a vision of himself leading the school away to feed in the southwest, but the longer he dwelt on the vision the more he realized that the west held no appeal; that his real desire was to turn back for the east. With this realization he dimly envisioned the Gulf of Guinea where he had lived his short span of freedom less than a hundred miles from the coast, over the shelf with its near-constant supply of food. He hovered still. That was surely the way to live, surely better than searching barren seas for unreliable pastures, despite the danger, even terror, that he recalled there in the turbid gulf, although remaining uncertain what had caused it. Lost in memories, he almost forgot where he was until the teeth of a dominant female and nudging beaks from behind ended his trance. He awoke abashed. The school was impatient, calling ahead of him over miles of unbroken sea. He raced, sensing excitement. A push was on. He doubled his speed and neighboring dolphins fell in at the rear, swimming all out.

But that night when they rested there was only the hunger again. Finally, after another day, with the ridge's western foothills falling behind, they came to a solitary rise, unmapped, but known to the open-sea dolphins for generations.

They came over it well after sunset and spread out immediately, diving and listening for deepwater sounds under the constant hiss of the waves. In previous weeks they'd fed quietly, but tonight there was tail slapping where food was thick. Synchronous diving soon began.

Squid and fish were plentiful over this rise that, at its highest, was only three hundred feet from the top, and there were crustaceans: pelagic shrimp. Still, the feast was poor compared with those of earlier years. They missed the ommastrephid squid once plentiful in these waters, and the male could sense their deep disappointment. When the sky grew light and the school re-formed, he left his place in the rear to join the leaders.

He was angry. They had swum tightly ranked, ignoring all possible pastures—only for this! Among the disconsolate groups he passed back and forth, as if to emphasize their stupidity. His sister felt anxious as she watched him. She feared he would be expelled.

When they swam again, they were only a little less tightly grouped than before. Now they were headed for a rise much more extensive than the last. There they hoped to find permanent shoals, for even with food, this constant travel was not to their liking.

The male, like his sister, was deeply attached to the school. He regretted his anger, and both suppressed their uneasiness. When they entered the push of the South Equatorial Current, the exhilaration of rivers washing over their skin melted down their irritation.

Tiny smelt swam with the current. The herd became very vocal. Skittering sauries and coasting flying fish shone like new money. The school spread out and fed again, young dolphins shooting after the flying fish while older dolphins feasted under the waves. The feeding slowed them down and broke their formation so that the young male, still excited, could nip and jostle among the females while the older dolphins dove. Throughout the herd a spirit of play replaced the somber mood of early morning and yesterday. Diving at last with the others, the young male tried to remember his precaptivity days, but as before, some half-remembered terror cowed his spirit. Turning his mind to less threatening things, he was chasing fish when a singing propeller tickled his ear. He hardly heard it at first, lost in feeding, but when it loudened, its peculiar frequency turned his memories into shapes of catastrophe.

94

He broke the surface. An elegant vessel danced gracefully on the horizon, very different from the squat container ships and bulbous tankers he usually saw. He could tell from its sound it was sleek and fast. Again he remembered the Gulf of Guinea. Without knowing why, he arched over backwards and scanned the empty sky for birds. Leaving her subgroup, his sister did the same. Both peered to the north, where something was slowly growing. A flock of jaegers and frigate-birds were soaring on motionless wings, then diving like hawks at the little roseate terns who panicked, dropping their fish. The shapes came closer till it was clear the fork-winged birds were following schools. Now both dolphins tail-slapped and whistled the call of distress. Instantly the herd stopped feeding. Both porpoised east to lead the impressionable young away from the birds. In a moment a hundred dolphins had joined the rout, unsure of the danger but certain there must be good reason for this fear. Older, experienced dolphins merely watched, then resumed their diving. Between these extremes the rest of the dolphins hung bewildered, swimming in rings. Then, as the ship neither neared nor shrank and the spiralling birds flew close, the synchronized diving grew general and the herd went back to its feeding. The followers of the brother and sister slowed, then started feeding as well, then turned and swam back, chagrined, to rejoin their elders.

The sister was now far away from her group of bachelors. Brother and sister hovered alone and gazed into the north. They saw exactly what they had feared. Out of the distance came a wall of Spotted Dolphins. The brother and sister saw their own herd open wide to accommodate the speckle-sided beasts. The Spotted Dolphins were chasing sauries down from the north, and where they encountered Common Dolphins, the silvery fish were damming up. Both brother and sister tensed. The feeding grew frantic. The mingling schools co-operated in driving the sauries to the top. Terns snapped them up, only to lose their catch to the frigate-birds as they rose back out of the waves.

The male was torn. His herding instinct drew him back toward the school, but the combination of waiting ship and Spotted Dolphins would not allow him to go all the way. He circled restlessly. His sister was once more afraid that the school would expel him. Then, in a moment, both heard albacore in the sixty-five-degree waters not far down. The rumbling pulse of the drumming tails decided the male. It was what he'd feared. The ship saw the jaegers and frigate-birds, which followed the tuna, which followed the dolphins. Where there were ships there were also dangerous fifty-fathom nylon nets.

Both brother and sister awaited the ship's approach, and the terror he'd only half remembered before became clear in his mind. Any moment now small boats would herd the dolphins into nets, and the tuna would follow them. Dolphins by the hundreds would suffocate. Both brother and sister called to lure their friends from the danger while there was time, but the initially peaceful sea had become a whirlwind of noise that extended from the slaughter underneath all the way to the sky, where jaegers, terns, and frigate-birds were wheeling. The young male sonared in all directions and, though he found no net, heard danger nevertheless: the snapping teeth of requiem sharks. They, too, were feeding on the fish, and, like the tuna, they followed dolphins, always ready to pick off a weakling or a calf.

The school spread out to chase the sauries, slim-beaked fish of less than a foot that kept breaking the top. Earlier nettings came back to the brother and sister. Both wanted to swim away and leave this trouble behind. They turned, but, as blue water widened behind them, their fear gave way to loneliness. At last, unable to go or stay, they hung at the outer edge of the herd. With nightfall the Spotted Dolphins quieted down and the Common Dolphins, hearing the fish thin out and fade, went back to their more leisurely, synchronized dives.

With his sister, the male edged closer to the school, but by now the vessel had closed in. It was a yacht, not a tuna ship, but only a man could have told the difference. Sportsmen hung a lantern over the side. They were casting for tuna, and when the curious dolphins investigated, the men looked down in delight.

The young male dove. It was still a tuna boat to him. He knew he must leave, but he could not bear the thought of swimming alone. In his fear a bold notion possessed him. He would form his own separate group and lead them away. There was little time. Ignoring decorum, he butted among the groups, roughly drove the females east and confronted the dominant bulls, facing them down one after the other until a good many of his trusting associations were destroyed. To the dolphins he seemed insane, a renegade. Still, the synchronous diving continued among the bulk of the herd. By now many bulls had grown used to the newcomer's aberrations. Many winked at them. A tenuous sort of friendship still remained.

Only when his females began to fight him did the dominant bulls attack, barreling in from all sides and using their teeth. Belly-up in the water, he whistled out the rising and falling signal of distress, but the sound had grown pointless with repetition. For a moment the feeding stopped, and the bulls drew together to guard their families. They raised a solid wall of teeth against him.

He regretted his rashness. He tried to rejoin the school, but every time he approached they closed their ranks against him. His sister cringed when she saw the school close ranks against her as well. Hour after hour both tried for a place. At last, realizing what they had done, the brother and sister turned. It was over now. They swam off, alone again.

Their isolation changed them. Now even the male's fellow dissidents were gone. He was desolate. The emptiness of blue sea seemed to put eons between them and the herd, and over the days, their half-formed sense of belonging faded from memory. The whales were gone. Completely alone, the pair were savages again.

CHAPTER

10

THE Blue Whale cow was in torment. She had been empty for so long that now her brain was absorbing pesticide and heavy-metal compounds which, in well-fed whales, lodged harmlessly in lipids in the blubber. As these poisons accumulated in her brain, the Blue grew farther and farther removed from reality.

She ached. It was the middle of October. She sensed that something mysterious had happened inside her, though in her distraction she wasn't sure what it was. She had a fleeting intuition that more than her own life was at stake in this gauntlet race for the south, but it soon passed out of her mind, even though the being inside her was nearly five weeks old. Even before she'd swum from Ascension an egg the size of a pinhead, lodged in her womb, had become a creature of half an inch, a fetus with head, tail, and the beginnings of forelimbs and legs. Now, still burgeoning, still expanding, it hung doubled over in the dark, as though it were brooding on its own heartbeat. Her blood flowed through it, drawing food from her dwindling reserves. It crouched in the center of her womb, magnifying its outsized cranium. It looked like the embryo of a man.

The Blue's unnatural ways had threatened it. Most pregnant Blues would have left for the south before mid-August and long since reached the food supply that would assure the embryo life. Her mother, whom the Blue remembered as lingering late in the tropical sea, had been the first to leave in the year she had been conceived. But the cow had held back, and now she began to pay for her hesitation. As time passed and the embryo took more and more of her fuel, her hunger drove her night and day in full-speed migration. Miles that she had taken for granted in the fall were paid for in precious blubber. Ten days went by. Poisons began to concentrate in her brain.

When her southwest flight finally brought her to the South American coast, the Blue turned south and swam without pause until she reached the Gulf of St. George, whose waters were red with grimothea, a postlarval stage of crustaceans that flourished from here to Cape Horn. When the Blue circled into the gulf, it was not the Fin who stopped her, but the sight of grimothea, as red as polar krill, and the sound of Right Whales feeding. Traces of heavy metals maddened her. In her delirium the Blue was sure she had reached the Antarctic sea, and so she sieved the teeming brit without revulsion.

It was midafternoon when she fed. As she swam through the patches of red, the sounds of Right Whales began to tumble over each other. Each time she ran on her side the nearest Right made a sound like wind across the opening of an organ pipe. The others took it up, adding moans and pulses from every quarter till the Blue Whale's mind was ablaze with Antarctic spring.

But this wasn't the Antarctic. Like the copepods farther north, these small munidas entered her mouth only to drift back out between her plates. Yet they were thick here—fathoms thick. The sight of them swimming all around her was a torture. She attempted frantically to enclose them, and as they slipped away, she despaired. This was an especially subtle hell, and she wondered at the change in the Antarctic.

The euphausiids were much smaller than she remembered. Slowly, after an hour's attempts at feeding, her madness passed. With no other choice, she was ready to migrate again. But, just as she turned for the open sea, a Right materialized out of the shadows. Hardly fifty feet long, it bobbed and glided down her sides, then watched her closely with one satisfied oval eye, belching and grunting as a second Right Whale grew out of the green.

It was the first time the young Blue had been close to such whales, pitch-black, with white callosities on their high heads and barnacle patches studding their faces like pieces of moon. She rose and they spouted together, the Right Whales making V-shaped jets in the wind. The one with a barnacle in its blowhole raised a sound as shrill as a kettle on the boil. Settling back under, they nudged the Blue to satisfy their curiosity, then exposed the towering ten-foot plates that stretched their faces into gargantuan frowns. They skimmed the grimothea, snouts in the air, and their fine, fine fringes held in creatures of less than a quarter inch. She heard their satisfied swallows. In desperation she tried to feed, sifting the water exactly as they did, but again the creatures ran out of her mouth by the hundreds of thousands, and the hunger that had been goading her turned into torture. She fled for the open sea.

When she wheeled, several feet under, sun cleared the clouds and unrolled over the gulf, penetrating the plankton. The Blue saw whales in all directions. Humped and buoyant, filled with food, they mowed clear highways through the brit, and where the highways opened up, long lanes of sun flooded the sea, as if the stocky, slow-swimming Right Whales were black gods unlocking the night. The Blue Whale moaned aloud. Then she noticed that here and there were Humpback Whales. She imagined they were outriders from pods she'd heard offshore. One weathered Humpback female with pocked, barnacled sides crossed in front of the Blue Whale, her throat ballooning with fish. The old whale opened her jaws, and smelt rose out from her mouth like escaping breath. In apparent sympathy she called to the young whale, as if inviting her to share the gleaming smelt, but, as always before with the Fin, the Blue refused. She swam away.

She was broken. With late afternoon, Rights congested the mouth of the gulf, most of them bored and full and thoroughly tired out with random mating, their vocalizations and rattling baleen drowning all sounds. One Right Whale called to the Blue, swam near and inspected her. Others lofted their flukes like black sails and ran with the wind till their ripples rocked the Blue Whale's sides. When she dove, she saw Right Whale calves, almost twenty feet long, still riding their mothers. The Blue felt anger and envy. She found it bewildering that these slower, bulkier whales should be able to live in these inland waters where, mysteriously, no hunters seemed to come, while at the same time her kind were harried almost to the point of extinction. Still convinced she was near the ice, she listened for catchers, looked up at the sky. And now, for the first time in a year, she made out a wandering albatross: the set, unbending wings white in the dusk, as though alight.

Those birds followed factory ships to pick at the remains of butchered whales. Farther down she saw petrels sway and dart over the sea, and petrels also made her remember the boat that had killed her mother.

She hovered, uncertain of her way, then, after some moments, turned to sea again and swam in search of krill. For the first time in some while, she called for the bull, but the whales, the waves, and the ocean traffic badly muffled her twenty-hertz call for the distant male. Only once did she hear a reply, or what might have been a reply: three expressionless one-second thumps, pitched lower than anything else in the sea.

The sound turned her north for half an hour, but it had been faint, and in her bewilderment and hunger she forgot it when it failed to come again. She dove for fifty feet and swam straight south for twenty minutes. Then, at the surface, swimming full speed, she followed a rhythm of spout-breathe-wait, spout-breathe-wait, taking one breath for every minute she had been under. During such times, when they saw their quarry run at full speed, the hunters said that the whale was "panting." This was often the prelude to death. The Blue was panting now, although, in actual crisis, she would have been able to halve her intake of air. Twenty-four hours went by. Her acuity waxed and waned but she kept on swimming.

The farther she went the harder the wind. The Blue lost energy. Even the calories lost in spouting counted now, when ninety percent of her lung supply went from warm to cold.

Many days went by and soon a quiet hour became as occasional as violent storms had been in the temperate ocean. Water temperature steadily dropped. The Blue swam over the eastern edge of the vast

101

Falkland Plateau, where whalebirds crowded the air and kingfish and blue whiting filled the sea. Now, each day she moved seventy miles toward the slaughter. As she approached the Strait of Magellan, parties of Humpback Whales appeared. They had increased in recent years, and here they fed happily on crustaceans that were plentiful north of the ice. Some crustaceans were large enough to be easily taken and there were no sounds of catchers, which would founder here in the violent sea amid screaming west-wind gales. Convinced once more that she was swimming Antarctic seas, the Blue Whale paused to eat subpolar krill: euphausia vallentini, a coolwater species. She fed heavily for a day, but as the krill thinned out she swam off for the west. After some hours she found more krill, but again they were spotty. Still imagining she was home, she continued to search and feed, confused. After eleven days she turned north and pursued coolwater euphausiids up the coast. Now she was calling, listening once more for rorqual sounds.

After two weeks, at the beginning of December, her mind started to clear. She realized she was north of Antarctic ice and simultaneously envisioned the catcher boats, the Antarctic slaughter. She felt afraid but knew she couldn't linger here in the subantarctic where euphausiids were too scattered to be more than a stopgap food. Unless she learned to feed on fish, her hunger would continue to push her south.

She quailed, remembering the boats, the guns, the Humpback cow in the Gulf of St. George whose throat ballooned with fish, and finally the Fin. She felt deserted, like a calf without its mother. Terrified of the whale ships in the south, she called for the old whale, but there was no answer. At last she turned north, seeking the Humpbacks and Rights in the Gulf of St. George, determined to join them at their feast.

Approaching the gulf, she moved from sunless sky with frequent sleet to a largely cloud-free sky where screaming west-wind gales gave place to an offshore westerly breeze. Sometimes she thought of the dolphins. She moved north past ascending terraces of rock where this eastern South American coast was still rising out of the sea. Fossils in the topmost rocks were sixty-five million years old. Keeping well in sight of land, she seemed to be always in green-blue water, though, wherever a river emptied through a deep-cut rocky valley, the inshore sea went brown with sediment.

She called loudly as she approached the Gulf of St. George. It was

shaped like a half-moon and penetrated a hundred miles into Argentina, stretching a hundred and fifty miles from cape to cape. No whales
answered her call. There had been storms, and the limbs of sea hedge
filled the water. With limbs as thick as a man and innumerable strands
of stems, these macrocystis plants grew from fifty- to hundred-foot
depths. Outside the gulf she ate euphausia vallentini that filmed the
top. Each time she swam over a stand of macrocystis she looked down,
for they sheltered many forms of life. Twice she ate swarms of crustaceans that hovered around them.

She entered the gulf. As she rounded the southern cape, the water
went red with grimothea as far as she could see. She called excitedly,
expecting that Rights had come to feast, just as before. Lost once more
in illusion, lead and mercury fogging her brain, she swam deeper in,
confusing the surface swarms with krill.

She circled the gulf three days, in sight of land. As off the coast,
there was terraced rock with wave-cut platforms more than twenty
million years old. She found no krill. Once or twice a brown-hooded
gull passed overhead, almost a speck in the pale sky, and, when she
looked north, she could see clouds of smaller specks that rose and fell in
flashing wheels above the high pampas behind the cliffs. Locust chatter
in the offshore breeze when the specks flickered and rose resembled
crustacean sounds, and the whale wasn't used to picking up such voices
in the air. Her mind stayed numb, dark with confusion.

On her last day in the gulf the westerly breeze gave way to a gale from
the southeast, and after it passed, the red munida stain had left the
upper sea. Fragments of sea hedge clogged the surface. Once, when
the filaments stuck to her flukes, the Blue Whale roared and slapped the
water in frustration. When she reached the northern cape, she hovered
still, uncertain where to go.

Still crazed and disoriented from mercury poison, she turned north,
swimming nonstop for four more days. It was afternoon when she
reached the eastern tip of Valdés Peninsula. A flood tide from the
south, twenty feet high, had covered the coast and swelled the San
Matías Gulf. Once into the gulf she suddenly found herself amid blue-
spiked rafts of camelotes, small water weeds washed here and there by
the flood. But there were no krill. The Blue Whale groaned and puffed
in frustration.

Disappointment drove her up from the south shore to the northern

103

cape. Here the violent Rio Negro, shallow and treacherous at its mouth, like all the rivers from here to the Horn, washed silt clouds into the water. The cow hung still and watched. She saw no crustaceans.

Over the next three days she swam inland for a hundred and fifty miles. The outbursts of locust chatter grew loud on the wind, but it was the silences between them that dazed the cow. Hardly noticing where she was, she passed within feet of the bobbing fishing vessels docked at San Antonio, its streets and boardwalks bare. San Antonio was on the northwest shore of the gulf. From there she swam south down the western coast. After a week, as the coast turned eastward, back to sea, she approached the Gulf of San José. There were still no krill. Her brain was clearing. As if awakening from a dream, she swam at sixteen knots into open sea and started a nonstop flight for the Antarctic, calling out continually.

After resuming her pursuit in early October, the Fin had sought the young Blue down the South American coast, but after two weeks, the youngster's pulses had gone completely dead. Though the Fin Whale had called continuously for days and nights in succession, there hadn't been even a hint of a reply.

That had been late in October. The Fin had turned north, convinced that the Blue was dead. She had lived through many losses and remembered them well from her earlier life in the Antarctic, but even so the nausea, the piercing cramps that no amount of food could palliate, and, later on, revulsion at food, were as painful now as when she first had felt them, decades ago. After a month, anguish and grief began to exhaust even her giant store of fuel. Her once-loved solitude had become unbearable, and in place of her former peace came a constant restlessness of worry. Wasting afflictions of body and soul wore down her strength as she mourned aloud: dull lowing sounds. Her lamentation for the Blue and for her family became, with time, a lamentation for all rorquals who had fallen to the guns, as if the old whale grieved for all the world.

It couldn't last. She would either go mad or assimilate her sorrow as she had six decades ago, a process of healing that took years. At first she felt she would never be whole again.

When she entered her seventh week of loss, she felt a vague, barely discernible sense of comfort in her chest, as if something open and raw inside her skin had closed up—hardly enough to make a difference, but enough to begin the process.

She started to eat again, and for the very first time since missing the Blue Whale, she began to sleep. Brief nods in the beginning, an hour or so at a time, and then the balm of full oblivion. Her appetite strengthened. She began to remember the way she'd lived before the cow had come. It seemed a millennium ago. Still, she was getting the rhythm back, the old life of food and dreams.

Once more she lived in the sheltering ark behind her eyes. Her mind grew populous again with the ancient rorquals she remembered. These dreams lacked the clarity they had had before her loss, but after two months she began to hope for a happier life. The ache of bereavement still oppressed her, but she sensed now that the pain would reach an end.

In late December the voice of the young Blue Whale came north again. Two months before the Fin would have pursued without hesitation. She was a hundred miles out from Mar del Plata on latitude thirty-eight. She told herself that this was not the youngster's call—and yet she didn't dare to signal, fearing to hear signs of excitement and recognition: more frequent calls or a change in the intervals between the calls that told her the whale was standing still. Reception between sender and receiver was never constant when whales were in motion, but once contact had been made and both whales stayed still, communication could go on for hours, depending on traffic.

The Fin stayed quiet for several hours as the calls continued to come. At last, in the hope there would be no more than the rudimentary response that stranger whales give one another, the Fin called out. She called only once, resolving to stay where she was and forget this other whale if there were silence or just a short, routine reply.

She hung far from the surface, clenching her lids, silently hoping to herself that the whale in the south would not reply. She seemed to be balanced above a descent, awaiting the silence or sound that would tilt her back to peace or draw her forward to destruction. The intimacy with the youngster which she'd been learning to forget became so vivid and immediate that her loneliness grew as strong as when she'd lost touch

105

with the Blue in late October. Remembering her hours with the cow and bull in September, the Fin Whale yearned for the excitement of the bull whale's touch. She yearned to join the two whales once again.

Over forty minutes passed. No answer came. She was surfacing and turning for the north, both sad and relieved, when a volley of mixed frequencies—loud rapid-fire thuds, urgent, bizarre—spun her about and put an end to dreams. The whale to the south was surely the youngster, for though the sound, as before, contained no information, this distant Blue obviously had reason to hope that the call she had heard had been a friend's.

The Fin felt compelled to follow the signal. Her maternal love for the Blue Whale was so strong she was willing to risk her life to protect her, though the chance of evading catchers was very slim. She would go to the ice—unless, even now, at the rim of the killing grounds, her calls could turn the cow. For a while the Fin called constantly, standing still. But although the Blue Whale answered as excitedly as before, she didn't turn. The Fin felt a sense of finality.

The reciprocal calls kept up for two days, but there was no turning the Blue Whale now. In less than ten days she would pass the polar front, homing into her midnight sun off the killing grounds around South Georgia and the towering Scotia Ridge. She would swim west of the South Sandwich Trench to the Palmer Peninsula and find the krill awaiting her by the million, blown counterclockwise around the ice cap by the steady East Wind Drift.

The Fin swam back and forth, eyeing the south intently. She spouted twenty times in succession, as if to expel her fear. A tanker approached from the east. She circled west. A sportsman's launch neared with a roar. Not ten feet off, a frigate-bird dove out of nowhere, hit the sea without submerging, snatched a halfbeak, and in an instant returned to the sky. The Fin looked up. The wings of the frigate-bird were forked, with the shoulders stretched far forward of the downturned eyes and beak so that the soaring bird appeared to have no head. Underwater, the Fin heard the voices of many whales from the south, from closer by, from some buried place in her mind. The sea was loud with motors. By now the voice of the Blue had been lost in the jumble of sounds.

The Fin called and swam south, catchers and factory ships looming dimly in her mind. She kept on seeing the whales of her youth, though the vision was nebulous and she hadn't been able to hear them in her head since the calls of the Blue Whale had been drowned.

Tired of dreams, she arched her body toward the pole, her skin firm and rich. Straight above now, the frigate-bird rode the wind.

CHAPTER

11

THE cousin left the Fin north of latitude thirty-four, about a hundred miles from northeast Uruguay. She swam west by southwest in early morning at ten knots, and after eight hours she was well inside the twenty-fathom line that marked the outer edge of the Uruguayan shelf. She had never before been near this coast and had only guessed it existed when the explosive calls of croakers, bottom-dwelling inshore fish that she recalled from her African youth, had grown loud to her west.

Sharks passed. Only occasional at first, they began to appear and disappear at a rate of one or two a minute in the twenty-fathom zone. None attacked. They would rise from the shadows, undulate into striking range, look, make circular glides, then calmly redescend. The longest were fifteen feet. Light gray with dusky splotches, these primitive seven-gill sharks had piercing emerald eyes that scared the cousin, and when they opened their jaws, she saw that their lower teeth were not like knives as in most sharks but rather ridged, joined, and angled sharply backward. Equally numerous as the seven-gills were the sand tigers, five to ten feet long, pointed snouts upturned and dagger teeth always displayed. Hammerheads rose as well, and the raylike angel sharks and guitarfish came up with them, gracefully wheeling, their pectoral fins like wings.

The cousin missed the Fin. When she'd swum with the whale, sharks had never approached her. She could tell these were eating croakers, since they were thickest on the bottom where the fish kept up their din. She slowed and called out for other dolphins, feeling lonely and deeply regretting the outburst of rage that had turned her away from the open-sea school.

None answered. She turned due west till land appeared, then swam down the coast. Northeast Uruguay juts three times into the sea within a space of a dozen miles, and behind each jut of land are calm lagoons. Soon she discerned Punta Coronilla, a maze of flat peninsulas. She swam straight past this first of the juts. Six miles south, off Punta Diablo, she spent ten minutes diving here and there near sandy inshore shoals.

Here the sea grew unbearably loud. Even before, while the dolphin was swimming with the Fin, the calls of croakers from the west had been like drums, collectively loud enough to screen out nearby traffic. During her shoreward swim the croaker calls had loudened even more. Interspersed with them were sounds like boat-whistle blasts, along with frightening, low-pitched growls.

The sea had shallowed out to thirty feet. Light mottled the bottom. Schools of croakers shadowed the floor when the cousin dove, few of them longer than a foot. Basslike fish of a pound or two with rows of barbels under the chin, they idled slowly over the sand, brown above, light gray beneath. Five-foot cutlass fish, eating anchovies, undulated over her head, and eight-inch midshipmen starred the shadowed floor with rows of gleaming lights. The cousin swooped low across the sand.

The sharks were not as numerous near shore, and the cousin felt little worry. There was a tension in the water when a shark was going to attack—she knew the feeling well and it wasn't there. She glided and hovered, very hungry, but these fish were unappealing. For a minute or two she played cat and mouse with a toadfish. Its tail half buried in the sand, the nine-inch predator turned at surprising speed without leaving its spot, attempting to face her down with its rows of jagged teeth. She could have killed it in a second, but, with its bristling dorsal spines and the pointed trigger before each gill, it was unattractive. It whistled twice in irritation: blasts as loud and piercing as a steamboat's. She rose for the anchovies, but their schools were very small. After a minute she dove again and fed on midshipmen. Triangular fish with jutting teeth, they looked as primitive as the toadfish, but their rows of photophores called to her mind the lanternfish, and to her surprise their flesh was sweet. She fed for an hour, then dreamed for a moment, imagining lanternfish over the continental slope and her two cousins feeding beside her. She ached for the school she had left, all because of the strange rages that unpredictably possessed her. Knowing she couldn't bear isolation for very long, she sent out sequences of clicks but, hearing no answer, turned to sea.

Soon sharks grew thick again. Evening had fallen and the cousin swam well down. Past the twenty-fathom line sounds of thrashing came from the darkness just ahead and, with it, a pinging, ringing sound. The cousin's clicks picked out a net. As she drew nearer she sonared its ten-foot height, but there seemed no end to it. Thirty-nine hundred feet long, it seemed to span the ocean floor. Her sonar didn't detect the sinkers or the splices where separate gill nets had been joined. Sharks were struggling in the mesh like flies in a web, and as the thrashing, struggling sounds intensified, the sharks still free were turning away from the shoaling fish to tear at the victims. Soon these sharks were snagged as well, and when the cousin drew close her snout brushed Franciscanas—five-foot dolphins—tangled tight, already dead, a few half eaten. Up close, her sonar picked out sinkers on the floor. In fear she rose above the net to find there were floats buoying it up just as the sinkers held it snug against the sand. It was a hundred feet from the floats to the surface. She rose above them, avoiding the dead dolphins, calling out in the hope a living one would answer from below. No answer came. The cousin rose higher, away from the net, and swam on south.

Sharks followed. They were aggressive now, excited by the killings at the net. Each time one rose, her heart beat faster. She dove like a harpoon to ram her beak into the chest or up the vent of any sand tiger or seven-gill who dared to venture near. The more she attacked, the more the spirit of her navy-training days came back to her. She remembered slicing rubber dummies with the bayonet that men had fitted to her snout, remembered the food that had rewarded her frenzied rages, and wished she were back in the open-sea pen with the men and the other captive dolphins. As she recalled the metal disks, the love rewards, the challenging games and shining weapons, she became wistful. Unlike the brother and sister, she'd long since tired of her freedom.

By the time she had left captivity, both her mother and aunt had learned to attach the disks to seafloor targets and to discriminate one gunship from another. She dreamed. There'd been safety there, companionship, deep love. Here there were loneliness and endless unknown waters.

When she awoke from her recollections Killer Whales were moving west from Torres Island just a few miles off the coast. They travelled soundlessly, a group of twenty-five, most with their eyes closed, half asleep. The cousin went still to let them pass. The towering dorsals looked frightening at only twenty feet off. They shone in the moonlight. Then explosive *huffs* rang out across the placid evening sea. The cousin remembered the Killer Whales whom she had fled when she'd followed the Blue with the three others. She shook a little. Sharks were predictable but Killer Whales were not.

The sharks, especially the seven-gills, were snouting up less often from below. Most had suffered enough buffetings and thrusts to leave her alone. But the whales were different. They swam placidly, off guard. There was a male of sixteen feet between two twenty-one-foot females. One of the seven-gills shot up and snapped a gobbet from the chest of the young Killer Whale. Almost immediately the other sharks closed in, but before they arrived the twenty-five whales had closed on the seven-gill and sliced it into pieces. While the sharks snapped at the corpse the cousin saw the Killer Whales submerge. She dove as well. The upper water was pale in the moon, but all she saw were wheeling fins and spreading clouds of dark red blood. There were grunts and thuds as sharks, intestines trailing, sank for the floor. She strained to see the whales, but the writhing sharks blocked her view. Rising, she glimpsed the tall black dorsal fins moving far off, nearing the shoreline, almost gone. The sea was as placid as before they had arrived. She swam again. Less than a dozen feet away, a seven-gill of fifteen feet rose from the dark and twisted in circles. The upper and lower ends of its body were both whole, but between these weights of pale gray flesh a part of the spine had been almost laid bare, and the dying shark appeared unable to stop twisting. Seconds passed before two larger seven-gills snapped the spine in two. As the head and tail parts sank together, the eager ripping from beneath almost drowned out the sound of bottom fish. When she stopped watching and swam again, less than five minutes after the whales had first appeared, the pod had completely passed from sight.

It was only two minutes more before the sharks started testing her again, stirred by the blood. She rammed them in the chest and once, as before, killed a seven-gill by thrusting her beak up its vent. Yet this time the sharks were undeterred. As they kept wheeling up from the shadows, she missed the Fin and the open-sea school of Common Dolphins. Eyes trained below, she didn't see the buoy with a bamboo pole and a flag till the last second. Thinking a gill net had been set on the ocean floor, she circled wide to avoid the buoy. Then, when her snout had entered one of the four-inch openings in the net, she saw that this row of floats stretched west, not east as before, and that the net had been set at the very top of the water. A dozen sharks swam into the mesh about two hundred feet to her west and, as they thrashed, the sharks below swam after them. Soon she heard ripping, slicing sounds, then once again the louder thrashing as the cannibals were snagged. This noise went on until the handful of live sharks who still remained veered and swam south.

Had she stayed level and reversed she would have escaped the net. Instead she attempted to push herself free by bracing one pectoral fin against the web. She tried to keep the flipper flat against the net, but as soon as she pushed, the tip of the fin entered the mesh. The nylon twine relaxed a little from the pressure of the flipper going in, then, stretched to its limit, it contracted and clung tight. She tried to push herself free with the other fin. It also caught. In rage she shook her head, twisting it frantically left and right as when she had sliced at the rubber dummy, but the mesh moved with the head, clinging and tightening on her snout. Still she had hope. Her flukes were free. In a desperate twist she arched her lower body down toward the net until her flukes pressed at the web. Again she tried to push loose but her tailfins caught in the twine, first the left fluke, then the right, leaving the rest of her body bent, both head and flippers tangled up, back arching out and in again. She hadn't breathed for twenty minutes, and though her blowhole was near the air, a film of water covered her head. The approach of suffocation was unbearable and she tried to shake the net to make it rise. It didn't move but her body did. Raising and lowering herself, she found she could jerk her blowhole out for one or two seconds at a time.

Her heartbeat slowed with relief when she drew breath. She sank for rest, then rose again, putting all her weight on her flukes and pushing down. This was an easy thing at first, although it stung. After five minutes her sensitive skin developed pressure grooves at the points where it pressed the twine. Her heartbeat raced. Very soon the grooves were bleeding. One and a half millimeters thick, the twine soon started to feel as piano wire would have felt on the skin of a man. Yet she had to breathe if she wanted to live. She looked to her west. The tangled sharks had long since died. The night was peaceful and their corpses seemed serene where they caught the light. She closed her eyes. She would have gladly given over the struggle to live, but the urge to breathe would not let up. No matter how long she dropped her head, the need to breathe would start the cycle over again: the unnatural inward flex of the spine, the gradual rise, the grooves of pain where her tailfins bled against the mesh. Six hours passed. The sea stayed calm. The cousin expected she would hang here till she died.

No one checked the thirty-nine hundred feet of bottom net at dawn, but a crew of five came putting out from the town of Los Cerros in an inboard *lancia* to check the *vaga* they had made by splicing two gill nets together. The men began their search at the shoreward buoy, disappointed to find only a dozen dogfish, along with a few seven-gill sharks. Every December the spiny dogfish swam in thousands down the coast, the schools so vast they could be netted at all depths. This year other species had come early, and the men had half expected a dogfish run the previous night. Mildly dejected, they hauled in net, forking the dead sharks off with long-knived poles and pushing them into the hold. When, after an hour, they came to the cousin, still alive though motionless, they merely poled her in with the others and closed the hatch.

113

She landed on top of a shark in three feet of water. Though finally free of the stinging twine, she twitched with pain, for the men had widened out the rips along her fins when they'd poked her body out of the net. She lay exhausted on a dead seven-gill shark in the wet pit, where after a minute, despite her rips, she felt the relief of effortless breathing. She was almost too weak to move. With a great effort she had barely raised her head when the hatch opened and a storm of salt came down and caught her wounds. She writhed in pain as the hatch slammed shut, felt the throb of the inboard motor as the *lancia* went putting back for shore.

In early afternoon the cousin saw one of the men climb down into the hold. With the hatch wide open above his head, the light poured in. He was tall and dark and a cigarette hung from his mouth. He held a bottle in one hand, and, before descending, he tossed his knife-tipped pole ahead. It landed beside her. Vaguely she thought of the bayonet and remembered the deep affection of the trainers who'd rewarded her sharp thrusts. Feeling a trace of the old rage, she moved one flipper. Reaching the bottom of the ladder, the man paused, then gave her a kick, not seeing that the flipper moved or hearing her faint sigh. Thickly gloved, he poled through the pile of sharks to be gutted later on. The half-dead dolphin by the wall was the only catch that needed flensing. He raised the pole with the two-edged knife, removed the blade, and went down on his knees. The dolphin still quivered in various places, though the writhing had let up. In less than five minutes he had made a set of incisions between the neck and the upper tail. He reversed the knife to use its rounded edge. Inch by inch he started flensing the blubber off. When her blowhole moved and a moaning sound came out of her head, he reversed the knife edge once again and cut it off. A half hour later the boat reached shore.

The seven-gills and dogfish went to Los Cerros, but the single dolphin carcass was left on the beach of Punta Diablo for the pigs. Soon there was little left of the cousin but the bones. Pigs squealed and tumbled, chasing her head. They sent it flying through the air to land snout-first in a patch of mud, where it stuck up like some curious weapon, remaining intact until late afternoon brought cattle flies and ants. A pair of gulls ate the eyes as the sun went down. The head had disappeared by dawn.

CHAPTER 12

THE San Matías Gulf and the Gulf of St. George were far behind, and at the tip of South America the coolwater krill had been exhausted. There were no longer enough for even stopgap feeding. It was January. The Blue Whale was swimming home.

She flew nonstop through almost eighteen hours of daylight and on into night, travelling well down at twelve to fifteen knots. Her hunger eclipsed the memories that had held her back before: the bull whale, the grenade harpoon exploding inside her mother. She swam like a machine, automatically lowering her path when the waves deepened. Though she blew every fifteen minutes, her spray was as indiscernible as the puff of a man in the white of a polar blizzard.

Near the end of the second day, the Patagonian shelf, five hundred miles wide, started its drop toward the bottom. The Falklands were behind. Ahead the Scotia Ridge swept a thousand miles east to South Georgia where it broke the surface, dove, then rose again in an arch of islands—Sandwich, Orkney, Joinville, Shetland—back west to Antarctica. Each island was an underwater extension of the Andes. Rising up at Antarctica, the ice-covered crags of the mountains continued unbroken down the Palmer Peninsula. Both the southern tip of America and the northern tip of Antarctica were narrow. Like fingers that at another time might have touched, both pointed east to the Scotia Ridge. It had been fifty-five million years since the tips of the two continents had parted.

When the whale swam south she could feel the West Wind Current, ocean-deep. It bulled its way unobstructed through twenty degrees of latitude until it hit the two peninsulas, six hundred and twenty miles apart. Its power was vast: a hundred million cubic meters of sea flowed over and under the Blue Whale's body every second, the farther she swam the greater the mass. Although the current was less than two knots, there was no escaping it, and she was tired. When she dove, the undercurrents brought no relief. They were mere crosswinds in a steadily moving storm. She lost a half knot of speed, but her eighteen-foot flukes kept their rhythm, moving as impassively as pendulums, seventeen hundred horsepower strong.

At first the whale was lost in her swimming, oblivious to everything else. Then, from the depth of her chest, like a whale's low-frequency call from far off in the ocean, the sound of her heartbeat reached her ears. It was a signal. She veered east till the power of the current was partly behind. Soon her speed slowed to twelve knots and the beat of her half-ton heart faded, a pulsing star that had momentarily flared in her inner night. After a rest her speed returned to fifteen knots.

To the south rose flat, bare islands with stunted tussock where giant petrels and blue-eyed cormorants hunched in the wind. As temperature dropped and the grass grew thin, the animals were crowded ever more tightly. Wherever an island appeared there were birds. Cape pigeons with patches of white on their wings slept in low cliffs. Petrels and sheathbills covered the ground, and in small burrows under the earth, the dove-sized whalebirds hid their clutches from the cold.

Night fell. Bergs came more frequently out of the darkness. Usually they passed to east or west, but when they approached head-on they swelled until they filled the whole horizon like low skies. Always the whale veered out of the way when she heard waves break against them.

During her adolescent summers near the coast, she'd never noticed the gradual rise in the water level, and to her the Antarctic seemed as cold as ever. The burrowing whalebirds still puffed their feathers against the wind and shivered on their nests. Even so, the burgeoning carbon gas from the burning of fossil fuels was warming the south, and the temperature rise of one degree a year which had gone on throughout her lifetime was causing the coastal bergs to calve with increasing frequency.

Flat as tables, they increased in number and size till they forced her to change route every few hours and swim as long as twenty minutes at a time along their sides. After they passed they left a wake of roiling chips that hissed as they melted and polished fragments like a monarch's train. She had seen them during each of her previous springs, and for the first three years their numbers had seemed the same. Yet over the last three springs they'd increased, and she could sense the greater delay as they turned her repeatedly off course.

She started to labor. The automatic motion of her flukes turned to an act of will. Normally she rested when her flight grew arduous, but the pain of hunger was worse than her swimming pain. The four-hour twilight brightened into dawn, and still she drove toward the southeast with the current swelling around her.

After an hour she changed direction. She had swum well past the Scotia Ridge but could not continue southeast without overshooting Palmer Peninsula, four hundred miles due south. The peninsula was the western border of the Weddell Sea, which stretched for over a thousand miles to the barren Filchner Ice Shelf extending from Coats Land to the peninsula's southern base. Experience told her the krill she sought were thickest near the peninsular tip where the easterly coastal current dammed them up.

She would have turned due south in any case. Like the wandering albatross that wintered seven thousand miles from its South Georgia home and every other year sought its nesting site, the whale was drawn instinctively to her ancestral home. Through millennia the Blue Whales had divided into families, with separate polar zones and separate calving grounds which, together, covered all oceans. Like other

117

rorquals, the Blues had emerged twenty million years ago, cosmopolitan, but thickest in cooler seas. In regions where krill were plentiful they had grown into specialized feeders, but they had always been free to seek warmth when the glaciers came. The glacial cold had trapped the Bowheads and the Belugas in Arctic basins, allowing only those who reproduced in the freezing cold to survive, while Antarctic Blues had retreated across the unobstructed sea to more temperate zones. But when the cold retreated they'd always come back in pursuit of krill. Through epochs the seasonal patterns of feeding and travel had been fixed.

It wasn't just freezing that caused the mass migrations. The last great northward extension of the rorquals' feeding range had occurred a hundred and twenty-five thousand years ago when a temperature rise had melted the ice cap and sent hundreds of thousands of icebergs and enormous floating ice sheets north to chill the temperate seas. The krill had gone with them, along with the whales. As the changes in the atmosphere increased, the same thing could happen in the young cow's lifetime.

The Blue Whale's weariness continued to come and go. Swimming against the West Wind Drift, always easy in the past, had turned into work. She breathed hard every seven minutes. The current flowed heavier the farther south she swam, and at its height of speed and power the water thickened. Static reached her, hardly discernible, but urgent—high-frequency chatter, like the conversation of ghosts. Again she turned southeast. The water temperature dropped from forty-four to thirty-nine degrees in less than the time between breaths. And out of nowhere there were krill.

They were adults, at first far scattered, some descending with their eggs. She picked up speed until their patches swarmed at the top. One raft spread ahead of her like a curtain. All in one motion, as if a dam had broken open in her brain, the Blue swam sideways, spritzed, bolted a bulging mouthful, then ran again, hitting the raft from every side. Over and over her throat-pouch swelled grotesquely into the form of an inverted chapel vault, destroying her streamlined shape. The krill hung close together, facing one way, in shoals that looked like rust-red clouds. She drifted with them, ceaselessly swallowing till the first of her three stomachs held a ton. Relief made her moan aloud with pleasure. She rested briefly, her digestion so fast she could almost feel the food pass on to her inner chambers. At the first hint of an opening she took more. The sense of fullness flooded her body with a well-being she had not known since meeting the bull. Oblivious to everything but her pleasure, she drifted and fed, and when her stomachs and intestines held two tons, she plunged into sleep.

At first she had no dreams. Like the ocean, black to its base, only its upper five or six fathoms opened to light, the part of the whale that envisioned and dreamed was very small compared to the part controlled by instinct. The thoughts that crossed her mind flashed out and died like meteorites, but the glimmerings of instinct were constant in the dark. Only when unfulfilled would instinct flare into the obsessive hopes and fears that killed her sleep. Her love for her mother and the male had been like suns inside her head. By their light she had struggled with choices. Now that the struggle was done she forgot the Fin Whale, many miles north. Drifting in food, she ignored the trawlers that crisscrossed methodically to her west, harvesting krill. The thud of the motors entered her head like a distant animal's heartbeat. This was the season when Antarctic whaling was at its height, and had she been hungry, the sound of the motors might have alarmed her. But the end of her hunger made her calm, uncaring. When she continued south, she swam slowly, pausing each time a new patch of euphausiids came to light.

There were catchers in the southern Weddell Sea, but for the moment she'd all but forgotten. The euphausiids fluttered and fed, feasting as eagerly as the whale. Like the Blue and the ocean itself, they had reached a peak in their cycle. When the northward-moving surface current met the southerly water, both plunged hard in a steep convergence where each female euphausiid released up to five thousand eggs. The current took them down to warmer water. There, in the night, the larval krill would drift to the south. They would pass through a dozen immature stages and at adolescence rise near the icy coast to drift back north. From egg to adult the cycle took nine months, but the krill didn't drift back to the north simply to spawn and die. After spawning the adults would follow their eggs into blackness, molt to a smaller, more frugal form, then drift back south in the winter night to repeat the round. Between the continent and the convergence were six hundred to a thousand million tons of them, enough to feed the world.

Light waned. In each of the past three days there had been a night, always shorter and grayer and brighter, but still a time of token rest when the scattering layer could rise to feed, and the rocketing herds of Right Whale Dolphins, tuxedoed in black and white, could snatch the fish that followed the rising food. Just north of the Falkland Islands, the night had been deep black, five hours long. As the whale moved south, it had dwindled to less than a four-hour dusk. Now, halfway to the Orkneys, the sun did little more than halve itself on the sea, an egg in a cup that dimmed the sky to a purple gray. Dark closed from the east like an eyelid, and as the main core of the West Wind Drift dropped north, the waves died down and krill that by day had been rust-red signalled each other with blue-green photophores till the surface was a firmament of lights.

The krill moved back and forth outside the Blue Whale's eyes like motes. Between mouthfuls she watched their firefly dance with interest. They also watched, as keenly as the whale. Their black-buttoned eyes were enormous compared to the size of their fluttering bodies. Just as the whale could pick out sounds where a man heard nothing, the huge black eyes could pick out signals in depths where a man saw only black, for their eyes were sixteen times more sensitive to light than the human eye. By day, crossing the line from cool to cold, the whale had come upon the krill as ghostly voices, ceaselessly chattering in the waves. Now, by night, they were controlled, miniature beacons. Each two-inch creature had ten lamps that it could flash in combinations. Unfeeling, brainless things, the euphausiids still sent signals to each other, a parody of communication. The arch of the whale's mouth was almost a smile as she channeled them in. Now the temperature dropped near freezing, and the Blue Whale felt at home, a creature the size of a locomotive feeding on sparks in a world where cold spawned light out of dark.

That night the cow heard whale ships to the south, but they never turned in her direction. Anxious at first, she looked at the krill and slept again. Dawn showed another world, unbroken and flat from sky to sky. The sun stood brilliant white in a nimbus that was rimmed with smaller suns. Ice crystals weaved and danced into whimsical shapes in shifting clouds. Though the whale was lost in feeding, when her sideway runs took her straight into the sun's white face, she paused. Long ago as a calf she had seen that same white face, these fields of perpetual light. She wheeled her eighty-four feet of skin up into the light and back under the sea with the sun touching every inch of her body. The tons of krill were just beginning to dull her hunger. She pictured the past. Then there had been three of them: herself, the sun, and her mother. Now, as she fed, the polar sun seemed warm on her skin. With dusk it still hung in the sky, never going down.

The whale still thought of her mother, but her recollections were different now from when she had lingered in the north. There she had felt yearning for her mother, but here her mind was at last at peace. Since over millennia her species had grown monogamous, her adolescence had been an interim of play between the deep love-bond with her mother and her second, deeper love-bond with the bull. After her union with the bull in mid-September, even before the fertilized ovum had entered her womb, the corpus luteum—a follicle of her ovaries, swollen to eight pounds, yellowish-pink—had been pumping progesterone into her blood. It lined the walls of her womb with a matrix of blood and webbed out lifelines for a placenta, and over months its accumulation dampened her desire. But, though her desire was in decline, the need for love remained, and in the absence of the bull, she had thought more and more of the months in the cold seas with her mother.

The sight of the whale ship that had killed her mother came to mind. Though she felt grief, she felt no yearning. Now she was strangely self-contained. All during the twilight she dwelt upon her body as if in love with it, while the first-year giant petrels from the Orkneys passed in flocks that would circumnavigate the Antarctic many times. Unready for mating, overwhelmed at their own strength, these aggressive birds would circle the polar sky six years for the love of wandering. Like them the whale could feel a sense of release. Once a satellite hauled by suns, now she was self-assured, a sun in her own right, a continent unto herself.

That dusk a catcher passed on the western horizon well north of the hunting boundary, dragging a string of whales. For a moment the five Minkes who had virtually been her foster parents rose at the back of her mind. This distant catcher hauling its dead whales was the kind of sight that had haunted her sleep in the north, and she felt fright while watching it, though she calmed down soon after it passed. Six months ago she would not have calmed so quickly, but her growing self-content had distanced her from immediate threats as much as from old yearnings.

121

Inside, the thing that had changed her steadily grew. No more than a pinhead in the fortnight after conception, it had first developed stubs of hind- and forelimbs and a giant dome like the forehead of a man. Then, at an inch, what would have developed into legs had been reabsorbed into the body. Eight weeks later, with the bull whale's pulses silent in the north, the creature had grown to the size of a human hand. And now, at three months old, the flippered thing stood upright with its tail facing her cervix, over a foot long, clearly a whale, with perfect pectorals and finely tapered flukes. It blinked. Sometimes, when she lurched, it seemed to waver, hovering quietly in the center of her womb. Though it fed constantly from her blood, as yet it took only two percent of her daily calories. The two long horns of the womb spread out on either side of it. As it burgeoned, its own weight would make it fall into one of the horns. There, doubled over, it could swell to twenty-five feet and almost three tons before it was born.

By dawn the whale had passed the Orkney Islands. As she came in to Palmer Peninsula under blue sky in a barely moving sea, she missed the drizzle that was constant near the cape. Behind her, the bergs had been flat with space between them. Here the pack ice formed an enormous jigsaw with gaps of narrowing blue. As the whale picked out her way, she could hear the other rorquals farther in. Minke Whales were often companions of Blues who fed at the edge of the shelf. Though their voices were higher than hers, the Minkes were using the bottom of the ice to transmit, and the roughness of the under-ice thinned out high frequencies. The Blue Whale listened closely as she swam, zeroing in. Here the Antarctic was helpful, for the ice that could trap the whales also carried the navigational signals that kept them free. Whereas in the north the long-range channels had been deep, here the chilled water at the surface and the ice itself provided the best line of communication.

The Blue was drawn instinctively to the coast, but the latter part of her flight had zigzagged wildly as she paused for rafts of krill. She had overshot the tip of the peninsula where the shelf ice, over a thousand feet deep, at last receded, leaving a bare rock beach with clumps of flowering plants. As she turned northwest in search of shelf ice, she felt no fear, for there were voices all around her. Each year the ice melted down in different patterns so that the krill were concentrated in new

122

spots. For under-ice whales the constant "talk" of the other feasters was the radar that steered them to food and breath. The Blue Whale dropped from sight.

The world beneath the ice was a weird twilight. Undulating with effortless speed, she felt shoals of myctophid fish thin as minnows flicker like pins across her skin. They flashed blue-green flames produced by the oxidation of protein, the same process that caused luminescence in most marine life, plant and animal alike. At first the Blue ignored them. She had seen these fish many times in the northern scattering layers, but some species were endemic to the Antarctic. She thought of the Minke Whales who had fed on them. These fish were young, only centimeters long, but in their plenty, they nearly blinded her, darting like sperm around her eyes. Small krill were abundant also. The myctophids ate them until it seemed each brick-red creature had been replaced by a pin with orange paint in its gut. And just under the upper dark the squid kept their patrols. From time to time they rose en masse like gray torpedos for larger fish. She shivered slightly, began to race. Five minutes had passed and the ice floe had deepened its smooth keel. Now in the shadows, sometimes scattered, sometimes in schools, she glimpsed the deepwater forms: the so-called dragonfish with crocodilian eyes and fins that ran unbroken over half the length of their bodies. These were fast, fairly vigorous fish, but here and there she saw schools of sluggish swimmers, two feet long, transparent, scaleless, rubber-boned: the Antarctic icefish who somehow survived without red blood. In sudden interest the Blue Whale tilted, but it was a cold black world that she saw when she turned on her side. The ancient fish sank out of sight and the sea seemed dead, but the floor was filled with flourishing life: starfish, algae, bryozoans, molluscs, hydroids, sponges, and worms. There were so many sponges alone, and such a variety, that, had it been possible, a native from the tropics could have taken a month's catch in just one day. Yet the water was always thirty-two degrees, and even without the cold, a diver would need protection, for the sponges had glassy spicules that could go right through the hand. As the whale pursued the voices down the keel, the ice grew thin again and white sun broke like crystal into the sea. Now she had entered the blinding world of the crabeater seals. Out of nowhere they surrounded her, twisting and turning through shoals of krill. They sifted the red meat through their strange, baleenlike teeth. Curious, they spun for a moment around her eyes, then went back to feeding and chasing each other.

She concentrated harder on the Minkes. Soon their steady low-frequency calls were interspersed with the fainter pings and scraping ratchets of short range. As she drew closer she heard trainlike sequences, each clearly an individual voice. The first came very fast, each separate impulse of sound a tenth of a second long. The Blue swam faster as a second sequence reached her, its pulses more closely spaced and briefer in duration. Her heartbeat raced at the sound of a third sequence composed of pulses fifty milliseconds long, since one of her childhood mentors had often called this way. The Blue roared loudly when a fourth sequence counterpointed the others, pitched very high. Behind her eyes she saw the images of the Minkes who had led her away from the catcher after her mother had been killed. Now they were near. The signature calls were unmistakable, and, as she approached, the Blue Whale almost shook with an inner laughter, hearing again the high-frequency pings that had confused the submarine, and then the clanging bell-like calls and the whistle trains. Glowing, she pressed her blowholes to an opening where her plume of spray was a geyser out of the ice. Then, after a shorter run, she came up in a sapphire sea. The pack ice stretched behind like unbroken land and, ninety yards ahead, sun caught the blazing ice cliff of the shelf.

Ten Minkes were grouped together in the brilliant blue, all females, none of them longer than the distance from the Blue Whale's snout to her fin. All had calved in the warm waters to the north, then mated again a month or so later. Their young, weaned at four months, had been left on the northern side of the pack ice, and these cows were nourishing fetuses, gorging hard on the teeming krill. Though small by comparison with the Blue, they were still gigantic at eight tons. As she rose and spyhopped, they surrounded her, the eleven grunting loudly back and forth in the way of rorquals, for they had given her good guidance under the ice. These were Brazilian Minkes, one of seven blood stocks, each with their own zone. After nudging and touching for fifteen minutes or so, the whale let them be.

A few yards farther south, four other Minkes, at first indifferent to the Blue when they had heard only her informationless call, were swimming north. Their thumps and pings identified three of them unmistakably as part of the group that had led her south to safety in the year her mother had died.

As the four drew near, two catcher boats came from the north, but both the Minkes and the Blue were so excited at their meeting that they ignored everything else. The ten other Minkes dove back under ice while the four who surrounded the Blue blew high conspicuous breaths and made loud breaches, totally clearing the calm sea. Unable to match their leaps, the Blue rose part way from the water and fell sideways, smacking the surface with her head. Then, as the bull and cow had done on their first meeting, the Blue and the Minkes turned on their sides and hung parallel to each other just under the sea. One after the other the three older Minkes touched their ventral pleats to those of the Blue Whale and pressed their pectorals to her mottled, blue-gray chest. Their length was still only twenty-four feet, and the Blue was so large at eighty-four that, while their pectorals, pressed flat against her chest, were unable to reach around her sides, her own enfolded them completely. One of the four was even younger than the Blue. For a moment all five were aware that a catcher had neared, but when they looked it was turning westward, out of range. The smallest whale, the new one, caught the Blue's special attention, for she knew that the Minkes would be pregnant, and she could tell from the shoulder patches and blazing bands of creamy white on her pectoral fins that this new whale was a daughter of one of the other three. Usually a whale this small would be lingering north of the ice to fatten up, but this fourth Minke was already carrying young. The Blue swam under her, running her snout along her throat before turning away. Scouting catcher boats had twice come back into sight on the horizon, though over the last ten minutes their sounds had faded again. The din the Blue remembered from earlier years had largely died, but there were still occasional motor sounds, unmistakably from whale ships. For an hour she stayed with the Minkes, who, as usual, swam for the shelf. Though her bond with them was strong, it lacked the urgency of the bond she'd felt with the Fin, and she enjoyed the Minkes' company more than even that of the bull, for she sensed in these pregnant whales the self-content that she herself was feeling, and the absence of passion was a relief.

She followed them south to the shelf. As she watched them swim at the edge of the ice she was curious where they had summered over the previous six years, but the Minkes couldn't tell her. The Antarctic sea was vast. Perhaps they had shifted their range to the east or west in search of richer fields, or safer ones. After a final farewell to the Minkes she swam up the strait between the pack ice and the towering coastal shelf.

Sun dazzled in every direction off the ice, and to her east, where the pack was melting, she heard a rumor of streams drip-dropping from ledge to ledge, the distant voices of little bells. The swollen panes of the pack ice stretched with groans and creaks. From time to time she heard explosions from the steep cliff of the shelf. Enormous icebergs plummeted free in thunder that shook the ocean. Crabeater seals lazed on the bobbing floes. Stuffed tight with krill, they stained the ice a pinkish red with their droppings. As the whale made powerful runs, incessantly gorging, she seemed small between the vastness of the cliff and the bobbing ice. Antarctic terns came down in brilliant flocks, their wings like summer butterflies, and snatched red krill from under her gaping mouth. After a while she paused, lazily drifting on quiet flukes, watching the terns. With her stomachs full, a sense of wonder and satisfaction filled her mind. All was the same. In another hour black-and-white penguins would come into view, tending their newly hatched chicks in crowded cities beside Hope Bay. She dreamed to herself and inwardly sang. In its evolution her brain had framed few abstractions, but, unlike the birds, she knew a sense of awe and beauty. The sound of the catchers, loud an hour ago, had totally died. Her friend the sun blazed harder and the floes, petrels, and icefish flooded her mind. It was all the same as before, the same. In its ark of bone her brain recorded them: the myctophids, the terns, the cliff-ice thunder. Her flight grew solemn and very slow. She glowed, blessing the flickering sea.

Through January and February the Blue repeated her swim along the ice shelf many times, moving back and forth between the peninsular tip and the feeding ground of the Minke Whales. Each time she visited the four they did little else but eat together, all five whales daily more aware of the life inside them. Still, their companionship made the Blue Whale feel complete. In early February, when the calls of the nearing Fin grew unmistakably clear, she gave only occasional answers, leaving it to the Minke Whales to guide the old whale in, though, surprisingly, the Fin Whale never appeared.

The Blue took little notice, though more observant than ever before of other things. In fascination she'd hang still while light-blue prions sifted shrimp out of the sea and the distant catchers roamed the other side of the ice. Each time she saw one pass to the north she grew a little less afraid, sometimes ignoring them altogether while the kelp gulls teetered from wing to wing in glides across the water. They were few and far away. With the endless eating and long days, the time passed tranquilly. The young male swelled inside her.

High above the whale, between six and fifteen miles above the pole, clouds and chlorine were changing the heavens. In early winter, when the temperature dove below minus a hundred, water vapor and nitric acid in the sky turned into droplets, still liquid in the low air pressure. Later, when the temperature dropped even lower, both the water and nitric acid turned into clouds of ice. Harmless in themselves, these clouds released the lethal potential in high-altitude chlorine gas from industrial sources far to the north. By freezing the water and nitrogen compounds that, as gases, would have reacted with chlorine, the clouds left it free to meld with ozone molecules and destroy them.

In late winter the ice clouds approached the edge of the continent, though they had yet to cover the coastal sea where the whale swam. With spring's return, ultraviolet light triggered a reaction between ozone and chlorine that, from mid-August to late September, reduced the ozone over Antarctica by up to ninety percent. Summer warmth always brought a partial recovery, restoring ozone through reactions between oxygen and ultraviolet light. Yet the cumulative effect from year to year was a steady decline.

Directly over the South Pole a hole in the atmosphere allowed the entire spectrum of solar radiation to pass unchecked. In early spring this opening spread to cover an area almost as large as that of the continental United States. If a time came when it reached out to the sea, the phytoplankton would quickly die and ocean life that didn't go north would starve to death. The Blue Whale hovered beside the shelf, never dreaming that two months before her arrival the invisible threat of death had approached to within three hundred miles of where she dozed, nor that this emptiness could overtake and kill her when the diatoms and krill rose from their winter sleep again.

CHAPTER

13

BETWEEN December and February
the Fin made any number of attempts to push herself to the Antarctic,
but, after the first hundred miles or so, memory and fear always stopped
her. Each time she resolved to forget about the Blue Whale; to live
again in her private world of feasting and dreaming.

And yet she could not. The Fin could sense a separate, stubborn life
inside her, and, just as the fetus in the Blue had grown, blindly
determined to live, whatever the cost, so the Fin Whale's love for the
Blue had grown from a negligible flicker of regard in early September to
a blind, irresistible obsession.

Still, her terror of the catchers held her back for many weeks. Though
calls that she heard as Blue Whale calls reached her sporadically, they

brought back memories of her family groaning and sounding as harpoons entered their flesh. She remembered the few occasions when her
courage had let her follow the harpooned whales in their spastic,
twisting motions, parodies of their former grace. To follow the Blue past
the polar front was to risk that kind of death, and yet her worry for the
young whale wouldn't die.

In early February she travelled south without turning back, growing
settled as she swam. There had been many abortive beginnings before
this, but now the balance between fear and desire had come down on
the side of desire. She was swimming home.

After the Fin left the seas over the Falkland Shelf, she entered the cold
Drake Passage where the West Wind Drift bulled its way around the
Antarctic. Listening constantly for the Blue Whale, she made little use
of her eyes. When on occasion she raised her head to scan the south,
she could see only fog and storm, spears of high pressure from the South
American coast turning to mist and rain as they hit the cold.

She swam for fourteen hours, well under the waves. The light was
gray. Near the polar front, deep waves and a wind of thirty knots
heightened the surface agitation to a turbulent thunder that muffled
sounds. The sea grew dim. The Fin Whale listened, feeling the change.
For hours great schools of Falkland herring had parted and joined
around her body. Hours ago she had heard them before she saw them:
they swirled plankton into gills that worked like baleen, and she'd heard
their fins pass through the ocean like a rumor before the actual schools
had appeared. Then, when the fish had turned together, there'd been
the low-frequency *thuds* that sudden mass reversals always made, as
though a thunderstorm had materialized from nowhere, blustered
straight into the Fin, and passed. But now, with the turbulence at its
height, occasional schools that formed and broke around her body were
only audible up close. Ahead and behind their sounds had gone.

Not only fish static, even sounds of other cetaceans were thinning
out. Once, when the Fin Whale broke the surface, she was startled to
see a school of Right Whale Dolphins pass no more than ten feet off.
Magnificent streamlined black-and-white fliers without fins, they butted at wind speed over the waves for just an instant, then were gone,
their ghost-high frequencies lost in the wind. She swam past the polar

129

front and felt the cold sea more turbulent than ever. All the while she strained her ears for the throb of catchers and large whales. The sea would have deafened a man, but the Fins' and Blues' calls were low enough to escape wind frequencies. They were ancient, the sounds that the large whales made. Thirty-six million years ago, when the earliest ancestors of Fin Whales had appeared over the cold New Zealand Plateau, the winds and oceans had sounded the same. Over millennia natural selection had favored air systems that formed signals below the lowest sounds of the wind. The Fin Whale swerved when a seamount appeared at the lowest level of light. She contracted her head sacs, sent out signals in all directions, bouncing her sonar off the shelf, then listening hard. But there was no answer, not even trawler or catcher sounds, only the ever-present echoes from far-off commercial shipping.

She drove through dark all day, calling and calling. Her tenuous hope began to fade, and in its place came disillusion and grief. It was unlikely that her omnidirectional signals would escape the Blue Whale's ears in these deserted seas swept clear by storm-force wind. She hovered in silence over the inky cold. Hunger had driven the Blue Whale south, hunger and instinct, but for the Fin, who had followed her out of love, there remained no reason to go on. She could not force the Blue to answer. Yet still she feared for her erstwhile calf, feared for its life.

The Fin Whale followed the current for the Orkneys, continuing her call. It was automatic, for, like the Blue Whale's mind, her mind was filled with dreams. Her love for the Blue had lured her south to this place of death and terrible memories. But the route she remembered as a hall of hunters' knives seemed suddenly barren. Not only barren of her kind, as she had remembered, but barren, as well, of catchers. Though she did not doubt that they still waited beyond the horizon, the whine of their screws, once inescapable, had thinned. She had yet to hear even one. She began to hurry and hope again. This sea was like the sea she remembered from ninety years ago, yet not the same, for the absence of ships had not meant silence in the old times. In spring and summer this part of the sea had been alive with calling rorquals, electric with living sound. The network of voices had nerved thousands of square miles of polar water into an underwater city with a gigantic population.

The endless whales were a flickering memory, too sweet and terrible to dwell on, and yet too powerful to ignore. That was the first city. And

130

then, with time, the second had come: the city of ships whose powers of detection and frightening speed had left the whales no hiding place. The Fin was returning to a homeland that had died.

She kept to the surface now, in the absence of ships. Her wheel of spray became a snowy, travelling eye to the low-flying whalebird flocks who hunted the troughs and breakers. Straight east she passed, ignoring food in her excitement. Soon she was edging north again—Fin Whales had always fed far from the ice. Icebergs were frequent, but, having lived for a hundred years, the Fin knew well that their numbers swelled and dwindled with the decades. In the past, times of strong solar activity had produced a warming sea and a melting of the ice cap. Though excess carbon gas was now trapping heat inside the atmosphere, making the warming and melting less dependent on the cycles of the sun, the Fin had witnessed the increase in offshore ice many times. As she swam north, she all but ignored it.

She was beyond the thick of it, in any case. The West Wind Current boosted her speed to seventeen knots, and after a day she saw dusk, then continued north through an hour of twilight, finally to enter a four-hour night. She strained her ears for catchers or factory ships but heard only the sounds of myctophid fish and innocuous trawlers. By dawn she'd turned to the east again. Through another brief night and a day of sunlit sea, she steered a passage for South Georgia, in her age grown quite indifferent to normal migration. At the back of her mind she saw the world she had remembered, the Humpbacks who used to summer close to land and the Rights with their harems, who'd basked almost on shore where the broad-billed prions slept the night away in tussock-covered burrows and left each dawn to feed in rafts as red as blood.

But she shuddered to herself when the island finally broke the sea. As before, its steep, dark bays ran like fjords between black slopes. But nothing was there. It stood in the distance, bare and black: vast spreading slopes skirted with screes that sheltered the long-deserted factories. Though the island was near the latitude of the Falklands, there were no streams or grazing sheep, only stone beaches studded with whale bones and rusty cannon mounts unused for eighty years. Where there was tussock, albatross, fulmars, petrels, skuas, cormorants, and other coldweather birds fledged as quickly as possible, then went back to sea.

The whale saw this in patches, swimming warily off the coast. She

131

eyed the spreading mouths of Leith Harbor and Cumberland Bay: the factory's doorway. She stayed out. It was here that the rumors had begun, the intuitions of spreading death. Sometimes the ocean off South Georgia had reverberated with cannons. She'd seen Humpbacks thrashing and bleeding on the tips of the harpoons. Slow and vulnerable, they had literally been blown out of the sea.

The Fin Whale remembered her youth more vividly as she circled past the bay. In human time it had been barely the twentieth century, yet already the rival whalers had divided the Southern Ocean into zones. She was in the middle of the place called Area Two: the zone where whales had returned to Antarctica from Atlantic American seas. Beyond her sight, extending east to the Kerguelens, was Area Three, where African whales and miniature Blues from the Indian Ocean had come in. Beyond that lay the zone where whales had returned from both Australian and Indian oceans. Off Wilkes Land and round to the east, more whales from New Zealand and Australia had come home; then, mid-Pacific whales; and finally, from the eastern Pacific to Palmer Peninsula, two separate flyways of whales had funneled from either side of South America.

Had a distant observer circled the continent in an airplane in late November or December of 1900, he would have seen them approach the Antarctic from every quarter of the globe like iron filings drawn by a magnet—indistinguishable except by general species: the Minkes, smallest of rorquals; breaching Humpbacks; racing Sperms; and the various lengths and outlines of the largest rorquals: Blue, Fin, and Sei. A man would have seen only that and the general tendency to concentrate on home grounds—if the vastly spread-out feeding groups could be called concentrations.

Men saw these things and divided their catcher fleets accordingly. But the Fin Whale remembered more than separate species; within the species there were families and subgroups, rules and decorum. Decorum or instinct, it had been rare for whales from one feeding zone to mate with those of another. Fifty years later the northern scientists would see for themselves that the whales in the separate hunting regions were quite distinct blood groups. An instinctive decorum. They kept to their own by unconscious choice. And it was old, the tradition they followed. Thirty-six million years ago whales from the cold New Zealand Ridge had spread to occupy southern oceans. Sixteen million years after that whales born from the north Atlantic, along with their southern brothers, had filled all seas. All whales had been one then, at least each species had been one. But, as the tropical oceans cooled through millions of years, the warmwater feeders had died away and hardier species had increased: rorquals and Humpbacks and Rights and Sperms, whales who had learned to feast on cold upwelling plankton, or at least on the creatures that ate the plankton blooms. They had been strong then, with every species a single tribe. But when the temperature hit bottom and the antipodes froze, whales from both north and south retreated into the sun to flee the encroaching glaciers. After each ice age passed and the oceans gradually warmed, the whales moved back into north and south, pursuing the cold and its upwelling food. The seas had been loud then, filled with vast odysseys homeward from the scattered places of exile—home till the next ice age came and drove them out again. North and south they had moved through ice age after ice age until for the wandering tribes there were dialects, colorations, patterns of blood, variations in shape, all barely discernible to men, but for the whales themselves a knowledge deeper than consciousness, like the sense of life itself.

The Fin Whale hovered off the coast. The sky had cleared. Beyond the ocean, far in the distance, scree-bordered slopes with peaks of snow spired into clouds. Here, long ago, the Fin Whale herds had passed on their way to the home grounds, some of them lingering for weeks on end to feed on krill. In the back of her mind the Fin could remember her parents swimming on either side of her, urging her on, while off to her west the putting catchers hauled the dead whales to the factories. She circled and dreamed. Out of that rumor of thudding screws and rattling chain a curious calf could hear strange sounds: muffled explosions; the creak of ropes; loud, desperate breachings; vomiting; sighs like the exhalations of monstrous chimneys. Over and over she had turned from her homeward flight to explore those sounds, and over and over her silent parents had turned her south. Still, by her twentieth month she had witnessed it all: first terrible, later unpleasant, finally accepted and ignored. The Humpbacks were slow and fell to the catchers. That was the way of it. But, with the passage of the decades and the vanishing of the Humpbacks from the sea, she came to miss the elaborate songs that had come with the spring, a sign that the rorquals were nearing home.

And the rorquals. Where were the rorquals? From previous seasons she could remember relict groups of them feeding fearfully under the guns. Their image had haunted her over the years and she had dreaded to see them again. But now there were neither whales nor guns. The sea was empty. When she sounded, she saw elephant seals, like miniature whales, following their radar out of the darkness into squadrons of thin squid. Scrawny and ravenous after their breeding time ashore, they wolfed the squid, then scouted on, leaving the whale to watch the snapped-off feelers writhe with a separate life. They sank into darkness. She grew wistful in the half light. Out of the distance came an almost inaudible *thump* that she followed in to the head of the bay. Here the aimless waves began to move for shore. She found three Fins.

They were two parents and a calf, grazing well off from one another in rough sea. Krill were plentiful, for though South Georgia was only slightly below the Falklands, the polar front swung sharply north as the Fin travelled east. She approached the three whales eagerly. A little more than five months ago she had paid no attention whatever to the occasional whales she'd met, and far to the north, the distant rumble of passing Fins had been frequent enough. Then her ears had been shut against it, her mind closed over like a scab, shut tight like an eye that has seen too much killing.

Now her old fears were forgotten. The catchers were gone, it seemed; the ancient fellowships, feasts, calvings, celebrations, all returned with a stunning clarity, filling up her head like a cast of characters that at any time might take living form and swim in the actual sea. An extravagant dream, a senile whim, except that the sea itself, so strangely empty of shipsound and teeming with krill, was the very ocean she had envisioned. Despite the absence of the huge herds she remembered, at least there were these three. She swam toward them, keeping herself at surface level where they were feeding, and breathing extravagant, festive breaths that stretched behind her in a line of exclamations eighty yards long.

She reared, as if she were greeting the Blue again, then circled the three with a vigorous run, rocking and trumpeting, clicking excitedly with her baleen. But there was no pause. These whales, who had never answered her calls, and whose muffled thump had only reached her coincidentally, did not even bother to change the course of their runs. They swallowed sideways, crammed their bagpipe throats to the brim, gulping impassively, like machines whose only purpose was to cut lanes through plankton. The Fin Whale stopped, then nosed the largest: eighty feet. She ran her rostrum against the pale smooth undersides. But it merely called and then turned away to continue its feed. As it turned, a combination of things—dialect, shape, coloration—told the Fin that this was not merely one of her tribe, but one of the few whose families had shared this part of the ice with her own. The way it turned away in the sea was a signal, an inherited gesture. It hurt the Fin that she had no way to communicate her recognition. In this part of the sea the blood groups and ancestries would all be the same.

The Fin Whale knew she was close to home. She swam in an S between the others, the father and calf. At seven months the calf was very nearly weaned. Though her baleen was still too sparse to filter krill, she copied the feeding runs of her mother. When the Fin Whale approached head-on, the calf turned on her side and looked, alternating the angle of her head to watch the old Fin Whale with either eye. The Fin ran her back beneath her, brushing her length with her dorsal fin. The ventral pleats shivered but there was no sign of delight or surprise. Slightly bewildered, the Fin veered off and eyed the grown ones. These were automata, like the survivors she had remembered. When she had left the Southern Ocean all signs of consciousness had been gone. As if they were shell-shocked, the whales had fed silently, bereft of relish or ceremony, as if the joy of life and the sense of living itself had been shot to pieces by the guns. Far in the depths a nototheniid—mindless, crocodilian fish—passed like a shadow, scouting for prey, and on the surface the three survivors swam as mindlessly as the fish. Yet the Fin could detect no ships. Quite likely the calf had never heard a cannon. The old whale circled again, then watched from a distance for over half an hour. The calf took milk from the mother's teat in a furtive way, as if at any moment there could be danger. Its parents, free in a shipless sea, made an ocean of ships in their minds. Barely acknowledging each other, they fed at a distance, never touching, never calling, insensible of play or celebration, as if the men, even while absent, had entered and eviscerated them until only the fear remained.

After she'd watched them for a while, the Fin Whale joined their feeding runs. Finally, bored by their indifference, she swam east.

Once she had gone, the female calf, still surprised by the playful run the Fin had made beneath her body, pressed her flippers to her sides,

135

shivered a little and hovered still. Her parents ignored her, continuing to feed. All down the length of her underside was a thrilling, unsettling feeling. At first bewildered by the sensation of the Fin Whale's touch, she dwelt on it for fully twenty minutes after the Fin had passed from sight. She looked at her parents. Never once had she seen them play with each other. Never once had they caressed her with their dorsals in the way the old whale had. She swam toward them, imitating the playful runs of the Fin Whale. She touched them both with her dorsal and pectorals, then, inverting herself, called out, wanting to feel once more the sensation that had come with the Fin's caress. They paused only to listen for catchers, then fed again. The calf made grumbling sounds, then checked herself and fed beside her father. After six hours the Fin seemed little more than a dream.

Ten days after the Fin Whale left, two catchers closed in on the three Fin Whales, from either cape of the bay, and despite a lifetime of caution, both parents fell within minutes, virtually paralyzed with terror now that actual ships had appeared. The young female didn't swim off. Instead she hung by the catcher boats with her head out of the water to watch the men insert the tubes and inflate both parents. After they'd finished, the men ignored the undersized cow. She circled her parents all day, never far from the bloated bodies which the catcher boats retrieved just before dark. She had been entering the stage where she could survive on krill alone, but she yearned for her mother's milk as she watched them tow her inverted body out of the bay. In her grief she raced impulsively after the ship, then nosed the long snouts of her parents as they bobbed like rubber tubes in the motor's wake. After an hour of this a deckhand caught the side of her head with a rifle shot. She hardly felt it but it prodded her awake. She turned and swam silently back for the bay.

She was bewildered. Like the Blue Whale bull in the north, she had been orphaned too early to have the ways of her kind firmly imprinted, and there were no other Fin Whales to be her mentors. Except the one. The memory stirred her. She spent a week swimming after the old Fin Whale, but by now she had lost too much time to catch her. Her voice was still that of a youngster, and it didn't carry far enough for the Fin to pick it up.

So the pair remained separate. After failing to make contact with the Fin, the female calf swam back to South Georgia, then, like the bull whale years before, set out on her own to seek a new life in unknown seas. Within three months she was feeding steadily above the Macquarie Ridge south of New Zealand.

The light lengthened again as the Fin Whale edged for the ice. After a day she skirted the southernmost Sandwich island. Macaroni penguins with trailing crests scooted on stubby efficient wings above and below her, darting for krill. The sky spawned swarm after swarm of birds. Plaintive, enormous, they dipped low across the water, sometimes brushing her back with their wings. Crabeater seals grew numerous again as she entered the ice pack. She called through the jigsaw puzzle of floes and water, and sometimes the answering *thud* of a Fin or a Sei would turn her north of the ice where there would be listless greetings and investigations, until she was reminded once again that the whales who came here now lived joylessly, intent on nothing but survival.

On the fourth day, six hundred miles from the Greenwich meridian, she finally heard the pulse of a catcher and turned south, using the ice to block out sonar. She could see Sei or Minke whales, no more than dots, swimming far off from the region of floes, as if indifferent to the danger. The catcher passed. She swam east again, uncertain what she was seeking. Many cetaceans rose ahead and faded behind, though most were scattered in isolated pods, each living as if it alone had survived. Toward the sixth day, she came upon Sperms from African seas, bachelor groups of half a dozen who dove for squid and, here and there, veteran bulls without females or calves. Far to the north the harem cows, smaller than the bulls, lingered behind with the first-year young. Like the elephant seals, the Sperm Whale bulls had bitter fights over their harems. Bobbing and spying, perpendicular in an opening of the ice, the Fin watched in fascination as an old, dark bull, whose wars had cost him half his lower jaw, blew geysers out of his forehead. She understood nothing about these whales. The battered bull, like all of his kind, had only a single nasal opening. The other passage had been modified for making spermaceti: fine, fine oil that filled the high cliff of the head. The Fin's streamlined proportions made her slim when her throat-pouch wasn't full. The Sperm, streamlined as well, had much rounder sides than the Fin, and each time he blew, his puff of spray shot at a forty-five-degree angle from his forehead. His skin was scarred by the teeth and suckers of giant squid on which he fed.

With a flourish of flukes he descended, leaving the bachelors alone on the waves. The Fin dove also, rose out on the other side of the ice, and approached the group. They clicked and circled, showing their teeth, one with the trace of a harpoon in the side of its head. Grown careless and open in her age, the Fin clicked back, imitating their sonar as best she could. Then, in an instant, their voices had climbed to frequencies far beyond her range. When, a half hour later, she swam on, there was still no sign of the bull. By now he could be scraping his tattooed head on the bottom, the oil in his melon balancing pressure and buoyancy.

The Sperm Whales heartened her somewhat. Alien creatures, they still showed energy and pride. As she moved southeast, whales dwindled out, but the few Seis and miniature Fins she encountered at least answered her greeting.

Still, out of all the whales she met, it was the Minkes who showed the most life. Some nearly as small as dolphins, they rose through their ice holes to greet her, curious, animated, and vocal, just as they'd always been. Compared to the Fin they were calves, and, on the eighth day of her journey, she travelled three miles into the pack ice off Queen Maud Land and the Minkes, her guides for navigation, began to accumulate ahead and in her wake. The bright sun glimmered through the ice, making a house of crystal under the sea, and, for a while, as she swam with Minkes on every side, her old vitality came back to her. She felt again the sense of belonging to a gigantic herd, of following the sun, swimming with calves. The Minkes, more vulnerable than the Blue Whale, were like the sum of her calves come back again to swim with her in the sunlight. Carried away, she began to sound and nuzzle at them, swinging her tail in great wide arcs, turning over on her back to present the region of her breasts. The squeaking bodies thickened around her, darting above and below, excited and loud, but after an hour the holes for breathing began to thin and they had swum well past their krill grounds. At last they disappeared to leave her alone. Submerged too long, she groped for air, bumping her head again and again on a half-melted sheet of ice. Finally it smashed and she rose straight out, her white throat gleaming with waterfalls. Dazzled and stunned by the light, she blinked her eyes sixteen feet above the ice, as though she had thrust her head straight into the heart of the sun.

After recovering, she circled back and haunted their region for several hours, but the busily feeding Minkes began to tire of her strange behavior. Still, they were friendly enough. They clicked and bantered with her, each keeping now to its separate ground. For another day she swam among them, clicking and chattering back and forth along the lane of breathing spaces.

At last she turned away, pointed northeast, the sense of wistfulness and lost time flooding over her again. Two of the Minkes watched her go, a conical shadow, eighty feet from end to end, the gigantic tail sweeping vast reaches of white water over her back. One of the Minkes followed a short way, then returned. They clicked to each other. Pregnant females who had been born well after the height of the whaling onslaught, both were mature in their second year, and this whale was the largest animal they had seen, a whale sharp-snouted and pale-bottomed like themselves, sharing even the light-colored chevron behind the head. They sent out trains of pulses in her direction, slightly distressed, for this giant double of themselves had not competed for their food; had seemed above it. And yet they had seen her as a Minke Whale. As she swam east and out to sea, the enormous tailfins dwindled and dwindled, and when the fins had disappeared in the distant gray, her thumplike calls spread wider and wider until, after seven hours, they were gone. Now the Minkes slowed somewhat at their feeding, watched each other momentarily, went back to their feeding runs, then, after a moment, watched each other again. Low-flying cloud darkened the ice as the miniature whales, eleven tons and twenty-five feet, fed on in stops and starts, feeding and wondering.

The Fin swam northeast for a day, uncertain of purpose. Age was on her and a sense of lessening, as there had been for the better part of her life. The rigidity and detachment of old age had made it possible for the Fin to keep to herself in the northern waters and to swim in silence through leagues of whalesong. Age allowed her to travel impassively south while whales aflame with sexual passion or big with calf swam for the north, or to travel north while hollow whales with aching bellies raced in thunder for the krill grounds. Her enormous head was an ark whose brain could have held a congregation of men. And the giant brain, partly alight, flickered and trembled as memories sprang to light and died away. The ocean roared now, gale-force winds driving her low. Deep in her head there was a sense of isolation, and she realized dimly that she had come to use her body only as shelter for her brain. The storm wind strengthened, driving her deep. She glowed with dreams; remembered her youth, when she had chased the sun to the north and south as unconsciously as a bird. Her body had been a sun unto itself for the desperate mate who had hovered around it. The ocean roared. She veered a little. She had ferried calves from Antarctica into the tropics, out of the ice fields into the warmth. She saw her newborn young vulnerable and guileless as the thread snapped off in a burst of blood. Drinking from her, almost a part of her. But separate they had grown. Butchered while she herself had gone unscathed, by chance out of range or in other seas, ferrying new lives, making new meat for the waiting men.

Thoughts flared as the storm winds screamed, then flickered, as always, into nothing, the ark of her head no more than a ferry for dreams, for visions of dead things. She had lived the better part of her life in this private way, awake for food, truly living only in the instants when memories lived. But the spaces between them were progressively longer now, as the bright mind cooled into age.

She paused in her flight. Four more days had passed. Under the hiss of the wind faint calls grew loud from the east. She had neared the realm of the Pygmy Blues: slim whales of up to eighty feet, like the Blue herself except for the grayer color, narrower head, and proportionately shorter length between the anus and tail. Now one of the few that remained was passing to the north, the upchurning water from its flukes making bubbles of sound as it spouted and rolled. Suddenly hopeful, the Fin turned after, relived her meeting with *her* Blue Whale. But this time it was she who ran a rocking-horse track through the dark, blowing garlands of bubbles, crisscrossing and bugling and bowing. And the stranger whale, as old as the Fin, merely ducked in a sign of warning. This was a feeding ground, no more.

Just as the Fin had learned to ignore traditional boundaries, so this Pygmy Blue was feasting a little south of her usual range, and on euphausia superba, not the euphausia vallentini which most Pygmy Blues consumed. When she drew close the Fin discerned another Pygmy, a just-weaned calf of fifty feet who appeared to be hiding on the far side of the mother.

Still the Fin Whale bugled, orbited joyfully in the waves, arched and undulated her body and swam circles around the unresponsive whale.

140

The feeling was sweet but very short. The Pygmy Blue bumped the Fin with the tip of her snout and clicked her jaw to make it clear she wished to be left alone. Normally the Fin would have swum away after such a rebuff, but, after a minute, loneliness made her dive under the mother and rise out on the other side to approach the calf. As the Fin Whale's snout drew near, the youngster called out and made a motion to nuzzle her but the mother stopped her, calling loudly and leading her off. The Fin pursued and cut beneath them both, then rose to face the mother whale, butting slightly, with only a trace of her strength.

Puzzled, the Pygmy watched the Fin; hovered a moment as if reflecting. The Fin made a friendly, affectionate sound, then dove straight down, waving her flukes in invitation. The Blue Whale watched her disappear into the depths. Her youngster followed a few feet before she stopped her a second time. As the Fin descended, a fragment of memory almost surfaced in the mother Blue Whale's mind. There had been times when she herself had nosed that distant night where sunlight never came; had sounded in concert with the others for no good cause she could remember: for friendship's sake, for play, for joy, for the love of sounding. Yes, but it was pointless now, and distant.

The Fin plunged down. As the networks of shoulder and midline arteries swelled to cushion ocean pressure, her bloodstream shunted through an alternate system of veins. Night filled her eyes. After a minute she turned and looked up to the shrinking light, a pale blue sky that grew shallower, wider, seemingly miles above her head. Gleaming yet gray, it flickered here and there with stars, the tabular icebergs shunting sunlight into the sea.

She looked down. Strange deepwater fins rumored and crackled, as if impatient for her to leave, and things were watching past the margins of her sight. Ten thousand feet down, where ocean stopped, enormous rocks, ferried by icebergs out from the coast, lay scattered like skulls across the floor. Many held fossils: fragments of spine, a canine or molar from jaws still specialized for chasing prey on land, though the creature itself, when it lived, had long since learned to kill and survive in the ocean. The Fin Whale hovered over the darkness, straining her ears, and out of the shadows came the whispers: fishes perhaps, dark noto-theniids, nothing more. Yet under the silence, frozen in rock or scattered in silica and dust, broken, recycled, lay the old ones: seventy-foot Basilosaurs, snakelike mammals out of the Eocene; the Dorudonts, strange dolphins from the ancient Tethys Sea who fifty-five million years ago had been the first to swim the Pacific. Other fossils came from later times, from the Oligocene epoch, thirty-five million years ago, when the Southern Ocean had finally isolated Antarctica. Deep in the dark those later creatures lay dispersed, and yet the interval of their extinction, perhaps a million years or so, was hardly a moment compared to the tens of millions of years they had swum the seas. Shaped like the Fin—to judge by their bones—they'd been unable to bear the cold, but when the Antarctic had been warmer they might have passed where she hovered now. Named Squalodonts and Eurhinodelphids, they'd been divided into families with vast variations of shape and size, some with jaws that stretched like shovels for over four-fifths of the length of the skull. Gentler creatures had passed here as well: Cetótherids, graceful whales of sixteen feet, the earliest ancestors of the Fin herself, slim whales whose jaws climbed unbroken over the very rim of the forehead, as in the Fin.

She turned back to the light. High above, the mother and calf were swimming away. As the Fin spiralled up, she could see the tailfins beat for the north. Her invitation had been spurned. For a moment she followed, but the mother speeded up when she heard her voice, and finally they both raced as though terrified, as though the thing that followed behind were more than a whale, or possibly less, perhaps a catcher vivified and fitted with fins. The Fin Whale chased for a quarter hour, then turned back. Alone again, she hardly noticed the contrast between the crystal calm she'd observed from below and the violence of the waves.

Her mind was dim again. Relaxing after her dive, she let herself drift for a moment or two while she filled her lungs. She was facing east. Her tail hung still. Then, as her nostrils closed, a wave hurled her down for seventy feet and tossed her back as far again, white throat grooves gleaming, tailfins clear for half a second, slapping at air as she arched her long back into a second wave and went down.

When she hit calmer levels, she faced west. Three hundred hours of haphazard flight had taken her all the way from Palmer Peninsula to the ice that bordered the Indian Ocean. And now she was swimming back again, her stroke as steady as ever. She kept well down. Climbing and falling through the waves could have been play, but her isolation had closed her mind. She swam woodenly, in oblivion, beating her flukes at a half-dozen knots, perhaps to return, upon awakening, to the half life in the north. The storm winds faded. Patterns of krill began to materialize under the waves. Fluttering close, the synchronized swarms spread around her eyes. She closed her lids. A day went by, then another day, or what would have been a day if the sun had left the sky.

She returned through a vacant sea. Six days went by. She passed the shelf of the Minke Whales. They paused to watch, but less often now. A steamlike fog covered the ice floes, and the ping-pong calls the whales passed back and forth bounced out and off her like a ball striking the body of a catatonic man. The others—the Sperms, Seis, Fins—had all shifted their ground, so that the blankness of her mind remained unbroken the few times she looked outside her eyes.

The fog hung close, then, after seven days, formed patches. Finally she found herself in sun, south of the Orkneys in the gleaming Weddell Sea. She paused and looked. A sudden motion from the mist caught her ears initially, then her vision. Right Whale Dolphins from the outer edge of the ice pack seized her sight, and as her eyes followed the shapes, her mind sprang open. Dolphin motion, like a single turn that starts the whole machine, snapped her to consciousness. The sun grew brighter now and, as she entered it, she signalled them and listened.

A ticking sound approached her from the west, a radio pulse at half-hour intervals, too faint as yet to get her full attention. The dolphin school had gone. The whale pursued, quickening her stroke to fifteen knots, but their voices faded. They stroked straight north at twice her speed. She called three times, trying to slow them, but their voices died away.

She wavered a moment. Far ahead, hardly discernible, a distant trace of night touched the horizon. In her mind she saw her old life: suns that waxed and waned, set days of easy dreaming. She was swimming north when a second flock came up, this time just west of her. The Right Whale Dolphins, great wanderers, were returning to their usual range above the polar front. She followed, turning west. Out of the air the voices multiplied, voices so high they faded quickly, but at close range gave out complicated talk in patterns impossible to answer. Then, from waters smooth as glass, their shapes came up, their eellike arches, dolphins nosing into the sea as if they embraced it, praying their way toward the north, fifty, a hundred, kissing again and again the surface of the sea, with numberless humps of them beyond—Eurhinodelphids,

143

Squalodonts—she had no names. When she came close enough to catch their flashing pectorals and backs, the dolphins veered, and, as they veered, the separate voices made a single whirring beam. The whale called out. Their silence silenced everything. When they were well toward the north, their talk resumed, thinned down to separate sounds again, then faded off. The Fin Whale circled in the strange glass of the sea.

And now from the west the sound of the radio caught her attention. It was a dead sound, dull and steady, without information, and pitched at a hundred hertz, a frequency the whale herself could use for signalling. The meaningless sound touched chords in her mind: compassion and memory. She pursued it. Then, in the distance, she saw what it was: a ten-foot flagpole. She swam on despite herself. When she drew close, she saw the Minke's bloated body. It floated, belly-up, the size of one of her calves, buoyed up and gleaming. She panicked immediately, fearing catchers. Every time they had killed a whale the men had buoyed it: it had floated aimlessly with a flag sticking out of it, and, inside it, a mysterious pulse had replaced the living heartbeat. That was the sound that she heard now: the implanted device that had displaced the living pulse. At the height of the killing that sound had come from every side, and every rorqual had known what it meant. She envisioned families in their panic, and in her head she heard the radios spreading out to fill the sea with their mocking pulse.

She plummeted northward at full speed, swam for a day till the sea grew rough. She was throbbing with fear. The Right Whale Dolphins on their northward migration had plunged by her as a sign. Deep in her chest far-off bereavements, dulled for years, sharpened again. The radio had faded. After a day a second started in the east. She drove herself past eighteen knots. Now, when she breathed, her open blowholes made a desperate sound. The labyrinthine ice that filled the south spread ever wider, opened unobstructed lanes where catcher vessels could make time. Blinded with panic, she flew only by ear, listening for radios and ships, while the bloated shape of her last calf rose up in her mind. Then, as she arched to breathe, the shape that filled her mind appeared outside her—dead ahead. She stopped her flight, approached again.

It was a Minke, one of the four the Blue had met on her first day, at hardly twenty feet too small to carry young. The six-foot fetus hung

144

precariously from the abdomen, a pendulum in the choppy sea, totally formed except for baleen and ventral grooves. Putrefaction had ruptured its mother. The Fin caught the stench in the sensitive membranes under her nostrils. They closed their valves. Yet she did not leave. Instead, she moved closer, nudged the calf. It broke away and spiralled leaflike into the dark, waving its shreds. From the mother's side a bloom of intestines fanned into the sea, but, where her belly broke the surface, she was whole. The inverted mouth was hanging open and made a vague smile when the waves caught the baleen. Only the tongue was gone. The Killer Whales had taken only the tongue. There was no radio inside. A pole had been planted. And there was a flag above the water. Far to the south the fog still stood, a solid wall, but here it had cleared. As the Fin Whale circled, the red flag flapped in rising wind.

She mourned her calves. Each time she blew now there was the accidental sobbing sound of her shrill, high-pitched panting. She hung still. When the mouths of her blowholes opened and closed they were as meaningless as mutes. Inside she sorrowed.

She was lost so far in memory that the sound of the catcher, bearing hard at first, then slowly drifting in, was like a sound in her own mind, a part of her vision of the past. Then it drew near and she knew it was real. She ran immediately for the north—it was only here in the Antarctic, after all, that she had seen one. The catcher roared now, opening up. Her giant tailfins, sixteen feet from end to end, powered her forward for two hours at maximum speed. But the catcher closed. When she heard it near, an ache had started in her fins. She gathered her wits and remembered the speed of them. But below they could not see. She sounded forty minutes to west, then ran to the east, the sound of her heart like a drum inside, the man at the wheel confused at first, the gray sea spreading. But, after an hour, the distance closed; he seemed to follow without his eyes. He didn't use the radar yet, for he could afford to make wrong guesses with the speed of the ship on his side. Only the dolphins could have outdistanced him, their arches far to the north. The ship closed in. The whale had risen for breath only twice in the last hour, and she needed over thirty inhalations to replace her oxygen, but now the danger was too great for extended breaths. Her inhalations and exhalations were crowded together as she kept rising in different places to keep out of range. Once she took twelve breaths in a row and the man at the gun almost got her into his sights. She sensed it

145

and cut the number of breaths to less than six. To four. To three. Blood swelled the *retia mirabilia* in her shoulders and her back. Her muscles could work without the oxygen of a man's but even the little that they needed was taken away with her breathing time. She breathed three times, the steep bow's blackness catching her eye. Then she circled aft, the black above her, waiting to kill her when she rose. She breathed behind, well out of range, but the flexible bow wheeled again toward her. Out of one eye she saw the gun, dead beast that tracked without an eye. Now it was clear. She watched it turn to aim yet she didn't dive, surfacing dangerously as her system screamed for breath. She inhaled in five-breath sequences separated by shallow runs of ten or twelve seconds. Slowly her muscles lost their pain, slowly refilled. But now there was sonar around her—separate pings at first, then tumbling over each other—the wake of her tail and the swirling wake of the boat intertwined, their mazes maddening—insects in and out of her ears, her brain aswarm. But still she kept to the back of the boat, turning and weaving it hour by hour in maze after maze till at last the sonar stopped. Just under the light she called. And far to her west her voice bounced back to her: the ice—her only safety.

It took an hour of full-speed swimming at great depth to put the last of the floes behind. The ship lost part of the ground it had gained. But, after the last berg, water lay open for half a mile until the next one. Had she turned back she could have sounded indefinitely. But the bergs were very wide, and though the ship could not follow her under, there was a danger of getting trapped. She had hardly a moment, the bow closing in. She listened hard. It seemed the distance to the ship was wide enough for a second run. Not a certainty. She hovered a second. Then from the west: a low-frequency call, at twenty hertz the sound of a rorqual. Or Blue Whale. She hurried west.

She raced with shallow dives, deep thundering breaths—she glanced behind. Now the ship had cleared the ice. The sonar came, ship thundering, sonar and motor louder and louder. Fifteen minutes passed, then twenty. She started to ache again. It loomed behind her. Wide.

She sounded and crisscrossed till the darkness covered her. It would have been good to remain in the dark, to live without breathing. Sonar pestered again like flies. But accurate now. Now no matter how dense her screens of bubbles or the currents from her tail the ship ignored them, kept her in gun range. She knew it was dangerous to rise but after forty minutes of flight the ship still loomed. Her great lungs ached. Her half-ton heart was swollen and loud. Pins of paralysis spotted her sides. They pricked and pricked her. The eons of gentleness that had molded her mind made rage a foreign thing, but, when it came, it took away all trace of caution. She soared for the ship, veered at the last and showered huge cascades of spray up over the side, then saw the gunner for an instant, swivelling and bobbing, sighting through spray. She breathed the cold air—sweeter than food—into her lungs. Desperate for breath, she waited too long. When the gunner fired it was only the toss of the ship that kept him from killing her outright.

The harpoon was five feet long and it went into her all the way, but wide of its mark between the shoulder blades—it entered in the area next to the flukes. As she took it down, unreeling rod after rod of line, her mind flickered to blackness and her flukes beat even faster than before, making the blood rise out, a trailing, widening cloud. The impact of entry opened the four prongs of the harpoon head so that the flight which should have dislodged it buried it deep. Still in her terror she did not feel. Her flukes beat harder: marvellous wings. A hundred feet of line flashed out in just three seconds. Then the grenade explosion: rupturing muscles and veins. The great wings wavered, slowed. She played out all of the forerunner, took four hundred yards of cable. But now her flukes beat only spasmodically, in jerks, a pair of cripples above her head. Hardly aware that she was watching them, she scissored—involuntarily—like a fish, then started to rise.

She edged back up, gradually slackening to the west. The light came slow at first, then fast—an illumination of red blood. She thought of her calves as it drew near. It lit the surface. It was the sun the rorquals had followed into the ice fields every spring, but larger and brighter than ever before, an enormous blaze. The light spread out as if to touch her and gather her in. Behind her eyes she heard the roar of it. She greeted it in thunder.

She rose to touch it; fell back down, smacking her side; sank under a little, but not deep enough to start a second run, the surface flickering. The light spread out as if to enfold her. Behind her eyes the roar again. But it was her own blood also she heard, and the catcher coming.

The thud of the lance shattered her backbone, punctured her lungs, severed nerve cords to her tail—killed a large part of her, but did not touch her brain. As she felt the pain of it, the great valves of her head

147

opened themselves. Her heart beat hard, as if it were laboring to empty her of life. Out of her head it came, dark crimson. Whalers watched it as it rose. The sun made lights and shadows in it where it fell back into the sea. But it was not sea. The whale was conscious when it broke from her; then, when it fell away: on her back and barely floating. The pectoral rose and then sank down—followed her mind toward the darkness it had entered. Far north the dolphins rode the waves. Far west the Blue Whale heard the death and fled the cape. The body dove. It would have gone under all the way but for the cable and hawser. Whalebirds screamed. The men hauled it up and towed it in through blue-gray sea.

CHAPTER 14

FIVE months before the Fin Whale's death, in the second half of October, the brother and sister dolphins, expelled from the open-sea school, swam stiffly on the surface of the sea. Often one or the other would overturn and float on its back or side like a half-dead fish, its jerks and twitches signalling vulnerability. No sharks had attacked, but an attack was inevitable if they kept on swimming this way. Their herd had long since disappeared on the western horizon, while to the south the Spotted Dolphins, whose appearance had so frightened the young male, had gone as well. Their isolation was complete.

Even so, they were hardly more alone than when they had swum with their cousin and the juvenile Striped Dolphins. Then they had spurned the hierarchies and meaningless rituals of the schools, unwilling to tolerate limits of any kind. But now, after acceptance and belonging in the open-sea school of five hundred, the solitude they once had sought was unbearable. Awake and unmoving, they were unable to do more than lament.

Two days went by. On the morning of the third day, the sister turned to face the rising sun. She travelled east, automatically stroking, just as the school had done each dawn, and the young male followed till they were swimming side by side. When sheer exhaustion put them to sleep, it was the sleep they had known in captivity and with the whales: a general blackness and oblivion with hardly any dreams. After some hours they woke again, swimming eye to eye. They watched each other, then fell farther into sleep. This time they dreamed more vividly.

As the pair swam on, memories of childhood, shut away from both waking and sleep since their captivity, began to surface. The female clicked to herself, then squeaked out loud as she saw her childhood days in the Gulf of Guinea. Their sleeping minds resurrected memory after memory, and soon, from the year both had been born, they remembered the dry season: something uncommon off equatorial Gabon. Both recalled the yellowfin tuna.

Temperatures soared as the dry season wore on. By January, yellowfin tuna were everywhere, and now, with the spawning that had come, their hindmost fins were sickles of pure gold. They laid a million eggs at a time, well out at sea. The smaller tuna kept to themselves, but, whether feeding or at rest, the larger fish followed the dolphins. Wherever the dolphins located smelt the yellowfin tuna fed in a frenzy. Often it seemed that the dolphins were merely guides for the fish. With their spawning done, the yellowfins filled both the offshore gulf and the water over the shelf.

Hoping to lose the unwanted escort of yellowfin tuna, the herd of the brother and sister fed farther and farther from shore, eventually joining Spinner Dolphins in the nighttime seas up to fifty or sixty miles from coastal Gabon. The Spinners were gray above, tan on the sides, whitish below, roughly the Common Dolphins' size. They were named for their extraordinary aerial feats, which included not only three or more longitudinal spins in succession, but somersaults in which they rose headfirst, slung their tails over their heads in spirals of spray, and re-entered tailfirst, slapping their flukes against the sea. At night, when the Common Dolphins fed with the Spinners, there were too many hunters and too few fish. Still, the herds tolerated each other. Each dawn the Spinners swam off to join the Spotted Dolphin schools, and soon some Common Dolphins went with them, though most of the Common Dolphins, including the aunt, returned to the coast for safety.

The mother of the young male and his sister had been swimming back and forth between the deeper sea and Cape Lopez for over a week when she changed her routine. By day she joined the nocturnal Spin-ners and kept close to the feeding grounds, using diurnal Spotted Dolphins as lookouts while she slept or fed her calves. The experienced aunt who'd accompanied her before did not approve; she had too much fear of the tuna boats to sleep in the offshore water. But the mother ignored her sister's anxiety, trusting the Spotted Dolphins to warn of any danger. She would spend a week or so out at sea, then return to the shelf for a couple of weeks. This made her sister so angry that fights flared up, and the pair drew blood as they nipped and butted at one another. Still, the sister took care of the twins when their mother grew tired, and in return, the mother served as guardian to her niece, the oldest calf, already weaned. On one of the days when she swam for deeper water, the mother dolphin, tending the niece, failed to locate her older sister, though she didn't try very hard, convinced as she was that her sister's calf would be safe in the offshore sea. She hunted that night and, with day, fell asleep among the Spotted, Spinner, and Common Dolphins who made up the offshore herd.

The seiner closest to the mother was less than three miles away, and the Spotted Dolphins who stood watch had been aware of it for some time. They were big males. Each had a white tip on his snout and, over his speckled coat, a mantle of white-spotted black that ran just past his dorsal. It would have been easy to swim away, but these sentry dolphins saw no need. Sets on dolphins in the gulf were not very common. These dolphins had only a little experience with the seiners. In any case, they knew the men wanted only the tuna that shoaled beneath them. Both had been caught five years ago, and both knew that, once in the net, it was calf's play to dive to safety through the bottom, leaving the captive fish behind. Though most dolphins were terrified of speedboats, once they got used to the roaring of the outboards it was a simple thing to dive under the boats, and the older of the two sentries knew from experience that this maneuver drove the speedboat drivers mad. In any case, there were no outboards after them yet. They bided their time.

Ever since the advent of large nylon seines, tuna ships had fished by netting dolphins, since the yellowfin tuna followed dolphins so closely that, even when they were driven into the seine by roaring speedboats, the tuna still swam beneath them. Once both dolphins and tuna were captured and the bottom of the purse seine had been closed, the men would let the dolphins go and haul the tuna aboard the ship. Ideally no dolphins would die in the process, but in practice thousands did.

As the ship came on, the watching dolphins could see a boom from the mainmast lower a cable over the first of the six boats on the upper deck. The cable lifted one boat, driver inside, and then the boom swung out and lowered the boat down padded rails until it was hanging clear. It was a calm day for the dolphins, a ten-foot sea. But already the speedboat swayed in the wind.

The eighty-horsepower outboard roared like a giant hornet, though the roar of auxiliary diesels on the seiner drowned the sound. As the cable came down, the sentry dolphins listened and other dolphins began to wake up.

The fifteen-foot speedboat had room for only one man and virtually no draft. When it touched the water, the driver reached up and loosed the clamp. Now the boat was free. From where the dolphins watched in tense fascination, the V-shaped bow wave of the ship seemed to tower over the boat, and the quarter wave behind it seemed even higher. The boat held its position between the two. Soon the boom came out again. In a matter of minutes the five other speedboats were angled behind the first like a formation of flying birds, but a cable still held the skiff against the sloping stern of the ship. Now the skipper barked through the PA system, and there was a whirl of rattling chains and flying corks as the forty-foot skiff, with one end of the seine, vaulted noisily to sea. The dolphins saw it raise white waves when it hit the water, then spin so its stern faced the stern of the ship and it held the towline stationary, standing still by revving its engines while the seiner pulled away at seventeen knots.

Now even the sentries grew scared, for it was clear that the ship intended to encircle them in a corral. They watched. One end of the towline was still aboard the ship. The net began to roll out. The seiner was travelling in a wide, white arc to starboard of the skiff. The sentries muttered: a sort of chuckle; but it was time to swim for safety.

Still, as if they were frozen, the Spotted sentries watched the six boats turning parallel to the ship in a formation they'd never seen. This novelty, with the overwhelming noise, deeply confused them. The din was deafening even well off from the ship in the rear of the herd, where by now all the dolphins had awakened. There were over a hundred Spinners besides the hundred and fifty Spotteds. They hung a little way behind, and the Common Dolphins formed a smaller group, maybe fifty, at the rear. Now all were watching to see what the sentries were going to do. But they seemed uncertain. The mother dolphin was in the middle of the ring of Common Dolphins, her calves beside her, one pressing either pectoral fin. Emotion and instinct told her to turn and flee for the shallows where the ship wouldn't come in, but the rest of the school were still waiting to see what the sentries did. She knew that the sentries had had experience with ships, and she could tell from their tranquil sounds they had not panicked. Nor did the rest of the groups appear to be concerned. But the mother dolphin had never encountered seiners before. Inside her head she heard the clicking admonitions of her sister, and she trembled.

Her fear was not for herself, but for her calves. All of the herd could sense that only a second remained before the sentries would make a move. And yet the second seemed to be infinite. Now the mother lowered herself and lofted two of the three calves onto her back. She wanted them solid against her sides. She had no language, but she felt that, if she could, she would like to enclose them; to have the brother and sister inside her once again; to wrap her bones around their bodies. A trickle of vomit passed out the left side of her mouth and into the sea. Her cage of bones seemed empty and cold. She froze with fear. If she should lose them the cage of her bones would be empty forever. She murmured low, and, catching her sorrow, all three calves cowered inside. But they were overwhelmed by awareness of her love.

Finally the skipper yelled "Pull away!" and the first speedboat driver revved to thirty knots. By sheer speed the boats had to get behind the dolphins and scare them into the net. Up till now the driver had moved at the seiner's speed in the calm place between the bow wave of the seiner and the towering quarter wave slightly farther back. Now the dolphins could see him nose straight at the bow wave towering high above his boat, shoot into air, and flip-flop sideways. They almost heard the driver shouting for fear the boat would come down on its side. But it hit flat on, slapping its hull. Then in a moment it was back up, literally flying from crest to crest. For a moment the driver lost control and zigzagged crazily over the sea. The driver veered left, and the five other boats followed his lead. The sea was kicking. Spray shot constantly over the bows. Only the ship had a clear view of the dolphins, and the skipper was preoccupied in keeping his mesh from getting caught and tangled in the corkline.

The dolphins could see the net unreel. By the time the skipper had set an eighth of his net, the schools were racing in the direction of St. Thomas Island, about two hundred and forty miles out from the shore. The skipper cursed but continued to lay out line, urging his boats by radio to herd the schools. The sound and the gleaming wakes of the roaring outboards panicked them.

The Common school led the flight, with the Spinner Dolphins close behind. The young male pressed his fins to his mother's back and cupped his flukes over her tail while each of the other two pressed one of her pectoral fins, not swimming at all, simply carried along by her speed. The calves felt terror, not at the ship, but at the strange bird whirring above them: a helicopter from another ship, only minutes late for the catch. Not far away the other ship was watching. As the helicopter veered off, the motorboats closed and raced all four hundred and eighty of their horses, easily overtaking the schools. They passed them and turned around to face them, then pursued to force them in the direction of the seine. With the speedboats thundering behind them, the dolphins all reversed and swam back for the ship. Not far off they could see it peacefully turning, unloosing well over two-thirds of its net.

It seemed huge as they drew near. One speedboat flanked each side of the school while the four others roared behind. The dolphins were bunched closer together. Directly beside one of the outriding Spotted Dolphins the first driver's boat raised flashing spray. Another few minutes and the school would be encircled by the net. The two Spotted sentries remembered the process. The boats would guard the gap between the two ends of the seine until the ship completed its turn, closing the gap, and the skiff and ship were back together. The plan was working. But the one Spotted Dolphin who raced calmly beside the first driver's boat leaped from the water. Before it went down in a wave of flukes, the driver caught the intelligent look of the eye, a mocking gleam. Another leaped, then a third, a fourth, and then, in a line, the Spotteds plummeted under his keel. The skipper was cursing so loudly into the driver's radio helmet the dolphins could hear "Son of a bitch!" The driver screamed a profane reply, craning his head. The Spotteds had surfaced directly to port and were calling the rest of the herd to follow.

"Tighten! Tighten!" the skipper shouted, but the boats did not maneuver well in the ten-foot waves. Still, the engines frightened the inexperienced members of the school. In their panic, most of the starboard dolphins were disobeying the sentries. They bunched more tightly than ever and headed away from the terrible roar—into the seine.

In terror of the motorboats, the dolphins raced for a quarter mile before they noticed the boats were well behind them. As their initial fear subsided a second terror took its place: their echolocation detected obstacles on every side. Dolphins who had been trapped before were calm at first and merely awaited the "backdown," when the net that surrounded them would be lowered away—but the panic of the novices was contagious, and the bulk of the school recoiled, only to face the boats again. When the boats moved off, the skiff and ship came together. The skiff returned its end of the towline to the ship, and a winch reeled it in. Now the circle was complete; the corral was closed. But the area inside the net had to be kept as large as possible to prevent the tuna from panicking. If they panicked they might dive through the open bottom. To keep the net wide the skiff held it taut with two cables and pulled away from the seiner so that the closed circle of bobbing surface floats stayed round and wide. Even so, the very presence of the floats made the inexperienced dolphins bunch together and start to dive. Soon they were tumbling over each other.

The mother and her calves dove with the others, and as she went down, she saw a strange assortment of fish swimming around her: yellowfin tuna, ballyhoo halfbeaks, skipjacks, dorados, and blue sharks, natural enemies forced together. The dolphins went down for three hundred feet. The mother saw the flapping tails continue into the

155

dark as some of the captives dove through the bottom. But something had happened to the young male calf: the tailfins of a yellowfin had knocked away his wits. He rolled to one side, then started to float. As she watched him rise toward the sun, she turned herself upright and nosed him, pushing him into air. A minute passed. He didn't breathe. She poked his stomach. A dribble of water came out of his head. He coughed and struggled while tuna, dorados, and sharks spun around them, spooked by the dolphins' obvious fear. She arched her body around his to protect him from their fins. The two other calves studied him closely. After a moment he shook himself and breathed again.

The net was a quarter mile wide. The dolphins could have jumped the corks and escaped, but instead they thronged the center in their terror of the line. Open-sea creatures, they did not know what to make of surface obstructions. Still, they were not in mortal danger. Only snagging in the mesh could take their lives, by drowning them. The tug between skiff and ship was keeping the net walls apart, safely away from the dolphins bunched in the center. The speedboat drivers had cabled the net as well, and they were pulling back on the corkline to make sure the net stayed wide. But the net had been inadvertently set in strong undersea current, and despite the skiff and the boats, the current made the walls of the net close in farther than usual.

As they closed in, some of the braver Spinners dove and poked at the webbing, but most fought to get close to the center, farther away from the walls. In no time the diving Spinners caught their beaks in the four-and-a-quarter-inch mesh. As they thrashed and choked about seventy feet below, the ones at the surface could hear them struggle. The dolphins at the center hurt each other, jostling in panic. The concentration formed a solid mass where weaker swimmers went down, unable to breathe. Some floated aimlessly, snout upright, semiconscious in their exhaustion.

The skipper watched from the deck. He wanted to set the dolphins free, but he couldn't afford to try until he'd closed the seine. At this point it was a three-hundred-foot-deep cylinder with a circular line of floats at the top and a circular line of lead rings to hold it taut at the bottom. The line at the bottom was the purseline. At the top the ends of the floatline joined, but the two ends of the purseline at the bottom were attached to separate cables. These ran up and over two power blocks on the starboard side of the ship. Now a motor started and a

156

winch began to haul the cables up. In minutes they were aboard, and the two halves of the purseline were coming up from the sea, drawing the cylindrical net closed at the bottom.

The dolphins could hear the tuna aimlessly racing. Forced from the top, the mother had struggled into an opening near the edge. She had been frantic before, but now, when the mesh brushed against her, she took no notice, noticed nothing except the exhaustion that gripped her muscles and the fiery rasp of hot air entering her head.

She was in shock. One calf was gone. Somewhere in the wild stampede around the net the cousin had slipped away from the mother dolphin and fallen behind. By the time she realized this, the mother had been trapped in the crowded center, fighting for life. Now she hung dazed, bodies bobbing all around her, most of them calves. In her stupor, she watched the surviving dolphins grieve. Some, guarding their dead, fiercely attacked other dolphins who came near. A few of them, males, dared at last to jump the corks to freedom. From close by the sentries were calling. It was lethally hot in the circle. In minutes all had grown accustomed to death. When, seventy feet below her, a dying dolphin gave a last kick at the mesh and sent a little ripple of death over her body, she lurched only slightly before settling back into inertia.

She felt lost, ready for death. Her sister's calf was gone. She trembled. Then the net moved again, and the cousin rose up from the depths. Pushed to one side, she had caught one flipper in the mesh while pursuing her aunt to the top, and her calls had been drowned by the gasps of the dolphin struggling below her. The other had died, but the cousin had managed to thrash herself free.

What had saved her, though, was not her strength but the narrower mesh that lined the top of the net, the so-called Medina panel, inserted to save the dolphins during the backdown. A hundred and eighty fathoms long and eleven fathoms deep, this one-and-a-quarter-inch mesh was too fine to snag most flippers; even the five-foot calf had caught only the tip of her fin. All the same, she had been close to death. She gasped as she broke the surface.

The mother embraced her when she rose free. Badly bruised and disoriented, she struggled against the mother, almost unconscious; she had never before been below for that length of time. The mother's spirits soared, then dropped again as she felt the webbing nudge her side. The young male, daughter, and niece huddled close to her while, at the back

157

of her mind, she recalled again her sister's apprehensions. Neither elated nor depressed, the young male watched her out of glazed eyes, youth protecting him from the grief that immobilized her. A half-dead triggerfish drifted by. He snapped at it, then swam to the wall and nudged the bright red buoys.

High up on the bridge the skipper watched the seine, deeply frustrated by the need to hold in the dolphins. He wanted no more of them killed, but it was essential that this raising of the net go off easily and smoothly so as not to spook the fish. When the purseline had been raised and the bottom closed, the net itself had begun to rise to a power block. The power block loomed above on a sixty-foot crane with a movable boom; it hung over the working deck. The haul would continue until the seine that remained in the water was shallow and snug against the side of the ship. Out of this "sack" the fish would be lifted up by brailers: giant scoop nets that were lowered from the skiff. When the load of fish in the water grew light enough for lifting, they might be taken aboard directly in the seine.

The Spotted Dolphin sentries were both free. They watched from just outside the corks, troubled and sad, encouraging others to jump free. None of them moved. The sentries could see the ship gather net. They waited tensely. When would the motors reverse to lower the corks for the backdown procedure both of them remembered from other seinings? This would make even the most terrified dolphins swim free. Both hovered and clicked in encouragement, awaiting the backdown, but all they could see was the net going up to the power block and down to the deck.

Soon twenty minutes had passed. Half the net had been raised to the deck.

On board, the men were laboring hard to spread the net without snags. Already the sentries could see tuna flapping up the side, tails caught in the webbing. Some, too tightly snagged for release, rose all the way to the power block on the boom, thrashing like birds, then plummeted free. Amid cries of "Comin' down!" and "*Ojos arriba!*" the two-hundred-pounders plunged fifty feet with a sound like giant zippers opening the mesh. Work slowed as tuna were dragged to the wells. The boom moved back and forth, positioning net. Then one of the Spinners, only half conscious after getting caught in submerged mesh, rose to the block, passed through its narrow, crushing aperture, and fell sideways. The mother and sentries watched the Spinner while the Spinner plummeted. In a sort of dream they could see the helmeted head of a man gleam beneath it. Then came the crash. Both man and dolphin were hauled from the deck.

Now the winch stopped and the sounds inside the net began to fade. One motor cut out, and over the background hum the dolphins heard only the yellowfin tuna, most more than six feet long, racing between the walls of mesh. From high up the dolphins could hear the PA. The skipper was shouting "Back 'er down!"

When the fish approached the ship, separating themselves from the dolphins, it reversed at quarter throttle in order to let the dolphins go free. The skipper knew from previous settings that most of them would not jump over the corks, that the corks had to be lowered well beneath them before they would swim away.

The net slackened farthest from the hull, allowing the corks to submerge. The dolphins near the outside edge could slip away. Most of the school stampeded for freedom. After some minutes it was mainly injured dolphins and corpses that stayed inside. Afraid for its catch, the ship moved forward to make the line of floats resurface, closing the wall.

But too many dolphins were still in the net. The skipper ordered the first speedboat driver to scare them free. The mother dolphin and the young male heard the skipper's words through the PA, recognizing only the menace in them. "Back down again! Hurry up down there! Get those whitebellies out of the net! We're losing time!" The ship reversed to lower the corks, and the driver swam to push the injured dolphins away, but just as he did, a squadron of tuna and blue sharks broke from the bottom. Dodging sideways, it was all the driver could do to balance his body on the net while they shot by. "Christ!" cursed the skipper. "Raise the corks!" The diesels reversed—a shattering sound—and for the second time the corks rose back into sight. The driver returned to his boat. Once more the net came up the side.

The mother's consciousness came and went. Now she came awake. Her calves were near the center when she decided to try a dive. She nosed the net, seeking an opening through which she could lead the calves. As with the cousin, all that could save her from entrapment was the tightly woven mesh. But the Medina panel filled only a fraction of the seine.

She struggled. Where Spinner Dolphins hung from the mesh, the nervous sharks were slicing gouges out of their sides. Each shark weighed several hundred pounds, and when it hit a Spinner Dolphin, it zigzagged its body to get full power into its bite. Unable to turn their collared heads, and blind to the rear, the Spinner Dolphins perished slowly, a foot at a time, with intervals of unpredictable length between the bites. By now the spaces in the mesh resembled gallows, some of the victims still alive, though fully half of their bodies were ripped away. Among the dead, heads still caught in the mesh seemed to stare at the mother dolphin as she swam by.

The mother nudged the Medina panel, then came up. The calves slid close to her, pressing her sides. She seemed catatonic, shocked by the spectacle below. Now, as the larger fish consumed the smaller, some of the sharks were snapping at yellowfin tuna as well. Dead Spinners were everywhere in the mesh, suffocated, hanged. The mother vomited. Some who were dead she had known very well. But now all that mattered was keeping the calves above the danger. She pushed the brother and sister up onto her head, lifting them clear.

When the dream stopped unfolding and the brother and sister dolphins shuddered awake, it was late afternoon. Immediately sensing their position, they knew they must have travelled many miles in their sleep. Surrounded by emptiness and totally isolated, they swam on with no destination in mind, only to appease an inner restlessness, hoping that another school would materialize from the vacancy that threatened to overwhelm them.

The sea was immaculate. The steady Atlantic sun grew hypnotic as they drifted back toward sleep and their restlessness took clearer direc-tion. Both felt an instinctive urge to move east, back to their home in the Gulf of Guinea. The male, who kept envisioning the northwest African shelf from which he'd swum to find the whales, only partly obeyed the urge to travel east, swimming northeast instead while his sister stayed at his side. Still, in his own way he was also pointed home. Though neither brother nor sister remembered, much of the inshore school at Cape Lopez was made up of Ivory Coast dolphins who'd fled their bountiful shelf decades ago to escape the innumerable fishing ships.

The light of the sun pressed down their eyelids as the brother and sister obeyed their homing instinct. They wanted sleep again, a quiet, steady sleep without frightening dreams, but the terror of the seine was returning to light. After a quarter hour, the vision had its way with both of them.

The mother was so catatonic she had let herself be trapped with the dead and injured inside the net. By now the skiff had cabled itself to the starboard side of the ship, and the dolphins were all in shadow between the skiff gathering net on its starboard side and the ship itself, still hauling net aboard. The mother struggled, lofting the calves above the fish. High overhead a triangular net with a long handle trembled un-steadily on two cables that ran from the skiff to one of the booms on the seiner. This brailer was so large that it took at least three men to control it. Lofted by her mother, the sister watched as if in a trance. Slowly the brailer angled down from the bobbing skiff, entered the seine, and went under—a giant mouth. Soon the sister could feel it beneath her, tuna solid against its mesh, gasping and dying. With her mother she dodged to one side as it rose out. Wavering in the wind, it jerked its way up the cables onto the seiner where chutes had already been lowered to tuna wells and a larger chute, for sharks and "garbage fish," had been extended over the side. The sister looked around. There were only moderate wind and swell, but the skiff rolled in the swell and pitched up and down in the chop, surging back and forth beside the larger ship. This lurching movement endangered the lives of the men who controlled the brailer and made it more difficult to release the captive dolphins from the net without injury.

Inside, wounded tuna and dolphins broadcast a signal of blood and low-frequency sound—the sound of thrashing, wounded fish—all over the sea. Along with the sounds of helicopters constantly scouting, low on the water, the low-frequency pulses attracted more and more sharks.

The sister looked up at the ship, but all she could see was a chaos of flapping fish and swinging wires. But, after some minutes, the tuna went sliding into the well, and one of the mates yelled, "Take 'er away!" The sister watched the five-foot brailer with its thirty-foot steel pole jerk back down the cables toward the skiff. Lofting her calves above the tuna, the mother lifted herself clear. She was starting to shake herself out of her trance. She saw the motion of the brailer on its cables and was acute enough to know that in a few minutes it would come down for the rest of the catch.

She braced herself. So did the driver of the first boat. Down from the crow's nest, into his helmet, came the sound the mother and calves had heard before: the PA carried it all through the ship. Though they couldn't understand the words, the voice sounded threatening, unstable; the weary skipper ordered his crew to scare the dolphins out of the net with rifle fire.

The voice was so loud it carried all the way down to the net without the radio, but the radio amplified and echoed it all the more. Now, beneath the thrum of the boats, the mother heard more voices: dolphin voices. She almost blacked out again when she realized she was hearing the sickening gagging sound she had heard before. Another netting was in progress, not far away. Soon from all sides she thought she could hear it, louder than motors now: the nauseating sound of the garroting.

The sister looked up. A row of deckhands had lined up dutifully at the rail. The dolphins saw gun barrels turn toward them. Shots cracked out and a couple of blue sharks, hit in the head, sank to the bottom. Now the dolphins heard the skipper speak again. "Okay! Enough." He talked to the driver, an almost pleading edge to his voice. "For Christ's sake, man, can't you move those porpoise out of the sack?" Just as the skipper spoke, the rail of the skiff bumped into the seiner, shutting the sky out. Then the sea heaved and the skiff backed up, knocking everyone off balance. Cursing was general, but above it came a sudden, piercing cry. The brailer jerked free onto the cable, the blood of the port man staining the handle as the skiff righted itself.

Inside the net the fish were so thick that the dolphins were barely able to swim. Teeth raked their sides. One skinned its chest on the thorn-rough denticles of a blue that was sidewinding by. The blue showed its teeth. Shaken, the first driver reversed, watched from well off. But now a hammerhead shark was cruising the outside water, swimming with great, wide sweeps of its head, expectant remoras thronging its sides like the heavenly host. Some of these slim fish clung to the shark with the suction disk located on top of their heads. All waited eagerly for scraps. The voice from the ship and the drivers' radios came again. Someone fired at the shark, but the bullet went wide. The first driver cursed. The mother dolphin could feel herself drowning in yellowfins. She pushed her calves into the light as the fins went over her, darkening her eyes. Above, the brailer ran back to the rail of the skiff, and the sister could see where a man on the port rail wrestled the handle.

Eventually two drivers turned back to the net, where one got out of his seat, crouched at the tip of the bow, and reached to grab the fin of an injured dolphin as the corks went down again. When the corks had gone under, a flurry of tuna, some half dead, spilled into the sea. Requiem sharks on the other side—silkies and blues—tore at the tuna, scaring the driver back into his boat. The brailer was descending for another scoop when the mako shark came in.

The sister was close enough to the side, and sufficiently anesthetized by shock, to follow the shark with her eyes. It didn't swim with an undulation like the others—instead, it seemed to use only its tail, just as an albacore swims, or a bluefin. The drivers froze. When the shark drew close, the eye was all pupil, blacker than night and very large. Just as the brailer curved into the seine the mako arched lightly over the side. The sister could see the sun between seiner and skiff catch the aquamarine of its back. Someone on deck tried a couple of shots. One of them hit. Enraged, the mako hit the net with his full power. The mesh withstood the impact, and the ship lost none of its catch, but the dolphin family fled. The sight of the mako jumping the corks, larger than life, had snapped the mother out of her trance. She pushed the young ones ahead of her and, forcing her way through the tuna, arched out to sea.

The sister did not remember the rest very well. The mother flew until a second ship appeared directly ahead. It was in its backdown, and there were dolphins breaking for freedom. Here the mother rejoined the herd. The calves hung close to her, riding her back and her pectoral fins. After the boats were well behind, she paused for a moment and circled beside the brother and sister, belly to belly, feeding, caressing. With every mouthful they felt themselves strengthen, come to life. The cousin bunted in play, and the heartbeat of the mother started to slow while the other dolphins stampeded by. The sister, cousin, and brother grasped her tightly, small hearts racing, convinced that she alone had saved them, as they had always known she would, for each of them was still too young for doubt. She watched them intently for a moment, holding them near without a sound, and then the four pursued the others toward Gabon.

When the brother and sister awakened to the cloudless sky, they realized they had continued to swim homeward in their sleep. They turned on their sides and looked at the stars. Only beneath the surface was there sound. Above the ocean, in the air, all was as quiet as the sky. Atoms of flesh and bone, they watched the immensity for several minutes. Vertigo filled them, darkening their mood, but at the same time they could feel the northeastern movement soothe their spirits. They travelled all night at seven knots in mindless calm. With dawn they slept and dreamed again.

Their dreams this time were pleasant. The mother was leading them back for Gabon when they encountered the mother's sister swimming westward with her other calf and calling out for the lost one. The siblings of the young male and his sister were swimming with her. After reunion with her youngster, the angry aunt was about to nip the mother dolphin when the sight of the scratches and wounds from the tuna seining held her back. The exhausted mother and calves were badly in need of calm and rest. For the rest of the day the dolphins hovered quietly.

A week later, over the shelf off coastal Gabon, they hardly noticed when a thirty-foot launch appeared out of the north, Common Dolphins from the inshore school at Cape Lopez riding its bow. Once they did, the sight of these others coasting in safety quelled even the aunt's suspicions. After the launch slowed to a stop, the aunt, mother, and three calves, along with the older youths, idled west to mix with the dolphins who played near the ship. Some of these had been trapped in the tuna seine and escaped during the backdown. There were interchanges of clicks, expressing joy and commiseration, but it didn't occur to the dolphins to fear all vessels because of the seiner. All their lives they had been riding at the bows of friendly vessels where sailors shouted greetings from the deck. This small craft bore no resemblance at all to the massive tuna ship.

Though they were used to friendly greetings, they were surprised when after two hours men in wetsuits came quietly over the side and swam toward them, something even the oldest dolphins couldn't recall having happened before. Curiosity overcame most of the group, dolphins who hadn't been in the seine. They swam up to the men, then beside them. A half hour later a rubber zodiac raft left the launch and putted toward them. Calmed by the gentle talk of the swimmers, the dolphins didn't turn to flee. When the raft drew close, the swimmers climbed in and lay with their arms over the sides, still talking playfully to the dolphins. That evening, when they turned east toward the coast, the launch followed quietly behind them. Many hung back to ride the bow.

The mother and aunt with their offspring made up a separate group. Over the next four days the friendly men in wetsuits, noticing this, swam beside the ten for hours at a time. On the fourth afternoon the family's sudden discovery that a net had encircled them while they'd played with the men came as a shock, as did their roundup by the rafts and their hauling aboard in canvas slings, something that made the rest of the dolphins call out in fright and circle the launch. Swimmers who'd joined them in the water talked to them gently as they waited in the holding tanks on the ship. The family was transported to Lagos Aquarium.

With daily stimulation and affection from the men, it still took the dolphins two months to adapt to their life in the indoor pool at Lagos, but after six months they had adjusted and, though they badly missed their school, felt little fear. The affection of the men made them relax. Soon they felt at home with their captors, as well as with the Bottle-nosed Dolphin and two Striped Dolphins already in the pool when they arrived.

Almost from the beginning there was intensive, daily training. Out of the ten new arrivals, the aunt and cousin were quickest to learn, but after six months all the dolphins came to the trainers on command, placing objects on the bottom of the pool, then surfacing and diving once more to retrieve them. At first the objects were simple things like balls, which they could carry in their mouths, but later they wore muzzles to which objects were attached. To retrieve flat disks the dolphins pressed them with magnetic plates muzzled onto their snouts. Soon they were taught to plant magnetized disks against metal plates on the side of the pool.

Unweaned at the time of capture, the brother and sister were late to begin their training and never caught up with the others, though their mother, whose training had also been delayed, performed very well. The two Striped Dolphins, only recently acquired, didn't learn well, but the Bottlenosed Dolphin, who had been with the men for years, had long since mastered all the tasks, although he couldn't learn anything new, and when not performing for the men, he showed no interest in the others, his eyes always set in a blank stare and his head pocked with tiny scars, each roughly the size of a pinhole. Often the others would gaze at him.

After six months, the dolphins were placed in an open-sea pen. By now the men could send the mother, aunt, and cousin to retrieve metal disks four hundred feet down. The dolphins also learned to place the disks against targets as far as five hundred yards away, taking directional cues from the men. They would swim in the pointed direction until the pinging sound of a buoy came into range, and then home in. The target was never the buoy itself but a metal sheet hundreds of feet below it. After eight months the sister accompanied her mother on these dives. This task of diving to undersea sites marked off by buoys had proven invaluable when dolphins carried tools and other necessities to aqualabs or workers at undersea oil wells.

The dolphins were not as happy with the men as they would have been at sea, but they were resilient and adaptable and the men had their trust and affection. Over the months of captivity only two things threatened to break their trust, the first a maneuver where a sharp blade was attached to the snout of the muzzle and the dolphins were encouraged to stab with it. All but the cousin refused to do this, for the rubber dummy target was shaped like a man. The other thing was the spectacle that occurred on their final day in the indoor pool.

The sister's memory of this was especially vivid. Men all dressed in the same green-and-white colors came to watch at one end of the pool. These men were black, like all the others. One of the trainers climbed a ladder and held out a cloth with vertical bars: green, white, and green. Then, on command, the Bottlenosed Dolphin leaped the pole from which the green-and-white cloth hung suspended. There'd been no difficulty involved—any dolphin could jump a pole—but for the first time, the sister felt a terrifying menace in the sounds the humans made. She sensed that the hateful enthusiasm had something to do with the green-and-white cloth. That dusk all the dolphins were removed to the open-sea pen. Over the following days the sister noticed the green-and-white cloth fairly often, most frequently on the corvette that the dolphins followed for maneuvers in open sea. The men on the corvette were very kind, but every time that she looked up at the green-and-white cloth, the sister's memory of the green-and-white clothed men shouting rhythmically in hatred and derision would hurt her and make her afraid.

Sharks awakened the dolphins from their memories. It was noon. Once in a while a fin streaked the surface for two or three yards, but most of the sharks kept moving up and down between the light on the surface and the twilight thirty to forty feet below. The male could see they were mostly blues, eight to twelve feet, undulating without urgency or aim. Once six of them soared in the dolphins' direction, one arching under the brother's belly to bump him lightly as it went down. Their long heads contrasted sharply with the broad, short-snouted head of the single tiger shark who swam with them, brown above, striped on the sides, pale white below. Thirteen feet long, it also rose toward the pair. The dolphins sensed no imminent attack, but they were reminded once again of their vulnerability, alone in the open sea. Perhaps the next sharks they encountered would be more aggressive. They'd make a fight of it if attacked, but against more than two or three both would be killed.

Calmly stroking, taking care to make no loud or sudden moves, the pair kept swimming to the northeast, hoping the sharks would move away. The sharks would vanish for twelve minutes at a time only to turn up again in the shadows after the dolphins had decided they'd gone for good. Stupid, reflexive things, the sharks lacked the intelligence for games, yet as the afternoon wore on and both the dolphins and the sharks maintained the same casual manner, it began to seem as if the brother and sister were being teased, that the sharks were awaiting the panicky flight or desperate dive that would betray a loss of nerve and give them the chance for a quick kill.

It ended when a mail and passenger ship seven hundred feet long appeared on the southern horizon like the answer to a prayer. It steered almost directly toward the dolphins. They hardly had to speed up or alter course to have their flight intercept the ship. As its bow closed in behind them, they positioned themselves in the forward slope of its swiftly advancing wave, using the pressure field to speed up to twenty-five knots. In no time the sharks had vanished. Once over their relief that the sharks had gone, the pair felt free to enjoy their effortless speed. This ship from Cape Town moved up longitude seventeen, less than three hundred miles west by south of Ascension Island. For the rest of the day the Common Dolphins rode at its black bow, slowly heading toward the African coast.

CHAPTER 15

THE Blue Whale spent the rest of the southern summer west and northwest of the peninsula, sometimes feeding beside the Shetlands, latitude sixty-four degrees. The Shetlands were rough, bare islands, spotted with rookeries, but both here and on smaller Anvers Island farther south, patches of pinks and orange-brown deschampsia broke the monotony of gray. There were mottles of algae, red near the melting snow and green in the freshwater ice, and where rookery guano covered the ground, crustaceous lichens splashed vivid patterns of orange and yellow over the rocks. Just at the tip of the peninsula, where drizzle was constant twenty-four hours a day, the light-blue flowers and three-lobed leaves of frail hepatica made points of brittle color under the rain.

Inland, the hole in the atmosphere continued to contract toward the pole. Nearly the size of the continental United States in late September, it had shrunken to the area of Ontario when the cow had fed by the January ice, and when the Fin had died in March, it could have fit into Texas.

The whale fed even more constantly now, as if she were compensating for the Fin's death, as if she were plugging up an open sore inside. She had heard the Fin Whale calling her through the fog and had heard the catcher close on the Fin. For days she mourned. But then, once she sensed again the rapid growth of the calf, she could mourn no longer. The summer lengthened into late March and her underside, once pale, took on a patina of brownish-yellow diatoms: small plants. They had spread onto her from the water and the ice, as if she were merely one more geographical feature. It was this color that in earlier whaling-days had given the Blues their old name: "sulphur-bottom."

She intensified her feeding. Unlike the Fin, she did not swim continuously. Instead she spent weeks at each of the feeding spots between peninsula and islands. And she changed. The steep, thin V of her back filled out. Her flukes, which had moved constantly in the northern seas, hung still for hours on end. She floated in fat. Her output of calories, roughly a million a day in the north, declined to hardly three hundred thousand—mainly for basic metabolism, since she swam little now, and, when she did, it was effortless propulsion. She swallowed three to four tons, four million calories, in an average day, fêting her calf. Her blubber thickened, storing up fuel for the time in the tropics.

As March wore on, her head grew clear. She shook off the fantasies of death that had sporadically troubled her since the death of the Fin. She shook them off even while mindful of far-off shipsound. Pesticide compounds that had been channeled into her blood by her shrinking blubber, threatening her lungs, liver, and brain, were reabsorbed now into fat, though it was too late to undo the damage caused by the traces that had already entered her brain and her vital organs. Even so, her system had been returning to normal ever since January, and, along with the calf, this partly explained her contentment over the summer. As if a depressant drug had been flushed out of her veins, she'd found herself glowing from head to tail for no reason at all—for her joy in the light, for the pleasure of living. She studied the creatures that she saw with a sense of well-being that had been building since her first mouth-

170

ful of krill. Inside her womb the unborn calf could hear the roar of her blood, lusty and loud, and it sensed, as well, the intense pleasure of being alive.

The calf grew steadily larger, three feet by the end of February. At first it had stood straight up with its hind parts facing her cervical opening. It had swayed with her motion, as if uncertain which of the two back-curving horns of her womb to enter. Soon its own weight toppled it over into the left horn of her womb—the near-microscopic egg it had grown from had come out of her left ovary. Since each end of the horn was attached to her abdomen, the calf could only expand by swelling the outer side of the womb, expanding it and bending it out like a tire. With each month it grew more quickly. It was folded at first, with the umbilical cord coiled around it. Then, as it spread, it literally bent itself over backward, with the bulkiest part of its body farthest away from the opening. The veins in the cord were tight and wide. Although the calf had not been conceived till more than a month after the normal breeding time between June and August, it was strong. A birth caul swaddled it in folds finer than gauze, and by mid-April it was six feet long.

But, despite its strength and its rapid growth, the earliest phase of development, from egg to fetus, had been very slightly retarded, as if the Blue Whale's time of hunger in the north had made itself felt inside her womb. Thus its length of six feet by mid-April was slightly shorter than the average length for a fetus at this stage. No matter how quickly it grew it never made up for the time it had lost at the start.

The intervals of daylight steadily shrank. At latitude sixty, mid-April sunlight lasted for hardly more than eight and a half hours. Ice spread out from the Palmer shelf. On the eastern coast deschampsia grass went colorless and dry and cyclone winds, sporadic in summer, blew all the time. Over the ocean, circling formations of high and low pressure spindled the clouds and whirled the atmosphere in cyclones that pummeled the vast peninsular bergs. The breakers from the single daily tide took wing and splintered over the rocks, and under snowflakes fine as pins, snowflakes like teeth, hepatica petals blew away, and the three-lobed leaves curled up and died. Only the moss and the freshwater lichen still bloomed. But soon their green light also faded into gray.

Feeding continued, though the north pulled ever more strongly. As the long nights deepened around the Blue Whale cow, Arctic terns and Wilson's petrels, creatures that followed the sun year-round, had long

171

since left for the northern warmth. Other less desperate birds were following up from the south: pintado petrel and black-browed albatross, birds satisfied merely to flee to the subantarctic, not driven to lead their lives in perpetual sun. The flocks came in all shapes—Vs and lines and scattered clouds. Wingclouds went by the Blue each morning and in the sea, as well, she heard migrating wings. Part of the growing population of Humpback Whales, south of their usual range, had been haunting the lower Shetlands, and now, as the breeding time came on, the sea from Shetlands to peninsula resounded with their songs: weird bugling sequences that ran through many frequencies for twenty minutes or more, strange songs, repeated again and again without variation. This was a sound from the old times, or at least a vestige. As she listened, the Blue could sense a terrible restlessness. She hesitated more often at her feeding, watching and listening. Up from the south Sei Whales with calves were arching their way to the warmer waters. In shadowy pairs, one large, one small, they swam together just at the outer edge of her sight. She could sense that the Humpbacks were also splitting into groups—from the past she remembered how nursing mothers were the first out of the south, to give their calves the maximum time in warmer seas. After the mothers, the immatures, and then the nonbreeders, and then the adult males, would follow into the north. The pregnant cows were the last to go.

By the time late May had come and the daily light had dwindled to six hours, the Blue Whale felt her isolation. Now even the pregnant whales had disappeared; even the late-feeding Minkes were gone. Those whales that remained haunted the austral seas to the north, as the Blue herself had done in her long-ago adolescence. South of latitude sixty, where the Blue continued to feed, the only conspicuous creatures were penguins dotting the ice floes and the bobbing crabeater seals.

As the temperature dropped, the outer edge of the pack ice started to inch toward the north. Farther south, where the Blue Whale swam, the krill grew sluggish and sank into dark. Once, when she sieved a patch on her side, they hovered still in crystals of ice. Sometimes the light would lure her north a few degrees but then she felt the krill declining as the polar front approached, and she always turned back. Just as she'd resisted the southern light for the sake of the male, now, for the sake of the calf, she resisted the north, the push of the longer nights.

At Deception Island, far south in the Shetlands, water stayed hot

172

from the breached volcano under the harbor, and on the shore, as at South Georgia, the ancient whalebones loomed like beams. She skirted the island two or three times, curious, uneasy, sometimes swimming close for a bit of warmth, for the sea was bleak.

Finally, in June, the time was right. With the blackness as bare as the ocean floor and the sea as chaotic as the deep before Creation, the Blue swam past the polar front, sculling with ease through hurricanes that would have devastated a catcher. Her mind was at peace now. She could sense she had eaten enough. She lazed her way north, ferry of fat with the calf inside. The creature had grown to eleven feet. Sometimes it moved, testing its strength against her womb. Each time she felt it, she pressed her lids as if she were trying to look inside, to savor the sight. She savored the waves that broke over her head, the roar and toss of them as she rode straight into the sky and sixty feet down. After the first few hours, such child's play ceased to amuse her. She swam nonstop at fifteen knots, already envisioning the place where the calf would be born, almost foreseeing the infant's entry into the waves. She swam well down now, avoiding turbulence, rising each twenty minutes to breathe, and the West Wind Current that had troubled her before split ineffectually over her back. Storm and fog blurred the light of morning. Swimming entranced, she hardly noticed the breaking day. By the second night she had passed Patagonia.

The return past Tierra del Fuego and up the coast was a sequence of long-familiar sounds through a constant background roar of storming water. Like ghosts from the past the echoes came to her: Right Whales bugling to one another in the Gulf of St. George and the Gulf of San Matías, Falkland herring turning in thuds outside her ears, and, at night, the croaker calls and the plankton sounds and the hiss of myctophid fish. On the twentieth night, the stormwinds died. Far in the distance she saw the lights of Montevideo twinkling faintly over the waves. Closer up, the red and green signals of cargo ships were passing in and out of the harbor. Shipsound, sparse in the Antarctic, climbed to its old annoying level. She turned away, swimming straight east till the lights blacked out, though the sound never died. Hovering quietly over the outer edge of the shelf, she dreamed to herself in the spreading dawn, and, from time to time, she thought she heard signals in the lower range of the spectrum; felt at times that the continental slope had been set into motion like a tuning fork. She imagined the Fin Whale passing.

She envisioned the Fin Whale, envisioned her mother, mourned to herself. Then in the depths of her mind she saw the northern bull and imagined she heard his call. The ocean was calm now, covered with plankton, blue-green to the east and north. She missed the male. The thirteen-foot fetus, flooding her body with inner light, flexed more frequently inside. She mused and hovered over the slope and imagined that other sun, the enormous male with his scars. Hardly thinking what she was doing, she started drifting northeast by east. A day went by. A week. A month. The fetus was more than five yards long. Inside her mind the memory of the bull, dull in the south, sharpened and brightened. Islands rose and faded behind. She passed the Tropic of Capricorn, where the wind blew steadily from the east and the western run of the sea was sweet against her body. Then the wind revolved to the south; there were southeast trades and a rushing sea and sooty shearwaters tilting and creaking against the wind. Sometimes commercial traffic faded out but, when it did, the thrum of military ships became almost deafening. There were explosions: jet roar and guns, like upper sea earthquakes roaring around her. At last, in late July, holding a fetus of eighteen feet, she stopped and waited where she had waited a year before: in the sapphire sea to the north of Ascension Island.

Weeks passed. September neared. For over eleven months the calf swelled in her womb, more than the normal time of just eleven months. The rhythm of growth in the calf, slightly slower than usual in the beginning, had increased the length of gestation. Unaware of this, the Blue Whale waited patiently, dallying up and down through seven degrees of latitude, north to equator and south to island again, and all the time she dreamed. There were earthquake sounds, genuine earthquakes now, not ships: erupting volcanos under the water. She imagined the male returning. If he were faithful to his migration route, he would cross the northern horizon in time for the calving. She called steadily into the north and listened hard, the undersea earthquakes roaring around her. She called from well down. Still, though she was eager to see the bull, the desperation of a year ago had gone. It was the calf that held her attention. The self-involvement of the feeding time grew even stronger. She would circle head to tail, admiring herself, or, like a Humpback, hover head down, flashing her huge flukes in the sun like a mermaid's fins. She looked up to admire them; waited passively, with pride, and, as the calf swelled out, her confidence became unshakable.

The male would come. She thundered, breached, and, despite the quakes, the seas were hers for the shaking.

At no time in her life had she known such calm. The male *would* come. And in the meantime there were spells of boisterous play and easy sleeping. Then, after four weeks, when the calf had swollen to over two tons and its length surpassed twenty-three feet, the breaching and splashing came to an end. She suddenly peeled her ears for motors. The earthquakes had stopped. Planes from the air force base on the island rose and landed and the rumble of convoys never seemed far away. Circling and watching, she had come to know the shipping lanes and, amid them, ranges of safety to the north and west of the island. She stayed there, hovering motionless on her back for hours on end, her calf so swollen that even her all-enveloping fat couldn't hide her womb.

Inside her, the calf had conscious moments well before the onset of labor. Off Ascension Island the mother's U-shaped womb spread out to occupy nearly all available space in her abdominal cavity, and, as it expanded, the calf was bent even farther backward than in the Antarctic till he himself was arched in a U, his head near the base of the horn and his tail not far from the tip.

It was well into September. Labor was approaching. Feces and urine, always frequent, flowed from the Blue Whale's vent in a constant stream. She flexed her spine in vigorous jerks, like the spasms of the Fin, though far more gentle, farther apart. To an observer on a ship she might have seemed to be half conscious, maybe awakening out of sleep. Two days went by and the automatic, reflexive manner of her swimming was more pronounced. She stroked so slowly she hardly moved. Then, toward evening, her defecations came even more thick; the rate of her breathing speeded up and she felt the first far-spaced contractions.

Well before birth the calf struggled on his own but he needed pressure from the closing womb to reinforce his strength. In the six hours before birth he grew more and more conscious.

He peeled his ears. Once the roar he heard had seemed to be inside

175

him. Now he could tell it was beyond the layer of fluid around his head. He had always heard the roar of blood but never till now had it seemed so clear, growing louder the harder he listened, with the steady pulse beyond. It was a slow and ponderous pulse, ten times a minute, very loud. The womb was as dark as the ocean floor but when he moved his head he could feel the amnion against his eyes.

A sudden spasm in the womb made him tense, and when it died he heard the thump of his heart more clearly than before and felt an itch in his dorsal fin, bent at its base and pressed to his back. He realized for the first time he could move it. He flexed it a little, then wiggled his flukes, which were folded down and toward his head with their tips tucked in. Just before the second contraction he felt the itching sensation again, this time in his flippers, fitted neatly in a depression in his sides so as to streamline him for birth, which now began.

The cow felt the pain and squeezed her lids as her womb closed in. For thirty minutes at a time the mighty contractions of the horn worked the fetus forward. It was the tail that stuck out first: blunt-tipped, its small flukes folded in. Her moans were piercing. Minutes passed. Her convulsion lengthened, squeezing the tail out inch by inch into the black of the nighttime ocean. Still the bulk of the calf remained inside her body. The female strained, hovering blind a dozen feet down, flexing her length. It seemed she was back in the south where darkness never broke. At last, in a rhythm far older than the rhythm of her mind, a rhythm that followed its own time, the abdominal wall picked up the contraction of the horn. With this new motion, the Blue Whale sensed a sudden lurching of the fetus. But another sixty minutes passed and the dorsal, curled and limp, still failed to appear. She moaned again. The soft-curved flippers stayed inside.

The unborn calf heard the contractions, thunderous grinding sounds in his ears. He couldn't see the closing womb but he could feel it tighten repeatedly over his forehead and his throat as he retreated by flexing his abdomen and back. At the beginning of labor the horn was shaped like a U but, by the time his head had entered the curve of the horn, it had

176

contracted to a J with his head in the curl of the J and his body in the stem that ran to the opening where his flukes stuck into the sea.

His birth took over three hours, at least an hour more than average. During a respite after the first two hours the calf could feel the coldness of the sea against his tail. He tried to withdraw it but as soon as he did the womb closed up like an eye; flexed itself down against his head as it had done a number of times before, but this time irresistible, determined, thrusting the lower part of his abdomen into the sea.

When the birth cord ruptured a half hour later, his head was still inside. The cervical opening started to shut, and he was left partially hanging out of the Blue Whale's body. The oxygen in his blood was soon used up. Forced to inhale, he breathed in blood. An instant later, when he jerked free and floated sideways, red stains rose out of his blowholes. He inhaled again and drew water into his lungs.

In agony in the open sea he continued to make the instinctive flexing motion he'd made in the womb, but his body was exactly as buoyant as the water around him and he neither rose nor fell. He began to see spinning shadows and, closer by, the enormous form of the mother whale, as he choked and shivered with the cold of the ocean water. She was spinning too, and it took her a couple of seconds to raise him.

Once she had pushed him into the air, she hung very still in anticipation of the breathing sound every mother whale instinctively expects after birth. When it failed to come she tensed. The young male's stillness gave her an urgent sense of something left undone, yet there was nothing more she could do. Seconds passed and the calf still failed to breathe. Her hours of pain and labor seemed to have been for nothing.

Close to panic, the Blue Whale had lowered herself in the water and almost allowed the calf to go free when a gurgling, sputtering sound came from his head. She was so overjoyed she let out a roar of relief and lurched upward, toppling him off into the ocean. Out of one eye she saw him twist, as if the shock had lurched him to life. In less than a second her head was under him again. A moment later, she heard him take his first lungfuls of air and she knew he would float, the most basic necessity of life in the water. Diving slightly to look from below, she

177

studied him, turning from side to side to watch with either eye, then rose to touch him with her snout till he coughed even more strongly than before and inhaled again.

She could see that the water out of his blowholes was bloody and dark. Fearfully she held him up once more with her head. She let him rest at the top for nearly seven minutes. He was breathing now. As dawn broke she arched away to study his body. Though he was small at twenty-four feet, his size and his first tenuous hold on life made the Blue Whale's love all the stronger. She lifted him up and called more loudly than before, a sound of triumph. The calf moved free and started to swim.

CHAPTER 16

E LEVEN months before the Blue Whale calf was born in September and eight months before the Blue Whale cow left Antarctica in June, the brother and sister rode the bow of a passenger and mail ship north on longitude seventeen. Though this required less energy than swimming, the dolphins had grown extremely hungry since leaving the open-sea school, and after four hours of riding the bow at twenty-five knots, they dropped away, having left their shark tormentors far behind. Now, in the last third of October, they were on latitude eight, two hundred and eighty miles due west of Ascension Island. Here the peaks of the Mid-Atlantic Ridge rose high. It was early evening and the scattering-layer creatures had neared the top. The

179

dolphins whistled for joy, seeing lanternfishes flash their blue-green lights a hundred feet down. They dove and fed.

They slept at dawn. When they awoke in the late morning both felt the homing urge again. Swimming between northeast by east and east-northeast, they averaged six knots over the following sixteen hours. That evening the lanternfish were thick. After four more days of this, with the ridge behind, the pair ate sauries and open-sea smelt as bos'n birds dotted the sky. Their direction unchanged, they swam a hundred miles a day at a half-dozen knots, feeling the sea grow deep and empty underneath them.

After nine days they stopped feeding. Out of the background noise of traffic the turbine engine of an oil tanker loudened from behind. With a roar and a high-pitched whining sound, it was moving in their direction, its destination the mooring buoy thirty-five miles southwest of Lagos, where undersea pipelines would fill its tanks. When the ship drew up behind them, a thousand feet long, it was doing sixteen knots. For a day and a half they rode at its bow, the tremendous roar of the turbine engine in their ears, along with the whine of the single screw. They dropped away to feed and rest for a day when fish appeared. When another tanker passed in the same direction as the first, they rode *its* bow. On their thirteenth day after setting out from the latitude of Ascension they entered the one-knot Guinea Current, slightly cooler on their skin than the South Equatorial Current which had caressed them for the previous twelve days. Birds became more and more numerous. They were still at the bow of the tanker, roughly sixty miles from shore. As the ship made for the mooring buoy, the pair saw other tankers to their west. Two navy ships approached from the north.

When they drew near, the sister could see that both flew the green-and-white cloth she so vividly remembered from her time in captivity. The ships drew up on either side of the tanker, which they accompanied toward the mooring buoy. The dolphins left the tanker's bow to swim beside the smaller of the escorts: eighty-three feet. They arced in and out of the water, closely observing this ship from one end to the other, for both were aware they were nearing Lagos, and from their days in the open-sea pen, they remembered the outlines and the underwater sounds of Nigerian ships that had anchored nearby. Looking up, they saw that the ship was virtually featureless for the twenty feet between the two gun mountings and the bow. Behind the mountings was the bridge and then, halfway toward the stern on the upper deck, two missile launchers that resembled the guns except for their great size.

This was a ship the dolphins hadn't seen before. It stayed with the tanker. After a couple of miles the second escort moved away to the west. As it moved off, the dolphins raced for a closer look, and the thud of its engine shafts along with the distinctive cavitation of its propeller struck long-familiar chords in the sister's mind. They raced beside it at full speed, the green-and-white flag high above the bridge. A radio tower loomed behind the flag and, when she looked lower, the sister discerned two pairs of guns, one sixty-six feet and the other a hundred and ninety-eight feet from the bow. Uncertain at first, she grew sure from the positions of the guns that this was the same corvette that used to ride at anchor and observe outside the pen during training sessions. The brother sensed her certainty and started to call to the ship. Both remembered the many times it had transported the dolphins for open-sea maneuvers. Recalling the friendliness of the men, both dolphins leaped and called as they moved toward the bow, but no one answered; the roar of the engines was very loud and the dolphins could make out no one on deck. Now that they'd recognized it, the thought that it might be transporting their family made both their hearts beat faster. They hoped that it would stop to let them look for their mother and aunt, perhaps even now waiting to transport metal disks from place to place or to find pinging buoys or to do one of the other seemingly pointless tricks that earned the men's affection.

The sky darkened. The ship speeded up to twenty-one knots. All night the dolphins followed, riding the bow wave and the stern wave, constantly looking up at the deck. Men came into sight from time to time but never noticed the two youngsters. By dawn the pair were tired and hungry but the ship didn't slow down. Nor did it move in a straight line, sometimes veering for open sea and sometimes moving well over the coastal shelf.

The dolphins had grown weary and ready to drop away when, roughly fifty miles from Accra off the Ghana coast, the ship veered sharply south. It was just past sunrise. Their curiosity slightly piqued, the dolphins rode at the bow as the ship roared out for sea, accelerating to thirty knots. When after ten minutes it slowed to five, the brother and sister moved off to one side, glad for the respite. Neither saw the other military ship on the southern horizon. Only binoculars could have picked out the radar antennae like blurred moons over the stern and the other aerials barely visible over the forecastle and bridge. The roar of the diesels faded. Signals passed back and forth between the watching ships, though the dolphins heard nothing, the radio frequencies many times higher than their upper limit of hearing. When the exchange of signals ended, the ship to the south moved farther offshore. Naval vessels from the south were never welcome, especially in regions of undersea oil.

As the corvette hung still on the water, the men on the deck at last took notice of the dolphins. The brother and sister jumped and squealed as the sailors shouted down at them. Perpendicular in the water, sculling backward with their tails, they heard the shouts of the men on deck and strained for voices they remembered.

They heard none, nor did anyone leave the ship to swim with them, and when they drew close, there were no sounds of dolphins aboard. Both felt their spirits sink. They ceased their sculling. The sister began to doubt if this was the ship she remembered from before.

After an hour the ship started travelling again, moving northwestward now at less than fifteen knots. As it moved away, the pair heard sauries. Both were hungry from twelve hours of nonstop flight. They hung under the early morning sun and clicked to each other. If they paused to feed on the sauries, the ship would pull too far ahead for them to catch up. They kept up their clicking for two or three minutes, so absorbed by their indecision whether to go or stay that they hardly noticed when sauries came within sight and then grew thick from the northeast. As the dolphins hung in the water, schools split and rejoined, swimming around their bodies. The pair once more swam after the ship. Despite the strangeness of the voices from the deck and the apparent absence of dolphins, the distant chance of finding their family was a stronger lure than the fish. Within a quarter hour they were riding the bow again.

It began to rain, not a brief downpour but one intermittent shower that lasted all day. The physical strain of riding the bow hour after hour, combined with the constant rain and the rhythmic noise of the engine, put both dolphins into a trance. The brother imagined he saw their mother reaching across the top of a bright-green metal drum in a storming sea. She was still in the open-sea pen, calling loudly to bring him back. In his mind he saw himself with his cousin and sister. Lofted

182

free by a towering wave, the three were uncertain whether to swim back into the open-sea pen or follow the two Striped Dolphins who were swimming slowly away. Their first impulse was to turn back, but when they tried to dive under the drums, they hit the net, and their fear of obstacles kept them from jumping back in.

The brother dwelt on the memory. When they'd left their mother to swim away to sea with the two Striped Dolphins, there had been no resolution not to return. Only later, after many hours of freedom, had they begun to sense the exhilaration of swimming wherever they pleased.

Yet now, that remembered exhilaration hurt. With his mother's image in his mind, freedom appeared a worthless thing. He recalled the short-snouted dolphins of open sea, sensing his need for membership in a school of his own kind—not a captive or nomadic community, but a rooted herd of families and lovers, thousands strong: the inshore school he'd left behind and had been seeking, although not always completely aware of it, ever since leaving the open-sea school. A deep yearning for companionship filled both the brother and sister. If only the men would free their family so they could be with their mother again, at ease once more with the thousands of others over the inshore shelf. Yet the deeper their yearning the less likely it seemed that their mother or any members of their family were on this ship. When evening came the pair was once more almost ready to turn away, for the ship was racing at twenty-five knots, taking them farther and farther west, away from their home ground off Cape Lopez.

In their disappointment they'd started to turn away from the corvette when it slowed down. They kept on swimming, but by the time they were a hundred yards away the ship had stopped. The dolphins swam back, gazed up through the shadows at the mast lights and the lights at bow and stern. The ship had turned. It was pointed south and they were on its eastern side. They called and splashed to attract attention. When no one looked, they both swam under the pulsing hull where the idling nine-thousand-horsepower diesels hummed and murmured restively. The sound of the diesels drowned out everything else for a moment, but when they swam clear the dolphins heard a clank slightly west of them, under the sea. It lasted a second. Sonar from the corvette was probing the floor. They were focussing on that sound when they picked up signals at the very upper limit of their hearing, near three hundred kilohertz, not from the ship but from their west. It was repetitive, with several seconds between each repetition, and the last pulse in the three-pulse signal modulated upward, gradually fading, as if the better part of the sequence were beyond their hearing range. They followed the signal west and in only seconds located the source: an orange buoy one meter high, circular, with a metal rod sticking out of the top. When they nosed the buoy from beneath, they saw that a line ran from it into the depths, as if it were anchored to the floor. They paused for a minute, puzzled, clicking back and forth. Then both thought back to the days of captivity. The young male dolphin remembered when the men had let him accompany his mother as she'd carried a tiny magnetic metal disk to a surface buoy. That had been early in her training. The more he dwelt on it the more this orange buoy seemed to resemble the buoy he remembered. It, too, had been circular with a metal rod protruding from the top. All at once the chance that his mother was on the ship seemed very strong. His heartbeat raced as he swam back for the corvette, and his sister quickly caught his keen excitement.

The intermittent rain that had fallen all day continued through dusk as the brother and sister watched beside the still corvette. After five minutes it started moving again, now heading back for the east. Ten minutes passed. It travelled slowly at three knots. No dolphins were lowered into the sea. Their hope declined. Then, roughly a thousand yards from the buoy, the corvette stopped. The dolphins looked up. The cover of cloud over the moon and stars dispersed. Seeing seamen at the rail of the corvette, the brother and sister leaped in greeting once again and there were shouts. Recalling once more his captivity time, the young male turned and swam for the west, his sister beside him. He signalled loudly in the air, as if he meant to show the men that he could track the orange buoy.

They reached it quickly. This time the line called to the sister's mind the day, eight months into training, when she had accompanied her mother on the diving exercise. On a sudden whim she decided to follow the line for the floor. She wheeled and dove. Her brother followed, the two of them turning in tight circles. The pair went down for four hundred feet into total darkness, giving out signals that echoed loudly as the upper edge of the continental slope rose up to meet them.

They nosed the place where the line came to an end. It wasn't just ocean floor as they'd thought; they were touching metal. Both started to sonar at high frequencies, moving back and forth to establish the outline of what they'd found. After a minute they had swum the length and breadth of it several times. They knew from the metal that it was something made by men but they had never encountered anything like it before. It lay still near the place where slope gave way to shelf, its shape like a whale's but larger than anything that swam, five hundred feet long and forty feet across the beam. A gently arching cone ran from four hundred feet behind its bow to the stern and when they swam to the stern they discovered a five-bladed screw. This, like the metallic hull and the turret that rose near the bow, told the dolphins they'd found a ship, but it didn't float and made no sound except loud clanks when the undersea current swayed its hull against large rocks. Undersea ships were new to the dolphins, since there were none in Nigeria's navy, nor in the navy of any other West African state. Two decades old, this one had come from farther south. Undersea vessels of major powers could signal distress to satellites, but, with its turbines dead, this could do no more than signal its home base twenty-five hundred miles away.

The dolphins rose and swam back to the corvette. They swam the length of it, calling out and splashing loudly, but the men who had watched them before had left the rail. An hour and a half went by and nothing happened. The two had swum closer, their fins almost touching the side of the ship, when a hatch opened up and two other dolphins came out of the hull. The youngsters almost breathed in water, opening their blowholes in a gasp as the pair appeared. They looked grotesque. Muzzles covered not only their mouths but the entire sides of their heads except for the eyes. The muzzles were metal and attached to the snout of each was a metal disk, so that, from the front at least, the two appeared half dolphin, half machine. Yet there was no doubt who they were. The first to come out of the ship made the signature call that only came from the mother, while the second, three feet longer and far huskier than the first, was the Bottlenosed Dolphin with the pinholes on his forehead where electrode implantations had crippled his brain.

Overwhelmed, both brother and sister tried to embrace the mother dolphin. The muzzle prevented them from nuzzling at her snout, so they dove beneath her and stroked her ecstatically with their heads, clicking and whistling, their bodies tremulous with delight. For two seconds she answered. In their rapture they failed to notice that there was virtually no emotion in her whistles and that her click combinations made only a

185

routine acknowledgment of greeting. After a minute the pair reflected, feeling a strange hurt rise inside them. Both remembered the repetitive clicks the Bottlenosed Dolphin had made in the indoor pool. Now both their mother and the Bottlenose sounded the same. When they swam close, they could discern circles of pinpricks on her forehead.

Unable to let her go, the calves clasped both her flippers, slowing her down. They embraced her again. She seemed perplexed. When the Bottlenose made a rattling sound, she speeded up, swimming beside him at ten knots, the brother and sister keeping pace, rising and diving and circling her body. When their ecstatic embraces resumed, the mother slowed down again, her signals still monotonous and flat. She hovered and watched her children, then swam in a circle, making confused, bewildered sounds. Her skin was trembling. Well ahead, the Bottlenose gave the rattle again. Less surely now, she followed him.

This kept on until the Bottlenose and the mother, swimming west, picked up the high-pitched sound of the surface buoy. By the time the Bottlenosed Dolphin dove for the sub, the mother dolphin was still on the surface about three hundred yards behind him. She had yet to express emotion at her reunion and still seemed confused about her calves, pausing and hovering in silence again and again, as though struggling to remember who they were. Then, two hundred yards from the sub, her signals changed and the two calves, stinging and crying with fear of rejection, embraced her even more fervently than before. Waking up, she turned and waggled her snout up and down as she used to do when she chastised them. She lowered her head and gestured "stop" with both her flippers and her tail, repeating the movement several times and clicking the pattern that meant "stay" each time she did. Both brother and sister sensed there was danger but were uncertain what it was. The mother swam on. She disappeared into the west just before the Bottlenosed Dolphin resurfaced and swam mechanically back for the ship. The brother and sister didn't notice that the ship was moving eastward at ten knots, but both could see that the Bottlenosed Dolphin's metal disk had disappeared. They remembered the captive dolphins pressing magnetized disks to ships and other targets, a feat as pointless as the other tricks and maneuvers in open sea. Yet they had envied the affection which rewarded the strange tasks. Forgetting their urge to rejoin the school, the pair raced west in pursuit of their mother. Life with the men seemed more attractive now that they'd seen her.

186

They wanted to join her in her task, swim back to the ship and share the reward of food and love she would receive.

They whistled loudly so that their mother heard them come. Reversing direction, she swam back to stop them again. Both could see the metal disk still at her snout. She whistled out in fear and anger, urging them angrily back to the east. Both brother and sister sadly obeyed. For over a minute they heard her chase them, clicking and whistling in rage and distress. At last, when they'd swum a hundred yards, she ceased her pursuit. Still they kept swimming.

After eight hundred yards they turned. Two torpedos hissed for the east just underneath them, then the corvette, nearly a mile away, exploded in orange flame. The dolphins dove. With the boom in their ears, they heard a second blast from eight hundred yards due west and four hundred feet down where the mother had dived to plant her disk. Forgetting the ship, which was now three fragments, all capsizing in a blaze, the dolphins listened to the sounds out of the west. The disk-shaped limpet mine of the Bottlenosed Dolphin exploded against the sub, then a bubble of gas spread out from the explosion. A shock wave ran ahead of it, smashing into them like a solid wall of lead. The bubble of gas collapsed and made a second blast just a little above the first. As the mother's limpet mine, planted later, split the sub, the brother and sister were rocked again by the spreading shock wave. They rose to the surface, stunned and sore. On the eastern sea they saw the flickering remains of the corvette. The pair swam west to find their mother. They had trouble staying down for more than twelve minutes. The submarine was split in the middle and there were metal fragments everywhere on the floor. After four dives the dolphins turned back east to where the ship had been. They heard no survivors calling and splashing in the sea.

Still, they found the Bottlenosed Dolphin. He was hanging just under the surface, slowly sinking. The metal muzzle was so light it left him buoyant, but when the brother and sister swam over his back and looked down they could see dark blood spreading out and up from just behind his head. He hadn't been fast enough to overtake the ship which had already started east, away from the sub, before his return. Porpoising and calling in terror of being deserted by the men, he'd been hit by a fragment from the explosion. The moonlight caught his shadowy back and the cloud of his blood. The dolphins dove to his either side and

187

looked in each of the dead eyes, their stare even glassier and more vacuous than in life. The sight made them cry in pain at the fate of their mother.

Late that night they started swimming east in earnest but by daybreak both were motionless with grief. They lingered for days off the Ivory Coast, just far enough from the sunken ships that salvage vessels searching the wrecks didn't detect them. They were fifty miles offshore of Abidjan. It was early November. It rained continually and fish were thick on the shelf, but the dolphins seldom dove to feed. Not till after three days did they lift themselves from their stupor and hunt again. In afternoon they started east, swimming only halfheartedly.

From the Ivory Coast to their home was less than a thousand miles as the crow flies but they took the long way, hugging the coast and never swimming more than sixty-five miles a day. When they reached Cape Lopez and the Ogooué rivermouth in early December, their crushing grief lifted only slightly at the sight of the other inshore Common Dolphins. Still, there was comfort in finally living as they were meant to live, free, among their own kind. Though they were in agony at their loss, their time of trial seemed over.

CHAPTER
17

THE bull whale passed the summer in a southeastern Greenland fjord he'd once shared with his mate, where thysanoessa swarms were inexhaustible. He dreamed of her while he fed. Sometimes he imagined her arching in and out of the water at the entrance of the fjord, or swimming up the Denmark Strait where a sound of thunder came from the towering ridge that joined Iceland, Norway, and Greenland. Seldom less than nine thousand feet high, the Greenland-Iceland Rise north of the fjord dammed the lower Norwegian Sea, and the part that escaped poured over the brim in undersea waterfalls that spread south just above the Antarctic Bottom Water, a current that flowed all the way to Antarctica. Each year the whale had heard it when he'd swum to the mouth of the fjord. Only this year did he hear the voice of his mate in the sound.

Now winter was far behind, though he remembered its silent days. After his second failed attempt to swim south to the cow, fear had turned him north till he'd rested in the doldrums. Vacant and vast, the equatorial zone was a still, quiet place in early October, where birds who wandered the open ocean, albatross, shearwater, petrel and tern, had disappeared. The sky had been empty even of wind, the water a uniform deep blue. The lonely bull had yearned for upwellings of green to chill the surface as it did in temperate oceans, raising food to the top and bringing flocks of birds to the vacant sky.

Simultaneously attracted to and repelled by the ocean below the equator, the frustrated whale had swum back and forth in the equatorial seas nine hundred miles south of the Cape Verdes while the calls of the cow grew fainter and farther off. The farther they faded the more the emptiness had driven home to the bull his isolation.

It tired him out. He'd entered a half sleep after a week. Though his lids had been wide and his flukes had continued to move, his mind had been less active even than during actual sleep, for he'd had no dreams. The nematodes had gone. There'd been no more sudden bursts of pain to prod him awake. Pursuit of the cow had exhausted his will, and instinctive impulse, all the stronger now for having been suppressed, controlled him again. Late in October, he idled north to pass most of the northern winter at roughly latitude thirteen north and longitude thirty west, where the Canary Current, cool and rich with plankton, swept down from northwest Africa.

Toward May, as his blubber thinned, the bull had dreamed about his calves on the harpoons. His time of peace was nearing an end. For weeks he'd felt his restlessness grow with his hunger and now at last he began to swim north in a haphazard way, stopping to sample rafts of crustaceans that rose in the dark. By June he was east of Newfoundland, steadily feeding, his mind ablaze with thoughts of his mate as the springtime madness gripped him again.

He turned back from the roar of the waterfall at the Greenland-Iceland Rise. It was plain now that the sound of his mate, so real a moment before, had been only illusion. He re-entered the fjord. Here his days

190

passed slowly, all the same, and his deepening loneliness was a slow descent into hell. Once in July, glimpsing a spout of spray to the north, he called and swam up the eastern coast, but when he reached the place where he'd seen the rising breath, there were only floes and the shelf spread blank beneath his eyes. He'd imagined his mate had returned from the south. Up from the floor the bouncing sonar of seals blacked out the brilliant vision. He swam back south and re-entered the fjord. That night, when he slept, he remembered affectionately the aggressive independence of his first bull calf, killed with his family of three in the south by a Panamanian catcher; the docile obedience of the cow who for almost fifteen years had swum within sight of him, then had left with an Iceland bull to disappear off the Faroes. He remembered the twins from his tenth year with his mate, both of them dead; then, still asleep, he saw the others, all of them gleaming in their great health except for the sickly calf of the final year. They rose up in his mind with his mate beside them, only to fade back into black, and for each one that passed he felt a deep perplexity, for, in every case, the disappearance had been mysterious, a thing that had taken place out of range, connected with sounds of ships but the connection always uncertain, since when he'd arrived both calf and ship had disappeared.

Sometimes the bull whale pondered, swimming alone in the vacant fjord. How had it happened that all had gone: that all the escape routes, the new migrations, had turned out exactly the same as the suicide route his parents had pursued? For sixty days he circled the fjord, pondering and dreaming. Sometimes, when visions came, he raced to pursue them, but when they disappeared, he went back to his shallow surface runs, puffing each seven minutes or so, revolving much but resolving nothing, the water around him now brilliant and clear, now dark with visions out of the past. He swam erratically. All his reasonings and dreamings came to nothing. In early September he left the fjord.

He was swimming at latitude sixty-four in the Denmark Strait when a volley of waves rolled up the shallow inshore shelves of Greenland and Iceland. Repercussions of water explosions, they travelled at heights of one or two feet where the sea was deep, but they slowed down in the shallower water where the energy that they lost in diminishing amplitude went into height. The whale was a half mile out from his fjord when the volley passed. He dove, but the waves seemed ocean deep and he was hauled toward the coastline where, when he reared, he saw one huge wave break on the rocks and run in seconds up the entire length of the fjord, over thirty feet high. He could not fight the tremendous thrust that pulled him in. In a matter of seconds he had been hauled at high speed through a wishbone formation of rocks whose sharp protrusions perforated both his eyes. In an instant the thrust reversed and he was sucked out, then in, then out again, back to sea. When the great waves passed, his memories had faded and he hung stunned, his muscles sore. Harp seals shivered by the ice floes.

He kept his lids closed tight. Both eyes were hurting. The sharp rocks had pierced the mucous coatings that protected them from the sea. For the next few days he swam with his eyes closed. Once, when he opened his lids for a moment, he saw only black.

Twenty-four hours after the giant waves had passed, helicopters clattered in and out of the fjord and up the coast. The whale had heard them before but there were more now, too many, he thought. The pain in his eyes abated slightly, and, as his troubling fits of memory started to wane, the sounds of the sea's advance and retreat seemed to tell him the nights were longer. Ivory gulls were heading back for the open sea. Their distant cries evoked the image of their pretty, ternlike flight. After two days the light came back and he made out shapes. He could hear eiders pass to his north from the colder fjords around Angmagssalik where the helicopters came down, transferring their loads to the larger planes that flew northwest to the land near Thule. The whale was blimplike, bulging with blubber. His mind went blank. The useless dreaming came to an end and the pent-up energy from his months of rest and feeding cried for release. With September still early, he started south.

It should have been a lazy time for the whale, now that he'd fed, but the injury of his eyes had made him anxious. If his mate were alive he'd have swum for the African wintering place off the coast of Sierra Leone, but his mate was dead and the old migration route was bitter with memories. He turned south-southwest, moved by restlessness more than by longing for a particular destination. After four days he was a few hundred miles off Newfoundland.

More and more each day, he was able to let the light into his eyes. It overjoyed him to see again, though his vision was not what it had been. As if to compensate for his period of blindness, he spent hours watching shapes in the upper water or gazing up into the sky.

192

Shorebirds from the north darkened the air with their wavering Vs, often so high that they looked like far-off lines of smoke. Among them were phalaropes who nested in northern Quebec and Baffin Island and spent the winter on the southern hemisphere sea, along with far-flying golden plovers who spurned the land. These were birds one would expect over open sea but, as he trained his eyes on the sky, the whale saw that migrants were far more numerous than he remembered from earlier years. The sky seemed constantly covered with birds. His eyes were too weak as yet for more than rudimentary discrimination, and even with normal sight he couldn't have told that land birds were forsaking their inland routes to migrate offshore, something virtually suicidal given their feeding requirements. Once at noon when the sky went dark he couldn't tell if he was seeing the sun die or merely the shadows of thousands of wings.

Having just left his own inner darkness, he was disturbed to see this midday dark in the sky. It made him curious and he swam toward the west where the dark was deepest. Before the actual coast appeared, the whale discerned a wall of cloud stretching north and south as far as his eyes could see, beginning at ocean level and towering beyond his field of vision. When he dove he heard the echoes of tremendous shoreline storms and, when he rose, he felt the kind of offshore winds that stormed and roared off northern Greenland.

Deep apprehension tempered his curiosity, but he was happy that the sounds of factory seiners had disappeared. After he rounded south-eastern Newfoundland he kept swimming for the west, toward the eastern Gulf of St. Lawrence and Cape Breton Island. As he swam, he sent out calls, vaguely aware that he was travelling the sea of his parents, falling in with an ancient pattern. Sometimes he peeled his ears for the sound of whale ships, but it had been decades since the catchers had chugged out from Blandford in Nova Scotia or Dildo and Williamsport in Newfoundland.

Not only whaling ships and seiners had left the seas; the whale could hear no traffic at all, and at first this brought him a thoughtless pleasure. The sea ran rough, bracing, astringent. Why had he wasted his time with regrets? This was the old sea, the sea his ancestors had known. The ships were gone. His blood raced with a prospect of new things.

Twenty-eight hours of twelve-knot swimming took him west into the strait between Newfoundland and Cape Breton, where there was another change in the light. He seemed to be under an evening sky in the daytime and when he could see Cape Breton Island he discerned another towering shoreline cloud and heard more blasts of thunder and wind. He swam on toward the St. Lawrence. Night, when it came, was merely a deepening of the dark.

That night the sea air grew so cold that even the bull, with his thick blubber, could sense the change. With the dawn, as he swam down Anticosti Island, he kept breaking panes of ice. Bonaparte's gulls, close to the waves, arched in a casual, slapdash way to take him in, then disappeared in clouds of dust that seemed to be flowing with the current down from the north. The easy wheeling of the gulls made them seem like low-profile patrols, casual outriders from the coast who kept an eye on things as part of the dawn routine. The bull swam high. It was the way they had always flown and he welcomed the sight. But the darkness deepened.

Cliffs rose, barely discernible through dust. The whale was swimming in shallow water so darkened by streams of silt washed out from the land that he couldn't see more than a foot. Breakwater bluffs and shattered headlands supported twisted conifers that grew sideways out of shale. Once, when he spouted close to shore, a kingfisher bolted and trailed a clatter of obscenities down the cliffs.

Toward noon, he heard a roar in the upper air. High-altitude winds were draping the coast with a dark snow of crystal and ash. On parts of the shore it withered leaves: a deadly talcum sometimes a centimeter deep. After two hours the "snowstorm" stopped, but still the film in the upper sky showed that the winds were bearing dust: the finer aerosols and ash, not ready as yet to come to earth. With part of the atmosphere cleared by the dustfall and ultraviolet radiation penetrating the ozone layer which upper-air gases had destroyed, there was a sudden dazzling glare. The whale reversed his flight, swam out for sea.

Morning found him once again off Cape Breton Island where a forest fire had burned its path to shore. Streams of char poured out from the land. Moving far enough offshore to put the coastal noise behind, the whale continued toward Nova Scotia, still on the shelf. He speeded up. Minerals ran from the burning coast into the sea, and wherever they ran, the algae burgeoned to a point where oxygen vanished and the underwater world went dead, though green. Sometimes it seemed that wherever

194

he swam there was a surface film of dead. The herring had thinned and the water stank from mantled plankton. It was a week since he'd left Greenland. Off Nova Scotia he finally turned for open sea.

He had been swimming away from shore for less than an hour when two coasters appeared ahead, rocking in waves, though this offshore swell, steadily rolling, was gentler by far than the inshore sea. The ships were stranded. He would have normally swum by, but the total absence of ships up till now made him pause to look, a thing he'd done only once or twice since his youth in Trinity Bay.

Each ship was two hundred and fifty feet long, high bowed, with derricks and loading equipment crowding its deck, and when he approached the nearer ship, he saw that two men had rigged a rope ladder over the hull where, feverish and giddy, they climbed up and down, splashing in water not far above freezing. As he swam close, dove a dozen feet, and surfaced at the bow, the memory of cargo ships he'd followed as a calf came back so vividly that he ached with the joy and bitterness of that time. As the men in the water raced to avoid him, kicking their legs, he was struck by their vulnerability. Yet they seemed lively. Weary of swimming through dead plankton, he called out loudly, a mountain of flesh that had come up from another world.

They raced for the ship. Both climbed the ladder, and as he saw them going up, he made a connection with the fishermen of his youth in Trinity Bay. These were the same, though pinker and frailer and lacking pipes. Their flesh seemed pale in the fading light, and when they turned, each face was a mask of rings and lines. He dove under the hull and looked at the four-bladed screw, then swam down the keel. The draft was shallow: a dozen feet. He paused in its shadow. Somehow they lived on this. He did not know exactly how, but they were part of it as the murres were part of the cliffs. Vaguely the catchers came to his mind, though he could tell by their size and shape that these two vessels were not catchers.

He surfaced again at the side and watched with one eye. The shadows were thick, and he couldn't make out the human shapes until the sun broke through for a few seconds. The men were shivering on the deck, dangling their legs over the side, with puckered bodies and chattering teeth. Something intrigued him about the faces. Clearly the naked men had minds, and though they were lined and pale, when they looked at him there was clear light in their eyes.

195

One of the men walked away and picked up a rifle. The other waited. His friend came back with a sweater on, steadied the barrel against the rail, took aim, and fired.

The bull whale dove. When he surfaced, a half mile off, they fired at him again, making small welts in the rolling water: little hailstones of hurt and hate. He cried to himself as he arched for the sea and his nineteen-foot flukes kept up the time to his lamentation. The bullet had entered the tip of his snout. He bobbed in pain. As he travelled, he saw more clearly than ever before the close connection between the fishermen in Trinity Bay and the men who had killed his calves, the close connection between all men.

He swam southeast as fast as he could. At first perplexed, now he'd grown frightened at the unnatural midday dark. Whole schools of herring, squid, and smelt bobbed lifelessly, fouling the water. There were acres of capsizing birds. They floated sideways, belly-up, head down, outstretched, with nothing to eat them, their long necks limp under the surface like dead snakes. The whale propelled himself to sea.

He was racing hard to get off the shelf when he saw black smoke fill the land rise to his west. Stand after stand of timber and orchards were going down to a forest fire. Here and there through the black he could glimpse the racing flames all down the coast. He hurried east. From well out at sea he could see smoke so thick and wide that it seemed a second low-hanging cloud had joined the other, perpetual cloud in the western sky.

The whale kept swimming at full speed. His eyes were wild. After an hour he plunged straight down until the surface noise receded and he was swallowed in a still, perpetual night.

CHAPTER 18

THE bull whale swam southeast. Northeast of Halifax over the continental shelf, he swam in the dark at a fifty-foot depth, wanting to shut out all he had seen. When he rose to breathe he glanced behind him but already the smoke had faded and overhead the sky was free of cloud. He shot out twenty puffs of spray, arching his body at the top. When he went down again, not as deep this time, he slowed to barely ten knots.

He crossed the outer limit of the Nova Scotia shelf fifty miles due south of Sable Island. Soon after that, near the limit of ice, a single floe rose up ahead and faded behind. In less than a day the water warmed. He felt the Gulf Stream, scarcely half a knot at first, but deeper and faster the farther he swam. Still bearing southeast, he covered roughly a hundred and ninety miles a day.

He was nearing the fortieth parallel when his voice bounced back to him from a series of mountains three hundred miles to his southwest. These ran out in a straight line from coastal New England, stretching southeast for a thousand miles: Picket, Balanus, Kelvin, San Pablo, Manning, Michael.

The whale was across the fortieth parallel, hearing his echoes bounce back from the mountain known as San Pablo, when he noticed that the light was starting to fade. At first he tried to ignore the clouds that had entered the sky, diving well down in a semi-sleep. Now he was five days away from Cape Breton and he could tell from his own echoes that he was over an extensive undersea rise. The semi-consciousness was impossible to maintain and when he surfaced, there was twenty-four-hour night.

Frightened, he picked up speed and swam nonstop until the dark sky paled to gray. Then, with the seven-thousand-foot depth of the Corner Seamounts just behind him, seven hundred and fifty miles east by north of Bermuda, he entered a region of sun where the Gulf Stream current died and thick sargassum weeds appeared in the surface water. He slowed down to savor the light, swimming high up despite the weeds that clung to him each time he arched to breathe.

Two days went by. He swam southeast into the southward-flowing arm of the Gulf Stream gyre where the weeds thinned out. Soon the Mid-Atlantic Ridge rose up beneath him. The sky was bright as yet and his sight seemed clearer than ever. He spent many hours hanging quietly at the top to watch the light, then started south again.

He was at latitude thirty-three, due east of Bermuda, when light and dark spangled the water and spreading canopies of high-altitude dust spread south into the sky. He raced for a day and a night till he left the dust behind.

Though he swam full speed to escape the spreading dark, the dust cloud followed a few miles behind him as he passed thirty degrees north latitude. By now the dark was constant to the north of latitude thirty, but since the canopy of dust over North America extended farther south than the one over Europe, the leading edge of the Atlantic cloud stretched farther south in the west than in the east. The whale was on longitude forty. Stretching down from his northeast, roughly from latitude thirty and longitude thirty-six, the leading edge of the dust formed a line that ran southwestward into coastal Venezuela. East of that line the sky was clear.

Seventeen days had passed since the whale had left his home in the Denmark Strait. He was swimming southeast, hearing sounds of fish from the south. When after an hour the dust drew up on him, he tried to swim faster at first, chasing the light.

But the cloud closed in no matter how fast he swam and at last, giving up, he paused and turned to look back at the northern sky. The advancing cloud resembled the prow of some monstrous ship with its bow in the center of the sky and its sides trailing back in a spreading V that encompassed all the northern horizon. He gave out little puffs of frustration as it advanced. Before, he had thought that his speed could outfly the spreading cloud, but now it was racing at over twenty miles an hour, so high that he couldn't see the top and yet so low over the water that it seemed the sky beneath was being flattened and spread out on either side. Its darkness made the sky beneath it luminous by contrast and as it advanced there was an effect of explosive brightness swiftly unrolling over the sea. The bull whale dove, then rose again when the light had gone by.

Once the tip of the cloud had passed and the dust behind it was spreading out to fill the sky, it seemed to the whale as if both the advancing cloud and the light had never been, for now there was only a uniform darkness wherever he looked, and this took away his sense of the cloud as something inscrutable and swift that hunted him. He continued to blow out jets of air in his frustration. The cloud was nothing but cold and dark. How had it started? Why was it here? Feeling beaten once again, he turned south and swam on.

He had swum at full speed before, but now that the darkness was complete he swam very slowly, having lost hope he could get away. There was nothing in his memory to account for this kind of night. He'd thought he had left it in the north. After an hour he slowed, then stopped swimming completely.

The shroud continued south. The lower part of it was soot but gases and particles of dust formed the upper layers. To the north, where westerly winds had assisted its movement off the North American coast, it had been a single towering cloud, but here, as it met high-altitude winds from the equator, its leading edge broke into streamers and jagged fronts, one of which had just passed south above the whale.

Though the cloud had been all but impermeable in the first weeks of its life, changes in weather did affect it. Even now, as the whale swam south, evaporation was making the sea air shine with vapor fifteen hundred miles to his east. Static highs and prolonged heat had brought sultry weather to the eastern Atlantic Ocean, and just a few miles south of the Cape Verdes, with surface temperatures over eighty degrees, the warm moist air kept rising. Here and there, where it met descending cooler air or where the wobbling spin of the earth altered the motion of the trades, it formed a gyre of whirling winds around a center of low pressure. As the whale swam south on longitude forty, this condensation fifteen hundred miles away had already lifted one vortex especially high and heated it up until it became a hurricane.

By the time the whale was slowing down, the hurricane near the Cape Verdes had already started to move. A three-mile gyre in the beginning, now it was thirty miles across and surrounded for more than a hundred miles by winds of over two hundred miles an hour. Lesser winds extended the width to three hundred miles. Beginning near longitude twenty-one, the storm moved west at first, at a speed of ten miles an hour, but when it reached longitude thirty-five it turned north-northwest and less than three days after that the low-pressure eye was two hundred miles south of the whale.

As it neared in the late afternoon he saw a deepening of the dark and felt a drop in the surface pressure followed by waves of seventy feet. He dove to calm where he heard the hurricane pass for the better part of the night. Each time he rose to the top, thick rain was pelting the sea. Then, when he surfaced toward morning, he found himself in an eye of calm, with stars and clear skies over his head. He stayed on the surface for over an hour, watching the stars. Then the ocean swelled again, and just at dawn, with steady sheets of solid rain, bursts of high-speed wind swept up from the south-southeast. The sea looked white. When a hundred-foot beam flew through the air with the grace of an arrow to hit the crest of a wave just past the Blue Whale's head, he wheeled and dove. A half hour later, when he rose cautiously to breathe, he sensed that the air pressure was rising. Even so, hurricane winds continued to blow until midafternoon, with nonstop rain and thunder and lightning. After the brunt of the storm had passed and the rain had thinned, west-blowing winds went by until well after dark. An hour before dawn, when he started swimming again, the storm was all but spent.

The hurricane made inroads into the dust cloud. As long as the surface water stayed warm enough for the hurricane to suck moist air from the sea, the eye of the storm had an inexhaustible fuel supply and the storm was so wide that more than a hundred and fifty miles of high-speed wind could sweep through the dust before the eye of the hurricane had even entered. Then, when its winds had cleared the way for it by sweeping soot and dust to the north and west and raining particles out of the air, the eye of the storm came into open sky instead of a dusty shroud. The eye sucked moist air up to a height of seven miles before dispersing it into the lower stratosphere to force the rain that cleared the sky.

The cloud slowed down. The only parts of it that continued unimpeded were the gas and the finer dust that floated more than seven miles up. Since this upper layer was more or less transparent, when the whale swam south it seemed to him he had left the cloud behind.

The hurricane swept on into the north. It was decreasing the size of the cloud, but the cloud was too massive for any hurricane to destroy. Also, the dust lowered the temperature of the ocean as the eye of the storm moved north, and this would kill the hurricane in two days' time.

The bull whale continued for the south. It was still September, twenty-four days since he'd left his summer home in the Denmark Strait. Now that the sun shone unobstructed after a night that he had feared interminable, he kept his eyes trained on the sky, swimming at fifteen knots, pushing hard to leave behind the partial cloud that remained to his north. The light was strong now. The freak accident on the rock in the Denmark Strait had damaged his eyeballs, leaving blind spots, but the pain had largely passed and he saw well. At first he swam at a twenty-foot depth, rising to breathe every fifteen minutes but, as blue sky opened behind him, he kept to the top, feeling a trace of the old defiance that long ago had led him to Greenland from Trinity Bay. The mood was brittle to begin with, so diminished had he been by a night that came with a will of its own to suspend the cycle by which he lived, but it took hold after an hour. The brilliant sunlight following hard upon the most powerful storm he had known almost convinced him that the dark had gone for good.

He made drumming sounds by compressing the sacs in his head. The farther he swam the deeper his certainty that the cloud had died and the louder the sounds he made. Once the dust was well behind he started to arch in and out of the air. The death of the dark made him expansive. He stopped his drumming and sent a series of ten-hertz signals in all directions, calling both in the air and the water, as if expressing his rage at the dust. After ten miles, he lifted a third of his length from the sea and fell to one side in a crash of spray. The day was brilliant and the ocean surface rocked with three-foot waves.

With this sudden release from the dark, memories returned with a new luster. He was still well above the Tropic of Cancer. He remembered the swim to Greenland after his parents had disappeared, the northward migration with the Iceland whales and the meeting with his mate after the Iceland herd had died. The memories warmed him, for each incident had brought happiness out of defeat and now the same thing seemed to be happening again. The dust had been an alien element, but now the noise of the sea as he picked up speed seemed one with the roar of his blood, and all the strange little sounds he heard inside his head when he was happy came back to him: the high-pitched humming behind his ears when he inhaled and arched from sight, the almost inaudible singing sound that filled his head when he lazed at the top in times of well-being, the swish and gurgle of surface water around his ears that was so different from the stillness under the dust, the defiant rush of his exhalations.

And always above him shone the light. Five hours passed. He swam very high, gazing steadily at the sun's hypnotic glare. Though high-altitude easterly winds kept blowing cirriform clouds across the face of the sun, its light seemed more brilliant than ever before. He gazed and gazed. In late afternoon he closed his eyes.

Far above, nitrogen oxides that had flown above the roof of the hurricane continued to spread southeast, blown by high-altitude winds. Wherever they passed they thinned the stratospheric ozone and let massive ultraviolet radiation strike the sea. Just as a man who looks at a welding flame with the naked eye might not feel pain till many hours later, so the whale, dazzled and dizzy from the light, closed his eyes and lazed on the surface in a self-contented trance as the sun went down, only to waken four hours later partially blind.

He moaned when he woke. The ultraviolet light had made fissures in the window of each eye, cornea lesions that caused him burning pain.

202

Since one of his ocean adaptations was a thick layer of mucous over each eye, there were no tears and his spastic blinking did nothing whatever to ease the burn. Given the thickness of the mucous and the shielding effect of the surface water, swimming well down might have saved his sight, or at least delayed the loss of it, but the sun had made the whale so happy that it had never occurred to him its light could blind. Now his eyeballs, damaged already by the rocks in the Denmark Strait and further weakened by the intermittent glare off Canada, were becoming dark and at the same time growing more sensitive to light. When the whale swam high the moon was soft on the ocean surface but now even it appeared to glare. He breached three times, then dove well down until completely covered by night. Here he kept swimming. He couldn't stop moving, since the pain gave him no rest. He stayed well down all the following morning, keeping his eyes closed when he breathed, swimming southeast now, away from the Mid-Atlantic Ridge.

After six hours of steady flight he sensed a deepening of the dark. Fearing blindness, he rose to the top, where in the blazing midday sun he saw only blackness and varying shades of white and gray. Despite his pain he stayed at the top and tried to hold his lids apart, for more than anything else he wanted reassurance he still could see. Out of his left eye he saw the sea and out of his right a Cory's shearwater, the first bird to pass in many days. The bird was flying just at the surface and as it approached, under his right eye, he saw that its long thin wings were actually breaking the waves. Confused and frightened, it hit his head and dropped to the water, stunned or dead. He watched it float, as if its death or survival had something to do with his. For the one or two seconds that he could see he watched the bird in fascination. Then the burning that was making all birds blind shut up his eyes and he dove again.

The burning passed but seemed to abate at the price of his sight, for though he rose and swam at the top on the second day after the blinding and was able to keep his lids apart for minutes at a time, all he saw was a general darkness, as if the dust, still well to his north, had overtaken him again.

Now the little sounds of happiness in his head either changed or died. The high-pitched humming that he heard behind his ears when he breathed and dove became an irritating drone, the nearly inaudible singing sound a vacuous silence. His inhalations and exhalations, like everything else, required more effort. Each time he breathed he seemed to hear his growing weariness reflected in the harsh, exhausted sound of his own breath.

With his sight gone he started listening to the sea with doubled attention but the sounds he heard were mainly his own breath and the surface waves. Near noon of the second day after his blinding, after swimming at fifteen knots for over five hours, the hush of the sea made him slow down. Where were the fish he had heard to the south just after the dust had blown away? He'd been swimming fast, but the sounds that had seemed just past the horizon two days ago were still far off. Why? Why?

He peeled his ears. At first no more than an absence of ships in the northern sea, this silence that followed him into the south had deepened and spread to the east and west. Once he had welcomed the vast hush. Now he feared it. It seemed a lifetime since he had heard the sounds of shoaling fish up close, or the calls of whales, or subsonic static from crustaceans and other creatures who rose and fell with the scattering layer. Gone as well were the startling whistles and grunts that drums and croakers made with their air bladders, and he missed the cries of birds on the distant sea.

He thought of the shearwater as he dove, calling loudly and listening for answers that never came. When he resurfaced to swim in silence, his sense of futility far surpassed his summer despair in the Greenland fjord when he'd remembered the lives of his parents. What did it matter now that he'd broken with the old, destructive ways, the fatalistic complacency that made the old ones live their lives almost in sight of the whaling factory? It occurred to him that he'd been wrong to go his own way. Forty-eight hours after the blinding he started to grieve for his vanished sight, for he feared that even the black-and-white outlines would never come again.

On the surface next day he could tell when the sun was bright, but he saw no shapes, and he saw no better a day later when on longitude thirty-six he passed below the Tropic of Cancer. From time to time he would stop swimming and simply float in the surface waves or let himself fall as he sometimes had during the winter, although too buoyant to sink very far after summer's feast.

But sooner or later he always resumed his southward journey, travelling at roughly eight or nine knots, the autumn restlessness still with him. When after a further two days he was over the Cape Verde Basin on latitude fifteen, he swam through another northward-moving storm, and two days later, at latitude ten, lightning flashed from cloud to cloud and from cloud to sea as he rode on the surface, craning and gazing, letting the flashes faintly illuminate his eyes. After the storm he hovered silently for days and the steady high pressure made him feel like he'd entered the region that used to mark the change from westerlies to trades twelve hundred miles north at the Tropic of Cancer: the zone where air that had risen at the equator came down again to blow back south as the northeast trades.

This made him pause, for he navigated not only by the sun but also by atmospheric pressure. It seemed wrong that this far south, at this time of year, the pressure should stay high. Although at the back of his mind he knew the change bore some mysterious connection with the dust, it was a shadowy, unfelt knowledge, and the downward-moving air that contradicted it instinctively troubled him. Afterimages of the lightning filled his head as he bobbed up and down in the surface waves, snout to the sky, straining for visual signs to assure him of his position. The continuous bobbing of his head in and out of the water made him look as if he were trying to wash the darkness from his eyes.

But he saw no signs. One time he roared. After a quarter hour he levelled himself to a horizontal position and continued south-southeast with a wind behind him. Aside from the wind and the surface noise, silence seemed to be filling up the entire sea. Yet his grief at the hush partly subsided when he entered a semi-sleep. He slept for a day, then snapped awake when he heard a Blue Whale call from well below the equator.

CHAPTER

19

AT the same time as the Blue Whale bull was swimming south in September, the mother whale was calling in triumph, seeing her newborn calf swim free. Yet the sound meant nothing to the youngster. His flukes wouldn't stiffen for hours and he floundered ineffectively till hunger drove him underneath her body. Seconds passed but he failed to find her breasts, located on either side of her genital slit and visible only as slight swellings of the skin that covered them. He rose. Her calls stopped when he breathed more water into his head. He coughed and sputtered till after a minute he took in air and dove again. No matter how much she may have wanted to direct him to her milk, she was helpless to do so.

The calf kept searching. The nipples protruded less than an inch from the Blue Whale's eighty-four-foot length, and he was disoriented and tired from his difficult birth. Once he swam beneath her body from side to side, then rose to breathe, then swam down her abdomen, head to tail, then rose again. Water continued to enter his head, and he kept coughing. The cow tensed in fear. Seven minutes passed as he searched. When at last he located his mother's nipples, he approached them first from the front and nudged at them. They gave no milk. He rose to breathe, then on his next try approached from behind, feeling so tired that it was a strain to hold his body in position to take the milk which finally squirted when he seized one nipple between his palate and tongue.

He fed only sporadically after that. His head was aching and he found it extremely difficult to relocate the nipple on each dive, for he depended on his sight as much as his instinct, and each time he dove her body had moved, while his eyes kept going dim. On the lucky dives, when he fed, his tongue curled lengthwise up to his palate to funnel the milk. Still, after a good dive, as often as not he would get more water into his lungs and the approach of suffocation would make him miss his mother's breasts the next time down.

It was a test that exposed whatever weakness a newborn calf might have and exploited it fully. If it weren't for the danger, there might have been humor in the way the outer edges of his flukes flapped up and down against the direction of each stroke, or in the way that he hung near his mother's genital slit and poked now here, now there, trying desperately to relocate the nipples. After twelve minutes he stopped diving and hung on the surface, feeling once more the impulse of protest he'd felt in the womb, awed by the difficulty of what he'd been called to do.

As he was lying on the surface in despair, he caught sight of a line of fifteen dorsal fins passing in silence less than a hundred yards away. Up till now he'd had no idea that other creatures besides his mother and himself lived in the sea. He was too tired to submerge and look at the black-and-white bodies of the Orcas, too dejected even to watch the fins for more than half a second, by which time all fifteen had gone. This whole perception was over in an instant and he forgot it immediately, but once it had passed he felt rested and he once more wanted to live.

He made a motion to seek the breasts again, but the mother whale, whose terror of the Orcas he didn't see, realized he was losing strength. She kept to the top and turned on her side so that the calf, although still feeding underwater, could breathe by simply bobbing his head without leaving her breasts. This was not the way that rorquals normally fed. Only after watching the worn-out calf had her fear made the mother remember another way. Her fear that the calf might die was as strong as her fear of her own death would have been. When she turned on her side and slowly arched in the calf's direction, it was because of a nearly buried recollection of a Killer Whale feeding her calf off Africa, a recollection the silent Orcas had brought to light.

The calf stayed still at first, closing his eyes. She hung on the surface with one nipple just a few inches underwater, close to him. When he awoke and saw the nipple just below, he stretched to take it. It was hard to elicit the squirting response without the approach from the rear, but now, with this access to the air, he was persistent, and the mother whale stayed perfectly still as he closed his tongue and palate over each of the nipples in turn, angling his head in every conceivable way to make the milk come out. When it finally did, his mouth was almost out of the water. For twenty seconds at a time the milk would squirt, its pressure so great that, for five or six seconds after the calf had raised his blowholes into the air, the milk continued to make pink-white jets in the sea.

When the calf stopped pausing for breath and hung so high that his blowholes were out of the water almost all the time, the mother whale, who'd been unable to direct him to her breasts or to protrude them in display, found she could squirt the milk at will by flexing the muscles around her nipples. Hours passed. The normal feeding rate for a new-born calf was at least every twenty minutes, but now he fed continuously. He forgot his despair. After five hours of alternate feeding and sleep he started to feel secure.

By the end of twenty-four hours he'd drunk eighty-five gallons, and he fed through a second night. As his desperation passed, he gradually mastered the normal way of feeding. Once during the night he paused beneath the breasts and vaguely marvelled that the task had once seemed insurmountable. When he rested, his sleep was haunted by the sight of tall black dorsals passing in silence.

208

When not feeding he stayed near his mother, one pectoral pressed against her. The temperature on the inside edge of his blubber had climbed to ninety-eight degrees, although the outside edge, at seventy-five, was almost the same as the sea's. But not quite. The sea was seventy-three degrees. Despite his long time in the womb his blubber wasn't as thick as an average newborn's. The cold of the sea kept reaching in toward his blood so that over and over, even after he fed well, there were spasms of shivering. The cow feared the shivering as much as she feared the cough, even though the calf, feeding constantly during his first three days, gained almost nine pounds an hour to thicken his walls against the sea.

After a week the shivering kept up, though the coughing decreased. He fed every twenty minutes. Between feedings he would hang by his mother's head and try to see the things she saw, for he imitated her constantly. In afternoons, when she dove into darkness and called loudly toward the north, the calf could sense that she listened more sharply than usual after each call. He listened as well, though he seldom knew what it was he was hearing.

At night the cow's attention seemed focussed most often through her eyes. She stayed off the northwest tip of the island. Killer Whales passed within sight, and he knew instinctively that she couldn't save him from them if they decided to attack. But, as before, they travelled in silence: a line of dorsal fins. Once, as he hung beside his mother, he could tell from the way she was pointed and from the things he saw himself that she was intent on three bright lights on the eastern horizon. His mother was close enough to land that he could hear breakers five or six hundred yards to the east where the three lights shone. The mother's attention would lapse for minutes at a time as she half slept, and then the calf would sleep as well, though never for more than a quarter hour. Usually when he woke he'd find his mother watching the lights again.

Even after six hours he saw only a dim relationship between the times of her watch and the times when a roaring or humming noise drew near. Although he had yet to see his first ship, he knew their sound and the look of their lights. He was far too young to understand why they interested her. She chose her place of rest in relation to the lights that beamed on the ships and on the horizon in order to avoid the traffic lanes. She needed to keep near shore, since the bull whale's long-range signals, if they came, would be channeled upward by the island.

The mother whale remembered the bull in flashes, but the sickly calf was always in her mind. During his second week of life he started shivering more intensely, from fever now, a thing she did not understand. She thought him still cold and tried to press against his skin. But the shivering went on and she saw that again, as when he had sought her breasts, she was powerless to help him. Her spirits dropped. After three days it hurt her to watch him, for discharge trickled from his eyes and oozed only slowly from his blowholes, though he exhaled with unusual force. If he surfaced for long, the thick green discharge from the holes ran down his cheeks to meet the other discharge spreading out from his eyes. His mother ached.

The first crisis came after ten days, when he went through hours of slow circling, deaf to her clicks. His eyes were fixed. The mother whale could not stop moving in her anguish. She swam back and forth beside him, sighing and puffing with her blowholes open almost all the time. Finally with late afternoon he slept off a thundering coast where northwest rollers kept all ships at sea, or would have, had there been any. But she was too anguished to notice the decline in offshore traffic.

Two days went by before he swam once more in the normal way. After three days, when he fed again, the strength of his mouth and tongue at her nipples filled her with joy, and, as he fed, she gave out low-frequency singing sounds so powerful they made avalanches in the nearby reefs. But, though his suckling improved and he followed when she swam instead of circling aimlessly, the discharge continued at blowholes and eyes and his hoarse exhalations put her on edge. She never relaxed.

Even so the calf continued to feed and grow, though not at the normal rate of an inch and a half a day. After the first fifteen days he had yet to reach twenty-six feet and was almost a ton underweight at only a little more than ten tons.

But the sickly calf survived. By the time the bronchial pneumonia became a head cold in late September, his length was nearing twenty-seven feet. Despite his growth, his mother still worried, for the shivering didn't stop, and one afternoon when a Blue Whale call came down from the north, she hardly thought of it at first, answering only after four hours and even then not starting to follow it until after two days.

But the call was not at all muffled, as so often the previous year, for there was a silence to the north, something else she had yet to take in. As she swam at a speed of half a dozen knots she kept on stopping to feed the calf, who, as usual, swam with one pectoral pressed to her side. While he envisioned the Orcas, the two stroked slowly toward the north in early October, the bull a thousand miles away.

CHAPTER

20

A T the beginning of December, ten months before the birth of the Blue Whale calf in September and nine months before the Blue Whale cow started north from Ascension Island in October, the young male Common Dolphin and his sister rejoined their school off coastal Gabon. They had been swimming toward their home for forty-eight days. It was almost evening when they began to hear other dolphins, not just the chatter of a hundred or so, a fairly common commotion out at sea, but rather the sound of many hundreds calling together. Both of them slowed, for there was no meaning in this sound—or too much meaning. The voices swelled and roared like an undersea waterfall. Could he have heard, the northern Blue would have thought of the Greenland-Iceland Rise over which the

Norwegian Sea dropped to the ocean floor to send currents all the way to Antarctica.

Despite their lingering grief, they both felt awe. When they drew close enough to discern the effortless motion of the outer ranks, the two kept close together. As they swam, some twenty feet down, the pair could see a whirlwind of fins. Like angels, the dolphins flew up and down and in every direction. The brother and sister had entered an animated maze, and, as they glided through the turning light, a steady background din again and again narrowed down into separate voices.

This first group was comprised of several hundred, but the others were far smaller. As the brother and sister swam down the coast, what first had seemed one enormous school became an endless succession of groups that ranged in size from two or three to more than two hundred. The two dolphins swam all day, thirty-five miles down coastal Gabon, and though they paused to greet each new group that appeared, they saw but a fraction of the school.

By early evening most of the dolphins had left to hunt in deeper waters. This made the male remember how his aunt had hugged the shore in fear of ships. He searched among the dolphins who stayed behind. There was no aunt, or any other relative he recognized, no older brothers or older sister. Still he was home, though only with dawn did he and his sister realize that this wasn't a dream. By then it seemed very likely their family was either dead or still in captivity. The pair felt grief, but when the sun cleared the horizon and the dolphins moved as one toward the east, they slept more deeply than they had since leaving the open-sea school of five hundred. With afternoon they socialized among the groups, and once more, as in open sea, there was banter and play with others their own age. Small groups seemed to be constantly coming and going between coastal Gabon and the northwest part of the shelf. Often, when an especially old or tired group returned, the brother and sister had the sense that it had come from almost as far away as they had.

Two days went by. One night, as a subgroup of six came slowly in from the north, wearily calling, the brother and sister picked out a signature call they thought they recognized. They answered and raced for the northwest. As their calls reached the dolphins drawing near, one of the females in the group raced out ahead with a young cow beside her. Dorsals breaking the sea, the brother and sister charged her so fast that in the moonlight it looked for a moment as if two sharks were closing in. Both brother and sister reached the cow at the same time. As they drew up on her they slowed and their calling ceased. The signature call they had heard had so closely resembled their aunt's that they had thought they'd found her again, while, for her part, the forty-four-year-old female, four times older than the aunt, remembered the pair from their infancy. Up close, she didn't remotely resemble their aunt. Her markings were strange. The others had blazing white patches on their pectorals, but in the moon the brother and sister saw that a white stripe had replaced the pectoral patch on one of this dolphin's fins. The grandmother of the cow swimming behind her, she nudged the pair with her snout when they drew close, and this apparent acceptance made them feel at home. Still, the gestures of welcome turned out to mean less than they assumed. When others came to greet her, the old female moved away to swim with dolphins her own age and she seemed indifferent, almost contemptuous, when the brother and sister pursued.

The hurt very quickly passed. Losing themselves in the hunt, they dove and fed for most of the night, then rested with the others. Mournful click trains that evoked earlier times passed back and forth between the two until a faint blue light had paled the eastern sea. With the rest of the school, the brother and sister swam for the east, automatically stroking. Flocks of ibis clattered across the face of the sun, calling raucously. The new day lit the sky.

Over the following few days the brother and sister separated, the sister joining females her own age and the brother joining a group of immature males. Coastal Gabon wasn't the richest part of the shelf, but the school remained there because it provided enough to eat and at the same time didn't attract as many ships as richer waters.

Still, for the brother and sister, inshore swims near the mangrove swamps were only a partial escape from the din of the fishing ships, far more distracting now than during their infancy. There seemed to be heavy fishing all the time. Stern trawlers made the dolphins wince at the scrape of the giant boards that kept the net mouths wide, dragging the bottom. When that noise stopped, they'd hear the five-hundred-horsepower motors winch their loads of bream from the sea, along with hake which the midwater trawls scooped up as well. The inshore seiners took shad and sardines while factory fleets for squid and shrimp drowned out the local outboard canoes, though that less powerful noise was always there when the factory ships shut down, and at any hour of the day the sister had only to raise her eyes to see a tuna seiner awaiting her on the horizon.

There was another kind of vessel, a wide-keeled launch of thirty feet, which never took fish. The sister grew used to the reappearance of certain vessels, but this less imposing ship attracted her special attention because it passed close to the school nearly every other day, carrying men in khaki shorts who sometimes watched the dolphins from the deck.

Ten days went by. One evening when the sister's companions were swimming around an inshore spit to join the rest of the school, she hung at the shore where she watched sediment flow at high speed up a channel filling with tide. Near the coast the channels were broad, but forty or fifty yards inshore they narrowed sharply, splitting and spreading out where mangrove roots marched like legs of giant spiders down to the sea. Wherever the roots advanced they broke the sediment flow and shored up land. To the sister the vanguard of roots looked frightening, and behind them, where the pale green seaward groves gave way to darker, older trees, the fading light made the swamp so large that for a moment she had a sense the land was advancing into the sea, and she turned away to pursue the others.

Just before leaving, she grew aware of a group of men who had been standing for quite some time eighty or ninety yards up the beach. They were just at the edge of her vision, and as she turned to look, she saw them peer at the sand and squint at bottles they kept dipping into the tide. Immediately she remembered the men on the launch who'd been dressed in khaki just like these. That night the sound of the fishing vessels especially disturbed her, but, not long afterward, the noises ceased for good.

They didn't stop all at once. The school hardly noticed when the first of the seiners and trawlers tooted their horns and moved off for the west. Still, more ships went home each day, and by the third week in

215

December, when neither factory ships nor skiffs came into sight and an armada of derricks bristled the horizon, the older dolphins searched their memories, unsure what to make of it, while the sister and her companions communicated in high-speed clicks for hours at a time beside the tideflats.

Soon after the mass departure the sister again saw men with bottles study the water, but this time they also scooped the tide with hand-held nets, and as she watched, she re-envisioned how the launch had trawled as well, in its odd way. Once it had circled her resting place for over a day, the strange men stopping every so often to raise their apparently empty trawls up to the deck where they would study them through glasses like those the tuna fishermen used to scan the sky—but these much smaller, and pointed down at the pale mesh, as if the men were trying to examine minute animals, or sediment, or plants. They would focus so intently they stayed absolutely still on the upper deck, but it was only because they'd lingered so long near her resting place on the outer wing of the school that the young female had paused to watch them.

There had been something else about them. She had noticed that their launch flew a piece of cloth identical with that the corvette had flown, and with those others at Lagos Aquarium and Harbor. Ever since captivity she had noticed that many ships flew pieces of cloth, but only the brilliant vertical bars—green, white, and green—held meaning for her. At first she had watched them with a mixture of fear and longing, but now they brought sorrow, each appearance of the launch recalling the sinking corvette, the exploding submarine, and the death of her mother. With the sorrow came a dread that, together, the launch with the green and white flag and the departure of the ships portended some new catastrophe.

She tried very hard to communicate these things to her companions, but though the others felt her distraction, she had no way of articulating her sense that the strangely observant men were somehow connected with the departure of the ships. At times, when her friends grew vexed at her obsessive worry, they'd glance at each other and slap the water with their tails to break her trance.

They seldom did. Her sense that the men somehow meant trouble would persist even at feasts as she dove for lanternfish offshore. Though she missed the exact nature of the connection between the corvette and the strange men on the launch, the green-and-white cloth she'd learned to fear united them.

While the sister worried, restlessness filled the brother, who hadn't weathered his open-sea trials as well as she. When he'd been small these inshore waters had seemed vast and bountiful, but, after his travels, they struck him as poor, and though the contrast didn't trouble him at first, the older dolphins he sought as friends were self-involved and he deeply missed his mother and aunt. His sister seemed to be happy with her juvenile companions, but his experience made him feel distant from his friends. He didn't know why the fishing ships had left, but now that they had, travel appealed to him even more, and he envisioned the days just after his release when, west of Freetown, the shelf had widened out to nearly a hundred miles and thickening plankton had raised the thermocline so high that, no matter how far from shore the dolphins had dared to swim, they'd seemed to stay in shallow water thick with life. For hours he'd remember that seemingly infinite stretch of fertile sea from which he'd swum to meet the whales. He would warm. The whales. And he'd envision their tapered flukes and their great size, dreaming and clicking to himself till the others watched him warily.

Near the end of December the male persuaded his sister, with several others, to go travelling up the northwest part of the shelf. As she swam away beside him, both renewed their bond from the days in open sea.

A week went by. There were numberless fish and with no background din, the coast seemed new and strange. The dolphins travelled in a stop-start pattern, pausing repeatedly for play, and after a fortnight they were near the border between Cameroon and Nigeria at roughly five degrees north. The brother and sister grew anxious nearing Lagos, but aside from that there was no sense of zones or borders, since the coast was largely the same wherever they swam, and the only significant change occurred between the in- and offshore sea. To swim inshore was to move over sandbars and around enormous spits beside a patchwork race of mud and mangrove swamp where, once in a while, flocks of ibis

217

flew off in alarm. To swim offshore until the trees were lost to sight was to feel the push of the southwest swell from midlatitude storms: a force far stronger than the one-knot Guinea Current or the trades. The dolphins would swim where the combers gathered strength, again and again lurching out from the foaming crests to splash belly-up, constantly calling, as if exhorting each other to stop expecting something bad to happen, for despite the sister's calm, some of the male's friends were anxious and unsteady.

They neared the mouth of the Niger River with its vast sediment flats, rested a while, then swam west for another twelve days, sleeping till noon. Soon no matter how far they swam they encountered Spanish sardines. When they passed Abidjan less than a mile out from the coast, their wanderlust died and in the second half of January the group turned out to sea.

Curiosity turned them out. For twenty-four hours they had been hearing the sound of ships from the southern horizon. They swam straight south till they'd lost sight of the Ivory Coast, rested a day, fed and travelled for a night, then rested again. Soon after they started to swim the next afternoon with the shelf just behind them, two corvettes and a larger warship came into sight, stationed silently at a buoyed-off zone where once in a while a smaller launch would make a run between two resting gunboats. None of the dolphins had seen large vessels since the fishing ships had gone, and they were excited.

Remembering the submarine, neither the brother nor sister had been eager to swim this far out, and for most of the way they'd been trying to turn their eager companions back. Yet, once the ships were in sight, the pair felt drawn to them, as if even now they had hope of finding their mother. It was the sister who finally dared to swim in close. When she began to pick out details, she saw that the ships had enormous guns and that all flew the green-and-white cloth. She received no answers to the long-distance signals she sent again and again in all directions. She started to worry again and her grief came back, as strong as ever.

None swam all the way to the ships or dove to the wreck of the submarine on the upper slope, but if they had and if they'd been able to pierce the dark, they'd have seen that its colors weren't green and white—rather three different-colored bars, the middle white and enclosing three other flags. Although the dolphins might feel the effects of the wastes the submarine emitted, they'd never see them, since the solids were fission particles from the core of its reactor and the liquid was pressurized water.

Each year when the southeast trades crossed the equator with the sun, the earth's rotation turned them inland so that they entered the north as moisture-laden southwest winds which accounted for most of the rain. When in September the sun retreated, the rain-bearing winds retreated as well, falling back before the dusty harmattan. Blowing as far as Morocco in mid-August, by late September the rain-bearing winds had died at Dakar at fifteen degrees north, and by mid-October the six moist months at Conakry at ten north had passed. The end of October saw the last of the rain at both Sierra Leone at eight degrees and Liberia at seven. Coastal Nigeria, at six, saw rain from March to July and September to November while the Ivory Coast, at five degrees, had a similar sequence of rain. Farther south, the coastal equator had essentially one season, moist and warm, and the water temperature seldom changed.

The dolphins turned away from the ships and started swimming home. By dusk they were over the middle shelf, six miles from the coast, where they took sardines till dawn. The brother and sister awoke at noon to see the others swim excitedly away, and as they followed, the Guinea Current warm on their skin, the southwest swell hit offshore sandbars and went brown with rising silt. The other dolphins started encircling sardinella aurita that thronged out from the coast, and as they joined in, the sea felt grainy on the brother and sister's skin, as clouds of silt kept swirling up from the bottom. Now the shoreline was in sight and they could hear the breaking waves.

The feeding went on for an hour, but the brother and sister grew sated before then and swam off by themselves. Although these fish, up to twelve inches, were often abundant, they were especially thick beneath this dry clear sky whose sun had been heating the surface water since the end of the rain in early December, while offshore wind, steady and dry, had pushed it south. Cool water from below was taking its place, lofting nutrients from the bottom till the entire shelf from Liberia to Lagos had grown turbulent with rich upwelling sea.

219

As most of these Common Dolphins had lived their whole lives over the shelf, they were used to alternating offshore lanternfish with the sardinella aurita or Spanish sardines, but for the brother and sister the inshore fish with their sharper, saltier taste seemed slightly exotic, raising memories of their first months over the shelf after they left the open-sea pen. Both remembered as well how the fishing ships had hauled out sardinella in their huge five-hundred-foot seines while strangely ignoring the tasty lanternfish who rose offshore each night. Most Spanish sardines were larger than the three-inch lanternfish, and they behaved differently off the Ivory Coast than they had off coastal Gabon. The group could tell from the sounds to their east that many members of the school had travelled west and were also feeding over the shelf.

All the sardinella were swimming east, and while the other dolphins fed, the brother and sister swam east as well, calling out toward the horizon. Among the signals that came back they picked out the signature calls of the elders, who generally swam with others their age. These were fifteen miles offshore. When the pair called out a second time and the elders, twenty miles to their southeast, answered eagerly as if in invitation, the two hurried southeast for the outer shelf.

The sardinella thickened as the booming inshore waves faded behind, and phytoplankton stained the water yellow and green until the dolphins began to see vast rafts of euphausiids eating the plants. Soon the feeding din of scad came from all sides, and when they faded the dolphins found themselves amid red and brown algae that thrived on the nutrients from below.

Despite enthusiastic long-range signals, many elders greeted the dolphins nonchalantly that afternoon, though after an hour there were tentative strokes and synchronized swims over the slope. The female with the pectoral stripe whom they'd met on their return was the first to swim beside them. After a day the rest of the elders warmed toward the pair, and in the nights of steady feeding that ensued, the rest of the school began to congregate over this shelf which, with its upwelling, was richer than coastal Gabon. With time even dolphins at first reluctant to leave their old home joined the others close to the continental slope off the Ivory Coast, where the sardinella laid their eggs and upwelling water raised more bottom salts each day, along with radioactive elements dissolved or in suspension, which the southwest swell would carry into shore.

By March the school was always in sight of the coast. Each afternoon the brother and sister and the elders swam the shallows by the tideflats, where their intense communication left them oblivious to the mangrove stands that lined the northern sky. The signalling went on for hours on end, and sometimes the elders grew so loud that fiddler crabs pushed the stone lids from their burrows to turn their stalked eyes out to sea, the thousands of tiny upward movements making flashes down the length of the tidal flats. Besides the female with the stripe on one pectoral fin, there was another female elder who was especially warm to the youngsters. She had known both the mother and aunt and often introduced their signature calls into sequences of clicks that she could sustain for a quarter hour without pause. The brother and sister felt especially close to her. The young male dolphin felt the sense of belonging he'd missed in early December.

The influx of sardinella from the west seldom let up, and the radiation continued to rise from below. What the fish drank in went out again through their gills, but floating algae off the coast absorbed radiation to a level far exceeding that in the sea, and while crustacean concentration varied by species, it was high, with the copepod concentration forty thousand times that of the water. Many crustaceans, especially larvae, ate floating algae, and the sardinellas' gills had more than a hundred bristles or "rakers" to sift copepods and smaller forms of plankton from the sea. With their slower growth, neither they nor the lanternfish absorbed radiation with the speed of the plankton they fed on, yet they ate nothing else but plankton and the inward flow of water from the slope and outer shelf was continuous.

Still, the upwelling would end with the rain, and with the adult sardinella always in transit, they absorbed less radiation than they could. Fish, like other creatures with spines, stored radiation in muscle and bone, cesium in muscle, strontium in bone.

By early May the sardinella populations had spawned several times, and the drifting larvae from the January spawn had long since reached the crucial ten millimeter length at which they approached each other head to tail with an instinctive shake that signalled recognition and formed schools, the smaller fish even now swimming above the larger to

221

let in the sun. Sometimes, in play, the brother and sister would try to break an adult school, but each time they did, it would contract until it looked like a spinning ball. When they moved off, the school would spread out, though never far enough for any one fish to turn around by itself. When the pair attacked and fed, the school turned several times a second, and when they had a school bunched tight, they'd watch the echelons of mouths open and close. Sometimes the dolphins saw sardinella feed on microscopic dots that reddened the sea, but at other times the fishes fed where nothing appeared to the eye.

The months went by, and though the fishing fleets never returned, the dolphins heard many offshore ships. Some missed Cape Lopez but most felt at home off the Ivory Coast, though several nights a month the brilliant deiopeia ctenophores lit the surface up like fireworks and sometimes then the school would pause at their feeding, half expecting to hear the sounds of far-off missiles, frequent by May, though even then less irritating than the factory ships had been, and finished by June.

On inshore swims with the elders the brother and sister were more restrained than with their friends, never having met such old dolphins at sea. The female to whom they felt closest was more than fifty, and though the pair didn't remember her from before, the loss of their mother made them envy the close intimacy they saw in her exchanges with adults three times their age. They tried to get closer to her. By June they swam beside her while she communicated with dolphins her own age. It lifted them to swim at her side, though strange inflections and unusual combinations in her signals puzzled them. Her messages almost always consisted of memories and the emotions they evoked, but, lacking a language, she could only hint at the memories by mimicking echoes (for example, the sonar patterns of "tuna" and "ship"). Still, this was more than aural charades, her high-speed sonar sometimes mimicking many echo sounds within a second.

Despite their confusion, the brother and sister swam with the old more than with youngsters. In June they both communicated memories of their own to the old female and other elders in her group. Yet, long before the height of rain in July, the two had come to the end of their memories, and this surprised them after all they had been through, especially when the old female, in recalling only a single thing such as

222

surfacing lanternfish, would signal longer and more intensely than the youngsters had in recollecting whole catastrophes. Now both understood why most juveniles kept to their families or to dolphins their own age, though the old female was never confusing when she signalled to them alone or when in August she swam between them to the nightly inshore feasts.

August dryness brought a second upwelling period, during which the feasts on squid and inshore shad made every dolphin see how the absence of ships, along with the richer sea off the Ivory Coast, had bettered things. Soon even those who'd been slowest to leave approved of the move from coastal Gabon.

When the brother and sister dove beside the female during these loud communal feasts, they started to realize the burden of age, for though her straight-line swims were fast, she seldom braked in one quick motion, and if fish darted quickly to the side, she often missed them. Sharp, quick movements hurt the joints between her body and pectoral fins. The female's "shoulder" was in fact the entire humerus or upper arm, which aquatic adaptation had contracted to one bone, largest at the ends, with the "shoulder" end inside the body and the "elbow" where the body joined the fin. When the youngsters moved their fins they didn't even feel the joints. Flexible ligament connections kept their motions liquid and smooth while their skeletal frames, primarily cartilage, not bone, were extremely light. Human cartilage joined bone to bone, but dolphin cartilage, buoyed and supported by the water, could function as bone. In newborn dolphins much of the skeleton was cartilage. Bone didn't replace it but rather augmented it as they grew, a lifelong process which gave the oldest the highest proportion of hard bone.

The growth of bone out of cartilage accounted for the old female's stiffness. It happened in three stages. First the cartilage calcified, then vein-filled tissue invaded it, and then, when bone began to form, connective tissue kept on building up around it so that it widened well before it lengthened out. With the years, so much bone had formed on the walls and in the concave ends of the old cow's humeri and in the vertebrae near her tail that moving her fins had become a strain. Sometimes, after feeding, the brother and sister would see the female hang on the surface and pant and gasp. They'd keep a good way off at such times, when she was usually surrounded by other elders who also panted, while the pair could hear the low-pitched sounds of pain and commiseration pass between them.

The two dolphins had first seen these things near the end of January after joining the group of elders near the slope, one of the rare times when the group had fed apart from the main school. Generally the old fed with the young in the communal nightly feasts. There the various hunting groups could herd the fish toward the old, something easier off the Ivory Coast than in the poorer seas they'd left behind and one of the reasons the school required a surplus of prey. The young male thought he knew now why the elders had moved west before the main part of the school, and why the school had so quickly followed. Care giving was instinctive among groups, whatever their size, but he hadn't realized before now that only large schools could let dolphins achieve old age. Occasional dolphins and whales survived alone, or nearly alone, after actually losing fins. Yet these were exceptions. By March it was clear that the oldest could have never sustained themselves without the school. This realization affected the male as deeply as the warmth of the old female. It seemed that, together, the dolphins had partial remedies for even seemingly hopeless things like bereavement and age, and he felt badly about his earlier impulse to leave them behind. His memories of swimming in open sea beside the whales began to fade. Though still confused when the old female communicated with other elders, he saw how dolphins older than he frequently listened at the periphery of the group throughout the exchange, and he paid closer attention, hoping to understand some day.

By September the female had grown unable to move her flukes and fins sufficiently well to benefit from communal feeding. Since family members, with other dolphins, started catching fish for her, she didn't weaken till October. There were no ultrasonic scans, since this was something without remedy which most dolphins had seen before, along with the thinning that persisted no matter how many sardinella the brother and sister brought in. This elder had lived more than fifty years and her death in October came without pain. The school positioned her toward the center, breaking less frequently into subgroups so that thousands of dolphins guarded her on all sides. After her death, they mourned and bore her up for a while before letting her go, yet the young

224

male missed the frantic grief he'd seen at other deaths. The school broke up into subgroups again, and communal life went calmly on. With the dryness past, the rain poured out of the rivers. The brother and sister were deeply hurt by the loss of the old cow, yet it wasn't the same as the loss of their mother had been, not because they cared that much less but because for the first time in their lives they truly identified with the herd. This bond consoled them and heightened responsibility to the school, and both the mourning for the cow and the resumption of day-to-day life after the mourning told them the others felt the same.

Still, well before the dark came down from the north in mid-November, the increase in deaths among the old had begun to erode herd unity, for there was no precedent nor any apparent cause for such a plague, and it seemed absurd to even the dimmest that it should happen after the ships had gone away and food had grown more abundant than ever before, here in the place the elders themselves had chosen as home. The young male's memories of the whales and open sea brightened again as the frantic mourning grew more and more like that of the mothers who'd lost their calves in the tuna seine. The constant splitting of the survivors, as group left group and family left family, made him mourn the approaching death of the school as much as he mourned the elders who'd already died.

A week before the dust, as more dolphins turned back for Cape Lopez every day, he swam with his sister out to sea. They swam slowly, in the way they'd swum from Lagos after escape from the open-sea pen, though this time neither turned to look back. When the sky went dark the rest of the dolphins panicked, and many swam off in separate ways under the dust, but the brother and sister saw none of this where they chased the thinning shoals on the outer shelf, alone again.

225

CHAPTER
21

THE Blue Whale bull was just past
latitude ten when he first heard the single pulse a little lower than
twenty hertz from a long way off. In the empty fjord he'd once shared
with his mate he had remembered her so clearly that he'd nearly
forgotten the southern hemisphere cow, but his thoughts turned
strongly to her now, and as he answered the call he began to pick up
speed. It came again after two hours. Though his sequence of breaths at
the surface was five minutes long, when he called he was usually well
down, for he'd been below the light when the arcing soundwaves he
pursued had risen to him from four thousand feet.

He averaged nine knots. Twenty-four hours took him two hundred
and sixty miles to the southeast. But then the calls, always sporadic,

stopped completely, and his memory of losing contact with his mate surfaced painfully.

He was pointed southeast. After another twenty-four hours had put him past St. Peter and St. Paul's rocks, four hundred miles northeast of Brazil's northeastern extremity, hope drove him faster, and though his speed of sixteen knots wasn't taxing him yet, he began to feel obsessed by his pursuit. The obsession was painful. He grunted as he swam. It could have been years since the beginning of September when he'd forsaken his migration route to swim off Canada. Faintly he wished for that time again, when the grip of nostalgia had loosened enough to detach him a little from grief and desire.

When the calls failed to come again, he returned to the despair that he had felt ever since pausing in the permanent high at the latitude of Trinidad and Tobago, twelve hundred miles from the place where his memory had said it should be. Both then and before, near the latitude of Bermuda, he'd turned to the sky to dispel his feeling of being displaced. But he had seen no light at all at the latitude of Trinidad and Tobago: ten degrees.

The sun had gone out for the whale, and his growing sense of despair was frightening him. The night in his head made him yearn for the light as much as he'd ever yearned for his mate, and as he hung still, he saw a dazzling succession of suns flare up and die on zigzag horizons off southeast Greenland and northwestern Africa until their lights seemed to blind him a second time. He felt totally lost.

His bearings quickly returned when the signal came again. He pursued it as swiftly as last year, but now he had no way of knowing when he'd passed the equator. His fear of going too far was very faint without the sun, but the long silence had dimmed his hope that the voice might be that of the southern hemisphere cow.

Whoever made them, the calls weren't moving in his direction. Still, he was lonely and yearned for a guide. The voice was the strongest sign there was.

By the time he came into sight on the northwest horizon it was well into October, and the Blue Whale cow had swum only two hundred miles from Ascension Island. All through the southern hemisphere winter she had called toward the north, but it had only been a week since she had heard the bull whale answer. Her preoccupation with the shivering of the calf had made her migration a stop-start thing. Long-range reception was never constant between two whales when source or receiver were in motion, but intermittent reception sufficed for a bearing. Still, it was necessary for both whales to keep calling, and there had been days when the cow, obsessed and in anguish at the shivering of the calf, had remained silent. Even now, with the bull in sight, although she speeded up and called loudly, she worried about the calf, who dove below her, slightly afraid of the strange whale who approached from the north.

The calf had never heard a long-range signal before the bull's, whose attenuated voice had travelled a thousand miles before hitting the slope of Ascension and coming up just off the island's northwest coast. His mother's interest in the strange, distorted sound had perplexed him at first, but later, on the journey northwest that followed, it had excited him to hear the sound from the north begin to grow clear. His mother had swum under the light much of the time, keeping him with her, and he had heard how the signals she followed, sometimes dead for five or six hours, were always stronger below the light where she also signalled. Exuberantly the calf had called too, but by the time the bull was drawing into sight his booming voice had begun to unsettle the youngster.

The bull and cow slowed slightly at a hundred yards apart. Thirty feet down, ahead of his mother, the calf could see the light on the surface turn them both to silhouettes. In the harsh light he feared at first that the two were charging in anger, but, just as the snouts were about to collide, the cow turned sideways, and the calf saw one of her eyes turn down toward him while the other faced the bull. She glided under the huge whale, gently touching her length to his. When her snout came clear of his flukes and she turned upright to poke her head into air, the bull whale, wheeling to join her, also poked his head through the top. The calf rose too, putting his mother once more between himself and the bull. Her eye was on him for an instant, then fell away as her head and the bull's crashed together into the sea, turning both of them horizontal, undersides touching length to length, each with one eye on the sky and one on the darkness below.

They hardly moved, each with its pectorals pressed against the other's sides. Head out of the water, looking down at them ten yards away, the

228

calf could see where the tip of his mother's snout touched the bull whale's narrow throat grooves and her flukes his abdomen, revealing her smaller size. His fear of the bull began to subside as he saw the two hang motionless. Throat to throat, they lifted their heads from the sea to breathe in unison, then swam apart, the bull above, just breaking the surface where he spouted several times. The mother whale came up beside him and for some minutes gently touched his eye with her pectoral fin. Then she lightly brushed his cheek before going down to rise on his other side where she touched his other eye and brushed more vigorously, trying to wipe the cloudiness of his eyes away with her fin, the bull all the while making forward and backward motions and inhaling with short, tense breaths. When the cow dove under he spouted loudly, as if relieved that she had stopped.

The calf stayed still, watching the thirty-foot spouts of the bull rise out of the sea while the afternoon sun kept dimming and clearing in the clouds. The strange appearance of the bull and the dazzling alternation of sun and shadow were like the flickering sights of a dream. Suddenly the hundred-foot whale touched him lightly with his snout and made an affectionate lowing sound, like the sound his mother made while nursing. Immediately the calf dove after his mother. She was a few yards under the water, but when the calf saw her lift her snout and stroke the bull whale's skin, he rose again.

The motionless bull was making gentle sounds. Suddenly bold and curious, the calf dove under his body. Above him, it seemed endless, the abdomen darker and much wider than the cow's, patterned here and there with circular marks and scars. Swimming down from his father's chest, the calf arched up to look at the silvery scar the harpoon off northeast Newfoundland had left when he'd taken it on the side. He shivered as he looked, slightly hurt by the sight of the wound. He surfaced, far less afraid, expecting the bull and cow to continue their strange play and ready to join them now, but the mother whale had started for the south. He was so disappointed that, even after his mother called, he lingered behind, head out of the water, to watch the bull.

He wanted to hear the lowing sound, but his father, facing south, was quiet this time. After a minute of uncertainty the calf dove under again, this time to nudge the place where the nipples would have been. He saw the pectoral fins were white on the underside, like his and his mother's.

229

When the calf came up just ahead of the snout, the returning mother whale was fifty yards off and he could see the two face each other, neither advancing nor retreating. He sensed their tension, feeling again that the graceful affectionate play had been only a dream. He moaned very softly, hungry now after twenty minutes. Still, he didn't join his mother, instead remaining between the pair where he started to circle, deeply confused that this estrangement should come as quickly and inexplicably as the caresses.

Watching the calf, the young cow wished she could turn the bull south, but, just as the bull whale's fear of the southern sun had faded with his sight, so her need to be with him had waned with her sexual passion. At most, Blue Whales gave birth every other year, and spaces of two years between births were not uncommon. Last year her intense desire had aroused the bull, and even the old Fin Whale had slowly lost her detachment after she'd caught the scent the young Blue had emitted into the sea. This year her drive was dormant, and though she had greeted him with joy, as soon as she'd sensed his grief and seen that her stroking did nothing to change his eyes, she'd given up hope of leading the bull whale south to her home. She'd never before encountered blindness and even now it seemed that the cloudiness of his eyes was just the reflection of some fear he carried inside. Whatever the cause, he appeared lost to her and time was running out. Last year they'd met in mid-September. This was October, well past the time when Antarctic rorquals started south.

Still, even without the sexual drive, the cow felt a fiery bond. The calf called more loudly, three strokes of his tail taking him halfway toward his mother, where he stopped, snout to the sky, bobbing to show how hungry he was. The cow immediately glided toward him, but after he dove to approach one breast, she felt so drawn to the bull that she glided farther ahead, moving the nipple away from his mouth and shooting jets of pink-white milk around his eyes. The calf caught up and fed, then hung near her head where he saw her submerged snout touch the snout of the bull and jets of bubbles fountain out of her blowholes. Swimming above her to let the bubbles break against his throat and sides, he saw the higher fountain that rose from the bull whale. After a minute he swam to the bull, hovered above him, then dove and returned to his mother's breasts.

As the nuzzling kept on, the cow remembered how mothers with calves had always been last to arrive on the krill grounds. It seemed for a moment that there was no need to swim away. She looked at the calf. Perhaps he needed more time in the warmth. Sated now, he was resting silently by the bull, and as the cow watched them together, she remembered how her own mother had lingered late off Africa in the year she had been born. First-year mothers always delayed the spring migration to give their young maximum time in warmer seas and let their blubber thicken before they reached the ice. Even so, her first exposure to polar water had stung her with hints of deadly cold.

She swam back to the bull and turned so they were parallel again with the calf between them. The sun stayed bright for another hour, and as the youngster slept, forgetting that he had ever feared the bull, the mother and father also rested, touching fins.

The cow repeatedly fell asleep only to wake again and listen to the sea, a constant pattern since her return to Ascension waters where, at the start, the din of traffic had never let up. Now she could hear no traffic whatever. Despite her joy at meeting the bull, the unusual silence was a goad, for though she welcomed the absence of shipping, the disappearance of other sounds was ominous. It seemed that the only noise she had heard from the north for days had been the usual background sounds that, like the sound in a shell, were always there when everything else had died. Over the previous week her growing apprehension at the hush had slowed her northward journey to a stop. It returned to her now. It was impossible to tell what the silence portended, but by the time the cow awoke she was once more eager to swim south.

Watching the bull whale's eyes, the cow felt even more at a loss than last year when she'd at least been able to scrape penellas off him. This year she couldn't help him at all. Before leaving, she ran her side down the length of his one final time and again touched one of his eyes with a pectoral fin. She groaned, but the bull gave only the gentle lowing call of before. The sound warmed and soothed her, and the three of them hovered there in a net of joy and sadness.

The bull whale seemed to be steadier than he'd been an hour before. During his half sleep, while the cow had heard the silence to the north, he had been hearing thousands of fins turning together where dolphin-fish made forty-mile-an-hour feeding runs through a school of sauries far to his south. His ears had caught each reverberation when the

231

sauries had zigged or zagged, sounds that reassured him the dust was well behind. As the cow prepared to leave, he raised his ears out of the water to hear the piercing high-pitched call of a bos'n bird and then, farther off, the echoes of other bos'n birds near the darkening horizon. He warmed inside. Lifeless compared to temperate seas, the doldrums seemed suddenly alive with birds and fish, as if to compensate for the silence under the dust.

When the sun had finally gone, the cow swam off, but the calf remained with the bull. Although she called him very loudly, it depressed her when the youngster at last obeyed, for it was her judgment that led her south, not her love or desire. After leading the calf three hundred yards away, she swam in a circle and called to the bull. When he didn't answer, she swam a little farther south at a dozen knots. Now, as he had every day on the northern journey, the young calf started to shake. She halved her speed, turning from south to south-southeast in the dark sea lightened only here and there by a lanternfish flashing its lights. The calf's shivering worsened, remaining even after he'd fed. He'd weathered bronchial pneumonia, but it had left him weak and the head cold that remained kept raising his temperature, so that he shook with fever and chills. The cow grew afraid. If the calf were cold in this tropical water, how would he bear the polar cold?

She had turned back north and just started to call when, to her surprise, the bull whale answered less than half a mile away. Had she not been worried about the calf, this would have filled her with joy, but now she followed the sound without enthusiasm, the calf still shivering beside her.

The bull surmised he was past the equator, but it wasn't fear of travelling south that had held him back when the cow had left him at dusk. Ever since the blinding suns had flared and died in his head, his mind had been moving in a dreamy, ponderous way. By now the numbness that had always followed his losses had begun to slow his reactions as well as his thoughts. Without the cow he would have re-entered the semi-sleep of the previous year. Yet the reunion made him realize once more how deeply he loved her. Partly leaving his torpor behind, he'd followed her after an hour, though even now the sounds of life entranced him so that he swam in a dream part of the time and often stopped when he woke up, for the calf stirred painful memories.

When he drew up on the young cow, he ran his pectoral fins down the

232

length of her back, feeling the slope from spine to sides, rounder than last year when she had left the Antarctic in April. Now, in October, barely four months had gone by since her fast had begun in June. Yet she was motionless with worry. He inverted himself and swam under her, touching her throat with his, then rose to breathe and arched his snout down from the surface to touch the calf.

He noticed the youngster's shivering and pressed to feel how thick the blubber was. The calf went tense, but as his father's snout arched up and he caught a glimpse of his cloudy eye and heard the explosive *whoosh* of his spout, the shivering stopped. He came up beside the bull, but this time the old whale didn't stroke him. The cow made a moaning sound as the shivering started again.

Ignoring the calf, the bull once more inverted himself and touched the young cow's throat, its ninety ventral pleats as clearly scored as his mate's. Bubbles burst out of his head as he moved his throat backward and forward against hers. When she didn't respond, he touched the calf with his snout again. The blubber seemed neither unusually thick nor unusually thin and the water was warm, but the calf still shivered. The bull hung still for several minutes, straining to keep himself in the present, but, from a little more than a year ago, the past grew clear in his mind.

They were off the Greenland fjord, crustaceans thick on the calm sea. The wheeling seals took hurried breaths and dove for cod. The world seemed cleaner outside the fjord. Its dirty icebergs, three years old, circled from base to mouth all summer long but never found the strait. Here the floating ice looked clean, covered with snow. He fed for hours at a time and, when the ache in his kidneys sharpened too much to ignore, dove under the ice as if to escape the pain. This had seemed to work in June, but now, in July, the attacks were worse, and he ignored the cow who hung eighty yards away with the calf beside her.

The calf had seemed well on the northward migration but now it had started to shiver again, and he knew she feared it would die if it didn't go south. Though he travelled apart from his mate more and more often, the bull had been present during her labor at the Sierra Leone Rise where she'd been vulnerable at the surface for two hours. The calf, only twenty feet long, had shivered even after a day's feeding. He'd hovered beside it and caressed it with his snout. Mutual worry over the calf had kept the bull and cow within sight of one another throughout the winter, but, unlike her, he hadn't delayed his northward swim for the youngster's sake.

After his silence made the cow swim up to him, the bull whale paused, then with a grunt resumed his runs through pink crustaceans. This time she chased, nudging his flukes and leading the calf through the lane of blue he left behind. He spouted loudly with an angry rasp that echoed off the cliffs. The cow was diving under the bull, angry as well and about to bunt him, when a pain attack sent him shooting ahead of her.

As soon as it passed she led the calf to his side. He nuzzled it briefly, then, feeling a trace of what he had felt when his family had first begun to vanish, returned to his feeding in an abrupt, dismissive way. The cow swam south without looking back.

At first she swam in silence and the bull kept making runs through the thysanoessa. When she called out again and he realized she was travelling down the coast instead of returning into the fjord as he had expected, he became sharply aware of the background roar from the Greenland-Iceland Rise. It had pleased him before. Now it disturbed him. He went still. The hurt he had partly felt when he'd looked at the calf was sending ripples out from his sides, making him realize he was trembling himself despite his thick coat of blubber. Thin after migration, his mate hadn't fed as well as he, and yet it was she who'd gone ahead with the calf. The bull turned away from the thysanoessa. Perhaps she would stop if he followed her, perhaps even turn back north again.

He had just started to swim when pain from his kidneys made him see how helpless he was. He remembered how impotent he had been to protect his calves. He paused. The cow was strong-willed and he had never been able to turn her from her premature flights before. The pain dulled. He went back to his feeding. Though grief for the calf, who would surely die, hurt for a moment, he refused to give it space. The pain stopped. He continued to feed even when day had dimmed to late-summer polar night, and only answered his mate from time to time. Her calls remained strong, and he could see there was no need to leave right away. The attacks of pain had ceased for now, and by the time he had stopped feeding, the roar from the Greenland-Iceland Rise pleased him again.

The memory passed in a second, and when the bull awoke to see the calf still shivering, he touched the skin in gentle arcs, beginning at the head. Despite his chill, the calf felt pleasure when the bull touched his upper jaw and the sensitive places on top of his head where there had been hairs before his birth. As the massive snout drew back he saw the circular wound from the bullet off Canada, and when it drew near again he discerned fine bristles on it. Small and not easy to see, they struck the calf despite his discomfort because his mother had them as well and his own snout still retained prenatal hairs where the bull was gently stroking him. The calf would lose the hairs, but the clustered nerves that had evolved from their follicles would always remain. They gauged the pressure of the water and gave him a sense of his relative speed. They tingled with pleasure at the bull whale's stroke, although the youngster's sides continued to shake.

Feeling the shivering persist, the bull moved back. He touched the pectoral fins and the spots on body and head where free nerve endings filled the skin. Though he couldn't actually warm the calf, he'd learned that pressure there sometimes stopped the shivering reflex. Soon the shivering let up, though this time the bull whale didn't stop stroking.

The shivering had been a movement of the muscles, not the skin, which on the calf, as on his parents, was only a few cells thick and, though moving somewhat with the water, very tight compared with that of a mammal on land. The nerves that cut down turbulence by making the skin respond to water pressure also made the skin more sensitive than a man's, and once the calf stopped shivering, the mother whale started running her snout down his underside while the bull whale's snout kept moving over his back. After the calf arched under his mother and started to feed, the bull whale stroked him from below, and when the cow made the lowing sound that often accompanied her suckling, the bull took it up, so that the youngster felt secure despite the lingering cold in the head that had made him shake.

After a day the calf seemed better and the three whales started swimming south straight down the Mid-Atlantic Ridge. The cow felt

235

no need to veer for the west as she had last year, but her migration was just as slow, since she wanted the young male stronger before he passed the polar front. The calf became more alert as his congestion started to clear. That night he could see blue-green flame surround his mother's snout, while to his rear he saw the strokes of all three tails leave blue-green lanes on the dark sea. He made loud rumbling sounds of pleasure and surprise as the cow brought her tail down hard on the water, making a blaze. Noctiluca, medusalike plants that shone when touched, kept flaring up for a quarter mile, twice making the fascinated calf break away from his mother to watch the lights. The bull whale circled, lowing and puffing as he tried to guess what excited the young male. Once, when the light blazed up beside his cloudy eye, the calf called out, thinking his father watched the plants as well. The cow called abruptly then and led the young male south. After ten minutes noctiluca on the surface dead ahead lit up a ring of Killer Whales who had encircled a fifteen-foot mako shark and were taking turns at slicing pieces out of its body. The shark had been driven up with every dive and now it stayed on the glowing surface. Each time it slashed, its target retreated or dodged aside while another whale to the rear of the shark tore out more flesh. Aside from the great white, this was the deadliest shark in the sea. Part of the spine was visible in the glowing light, crawling with worms. For a second the calf hung still in fascination, never having seen this kind of lingering death. Terrified and angry, his mother and father urged him on. After thirty hours he saw Ascension break the horizon, and the bull could hear the echoing calls of frigate-birds and terns.

The shivering stopped for good after two days, and after three the lingering congestion from the pneumonia went away. They followed the ridge for nine days after passing Ascension, never travelling at more than ten knots. Each time the cow suckled the calf the bull caressed him, and after five days the young male sometimes swam with one pectoral fin against his father's side. Each time he did the bull remembered the sickly calf who had found the Greenland sea so cold and who'd have known better than to press the side of its indifferent sire. The fin felt sharp when it brought back memories of those times, but only then. Often the three were only inches apart as they swam. The bull began to feel alive again.

The calf was fattening. Over the forty days since his birth most of his food had become insulation, the first priority for every newborn whale, and by the time they approached the eighteenth parallel in late October, his blubber was thirty-five percent of his weight, nearly double what he had been born with. During his first four weeks his fins and flukes had ached when he was cold, and the insulation there stayed thin even after his blubber had thickened. His veins could retain heat by reducing the blood supply to the outer edge of his body, but the blood supply to the flippers and fins was always rich.

By late October the calf was nearly thirty feet long, and as he grew larger, the changing ratio of his size to his skin surface would make it harder to lose heat than to keep it in. As the whales moved on, the calf became hot from prolonged swimming, and on the tenth dawn, when the cow decided to stop, he swelled his throat-pouch with water and waved his flukes and fins in the air to drain the heat.

His mother welcomed this as a sign of health, though she still worried. She halted well before the southeast trades gave way to westerlies, recalling again how her mother had delayed the southward flight in the year she'd been born. After she stopped, the passive bull, last year so restless, hardly ever left her side. Roughly three hundred miles southwest of St. Helena, he listened for hours to shoaling fish and distant birds and kept reminding himself that the dust couldn't come this far. When memories threatened to hurt him again, he caressed the calf, drawing strength now from its fin against his side.

Yet the bull was uneasier than he had been nine days ago. The sounds of life still made him happy, but the scattering layer's rise and descent were daily reminders that he was blind. And his blindness gave him a heightened sense of the earth's magnetic field. He didn't know why, but his sense of direction was most acute when undersea echoes focussed his mind on the Mid-Atlantic Ridge six thousand feet below, almost as if he sensed the intenser magnetic field over the ridge where rock was rising and spreading west by roughly an inch and a half a year. For the first time in his life he felt uneasy at having the ridge directly below. He didn't know that two hundred miles west, where the rock was half a million years older, the magnetic field weakened, then strengthened again over even older rock still farther west. The alternate zones of strength and weakness ran out from ridge to coast in parallel bands where every million to two million years the planet's polarity had reversed. The bull whale could feel a new, stronger sense of direction, and he feared it would come to control him just as his sight had controlled him before.

Yet the fear had opposition, for almost as soon as he began to grow uneasy at moving south he started to sense that the dust and silence were approaching from the north. No more than an intuition at first, the hush he heard to the north seemed to grow at the same rate as his sense of the earth's magnetic field. Simultaneously he felt pulled to the north and pushed to the south. After ten days his sense of the hush became unmistakable and fear of the dust tipped the balance of tensions inside him. The urge to flee south superseded everything else. The cow wanted slow migration with long intervals of rest. The bull repeatedly hurried ahead, calling her and the calf to go faster. After two weeks, with the calf over thirty-one and a half feet long, the mother whale began to hold back less.

They passed the Tropic of Capricorn in early November, still over the ridge, and the steady trades gave way to light, variable winds. Twelve days went by. The calls of Right Whales had been coming from Tristan da Cunha for over a week, and now the calf moved out a little ahead of his parents and called in answer, pleased that his voice at over a hundred decibels was so much louder than a month ago when he'd tried to answer his father's long-range call.

Tropical sea streaked with flying fish had given way to gray westerly swell, and as the calf pursued the whale calls into shore, he swam at the surface, butting the waves and calling constantly to his mother, who swam behind. Despite thick cloud, both mother and calf could see the cone of Tristan da Cunha, a single peak rising nine thousand feet from the floor to stretch a further seven thousand feet above the sea. The gray silhouette covered in thunderclouds at the top showed streaks of snow around its summit and white mist where waterfalls roared down the cliffs. From two miles off, the calf could hear the spouts of the Rights, rough sounds like heavy timbers dragged over stone. Soon a group of six came into sight, feeding between patches of red kelp not far from shore. The calf slowed down until his mother was beside him, then they approached the Rights together.

The bull's heightening sense that the dust was near kept him off-shore, where he hung vertical at the top, head in the air as if to gauge each change in pressure with the nerve ends in his snout. He'd grown obsessed with the dust well before there'd been clear signs of its approach, and even now the things that he took for signs would not have disturbed the inexperienced cow. It seemed to the bull that every lull in ambient noise made the background silence more closely resemble the lifeless hush he feared. Sometimes, when they rested, the cow and calf could faintly hear the hush as well, though their sight and the sounds from the south distracted them. Sometimes the bull told himself he was wrong and rested for hours with his family. Yet sooner or later the urge for flight always returned.

When the mother and calf came close enough to the Rights that the youngster could see the white callosities on their heads, the fifty-foot females took no notice, spouting in feathery Vs and upending themselves at random, as if too modest to look the Right Whale bulls in the eye. The round black whales kept pairing and parting, every approach bringing exchanges like amplified snores, and afterward, the bulls would withdraw, call, and upend before approaching another cow. The cows would start bearing young in December, and from December to March the adult whales would mate, but for now there were flirting games. The Blue Whale cow called out, remembering the Rights in the Gulf of St. George who had been curious about her, but these Rights gave no reply. The pair watched the whales now from above and now from below until shrill EEEOOOs from above the cliffs made them look up to see the albatrosses soaring in the updraft.

The bull whale heard them where he waited well offshore, and though he couldn't see the sooty albatrosses who made the long EEEOOOs or the wandering albatrosses whose eerie howllike calls were loud on the wind, the inshore noisiness of whales and fish and birds formed such a contrast with the silence that he sensed was drawing near, that he called urgently and started south again.

The cow led the calf to sea, but when the bull kept to a steady fifteen knots, she let him go on, slowing down after five minutes and after five more completely stopping to feed the calf. The bull turned back, remembering how even alone he hadn't outsped the dark. When the calf had fed, he led them south again.

Over the next four hours the hump of Nightingale Island rose in distant silhouette, and when it drew near, the bull could hear the greater shearwaters who nested there in tunnels under the six-foot tussock grass. The albatross calls had been new to him, but he'd heard these cries before off Canada and Greenland where the birds lived

239

through the southern hemisphere winter. These flocks had left the north between June and September, before the dust, and now, with the southern hemisphere spring, five million breeders had congregated at Nightingale Island. As he neared it just before dusk and the familiar cries made him break the sea with his head again and again, the bull could see the northern coasts he'd left behind rise up toward him, black with birds. The cow heard his agonized rumbling under the sea as he envisioned Greenland cliffs teetering crazily toward him. Above the sea the din of birds drowned out everything else.

He swam at full speed until the island was well behind, the cow pursuing him in fear, for it seemed he was growing as distressed as he'd been last year and she didn't know why. Calling in sympathy and confusion, she made the calf swim at her speed till her mate slowed down and she caressed him with her snout. The bull slowly calmed. While she fed the calf, he swam in circles around the pair. After the feeding he continued south at less than a dozen knots.

With their constant stopping they moved slowly and by dawn were about a hundred miles above Gough Island. The crack of light brought a lull in the westerly wind, and as the calf swam now by his mother, now by his father, he could sense that his mother was shaken. Soothing and tender before, by now her incomprehension had made her more deeply afraid of his father's fear. With both afraid, he felt his security shrink away, and, not knowing what they feared, he called to them both. Neither responded as the sun cleared the horizon. The Killer Whales rose up in his mind, not the ones slicing the shark, but the mysterious line of dorsals he saw in his sleep. He knew what the black fins meant now. They were death, liable to strike wherever they chose and, as he had seen off Ascension Island, equally liable to swim on by.

After an hour of silent swimming he yearned for his parents' attention. In early morning he swam up to his mother's eye and dropped below as if to remind her of his presence, for she'd been self-absorbed since passing Nightingale Island. When she merely swam on in silence, he swam under his father's eye, and when his father ignored him as well, he rose above the eye and looked down. Unlike his mother's, it was pale and never moved. On a sudden impulse he touched the very top of it with his fin. It still didn't move. The calf had long suspected his father had gone blind. Now he was sure. He felt both fear and wonder.

The bull remained at a depth of thirty feet, but as they moved on, the

240

calf swam higher until his vision to either side was very bright. Tilting down, he saw his parents' blowholes fade as the pair exhaled under the sea. The bubbles rose past him. When he swam higher and looked down again he could see more bubbles rise from the dark where his parents' heads were no more than blue-gray blurs. A month ago he wouldn't have dared to swim so far away and even now he felt frightened, but it lifted him to hear both parents calling in concern instead of stroking dumbly on. When he answered their calls but stayed near the top, the eye of his mother rose toward him as she arched up on her side, and it suddenly struck him that he had never seen his father make the same casual motion. The realization hurt him and he felt sympathy, envisioning his father's cloudy eyes. When he focussed past his mother into the nearly total dark thirty feet down, he could hardly see the bull whale's back. It occurred to him that his father never swam in the twilight place between the upper sea light and the total dark except with his mother at his side. Again he envisioned the cloudy eyes, and vaguely wondering what a life of perpetual darkness would be like, he dove and pressed one pectoral fin to his father's side. Bubbles rose from the bull whale's head and he gently called, leading the youngster farther down.

Here the twilight quickly faded into night and when the three whales rose to breathe the sun seemed hidden in high cloud. They dropped again, but not as far, for the mother liked to swim in the twilight.

Though the adults stayed below for a quarter hour at a time, the calf breathed every two or three minutes, and every time he rose, the light had dimmed. When his mother suckled him in the twilight, the bull kept calling her to dive, but though they both sensed falling pressure, neither mother nor calf could see why the bull kept trying to lead them down to total darkness when the much more pleasant twilight zone began just a few feet down.

As the hours passed, the mother was more and more aware of the hush to the north, though she didn't see its association with fading light. The farther south they swam the shallower the sunlight's penetration, but the sun remained high in the sky. Eventually this frightened the mother whale, and both she and the calf called out in panic. After an hour they started lingering at the top in desperation while the bull roared from below. Though they always followed him down, they delayed more and more with the dimmer light.

Air temperature dropped. In the afternoon, when he rose beside them, the bull could tell from the chill that the dust had caught up with him. He stopped trying to protect the eyes of cow and calf by leading them low, since the temperature drop showed that here the cloud had come over him all at once. Unlike in Canada or the northern seas, there'd been no alternation of darkness with blinding light.

By late afternoon it was dark overhead and to the north. The bull kept swimming, for he could hear loud storms accompanying a cyclone to the south and he remembered how the dust had slowed when it met the hurricane. A cyclone raged not far ahead, but the stormiest weather was past the southern horizon, at latitude forty where the expanded tropical air mass met the mass of compressed polar air and the pressure difference created a high-speed wind six miles above the sea. This easterly wind, with high-altitude westerlies farther south, was what the dust would have to subdue if it were to reach Antarctica. Throughout the southern winter high-altitude westerlies circled the eye of Antarctic cold, blowing concentrically at heights of eight miles and up, from latitude ninety out to latitude forty-five and sometimes beyond. Now, with November and the southern hemisphere spring, the pressure differences between the high-altitude cyclones grew less steep, slowing them down. Even so the easterly wind on the fortieth parallel, a so-called jet stream wind, blew at a hundred miles an hour at its six-mile height and faster higher up, circling the globe with a band seldom less than ninety miles wide.

Though the fleeing whales knew nothing of the hole in the atmosphere above the pole, these cyclone winds could either keep it from killing them or help it advance, and the hole was fully as much a threat as the cloud of dust. Sometimes the southern winds blew only in fixed, concentric rings, never veering off their course to mix with warmer, moister systems to the north and start the mid- and high-altitude storms that would carry heat into the southern stratosphere and prevent the freezing of water and nitrogen. It was this freezing that freed gaseous chlorine to destroy the ozone in the spring, and if the whales should survive the dust, they could be faced very soon with the total disappearance of polar ozone. Whether the cyclones would interact with warmer winds or merely keep to their fixed courses was uncertain, but an increase in the power of the sun would heighten the chance of mixing winds and the penetration of warmth below the polar front.

242

After a decade of weak sun activity, solar radiation was peaking once again, bringing more warmth to the stratosphere. If the whales could survive the dust, there was a chance the deadly vacuum spreading outward from the pole might never reach them. But the polar stratosphere would have to warm.

The bull swam for the south. Perhaps, if he led his cow and calf into the cyclone, it would hold the advancing soot and dust at bay. Yet sooner or later the mere vastness of the cloud, thousands of miles in length and breadth, would assure its advance to the South Pole. The bull whale couldn't know this, but his experience in the north was clear in his mind, and even while leading the cow and calf toward the storm, he felt an unreasoned fear they might never escape the dust. Still he swam hard, and in a little less than an hour the three whales entered the cyclone.

CHAPTER

22

T HE mother whale followed the bull whale for the stormy sky to the south, but she wished she could lead the calf to warmer seas. On previous migrations she'd barely noticed the convergence at latitude forty where subtropical gave way to subantarctic surface water, to lower the temperature at least by nine degrees. This year she'd anticipated the change as soon as they'd passed Nightingale Island, for, though she didn't remember a great deal of her first southward migration, she knew she'd been free of colds and bigger than the thirty-two-foot calf when she'd first crossed latitude forty. Still, there was no turning back with the dust closing behind.

They swam into the cyclone all that night, while the cyclone itself moved steadily west, the wind at first from the northwest with constant rain, then, after midnight, the northeast, then, after thunderstorms and downpours, the southeast, with the southeast wind the coldest. At dawn the ocean top was sixty-one degrees, though the young cow knew that another hundred miles would lower the temperature even more. The bull kept pressing for full-speed flight, and when she hung back to rest the calf, he pushed at its blubber with his snout as if to show it was thick and warm. The young cow hesitated more often the farther they went, as she could feel the cold increase.

When the sky cleared two hours after dawn and the cow saw bright sun overhead, she called for joy and went totally still, as if the dust had been a storm she'd left behind. She sensed it was more, but like the bull in the beginning, she couldn't conceive of permanent cold and dark outside the polar night. The frustrated bull was unable to tell her what he'd seen. Still, he kept encouraging flight, and the young male, sensing the tension, hung between the two till they swam southwest in a compromise, keeping to twenty feet while the youngster swam at the top.

The southeast wind died down, but all that day there were storms to the north, as though the advancing high-altitude heat above the dust were doing battle with the uncontaminated southern sky. This background tumult made it impossible for the whales to tell how near or far away the silence was until three hours before dusk, when the cow looked north to see the dark advance in a line that ran from the eastern to the western horizon. She started to race, but this time the bull whale hung behind, having sensed by her flight that she'd seen the dark. If the dust had come back into sight this soon, they'd never escape it. Still, when she kept on racing south, he followed her.

When the scattering-layer creatures started to rise in late afternoon, the bull didn't shut his ears against them as he had when their daily movement had only reminded him he was blind, for he knew that under the dust cloud they would die. He called repeatedly, cocking his head after each call to hear the false-bottom effect the creatures made. As always the echo was strongest from the air-filled lanternfish at two thousand feet. It was an old, unremarkable sound but the bull kept calling. Now, like the long familiar sound of the shearwaters, the echoes of the lanternfish would pass, as would the static of the euphausiids at twelve hundred feet and the louder noise where sergestid shrimp crackled their armor seven hundred feet below. As he remembered how

245

sounds of life had died in the north, he shivered a little and hung back from the migration.

For the rest of the day, as the three continued south in a stop-start pattern, the calf kept looking behind, half doubting his eyes. When the halting swim began, the dust filled a third of the sky. Although he couldn't see it move, each time he turned around, it had risen a little higher. Whenever his parents paused he turned and stared at the sky, determined to catch the cloud in motion. But never did. He kept his eyes on its upper edge where the dominant black gave place to brown and streamers spiralled up in graceful formations. Imperceptibly they rose and spread.

After an hour the dust was gaining ground so fast that the cow stopped. The bull, subdued and sad, remained intent on the scattering layer, for there was nothing to be done about the dust. The calf remained at his father's side as he stroked through slicks of phytoplankton. The sun still shone and the spreading cloud, though soon to fill the entire sky, had only started to dim the sea where the whales swam. Most of the scattering layer wouldn't rise till dusk, but when his father paused to listen, the calf paused too, swimming off from time to time to explore the yellow-brown diatom clouds that spotted the top. The calf expected to feel them against his skin when he entered them but he never did, although a few of the plankton clouds, chalk-white or rust, faintly suggested the consistency of fine sand when he let them enter his mouth and pressed his palate with his tongue. What he felt were foraminifera, near-microscopic animals whose shells coated millions of square miles of the ocean floor, just as farther south the diatom ooze encircled Antarctica. Watching the two males swim together, the mother whale hovered in silence and waited for the calf to grow hungry again.

An hour later, after he'd fed, the dust had filled half the sky, and when he looked up to see that the delicate formations had disappeared, he pressed his fin to his father's side, getting a physical sense of the cloud's immensity. His mother sensed it also and reflexively moved south a little way. The bull whale followed with the young male at his side.

A few minutes later the dust passed over their heads. The bull kept calling into the deep, but the false-bottom echoes had grown more faint, for the concentrations were dispersing as the creatures started to climb at greater speed, drawn by the dark. Behind his eyes the bull envisioned the tiny shapes he'd taken for granted when he could see. They seemed enlarged, and he could tell by his ears that the onset of the dust had made them rise faster. They came up as if they were eager for the night. From twelve hundred feet the one-inch euphausiids, white and pink with huge black eyes, climbed at three hundred feet per hour, while from seven hundred feet the white and red sergestid shrimp, less than an inch long, rose at two hundred feet per hour, and red calanus copepods, each roughly the size of a grain of rice, came up at fifty feet per hour along with ctenophores: zeppelin-shaped predators of an inch who rowed for the surface with hundreds of ciliate legs. In motion since noon, the specks had accelerated and spread as if impatient, many emitting brilliant light. After the dust unrolled above, a lane of light spread out beneath it, and where he swam behind the bull, hearing him call, it seemed to the calf as if his father were summoning lights out of the sea. In his excitement he didn't see the rising swimmers, only the glow that they gave off, and he continued to miss their outlines even after his flight had slowed and the plankton floated on top for the last time, some of them shining, most merely set off in the light of the others: transparent arrowworms, thin-armed siphonophores, red my- sids, glowing jellyfish, pulsing medusae, the bug-eyed translucent larvae of crabs, fish, worms, prawns, and a thousand other creatures, most of them visible but very few much more than an inch in length.

After the creatures came to the top, the cow went still. The air chilled quickly but the surface temperature stayed above fifty-nine, and she didn't start swimming south again till the black went brown with breaking day. Still north of latitude thirty-nine, the whales followed the ridge. Instead of diving as they usually did near dawn, the plankton kept gathering on top till the lanternfish who'd come up with them were joined by other midlevel fish, and wherever the youngster turned he could make out flashing lights. He followed his father between feedings, since the blind bull seemed less altered than his mother by the dust, and when the cow's growing withdrawal began to frighten him he nudged his father's side and made the sound he made when hungry, till the lowing bull caressed him with his snout and touched the sensitive places on top of his head to reassure him. After six hours during which she never swam at more than two knots, the mother whale caressed him as well. During what would have been afternoon the bull curved his body

247

so that his flukes caressed the calf and his snout the cow. The three hung motionless in the dark, drawing strength from their love for each other.

By now the predators who would normally have fed on the scattering layer as it descended had started to search the upper sea. Differing temperature and salinity kept some of them below, but many rose all the way to the top, and when the calf entered an area where luminous phytoplankton lit up everything that moved, he could see squid made entirely of flame dart to and fro just under the surface where they hunted lanternfish who virtually wrote in the upper sea, turning together in blazing schools. Forgetting the dark, the calf slapped the water with his tail and dove well under, arching away from his father and mother, who also blazed. Concerned, his mother submerged to watch with one eye, then sadly surfaced to resume her two-knot swim, completely indifferent to the light that covered her body. After a mile or two the dinoflagellate plants that made the light washed off the whales and the brilliance died.

Next day they reached latitude forty, where the temperature dropped to fifty-one. The calf's head cold was gone. He didn't shiver in the subantarctic water, but after a minute the cow whale gently turned him back. Though she had hoped to catch the sun, the bull whale's lack of enthusiasm had dampened her hope from the beginning, and with the temperature drop, she resigned herself to a period of waiting.

The calf felt a great letdown. For twenty-four hours after the dust had covered the sky, the surface had shone with glowing light, and while they'd kept moving and calling out, he'd had an instinctive sense that merely staying close to his mother and father would keep him safe. Now, with the light starting to fade, both whales went still. Feeling alone, he took to poking their motionless backs to get attention. Always one or the other would call and stroke when the youngster grew demanding, but the longer the dark the more reflexive their strokes until eventually he started butting their sides or, when he fed, deliberately squeezing his mother's nipples in an attempt to anger or hurt her, for the monotony was intolerable, not merely his parents' daze but the unvarying westerly breeze and the constant near-calm of the sea.

Centers of blackness started to spread toward each other on the glowing ocean top, their gradual motion indiscernible, like the dust's. After seventy hours the light and dark seemed equal on the sea, and seeing the change, the calf called out, eager to hear his soundwaves carry past his sight. He stroked his mother with his head, then far below discerned a brilliant blue-green flash. He pursued it impulsively, diving straight down till he saw fish with marble eyes and ribbon bodies rise toward him. One, which was fleeing the other fish, had its jaws locked around an unrecognizable creature ten times its size. As the calf drew near, the fish descended. Yet their lights stayed bright for well over a minute and this transparency showed that the water held no life. Frightened, he rose back to the top. Then, as he looked across the web of light and dark, he saw the pattern move at last, the centers of darkness joining each other and the lights dividing and shrinking into tighter and tighter rings. The next time he dove, the background noise amounted to little more than the hiss of surface waves. He rose again. Unable to rouse his mother and father, he watched in silence till the last of the lights went out. After it died, flickers continued to come and go but he didn't notice them. Darkness held the sea.

It had been ninety hours now since the sun had gone out. The youngster poked his father's head till one of the cloudy eyes came open. The night was so dark that, with his eye nearly touching his father's, the calf saw only an oval of gray where the milky film emerged from the lid. His father tilted to show him the light-colored underside of one pectoral fin, the only part of a Blue Whale's skin that was solid white. The snowy underfin, gray in the night, faded out as the calf moved less than a foot away. Shivering with fear, he called for attention.

His father stroked him with his snout, then stroked his mother, who briefly awakened from her daze. Terrified of being abandoned, the calf poked sharply with his snout when he saw her eyelid close again, and till the sun lightened the dust from a deep black to a brownish gray, he kept on troubling his mother and father. Both parents stroked but he could sense in the very feel of their fins uncertainty and fear. Sometimes, to pacify the youngster, they would set off toward the south, pretending to migrate. This calmed him down, although he knew it was just a game. Once he'd calmed, they would sleep once more, waiting things out. Weeks went by. He became more and more afraid.

After twenty-one days, his panic gradually gave way to acquiescence. By now he'd found new ways of getting his parents' attention. Though his mother was usually still, if he prolonged the time between feedings until his hunger actually hurt, she would awaken to push him under, loudly urging him to feed, and her concern showed she expected him to survive, despite her depression. Along with his father's inscrutable calm, this sustained him through the thirty-nine days of darkness that ensued.

He yearned for change. If the faint wind strengthened or ebbed by as much as half a knot it was a significant event, and the calf grew excited whenever bodies floated by in the westerly drift. After six weeks the youngster saw bloated rockhopper penguins collect at his father's motionless side where they bobbed like weeds, one of them moving back and forth in surface waves so that it seemed about to peck his father's eye. When the bull didn't push it away, the calf remembered how his father had never swum in the twilight place between the upper sea light and the dark of the lower sea without his mother at his side. The penguin reminded him of what he'd guessed when he'd watched his father's eyes. The bull lived in darkness all the time. The calf began to be less afraid.

The penguin had blood at the anus. Suddenly angry, the calf shot forward to poke it aside. It floated off, its white belly vanishing instantly into the dark. When the bull grunted and dove, the calf saw the rest of the dead birds fade into night. After they passed he caressed his father.

Aside from two or three times when bodies passed, the sea seemed empty. The whales took to swimming in great wide circles to pass the time. Two weeks after the penguins, a glowing squid passed under the mother. Barely alive though still spasmodically shooting water from its jet, it rose and fell like a failing eight-foot heart. The squid had brilliant light at the eyes, and as it passed, the cow whale panicked at its strangeness, having become unused to life of any kind. She pressed her head to the bull whale's side and the calf could see her shake with fear. He stroked her skin in soft slow circles. When he paused to feed, the bull took up the stroking. In minutes the mother's trembling ceased.

They had no idea if the night would ever end. After two months the calf was just as subdued as his mother. Still, he kept on feeding. The love among the three was fathomless. Their nerve stayed steady as they comforted each other in the dark.

CHAPTER

23

DURING an average month there were no deaths in the school of five thousand dolphins. Between mid-October and mid-November three hundred among the oldest in the school died of disease. By mid-November over two thousand had left in the fear that the sickness would claim them next, some swimming east along the shelf toward coastal Gabon, others swimming west or out to sea. Most left in family groups of at least four, though lone individuals and groups of up to a hundred also fled. Whether in groups or alone, most dolphins left in the hope of forming or joining another inshore school in less troubled waters.

The brother and sister swam south for a hundred and fifty miles and stopped at the outer edge of the shelf, well east of the wrecked submarine, fleeing not only to save their lives but also to put the sight of the school's disintegration well behind. Some of the larger groups fled even farther out. At first the youngsters were relieved to be away from the quarrels and deaths. Then, after two days of rest and feeding, the great loneliness they had felt after leaving the open-sea school returned to hurt them again. Instead of turning back for the Ivory Coast, they followed the African shelf toward Gabon in the hope they could form a new community with others who had fled.

After four nights of eastward swimming, as the dolphins started south off Cameroon, the cloud of dust covered the sky. Dejection stopped them at first, but, unlike the whales, they couldn't wait the darkness out, as they needed food every day. When, after two days, they started swimming south again, more slowly now, they could hear thunder and whirlwinds on the coast.

Despite the difference in climate, the effects of the cloud off Africa resembled those the Blue Whale bull had encountered in the north, since the cloud chilled the earth wherever it passed, and where the cold and warm air met along the coast, the spiring vortices of wind rose more than five miles into the sky, here, as off Canada, impeding the advance of the lower dust and allowing nitrogen oxides at the top of the cloud to thin the ozone layer. Dolphins who were swimming close to shore looked up from the stormy sea to see either a cloud of darkness or a strangely brilliant light. Many, bewildered by the unnatural midday night, stared up at the sun in fascination when they entered a bright region, only to lose their sight within a day.

Prey died fast beneath the coastal sun, but the brother and sister were far enough out that the perpetual night kept the scattering-layer creatures at the top. Within a day of the dust's appearance inshore dolphins who weren't overwhelmed by the dark or grieving for their sight began to feed farther offshore. As the brother and sister continued south they encountered some of these fleeing dolphins, desperately hungry, preying eagerly on lanternfish and squid. Within twenty-four hours a dozen had joined the pair.

The glow of the scattering layer dimmed after thirty-six hours, and less than three days after that the shoals of fish and squid began to dwindle. Groups swam in from open sea to hunt on the shelf. By the time the pair were off Equatorial Guinea their group of fourteen had swollen to a hundred, all swimming farther inshore in search of food.

252

By now coastal turbulence had died, though zones of clear sky still remained. After twelve hours of swimming east the brother and sister saw the dust begin to thin. A bright blue sky appeared ahead. They swam toward it. The dolphins with them, dusky figures for two days, grew clear in outline, their blue-black backs, flashing bellies, and hourglass patches appearing more vivid than ever before after the dark. Those from inshore kept reiterating the patterns of clicks that signalled "sun" and "light" in tones of dread while those from the open sea made sharp, querulous answers, eager for daylight.

They neared the light. Straight overhead the sky was gray and streaked with wispy streamers of cirrus. It brightened to blue as they moved on. Soon the dirty part of the atmosphere seemed a low line to the north, the south, and the west, but there was a towering wall of darkness to the east, over Africa. Above the wall the sky was brightening. The brother and sister stood up in the water and moved their heads from side to side to watch the light with either eye.

Only now did the youngsters realize how much they'd missed the light. They started to celebrate, calling and racing and somersaulting high in the air. The sun had yet to clear the wall of dust on the eastern horizon, but its rays were brightening the sea, and as fifty others joined them, leaping as high as they could and flashing the hourglass patches on their sides, it seemed to the pair that their group was more than a desperate assembly of fugitives; they felt a vestige of the old sense of community. All the dolphins were under twenty, most the brother and sister's age, although there were none of the close friends from happier days. Hunger had united them before, but now that they celebrated together, recollections of communal feasts and games in the school of five thousand were bright in their minds, and they began to arch under and over one another, exchanging signature calls as dolphins do when pairing.

In their exuberance they didn't notice at first the group of fifty approaching from the east, although their complex calls had preceded them for nearly a quarter hour. As they grew larger on the horizon, the celebration gradually ceased. The brother and sister swam east to meet them, and when they drew near, they recognized the signature calls of elders from the old community. Oldest of the survivors, these had remained behind even after more than a thousand had swum away, trying to keep the school together. Since the groups swimming away had never been larger than a hundred and had departed in different directions, it had seemed at first that clinging to the Ivory Coast had been the way to keep the school alive. Then, when the deaths from disease had passed a hundred and fifty, these old dolphins had turned south for coastal Gabon. Now, as the dozen elders approached with their group of followers, the brother and sister heard the complex signal trains that only the oldest made. Both remembered the old female and dipped their heads to make mourning sounds in the sea.

The signals of the elders had changed, however. They called more slowly, as if exhausted. When the youngsters drew up on them, the male called out. To his surprise the elders answered him in sequences of clicks he could understand. They were simple signals: the echo patterns of "fish," "squid," and other prey, all associated with "sun," as if the elders were encouraging the male to remain in the light.

The brother and sister forgot about their group, many of whom were swimming west to enter the darkness once again. Those who hadn't been celebrating had long since seen that the region of light was barren, while under the dust there was at least a little food. In the group of one hundred dolphins were a dozen who had broken off a week ago from the group the elders led. As earlier in the darkness, these were clicking out the signals that meant "light" in tones of fear, urging the others to follow them back into the dust.

Twenty minutes after they'd entered the brilliant light, more than half of the one hundred dolphins had turned for the west while simultaneously the elders' group had spread out into many small rings that virtually stood around in the water, each encircling a lone dolphin who'd stayed behind. The male looked closely as he passed each of the groups. There was something suspicious about them. They welcomed those who remained too loudly, too excitedly. The sun began to burn him as he passed from ring to ring, uneasily whistling his signature call.

Suddenly, to the north, he discerned the dolphin with the single pectoral stripe. She was clicking in welcome, greeting dolphins who'd remained. As he drew up close and clicked to her, part of her ring turned away from the newcomers they were welcoming and swam up to him, blandishing, stroking, all too eager to have him join their school.

The female with the pectoral stripe went silent. He met her eyes as she turned toward him. They were white, as blind as bone. He looked at the others who welcomed him: stone blind as well. He noticed these dolphins were far thinner than those to the west. Radiation had killed their food along with their eyes. When he looked at the ones who were being welcomed, he could see that they hesitated to remain, but every attempt to leave was met by the eager cajoling of the blind who, dying themselves, took perverse comfort in increasing the number of dead. After she turned to the brother and sister, the female with the stripe suddenly stopped making welcoming sounds and, urging them away, clattered a warning: a loud series of rattling clicks. Just as she did, the pair spyhopped and turned through three hundred and sixty degrees. The sun was high. It had long since risen but only now did it clear the dust wall to the east. Feeling again the exultation they had felt at first discovering the light, they looked up at the sun.

In sudden pain they were plunged into blindness, clenching their lids. Behind their eyes the glaring light had made a maze of blinding mirrors. They dove through the ocean till it was dark, then opened their eyes, but still the mirrors blazed all about them. They moaned and twisted, plummeting headlong through the black.

After some minutes the yellow blaze faded to huge, translucent rings—gold in each eye—then orange, then red, then only the blackness of the ocean. They angled upward, eyeing the blue light at the surface. There was not a trace of plankton, the upper thirty feet as transparent and empty of life as the ocean air.

They swam for the west, keeping low in the water, with others beside them. Only two of the oldest finally chose to remain. Within hours all sighted dolphins who had looked at the sun went blind. For some it was permanent while others, like the young male and his sister, saw again in a couple of days. All became ravenously hungry. Hunting in far-spread groups that stretched for nearly twelve miles under the dust, every day an individual here or there would find some fish, though when the others arrived to share it most of the sickly, half-dead shoal would have been eaten. In any case it brought no relief from the hunger pangs, hardly bearable after four days. The sardinella were barely visible in the black, and, close to the eye, the little fish resembled swimming spines.

After a month the sea became barren and the dolphins swam back east to join the elders, since the air was very cool and they wanted the sun. But now even close to shore there was no light. The elders had gone. The dolphins didn't know if it was night or day, but, hoping it was night, they waited for sunrise five miles out.

It never came. By the time the brother and sister died, over twenty-five others were floating dead around them and the seventy living were equally motionless except when they drew breath. The sea was so still under the dust that after they died the two didn't drift. United at least with a small fraction of the inshore school of five thousand, the brother and sister hovered together with open eyes as if even now they awaited the sun.

CHAPTER
24

B<small>Y</small> the time the cow saw light on
the southern horizon she had long since ceased to expect it, and despite
their love, the nerve of all three had started to wear down. January was
almost over. Had the light returned a month earlier it would have
brought wild celebration, but the adult whales were hungry and the
hunger pangs took the edge off every emotion except fear. The mother
still had milk but feared it was drying. Since she'd fed in the Antarctic
until June, there was no chance of her starving this instant, and the bull
could have lived without food for many more weeks. Still, their hunger
was sharp. The total absence of life made it seem even stronger than it
was. More irresistibly than ever before the adults were forced to face the
possibility they could starve.

When the sun broke through the dust it didn't occur to the cow to admire or praise the light. She simply followed it south in a joyless search for food. As she swam ahead of the bull, she remained uncertain whether her mate could see the light. The cloudy appearance of his eyes told her his vision was impaired, but since she communicated primarily by sound, she didn't know the extent of his blindness, and as neither she nor the calf was jubilant, the bull couldn't tell their swim for the south was meant to do any more than break the monotony.

Only after the dust fell behind on the northern horizon and they entered a zone of blue unclouded sky did the cow and calf call out in excitement to the bull, each facing one eye. He answered their calls and caressed them both but never once tilted his head to look at the sun, so the young cow, growing certain of what the calf had long since guessed, attempted to show him what had happened by swimming south at full speed for over half an hour as she'd never done when the dust had hung on all sides. After thirty-five minutes the bull awoke from his semi-sleep and lofted one pectoral fin until he felt the sun. Neither breaching nor crying out, he swam south toward his family.

His first response to the light was caution, not abandon. As he felt it and heard his calf call out to the sky, he remembered the time just after the hurricane when *he* had swum on top to watch the sun, only to wake up blind in the night. This memory made him race. When he caught up he rose over the calf and forced him under, then reached down to soothe him. As the mother submerged to stroke him as well, the bull moved forward to shadow them both. His urgent calls made them remember how before the dust he had constantly tried to turn them from the light. They didn't understand his behavior any better now than before but they followed him down to thirty feet, and as the southward flight continued, he grew so distressed each time they lingered for even a second or two at the top after drawing breath that their concern made them keep on swimming low without knowing why.

The sooty cloud, gradually thinning ever since it left the north, had lost so much dust in polar cyclones that the Antarctic sky had been the last to dim and the first to clear. Chlorine gas had been in the stratosphere long before the cloud had come, and once the clearing was complete, it remained a threat to life. But the threat was slighter this year. One effect of the dust had been to heat the upper sky, precluding stratospheric clouds that could only form at temperatures lower than minus a hundred and seventeen. Without the freezing of water and nitrogen into ice clouds, the chlorine gas would react with them instead of with ozone, so that the dust, which depleted ozone everywhere else, actually lessened the loss at the pole. There the ozone decreased through reactions with nitrogen oxides, but these had thinned as they'd travelled south, and by the time they'd reached the Antarctic they couldn't rival chlorine monoxide at punching holes in the upper sky. If the whales were to die, it wouldn't be from the effects of radiation but because their prey had died under the dust.

Moving steadily southwest from longitude fifteen and latitude forty, they crossed two parallels every three days. When they passed the polar front the temperature on the surface dove from forty-seven to thirty-nine, and even the cautious bull could tell from the feeble warmth of the midday sun that it was milder than the glare that had put out his eyes. All three lingered more often at the top. The mother whale stayed by the calf, watching to see if he still shivered, but he gave no sign whatever of being cold. Though the general vacancy troubled the cow, it didn't surprise her after the silence to the north.

A day later, off South Georgia, there was further disappointment. The sea was empty of Falkland herring and blue whiting, always there in previous years. There were no birds, though this was the very height of summer, the time when most birds would normally have been fledged. Although the dust had gone, the sky was still a dusky gray. The strongest vestiges of precloud times were gales against the cliffs and the bite in the wind, for, despite the relative warmth of the air at thirty-five, its dryness made it as bitter as polar air.

More watchful than ever after the dark, the young male paused at a rise that broke the sea two hundred yards from shore. When he hung vertical to look at the concave rock, he saw a circular indentation where two pairs of wings lay on top of one another under pebbles with which waves had filled the hollow they'd worn down. He poked at the birds but his mother ignored them, having seen such sights before. Thick-billed prions who nested on subantarctic islands hunted krill in open sea during the day and were forced to return to their underground nests under cover of night to avoid the skuas who waited to seize them as they came down. Here off South Georgia some of the prions may have

259

hunted under the dust when it first came. The skua who'd taken these two had left just the bones and wings, the sole remains of life the young male saw.

The whales continued southwest for another five days to skirt the westernmost Orkney Island. Unable to nurture even the hardy tussock grasses of South Georgia, the Orkneys were always bleak but never before had they been devoid of life. Yet here the cold grew bracing as the westerlies blew at full speed in the moister air. In desperate whimsy the whales started to play, and when a southwest gale blew up in the early afternoon, they tried to see how long they could drift, now hitting a crest, now hanging still in the eerie calm between two waves. What at first seemed a thin white band far to their south swelled and neared with unnatural speed until the cow and calf were hurtled a hundred feet toward the sky. The games they'd enjoyed before the dust made them briefly forget their plight, but after five minutes their sense of danger came back again, stronger than ever. They continued southwest at seven knots beneath the storm, moving their flukes in a grim silence.

Just as the Orkneys began to fade, thin rafts of krill appeared on the sea. Overwhelmed with relief, the adults roared for joy and fed. Though the krill couldn't fill them, their spirits soared, and when she dove, the cow discovered shoals of whiting searching for prey at shallow depths. She followed the whiting. First myctophids, then shoals of krill appeared. Again they paused to feed on the sparse rafts. Minutes later more shoals of myctophids flashed by, followed by Patagonian hake hunting above their normal depth, and the cow remembered the myctophids darting around her as she'd swum toward the shelf the previous spring. More krill appeared. She fed again. Though the krill only lasted a few minutes, the three whales glowed, as if these poor meals had prefigured feasts to come.

Hope lightened the southward swim as they dodged the icebergs, thicker than ever. The night, ten hours long at latitude forty, shrank to barely more than seven as the Orkneys dropped from sight. After four days they neared Palmer Peninsula.

The calf swam with one pectoral fin against his father's side while the mother whale scouted ahead, calling loudly in the hope that false-bottom echoes would show up shoals of undersea krill. When her calls revealed nothing, she started edging through the jigsaw floes of the pack ice, diving and calling, hoping the underside of the ice would carry her voice to Minke Whales feeding close to shore.

She called with confidence at first. Like herself, the Minkes were fasters, and well fitted to wait out the dust. But no answers came. She looked around. There were none of the birds who had always filled this part of the ocean in the spring: fulmars, petrels, dove prions, and dozens of others who hunted for krill in the outer pack ice. She turned her head from side to side, scanning the sky, then lowered her eyes in disappointment.

After four hours of diving and rising they were south of Palmer Peninsula's northern tip, where they found a channel of varying width that ran southwest with the curve of the land. They followed this strait, the pack ice reaching in to within a hundred yards, then receding by as much as half a mile. There was always a strait between the shelf ice and the pack ice, created by current and melting patterns. Normally krill were thick along the eastern peninsula shelf, but generations had been wiped out by the dust and their replacements, still asleep, had yet to rise. The cow turned east into the pack ice.

She slowed. It was pancake ice, shredded by waves, partially melted by the sun, then refrozen into jagged, irregular sheets. On a small scale this was neither help nor harm, but over and over there was evidence of melting and refreezing. The total effect was dangerous. Once, when she penetrated for several miles, the ice panes visibly stretched, and she saw ridges of over twenty-five feet where giant floes had met under the dust and forced adjacent ice to rise. Under these ridges there were keels of a hundred feet, most of them solid, though a few had been eaten away by the concentrated brine that rotted the floes from the inside, giving them the look of Gruyère cheese. At last, when she turned back west, the ice feathered out into sludge and slush as the temperature wavered back and forth between twenty-nine and thirty. After feeding the hungry calf, who grumbled now, she didn't return into the pack, preferring clear sea. The melting ice had opened wide inviting lanes, then quickly refroze under the dust. The temperature change had only been slight under the cloud, but still, a reduction of four degrees over two months could have reversed the breakup completely.

Resigned, the whales remained inside the strait. When the adults dove they located krill—but they were patchy. The bull fed opportunistically, taking myctophid fish and tiny squid with various kinds of plankton. None of these were very abundant, but after several hours he quelled his hunger. The cow remembered the opportunistic feeding of the Fin and took fish also, but expended much more energy than the bull in seeking krill. After two hours she fed heavily on any kind of crustaceans she could find. The pain of her hunger briefly passed. In the final hours before dusk she led the bull and calf around the peninsula tip to the western side.

They swam in a dark-blue light, the sun just about to meet the western horizon. Here and there rafts of crustaceans spotted the sea, and the bull resumed his feeding while the cow, forgetting her hunger for the first time since South Georgia, looked at the rocks of Trinity Island and the guano that was visible even at dusk on the western shore. She swam toward it, the calf behind, then stroked up and down just off the peninsula's west coast to look at the penguins who now, with dusk, had started returning from the sea. Every year of her life these Adélie penguins had covered the snow-free rocky shores around Hope Bay, breeding in early to mid-October and taking turns at tending the eggs through the following month. When she was a calf, her mother had led her close enough to see the elbow-to-elbow crush of identical chicks who gaped and swayed on nests of stone.

The cow and calf swam slowly together and watched the penguins who remained. Once there'd been two hundred thousand. Now maybe two dozen had come in. Her home was dying. Though there was fishsound in the sea, it was weak, sporadic, and, while she heard birds in the evening sky, the endless flocks that once darkened the sun and moon had disappeared. The cow nudged the ears of the bull, who had drawn close. Though the ocean was far from bountiful, it held food, and she had her mate and calf. Yet she felt hollow. As they rested through the half-lit five-hour night, the cow and the bull were seldom more than a foot apart.

The bull remained alert while the cow slept. The night seemed silent, but after a couple of hours the instinctive sense that had let him feel the earth's magnetic field over the Mid-Atlantic Ridge made him aware of other electromagnetic fields passing into the sky. Farther south, in winter, these fields were carried in the aurora australis or southern lights. Though now they left no visible sign, the bull was so sensitive to the forces in the sky that the restlessness he had felt over the ridge started to trouble him once more. To dispel it, he took to swimming back and forth in the ice-free water. After a minute or two it passed and he rested again. Then, after midnight, just as he settled down to sleep, he sensed something else. Electrical waves two seconds long plunged from the sky. They dropped in an instant from thirty thousand to less than five hundred cycles a second. As with the electrical fields before, the bull couldn't hear them but he felt them with the part of his mind that told him his direction, and the feeling brought an overwhelming nostalgia for the Greenland fjord and the summer days with his mate.

He grunted, hurt that this yearning, long subdued, should trouble him while he slept by his cow and calf. His heightened awareness of the electrical waves soon passed, but the memory made him feel uprooted. As he watched his family sleeping nearby as if they'd been with him all his life, he couldn't fathom his discontent and he swam in narrow circles, on edge again.

He couldn't know the power he'd sensed had been a lightning bolt near the north magnetic pole, its sound carried south in the ionized channels that layered the earth with an aerial skin, nor that the farther south he swam the stronger his sense of these polar disturbances would grow. Perhaps if he'd still had his sight he'd have noticed them less. They didn't trouble the cow or calf. He puffed and sighed as he went still. After an hour he grew more settled. For weeks it had seemed that the Greenland fjord meant nothing now and might as well have never been. The night grew unusually calm but he didn't sleep. Two hours before dawn the cow and calf awoke and led him back into the strait off the peninsula's east shore. He followed numbly, as if two strangers were leading him. Then, as the feed proved even more meager than yesterday, the pain of hunger superseded his sense of displacement. Mindful of nothing else, the three hunted together down the strait.

263

CHAPTER

25

THOUGH high radiation levels had
entered the foodchain in the Antarctic just as they had everywhere else,
the highest concentration had been in diatoms which had died for lack
of light before the three Blue Whales had passed the polar front. Krill
who had risen from their winter sleep before the nuclear night had
starved when the diatoms had died. Each year the dormant krill from
the previous winter rose in a series of blooms, with the oldest rising first.
The last to rise had only been eggs the previous year, carried downward
in the convergence at the polar front, then southward in the currents
near the floor. When upwelling stopped under the dust, dormant krill
ceased to rise until the light returned.

Thus the Blue Whale bull and cow, who had fasted farther north, had absorbed only slight radiation after crossing the polar front. In this they were luckier than other whales who had entered the Antarctic in early spring and steadily fed until the initial bloom of diatoms and krill had disappeared. Some of those earlier arrivals had sunk to the bottom, while others were visible only to seals or McCormick's skuas who, flying north in the deepening cold of the polar dusk, might glimpse a frozen side or fin slightly protruding from the pack ice like the tip of some splintered hull that had gone under.

Since gaining Palmer Peninsula the bull had eaten squid and fish along with the sparse krill. The cow ate fish as well, though her ever deepening hunger for euphausiids sometimes drew her into the ice. Near the middle of February, rising to breathe at a crack in the ice, she saw the snout of a dead Minke sticking up from a ridge where expanding floes had met. For some time after, she resigned herself to the meager yield in the strait.

They continued south toward the Antarctic Circle. The day was eighteen hours long. The time of dormancy was ending for some krill and the number of shoals slightly increased. There seemed to be more birds the farther the whales swam, but the krill never even remotely approached their former numbers. They had travelled fifty miles down the peninsula when the female heard the calls of Minke Whales.

They were calling from inside the pack ice, and when she heard them her first thought was that they were feasting on polar krill. Unable to see them, she entered the ice for the final time and after fifteen minutes finally discovered a breathing space. She pushed her snout out and bobbed up and down in an effort to widen the crack. Rotten ice peeled off like skin till she pushed out the upper half of her head. As soon as they saw her head rise out, the frantic Minkes gave out desperate high-pitched calls. The sounds made her heart stop. The three were trapped in a water-filled basin on the surface of the ice, and now that she was closer, their ratchets and pings identified them unmistakably as three of the four she'd embraced in the joyful reunion of last year: three of the whales who had saved her life.

She pushed strenuously at the ice hole with her head until she could see the creamy shoulder patches and blazing bands of white on the pectoral fins. Suddenly joy eclipsed her hunger. She let out a roar, then

265

dove and swam a zigzag course in their general direction, looking up for places where light poured in through cracks.

She intended to free them, but cautious after seeing the dead Minke, she sought openings from which she could pummel the ice without getting too far away from her air supply. After three minutes a narrow space of open water appeared ahead. She rose and breathed, then, swimming on, called explosively to the bull and calf who'd started to follow her in.

The closer she came to the Minke Whales, the more open water there was. Soon she saw krill in enormous swarms. She called again, especially loudly. Then she dove, the Minkes two hundred yards away. In a matter of seconds their calls were vibrating the ice above her head.

The Minkes had been resting, half-awake between two floes the sun had hollowed, when a sudden shift in adjacent ice had pushed the floes together. In both a concave hollow a few feet deep ran lengthwise down the top. With the Minkes resting on the surface, the two hollows had enclosed them. They had awakened to find themselves trapped in a concave depression slowly filling with meltwater, solid ice beneath and around them. As the bull and calf joined the cow under the hollow where the Minkes slowly starved, they heard the three whales *ping* and clatter and give out a hundred high-pitched sounds. The signals stabbed the female Blue, bringing back the death of her mother, her childhood rescue, and the days of happy feasts with her foster family. As soon as the bull was at her side the mother dove, then rose for seven hundred feet, levelling slightly near the top to hit the ice with her upper back. The Minkes made loud excited clatters, feeling the ice vibrate beneath them. The cow swam back to breathe at the opening, two hundred yards west. The calf went with her. Both heard the bull whale strike the ice and then once more the Minkes' calls.

After swimming back to the whales, the cow became frantic when she surmised the ice wouldn't break. Remembering reunions of before, she went belly-up beneath the keel, pressing her pectoral fins against it, as if to embrace her terrified friends on the other side. She strained to see them through the ice, but it was far too thick to reveal them. Even so, as she heard them clatter, she warmed inside at their unique signature calls. More memories rose. Dimly she saw their effortless breaches and remembered them herding myctophids to the top, remembered the searching submarine. Staying still, she imagined them shivering above her with their pectorals pressing the thick ice in the same place as her own. Her pectorals warmed despite the cold. It seemed likely that the Minke Whales would die. She roared and struck the ice again.

An hour passed. With the bull and calf she pounded the ice until blood spotted her head, but it only splintered into chips. The keels stayed firm. She rose again and again from nearly nine hundred feet to hit the ice, and, every time, the Minkes made loud, excited noises, feeling it vibrate. They were still clicking in frequencies she had heard in childhood, and she could see her mother clearly in her mind, so absorbed in her vision she failed to notice how the krill had begun to burgeon on every side.

The Minkes never stopped their encouragement, but after two hours it was clear that the thirty-foot thickness wouldn't break. The Blue Whales breathed at the nearest space, then, instead of returning to the Minkes, continued on toward the strait. As soon as they saw this the Minkes made chilling, high-pitched screams, and the mother whale began to race to get farther away.

They reached the open water she had discovered by swimming toward the Minke Whales. The water extended for only a few square yards—yet it bled with krill, the swarm extending down for several hundred feet. The Minkes screamed even more loudly as the Blues engulfed the krill. Both adults moaned with pleasure as they tightened their swollen throats. Eager at first to leave her friends behind, now the cow closed her ears against them, feeding so noisily that, under the sea, her own ecstatic grunts drowned out their screams. Suddenly nothing mattered but krill. When after half an hour the adults paused to rest, both could feel upwelling water against their skin. When after an hour the bull led the calf back to the strait, swimming southwest, he could see that krill were swarming both to the north and south. It was as if the Minkes had come into sight at the same time as the diatom blooms, the upwelling sea, and the sun had ignited the dormant shoals and lifted them to life.

They feasted for hours in sight of the Minkes, the sirenlike screams constant at first, then more and more sporadic with exhaustion. The bull and cow fed all that day and well into the night, literally eating their way south, away from the Minkes, the high-pitched cries still coming occasionally from the horizon long after the creamy shoulder marks and pectoral stripes had passed from sight.

The mother mourned after feeding but didn't turn back. For the rest of that week they ate very well, but when they ventured into shore they could feel ice starting to form beside the shelf. This surprised the bull and the calf but not the cow, for though it was only mid-February, this was the Weddell Sea where the clockwise motion of currents off Palmer Peninsula sharply isolated the water from the seasonal weather patterns farther north. The cow didn't notice that the ice was a little later and a little thinner than usual. Krill stayed thick wherever she swam.

She started heading north. Her memory of the Minkes hurt her deeply. Besides her family, they seemed to have been the sole survivors of the dust. Each time she looked at the ice she burned with grief and frustration.

The channel was wider now, and despite the thin new ice, wind was rafting offshore floes farther apart. The Minkes were dead when she swam past, no longer in sight, since the basin had deepened and the keels were finally breakable, too late. She could make out giant petrels half hopping and half flying as they rose in and out of the basin to pick at her friends. These were the first giant petrels the cow had seen since the dust. There were just three, and yet she had the sense the Antarctic was filling up with survivors.

During their northward swim the bull and cow seldom stopped feeding. The krill kept increasing, sometimes thickening hour by hour as if racing to keep up with the plants. Between the krill and the spaces of blue-green water the diatoms browned the sea for miles. More and more often the calf would try to eat with his parents, swelling his throat in sidewise runs, though his baleen was still too coarse to hold in krill. By the end of March, still suckling at a length of forty-eight feet, he finally supplemented his milk with euphausiids while his parents fed almost twenty-four hours a day.

By mid-April they were back at the northern tip of Palmer Peninsula. The night was almost fourteen hours long, and low-altitude easterlies, virtually constant off the coast during the winter, blew more often, bringing drizzle to the peninsular tip while slightly warming the air. Surface easterlies also penetrated inland, covering both the Filchner Ice Shelf and the perpetual snow beyond. Over the pole the hole in the atmosphere was the size of New York State. Ever attentive to the sky, both bull and cow could sense that the pressure steadily dropped when they swam north. This continued out to latitude sixty-five, where open sea westerlies were brushing coastal easterlies to start a high-altitude mix. This year the stratosphere would warm. Already the turbulent, swirling air created storms that carried heat down from the north to raise the temperature in the lowest part of the stratosphere, eight miles above the dry, snow-covered land.

The strengthening wind and lessening light made the cow restless. Her summer feed had been adequate and she was eager to swim north, pushed partly by sex but also by her memory of the Minkes. With their death the entire Antarctic seemed to have changed. Its emptiness had saddened her already before the Minkes had come into sight, but now it hurt her even more, reminding her constantly that they were gone. She began to listen to the sky for minutes on end, as if she could hear, or sense, the stratospheric cyclones overhead. The advance of the dust had slowed the cyclones in the spring and reversed their direction in early summer. Now, when she slept, a part of her mind could hear them whistle and roar in the old way, many miles up. The upper altitudes to the north were growing clear, and all three whales could hear great vortices of cloud blow in from the north, swollen with rain, for the temperate sky held water, something impossible under the sterile cloud of dust.

One day the cow swam north for fifty miles without looking back. The bull followed passively at first, while the calf at his side made grumbling sounds, sensing the timing was all wrong. The cow remembered from earlier years that females with calves were always last to arrive and first to leave in the short Antarctic summer, but she forgot that first-year calves were always weaned before the fall so they'd be able to feed themselves in their austral winter north of the front. Born late, this youngster wouldn't be weaned till May at the earliest, and he was eager to keep up his krill intake at least until that time. Neither the bull nor the calf wanted to leave.

The icebergs were less frequent and the floes farther apart as dusk came on. There was a fight just after twilight when the bull, with great reluctance, butted the mother whale from below. She butted back, but when he led the calf away she followed him.

When the calf was weaned in mid-May he was fifty-three feet long, and at the tip of Palmer Peninsula day lasted less than eight hours. Having survived so much with his parents, he was unwilling to leave them now. His mother's body was still responding to the changes in the light. They told her to move, for conceptions occurred in the warm sea.

Again at her instigation, they swam north. But in early June, when they approached latitude forty, the sun was harsh against their skin. There were no scattering-layer sounds nor were there birds when they swam past Nightingale Island, no Right Whale calls from Tristan da Cunha.

Still, they continued north, the cow in the lead. The glare was stronger than ever before, not from chlorine, which had no effect at these latitudes, but from the depletion of the ozone by nitrogen oxides that had been borne by the cloud of dust. The painful glare, along with the emptiness, turned her back in the middle of June. Until July the three whales rested in the southern subantarctic, where overcast sky and constant storm shut out the sun. More and more often the cow would touch her genital area to the bull's and blow bubbles and flirt as she had on their first meeting. Her desire increased each day, and as the bull responded more and more passionately, they caressed and played for hours at a time, never far from the calf. As conception approached, the courtly play intensified with every hour. The adults glowed. Sometimes, as they spun through shadow and light with their lengths touching, the calf would fit his motion to theirs, but he could feel his separateness. The female had ceased to grieve at the desolation of her home, and with the resurgence of her sex drive even the Minkes faded from mind. Only the bull and calf held her attention.

In early July the image of the young male dolphin entered the bull's mind, though there'd been nothing to evoke it. Its abruptness troubled

270

him. It lasted all one day. It would fade, then rise up again, and he stopped his play with the cow each time it came.

Early in the second week of July, he realized one morning that there were ripples and faint hisses not far off, the kind of noise that came when large schools tried to travel without sound. He hung still, watching the image in his mind. It frightened him. The dolphin was lingering to admire him, though two of the others had already fled. The old whale pondered to himself. Where had that been?

He tensed at a sound in the water. But it was only the female breaching at his side. He touched her fin. She was hovering in fear, all her attention in her ears. Orcas were coming.

26

THE Killer Whales had been mov-
ing toward the Blues for several hours, drawn by their calls. The shaking
bull started to flee as soon as he realized they were near. Both cow and
calf stayed silent as he led them back toward the polar front. No matter
how fast they swam the Orcas kept closing. The calf's heart raced as he
caught his father's fear. When the Orcas had closed to a couple of miles,
the bull whale stopped, faced the cow and calf and urged them south,
then turned to race full speed for the northeast, calling loudly. He
couldn't know whether the Orcas would pursue him or his family or split
up to go after both. Conceivably they could kill him and go on to kill
the calf and cow, for the Orcas were fast and could overcome the head
start, though absolute silence might save the two. When the whales

272

split up, the Orcas knew they had been heard, and they began to utter the terrifying screams that sometimes paralyzed their prey. All three Blue Whales maintained their speed and direction, and the Orcas seemed to waver. Their target had been the calf, since they had weakened under the dust and it required much exertion to kill a big Blue Whale. They hovered for a moment, still. Then the bull paused and called a dozen times. The Killer Whales swam after him.

The cow and calf, continuing toward the polar front, were two miles south when the Orcas started to close on the bull a second time. He swam at full speed in the arching motion the whalers called panting, at the surface constantly, but he couldn't push himself any faster than eighteen knots. A strange abstraction overtook him as he realized they would reach him very shortly and probably slice him apart. He remembered how the Orcas in the north had headed him toward the whale shark and the Spotted Dolphins, finally letting him go, and found himself urging someone or something, perhaps himself, to make something similar happen again. When he grew vehement in his urging, he started to moan, as if the high-speed swim were wearing down his strength.

But there were no other targets in swimming range except his cow and calf, and no matter how much he feared for his life, he would sooner perish piecemeal from the Orcas' teeth than have his family die. He tried in vain to increase his speed. The Orcas called once more and he could tell they were a quarter mile behind. In his mind he saw the towering dorsals, and memories came in rapid succession: Beluga Whales rolling belly-up in terror and submission; the gobbets of flesh jerking down the Orcas' throats as the Spotted Dolphins were ripped and bolted one after the other; the young male dolphin who'd admired him before turning to flee. In his desperation he made spastic exhalations, for he was weeping now in his way, and still he saw the young male dolphin in his mind.

The Orcas closed till a cluster of five or six were swimming beside and below each eye. The bull's inability to see tormented him. The look of their eyes or their bearing might reveal that they had approached him only out of curiosity, for they were as intelligent as the dolphins, and when they were full, they often inspected passing rorquals out of interest. Their high-frequency clicks surrounded him, and in his terror he tried to guess what they might mean. Ten minutes passed. Against

273

his will he'd been slowing down ever since they'd come. If he sped forward, seven Orcas at his snout slapped his head with their flukes and swam shoulder to shoulder, making him slow for fear of angering them to the point where they would turn and use their teeth.

He was larger than they'd expected. They seemed undecided whether to kill him or seek smaller, easier prey. After an hour it was clear that, if nothing else, they meant to control his swimming. Twice when he tried to dive the dozen beneath him butted his stomach and chest, and his first injury wasn't a deep bite but a shallow rake across his undersides. The sight of that opening seemed to decide the Killer Whales. He swam high to placate them, and yet, when his head had risen clear, a dozen advanced from behind and more from the sides to breach and drop on his rostrum, each between five and nine tons.

He felt his skull was breaking. He dove in pain, a ringing sound inside both ears, and yet no sooner had he dropped below the top than the dozen Orcas underneath him started using their teeth in earnest, ripping out gouge after gouge of flesh. They were excited now, and that made them stronger. This was the worst pain he had ever felt in his life, deeper by far than the pain of the long-lined harpoon he'd taken in his side off northern Newfoundland, incomparably sharper than the dog-fish slicing pieces from his sides. He started to groan again, more deeply this time, a labored, low-frequency pulse from his larynx and head.

He lifted his head, exhaling desperately. Yet, when he tried to breathe, the whales swimming beside him breached and fell, bringing their sides down hard on his blowholes while the dozen below rose like battering rams at his chest, trying to force the breath from him.

He took in water as much as air before the succession of surface blows knocked him under again. His lower jaw dropped open as he vomited. As soon as it fell four Orcas ahead of his snout wheeled to slice pieces out of his tongue, while others closed their teeth on the outward edge of the open jaw and hung there, weighing it down while the others fed. With a great effort he managed to close his jaw, but now the cavern of his mouth was full of blood, which streamed out of his lips. He went vertical in his agony, trying to dive, waving his flukes high in the air like a Right Whale, but as soon as he did the Orcas behind him leaped from the water and closed their jaws along the outside edge of his tail.

The bull had no teeth and, though he was fast, the Killer Whales were more maneuverable and faster. When unweakened by disease, they could kill even Sperm Whale bulls, and the Blue was their natural prey. It had always been so. All his life, even before he had seen them kill, he had instinctively known that the tall black fins meant death to Rights and rorquals. Even before he had learned to fear the catcher boats, he'd known enough to avoid Killer Whales. And yet there'd been times when he had dared to face down a solitary or pair for the sake of his calves. He waved his flukes in the air to shake the Orcas free so he could dive. The teeth bit deeper. He roared, then exhaled again with the desperate crying sound of before but this time more powerfully, as if he were trying to empty himself of fear. The cow and calf had turned back north a little way and they heard his roar. Thrusting upward with a violent twist of his spine, he lofted his tailfins higher into the air and thrashed them back and forth until the Orcas who had been biting them fell back into the sea. His head under the surface, he heard them break the waves. As soon as he did he brought down his flukes with a force of impact that could instantly kill them, but in a split second the Killer Whales had darted out of the way and as soon as his thrashing stopped they were on him again.

By the time he started to dive they had sliced so many pieces from his flukes that they were ragged and couldn't propel him effectively. Concentrating entirely on his tail, they splintered the place where the flukes were attached to the vertebrae, and despite the strength of the ligaments, the caudal vertebral connection came apart. Now, instead of pushing water, the flukes waved uselessly back and forth, up on the downstroke, down on the upstroke. Still, he dove a little way. In sudden fear that he might get away the Orcas descended en masse to bite at his undersides, slicing out gouges six feet wide. Blood from his body filled the holes. He rose again, and again as he cleared the top the hammer-blow breaching drove him under. But the Orcas were laboring painfully. They alternated roles, five or six feeders slicing gouges out of his sides while the rest of the pack kept up the herding. The next time he rose there was a bleeding hole where his dorsal fin had been, and on his next descent one Orca raked its teeth across his head and bolted ovals of white meat. By now the flukes were completely gone and the bull could only move by stroking with the lower part of his spine.

In earlier crises he had been able to escape his pain by entering a semi-conscious state. There was no anesthesia for this. He no longer roared, but his low-frequency sounds never let up, sometimes rising in pitch and lasting for five or ten seconds when the Orcas took an especially large piece, though mostly he groaned in a rhythm of labored bursts with a second or two between.

The Orcas' labor steadily wore them down. Though they seemed strong, they were all half starved and ailing from their time under the dust. They had survived by taking seals, penguins, and fish in the subantarctic and below the polar front. All had ingested radiation. Out of more than a hundred, these thirty alone remained, and the pod was shrinking by two or three every other day. With evening they groaned and puffed almost as heavily as the whale, tired out from their work.

Exhaustion ended the feast. Those at the head were the first to stop and move off. The others followed ten minutes later, though the bull was in such pain and shock he couldn't tell when they had gone. The white-water boil moving across the sea all day had brought a few prions who'd watched for a moment or two, then turned and flown away. Both sea and sky seemed bare of scavengers.

The bull hung still on the rippling surface, though he had to stroke with his stub of a tail to keep from sinking. When the calls of the cow and calf came from the south he didn't hear them. His groans kept up, but they were higher now. The sound didn't carry far under the water and the steadily searching cow and calf didn't pick it up for several hours. When they found him, he was stroking at barely two knots with his stub.

The cow and calf accompanied the bull, one on each side, the cow making submissive calflike sounds and sometimes bubbles as she had on their first meeting. She touched her fin to a place on his side where the blubber was thick, a ridge between two arching holes. The calf swam silently, in shock at the sight of his father, finless, gouged from nose to tail with crimson openings deeper than half a foot, most of them high and wide enough to hold three or four dolphins inside, all trailing blood, as did the mouth and tail and the crimson pulp around the cloudy eyes.

The bull only groaned, never acknowledging the calflike sounds of the cow nor giving any sign that he knew the youngster. Though it pained him to flex his lower spine, he stroked constantly, seemingly intent on some destination, never stopping even when cow and calf swam under him to cushion part of his weight. When after forty minutes they moved away, blood covered both. Now they were roughly

276

sixty-five miles north of South Georgia and the polar front. The bull swam at only one knot, yet he still kept stroking toward the south, as if some remedy awaited him beside the winter ice.

His stroke finally stopped. Both cow and calf followed his dive. It began snout-first but after eighty feet was haphazard, with now snout, now tail, and now one of his sides facing the top. As they followed just behind, the cow and calf remembered the times he'd led them both toward the sunless zone and the times when he'd hung silently in the twilight to hear the scattering layer rise. They followed him far into the dark, past five hundred feet where all the shining fish had dimmed, the glowing shrimp, the ctenophores, the fiery squid. After a thousand feet they turned back up again, letting him go, and, when they broke into the air with heavy breaths, the surface seemed as bare as the deep. Neither made loud sounds, though they bobbed for over an hour in the waves. From time to time the cow made curious low clicks that had no meaning. The pair hung still for nearly two hours. Then the cow called very faintly to the calf and, together, they swam for the polar front.

CHAPTER
27

OVER the next five years the mother whale seldom travelled far beyond the polar front, although the male would sometimes swim for temperate seas till she called him back, remembering the glare and the area where she'd first heard the Killer Whales. He always returned.

He grieved whenever he saw his dying father in his mind, yet after six months, when the cutting pain became tolerable, he would find himself waking from dreams with his father's roar in his ears as it had come down to him from the north during the combat with the Orcas. The sound aroused pride as much as grief, and after two years, the memory of his barely conscious father stroking beside him at one knot, ripped to pieces and laboring blindly for the south, began to be balanced by his ever more substantial dream of the fight against the Orcas. All his life the male had been haunted by the image of Orca fins. They'd first aroused him off Ascension after his birth and he had dreamed of them often since then, especially since his father's death. In the isolation under the dust he had come to know his father's love more deeply than other calves. It hadn't surprised him to see his father offer himself to the Orcas to save his family. There had been rage in the bull's call out of the north, and the memory of it stirred the young Blue Whale. The desire to mate and to shield his mate and calf from danger was blind instinct, and yet because of his father it also stirred his waking dreams. But he and his mother lived in isolation. During the hours when he wasn't dreaming, feeding, or sleeping he felt imprisoned.

Sex heightened the torment. While the bull had lived, there'd been sexual excitement in the strokes and pats the three whales had exchanged, and as the male became mature, his calflike gestures—nudging his mother's breasts or pressing one pectoral fin against her side—took on a new significance. By the time he was seventy-four feet long at five years old, the mother whale would run her side along his side as they nudged each other's genital zones. This play relaxed the male, who in normal times would have flirted with juveniles above the polar front. The cow remembered the young bull she'd met one year in the austral seas, and it hurt her to see the calf's loneliness.

The hole in the atmosphere over the pole began to shrink, and the Antarctic ice became more populated each year. Maneuvering their way through pack ice in late September or October, the bull and his mother would see silken-coated seal pups swim over the snow with lateral strokes of the fins and tail. Diving, they'd hear crabeaters feeding noisily on all sides, their voices amplified by the ice. They reminded the mother whale of the time before the dust, but the population, maybe six thousand, was small compared with the hundreds of thousands there had been.

The birds recovered more slowly, though every spring the returning flocks cast longer shadows on the snow. The cow saw birds she had forgotten: Wilson's petrels, blue-eyed cormorants, Antarctic petrels, Arctic terns. Sometimes the sky was loud with flocks of black-backed gulls, and once in a while a Kerguelen petrel came from far inside the

279

coast, usually high, steadily stroking as if intent on some far destination. More delicate and erratic was the flight of the snow petrels, which made the cow both happy and sad, for, like the Adélie penguins on Palmer Peninsula, these were birds she had missed when the bull had been at her side.

Like the bull in his fjord, the cow lived in the past. The burgeoning strength of the male and their tender erotic play lifted her more frequently as time passed, yet both remained lonely.

They listened for other whales. More and more frequently they could hear Right Whale Dolphins or Killer Whales pass in isolated groups of two or three. Since the passing of the cloud, Right Whale Dolphins had begun to live below the polar front. Always the sounds of Orcas inflamed the youngster. Yet they never heard large whales. It was as if the nuclear night had pushed the smaller Antarctic cetaceans almost to extinction, but had reserved oblivion for the giants alone. The pattern of feeding that had saved the cow and calf had especially endangered other whales. While they might fast for half the year, large whales made up for it when they fed, eating tons of radioactive crustaceans every day. Their sky had darkened so gradually that both before and during the nuclear night Antarctic whales had far outstripped Ivory Coast dolphins in the speed and scale at which they'd absorbed radiation. Because the Blue Whale cow and calf had arrived late in the year of the dust, they'd missed the extinctions. Now, in the midst of returning life, they were alone.

It was September. The male had entered his sixth year. As in every other year since his father's death, he'd wintered with his mother just north of the polar front. Though his mother feared to go farther north, she led him farther west each winter, hoping to locate other whales. This year they had almost circumnavigated Antarctica.

Just east of the Kerguelens, the mother whale fed lightly on the early spring euphausiids, sparse as yet. The male hung off by himself in the rolling sea, watching the sky. For five years he had seen sunlight wax and wane above the ice. In previous years the lengthening light of September and October had meant only that the krill were on the rise and that he and his mother would soon swim toward the land. This year it meant more. Under the muscles of his back his cylindrical testes had matured. They produced sperm in response to the season's light.

A restlessness stronger than any he'd felt before began to possess him, despite the fact that he'd just travelled six thousand miles. Frequent sleep, slow speed, and lack of a destination made the westward swims more restful than northward or southward migration. When the male and his mother had first begun swimming west in wintertime they'd always returned the way they'd come, travelling a thousand miles at most. This year they'd never bothered to turn back.

The male kept watching the sun, anxiously swimming back and forth. He wished to be calm, wished he were still swimming west in his winter daze. He remembered March, when they'd swum among flat, tabular bergs off the Amundsen Sea and the seven-hour light had only made him sleepy. In May, off the Ross Sea, the slightly longer light had found him drowsing while he swam.

The male had only awakened when the cow called to a pod of Minke Whales who'd wintered just at the edge of the ice. There'd been excitement as he and his mother had passed among them, and both envisioned the ice-bound whales they'd tried to help. He clenched his lids, darkening the light behind his eyes. This wasn't the first year since his father's death his mother and he had encountered Minke Whales, but each time it happened they became hopeful of finding Blues.

There'd been a tense expectancy in the mother whale after the Minkes had passed from sight, but after a month it had started to die. The male remembered the hours off Wilkes Land in mid-June when they'd hung close to the permanent pack ice off to the south. The light hadn't lasted six hours, and gales had kept them at depths where it had been black as midnight all the time. Looking back on it, he remembered he'd been at peace. He missed the dark. July found them at latitude fifty-five where the day had been eight hours long again. Now, near the Kerguelens, it was ten.

He opened his eyes, no calmer than when he'd closed them. The sun still blazed. He trembled, feeling raw inside with the knowledge he'd never mate.

* * *

281

The upwelling and melt had begun especially early, and the euphausiids thickened over the next few days. The cow began edging in for the permanent pack ice. During the great feasts that ensued, the days were thirteen hours long.

The male fed well, but often the cow would pause to watch him from a distance. He'd hover vacantly, head down, only his back breaking the sea. When he'd been sexually immature there'd been erotic play between them for hours at a time, and it had been satisfying then. Now, even though she caressed him as before, she couldn't ease the ache of his mating drive.

She never stopped trying. Sometimes she imitated her mate, stroking the sensitive spots on the young male's head and back and lowing very softly. The male would reply in kind, but she could tell from the feeble pressure of his fins that the strokes were dismissive. He seemed beyond help, as so often before. She remembered again her own loneliness before the bull had come, knowing all too well what the young male felt.

The feeding below the Kerguelens was as good as off the Palmer Peninsula. The pair stayed put until January, when they heard what they thought were whale calls from north of the polar front. The cow replied and swam at once for the Indian Ocean, with the male racing ahead.

They passed Heard Island, the two McDonald Islands, and then the Kerguelen archipelago, at full speed. As if enraged, elephant seals roared from the shores of the Kerguelens, but the Blues had ears for nothing except the signal to the north: a twelve-hertz *hrrrooomph*. The male's heart raced when at dusk the whale came into sight.

She was lighter than the cow and calf, an almost silvery gray, and, while she greeted the male, the mother whale held off and watched from the side. The stranger hung near the surface where the light silhouetted her. The mother gazed. She'd never seen such a whale before.

The stranger measured sixty-six feet from her snout to the notch of her flukes, nine feet shorter than the bull, and yet her length from throat to anus was conspicuously long compared to his. Her length from anus to flukes was shorter, making her look almost top-heavy.

The pair were shy with each other. The male swam parallel to the cow as they called softly back and forth. When the cow turned to face him directly, he saw that her head was narrow, its middle width maybe a quarter of its length. She puzzled him, as he sensed an affinity despite her strange appearance.

Aside from her mother, this sexually mature Pygmy Blue had seen only one other rorqual the size of these two: the Fin who had come from the west six years ago. She'd been disappointed when her mother had led her away from the lonely Fin, and when the female Blue drew up to forty yards, the Pygmy wheeled, waving her flukes in invitation just as the Fin had done, and diving at full speed. Both mother and calf followed her down. The Pygmy Blue had been alone for so long that the two huge whales beside her looked like images in a dream, and she kept veering from side to side between the pair, touching them both to reassure herself they were really there. When all three surfaced she started feeding again on euphausia vallentini which, unlike the euphausia superba, had taken years to recover from the dust cloud. Seeing the small krill thick on the sea, the mother remembered her months of confusion off Argentina in the year the calf had been born. Stirrings of sympathy came with the memory. She virtually ran at the other whale, caressed the length of her throat, then continued down to the notch between her flukes. The Pygmy bubbled. Together the three made runs through the krill.

The difference between the Pygmy Blue and the bull involved more than appearance. Less specialized than the giants, Pygmies fed mainly above the polar front, and when the big Blue Whales moved south of the front on feeding migrations, the Pygmy Blues went north to breed or give birth in subtropical sea.

The rest of the Pygmies had been wiped out by the dust, though the only death this cow had seen had been her mother's. She had been close to death herself when the dust had passed, barely surviving the fever, vomit, and gastrointestinal pain that had come with the radiation. Now she lived calmly, unreflectively, seldom travelling very far, much as her mother had lived in the years before the dust. This year, as throughout the previous five, the Pygmy cow had been alone.

The next day she followed them south of the polar front, but by noon of the day after that she'd turned back north again, preferring euphausia vallentini to the larger polar krill that had sustained her in the first years after the dust. Still, she wouldn't have returned all the way if the bull hadn't followed. She was in estrus and had an instinctive desire to migrate north to a place west of the Mid-Indian Ridge where she envisioned mating with the young Blue. She had only been there twice before, in the year of her birth and the year of the dust, but her mind filled up with a beckoning light when she recalled its sun at noon. She saw herself and the male together, swimming off islands twelve hundred miles from Africa, over the black Mauritius Trench. During the years since the dust she had ceased to have dreams and desires, and that emptiness made this vision all the more brilliant. She spent every hour with the young male.

Two nights went by. The daylight lasted more than seventeen hours. Sex hormones flooded the young bull's blood. On the third morning the Pygmy cow turned quietly for the north and swam without stopping. The young bull followed immediately. His mother came too, though delaying an hour for a solid feed of krill. From the beginning the young male had been adaptable in his feeding, never forgetting how his mother and father had eaten squid and fish during his first Antarctic spring. As he swam north, he called out to his mother but didn't slow down. She meant to follow till dusk and rejoin the pair under the stars.

At noon the mother whale heard Killer Whales swim by in the male's direction, and she called loudly to turn them around. When they did her heart rate doubled. All three were in sight by midafternoon, and as she watched them, maybe eighty yards to her east, she could see they were systematically searching the ice floes that had drifted up from the south. She watched for twenty minutes as they craned their heads over one floe after another, seeking cowering seals, and finding only penguins.

The birds were dead. She watched in amazement as the Orcas rocked the small floes back and forth until the birds dropped into the sea. They nosed the bodies, as if they were going to eat them. All three were scrawny compared to others she had seen, but the death of her mate had made her cautious about Orcas, whatever their size. Finally they left the floating birds and swam toward her. As they approached, the mother shook and tensed herself against the screams she recalled from when Orcas had chased her mate.

The screams never came. Just before they drew up on her, the first bull dove and the other two followed. They were much shorter than

284

those she remembered, only seventeen feet long. Soon from below she could hear rapidfire clicks as they herded fish. The hunting kept on for a quarter hour within two hundred yards of the cow. She shook again as she waited to see what they'd do.

At last fear overcame her and she headed south in panic, racing hard. When she looked back the Orcas had surfaced and she thought they were going to follow. They dove and she fled again but after a quarter hour of silence she paused, then waited for half an hour. No Orcas came. If it hadn't been for her memory of the attack she would have forgotten them.

With late afternoon she followed the young bull but didn't call, wanting no answering sounds that Orcas might overhear. By dusk, when she thought it likely the Orcas had gone, she signalled loudly, eager to join him.

At first no answer came, but she wasn't surprised. Long-range calls evaded the ears of both the sender and receiver more often than not when they were in motion. Her hope of rejoining the calf dimmed when after twelve hours she'd still heard nothing. After six weeks of haphazard search and fruitless calling in the unfamiliar sea, she started home. She thought of the Fin. By the end of February she'd rounded the Cape of Good Hope and turned southwest.

In March the polar krill moved clockwise around the gleaming Weddell Sea, and the sky, though hardly alive with wings, was seldom bare. The cow would feed in desperate rushes despite her enormous blubber stores, calling loudly, as if there were other whales nearby. Sometimes an Arctic tern would swoop to see what had caused the commotion, and as it neared, the cow's distended throat and side-turned head would grow huge in its eyes. The bird would snatch krill and fly on, dipping repeatedly till almost out of sight. When it returned minutes later, still dipping and feeding, the cow would as often as not be still, her regular spouts rising brilliant white from a single place in the sea. Some nights, off the western coast of Palmer Peninsula, the hundred Adélie penguins who'd yet to leave for their wintering grounds could hear loud *huffs* come out of nowhere. The noise made them uneasy, as they were either too young to know or had already forgotten the sound of the great whales.

In early April the cow swam northwest toward the South American coast to seek out companions. The krill had been thick. Floating in fat, she recalled her time with the unborn calf. Past the polar front the light stayed soft, like the light on the Indian sea. Yet the ocean was bare and she discerned no birds in the sky.

She swam to the Patagonian shelf and up the coast, remembering Right and Humpback Whales eating grimothea in the Gulf of St. George. The sky stayed bare, but plankton grew thick over the shelf. By mid-April she was well past Santa Cruz, approaching the gulf. In the middle of May, after a month of fruitless search, she turned back for Antarctica.

She returned at a leisurely pace, not regaining the austral seas till late July. When September came she tried once more to find the bull in the Indian Ocean, remaining there till late December, once in a while seeing an albatross or tern or school of fish, but never hearing any reply to her long-range calls. In January she swam back toward the sea off Palmer Peninsula.

The euphausiids were thick. Feeling the sun warm on her skin, she closed her eyes to hear their strange subsonic chatter and the dull low-frequency sounds of the nototheniids who fed on them below. An ice floe creaked. She opened her eyes and faintly saw the thousands of krill all angled one way.

The sun climbed high. The whale recalled its noon elevation off Ascension where the newborn calf had struggled to find her breasts. She closed her eyes. The krill moved north, abundant as never before. There were more predators as well, terns, prions, penguins, seals. These creatures fed steadily, yet couldn't deplete the supply. Krill by the million drifted north and millions arrived to take their place. Their rust-red stain never faded where they surrounded the jaws of the whale, half asleep, who hung among them and remembered.

CHAPTER
28

~~~

THE Blue Whale bull and the Pygmy Blue Whale cow swam north. Unlike the Blues, the Pygmy Blues came into estrus between November and February as well as during the austral winter, and the Pygmy, excited by her vision of the mating west of the Mid-Indian Ridge over the black Mauritius Trench where she had been born, swam at thirteen knots or more most of the time. Both she and the bull had lived most of their lives in the Antarctic and subantarctic, where in the summers they'd fed on krill and in the winters on squid and fish, and the suspension of normal migration with its cycle of feast and fast had made their blubber especially thick. The bull didn't worry that he might have to go without food for several months in the vacant northern seas he remembered from the year his father died.

The mother whale might as well have been silent during the first few days of flight when the pauses for lovemaking made both bull and cow hear only one another. After four days the bull picked up his mother's signals and turned back south, but the cow was eager to continue the northward flight and her attraction had overpowered him to the point that he would not defy her will. He called to his mother in the intervals between love play but his sounds never came within her hearing range, though more frequent calls would have reached her eventually. The bull forgot about his mother again and again. The cow made a game of trying to outswim him, and despite her smaller size, she could hold the lead for many minutes at a time, tantalizing him with her voice. Each time she slowed and he caught up, the long pursuit would make their caresses all the more passionate. Most of the time they were either swimming all out or hovering together, completely indifferent to all they heard.

After ten days, when they had put the Kerguelens eight hundred miles behind, they felt the South Equatorial Current reaching into the cold sea. They would swim for twenty minutes through the cold of the West Wind Drift, then feel a shallow stream of warmth for five or six minutes at a time. Icebergs grew rare, then disappeared as they neared the latitude of Cape Town. They swam on under clear sky into temperate ocean.

When they came over the Mauritius Trench in the first half of February, the mother whale's calls were blocked by the peaks of the South West Indian Ridge. The ridge ran northeast from seven hundred miles below Africa to a point east of Mauritius, where the bull and cow hovered silently over the trench. The sun was bright and the surface temperature more than seventy-eight degrees in the tropical sea.

Mauritius was little more than a large mountain. In its eruption millions of years ago its peak had been almost completely blown away, and from five miles out, the whales saw a wide central plateau flanked by low crags. As they swam closer they saw that the crags were lined with gorges and waterfalls. Nearing shore, they could feel the power of the swell build up beneath them. Off Mahebourg Harbor, a quarter mile out, they saw where weather and sea had hammered the coastal rock into crooked arches, caves, and stacks. They turned back out, sounding

288

the bottom with low calls. After a quarter mile both heard their voices echo from coral reefs. They turned to look back. There was still a lighthouse on two of the inshore islands to warn of reefs, and lines of buoys dotted the sea, but there was no sound of traffic. The southeast wind whistled loudly into the harbor, and the whales could see great breakers smash at the lighthouses and cliffs. This whistling, with the incessant roar of the waves, was the only sound. The Pygmy Blue remembered the time just after her birth when freighters, tugs, and tankers hooting in and out of the port had been the first sounds she had heard. Later on, after the dust, the sun had revealed a static harbor where the remains of ships capsized in coastal storms had floated haphazardly among deserted vessels.

They moved farther offshore where they coupled repeatedly in a nearly vacant sea. Conception occurred at the end of February over reefs a half mile out where successively higher columns of dead coral rose from the floor. After the coupling the cow fell away on her back to see great rings of light spread and contract on the rolling floor and hear the sounds of scattered parrotfish who'd made the water gleam with their giant schools in the year she'd been born. The slowly expanding schools of the survivors pecked continually at the reefs, finding here and there formations that held life. Yet by and large the reefs were drab and barren. The pair saw no birds. In March they moved east till Mauritius disappeared. Each time they called toward the bottom the interval before the echo changed. The cow remembered this game from her childhood and, with her larger mate at her side, began to feel like a calf again. The feeling gave way to a greater happiness in June when she sensed new life inside her body. Back at her birthplace, with gentle light instead of the glare after the dust, the world seemed kinder than she had even dared to hope during her barren years alone.

By the time the fetus had toppled into the left horn of her womb in early June, the passionate sex play had long since ended. The pair swam south in a leisurely way, always together, but now the blood of the bull was calm and he no longer submitted to the Pygmy's will. She wanted to press straight south to feed on euphausiids in the sea above the Ker-guelens, but, missing his mother, he turned down the South West Indian Ridge, and after a brief quarrel, the Pygmy followed him.

They paused at the latitude of Cape Town, due south of Madagascar, where euphausia vallentini reddened the sea and shoals of fish and squid

289

were numerous and thick. They gorged for months, starting southwest again in September, just as the mother whale swam east to the Kerguelens where she first had heard the cow. In October, at the polar front, the bull whale fed continually on krill, and the Pygmy Blue, forgetting her preference for the euphausia vallentini, fed as well. The fetus grew larger. In early November, feeding as they swam, the pair continued on to Palmer Peninsula.

The bull whale called for his mother along both coasts, finally turning into the eastern strait to retrace the route of his parents in the year he had been born. After a hundred miles the cow began to hold back, and the two whales butted one another till he turned north. In late December he gave up and ceased his calling, as the mother whale also stopped searching and calling for him in the Indian Ocean. While the bull and cow swam homeward up the South West Indian Ridge, the mother whale, having turned south and made one final search around the Kerguelen Islands, started straight west in Antarctic latitudes, heading silently back to Palmer Peninsula and her life of dreams.

Swimming at the young bull's side, the Pygmy began to forget her time of sickness, as if the radiation had never entered her body. Yet it had altered her chromosomes just as the lesser radiation the bull had sustained had altered his. In January, when the calf was born due east of Rodrigues Island, its streamlined shape made it look like its father, but it had no flukes or fins.

When the two-hour labor was over and the calf was breathing and floating on the surface, the mother and father ran their pectoral fins down its length and looked at it closely, the peakless lava lump of Rodrigues with its cabbage palms looming less than a mile away. Over and over they studied the calf, repeatedly turning away as if to distract themselves from their rising grief. Five times they turned away and looked at the island to see the swell shoot up in whitecaps at the ring of coral reefs half a mile from the shore.

The calf had no eyes. The mother grieved as if the thing were already dead. The bull was swimming away in confusion when the mother whale called out. He turned and looked back. The calf was thrashing with its caudal stub to get beneath the mother and find her breasts, but it failed to do more than submerge itself for a second or two. She swam toward the bull in deep dejection, putting him between her and the calf. Despite its blindness the calf followed, a silvery shape that swam up to the bull's right eye. It moaned and shivered, then dove again, and he could feel it feebly nudging against his sides, unable to get beneath his body. The feel of its snout against his skin made his heart beat faster, and memories of his father crowded his mind. He swam forward, letting the calf rejoin its mother, then turned back, his seventy-five-foot length lying parallel to hers with the youngster between them. She rolled sideways, turning her underside toward his. The calf still hovered on the surface, facing the head of the mother whale. The bull whale shifted its position with his snout, and once it was facing the mother's tail, the calf inched forward, half swimming and half riding its father's snout. When the tip of its snout reached the one nipple that had barely cleared the sea, the bull stopped pushing. After five minutes the blind calf seized the nipple between its palate and tongue and tried to drink, its father's head just a foot behind. When it failed, the gentle lowing from the mother intensified. After two more attempts the calf drank for a few minutes. The mother whale remained on her side but arched her body so that her snout nuzzled the calf. Both the mother and father stroked it with their snouts. The second time it drank for twenty minutes. The Pygmy Blue felt suddenly happy, and the bull, who'd been more than ready to give up on the calf a few minutes before, began to circle both it and its mother in tight protective rings, calling to warn intruders off, although the sea was empty.

Despite its blindness and lack of fins the calf survived and grew steadily. It was a male, and although it couldn't travel faster than one knot, it put on weight very rapidly, growing from twenty-one feet at birth to twenty-six by late April. The mother's store of milk was large and the three found travel unnecessary. The bull kept close to the peak of Rodrigues to listen for long-range signals. They were never more than a mile from the sandy coast.

Over the weeks the deformity of the calf troubled the parents less and less. In normal times it would have been abandoned or, if not, killed by predators as it fell behind on the annual feeding migration, but here there was little other life in the sea. As the blind calf grew, the bull felt more and more content. When it moaned or shivered he would spend hours stroking the places on head and back where his father had nuzzled him to stop his shivering. By mid-April it appeared strong, and the bull whale, glowing inside at his new sense of himself as father and protector, started diving and swimming off a little way to seek out fish. Shoals were rare, but once he enclosed a few dozen juvenile etelis in his mouth. These pink, predatory fish, up to three feet long, had once been common off Rodrigues and Mauritius. He brought them back, turned on his side, and let them swim out by the mother whale. She trapped them in her mouth and bolted them.

Yet the surface life was too meager for more than token offerings. The bull made dives to the underwater slope of Rodrigues Island where after a week he found squid like those his father had eaten by Palmer Peninsula. They seemed to be migrating north, and the deeper he dove the more there were. Soon he was surfacing with his throat stretched tight and full. He would turn on his side, open his mouth, and move his lower jaw back and forth to free the squid, but some fled deeper into his throat-pouch instead of escaping so that they came out in a series of shoals beside the mother. After each feeding she made the submissive low-frequency sound the blind calf made when he took her milk. The bull caressed her, touching his throat to hers and stroking, and this would go on until the calf was ready to take her milk again, when as often as not the bull would dive to find more squid.

The squid soon disappeared. Seeking other food, he dove for deeper depths until, instead of the usual forty-five-minute limit, he could stay down for as long as an hour at a time. As he descended he would call out to the cow, remembering the way his diving father had called to his family. Behind his eyes he began envisioning himself in his father's shape: a hundred feet long and patterned with scars. Envisioning his mother, he listened for long-range signals deflected up by the island peak.

The three moved slowly closer to shore over the weeks, until the white sand beach and palms of Rodrigues Island were in clear view all the time. Once in a while, spyhopping to look to the west or coming up from a dive, the bull could see shapes on the white sand. They seemed little more than dots, but he saw they were moving. Each time he noticed them he would lead the cow and calf back out to sea a little way. Then, when he looked again, the dim shapes would be gone and he would forget them. April stretched on. No long-range signals came. There were occasional storms from cyclones farther south, but most of the time the air was clear and the temperature well above seventy-five. Over and over the bull admired the brilliant dawns and the gentle light of the morning sky.

One morning in late April, as the diving bull was pursuing scattered squid, he heard a motor for the first time since the passing of the dust. It was on the surface not far to his west. Immediately fearing for his family, he soared for the top, and as he cleared the sea, he saw a twelve-foot outboard closing in on his mate and calf. It held three men, one at the rudder, one in the middle, and one at the bow. All three were naked except for skins around their waists, with hair to their shoulders. Their bones showed clearly through the skin. The one at the front was aiming a rifle at the Pygmy cow, her calf too slow for flight. After several shots she went under, trailing blood, and the bull could see that the blind calf bled from several places on his forehead. The caudal stub twitched in a spasm that ran the length of the undersides, then the calf was dead. He instantly sank and the man at the bow, surprised that rorquals sank when killed, cursed and shouted as he aimed the gun at the bull. The shots hit the back, the bullets lodging harmlessly in the blubber. The bull whale dove to join his mate, who was hovering in shock thirty feet under, looking down into the dark while the blood rose from her back.

The motor suddenly stopped and from above there was more shouting. The bull inverted himself, went down for two hundred feet, then rose to hit the boat so hard that he felt his head was going to crack. His eyes went dark. When they saw again, the men were thrashing about in the water, their boat overturned. He watched them stretch their arms across the hull, straining for purchase on the wood. When the three were hanging from one side, he rose beside them and called to the cow who rose as well, her wounds washed clean. They watched the three men swivel their heads to stare in fear. Two started to swim but one hung on. After a moment the bull made a shrugging, sideways motion, crushing the man against the wood. He glided under and past the swimmers, lifted his flukes and brought them down against both men at the same time, crushing their heads. Still in a rage, he turned back for the boat, battering its wood with his back and head. When he had finished, the cow was hanging on the surface at his side. He breathed deeply and dove to the slope where he searched and searched for the calf but could find nothing. When he came up again, his mate had started south, eager to leave the place behind. He followed numbly for twenty miles, then the two whales hovered together and made sounds of grief. It was early morning. Noon found them still in the same place, stiff at

293

the top, eyes in a stare. The following morning, when the bull whale saw the light, he felt much smaller, as if he were calf-sized once again. The cow swam wearily ahead of him, turning west for the Mauritius Trench, where they stayed until the spring.

Nine years passed. The Pygmy Blue bore a calf every other year, but each one was either stillborn or died from a birth defect, making the memory of the finless calf especially dear. Like his father before him, the bull was at first perplexed by the deaths of his children, then, with the passage of time, weighed down by the realization that he was helpless. In the tenth year, after four calves had been born dead, the cow gave birth to a calf with no tail and several tiny pectoral fins instead of two of normal size. The bull spent a day stroking the calf and keeping it close to the mother's breasts, but it didn't suckle, and when it died and sank for the floor off Mauritius, the bull looked down at the truncated shape and began to swim in anxious circles. He puffed loudly, some-times butting at the cow, who also circled in distress. The hunters had disappeared, the ships had gone, the light of the sky was gentle again, food abundant in the Antarctic and subantarctic and increasing every year in warmer seas. Yet the calves died. The whales felt beaten.

Sometimes, as she hovered by herself, the cow would slowly grow aware that the bull was scrutinizing her. He'd envision his mother and father and then dwell on her stockier shape, on the abruptness with which her abdomen narrowed into her tail, on her silvery color and smaller size. She was the only one of her kind he had ever seen and all her calves had been deformed. That spring he was slow to journey south, letting the cow go on ahead. When he finally did begin, he swam once more down the South West Indian Ridge to look for his mother. He never found her, though over the following years he searched again and again, the cow going south to feed on euphausia vallentini near the Kerguelens, and the bull going southwest to Palmer Peninsula.

The pair swam apart more and more often, but never for more than six months at a time. When the cow was in estrus, each alternate year, they'd reunite with a heightened passion, following one another's voices for hundreds of miles and, when they discerned each other's spouts on the distant horizon, diving and coming together as if for the first time.

294

Afterward, the pair would feel almost as close as in the beginning. With spring they'd swim south together, and, as they feasted side by side, the cow would grow quiet and self-absorbed, feeling the flexing of the calf inside her body yet not daring to envision the calf's birth. Their journeys back to the tropical sea were always halting and slow, and after the birth, when the mutation or stillborn calf was slowly sinking, the sense of estrangement would come again. With spring the cow, migrating first, would leave her mate with more relief than hesitation, and later on he'd seek his mother in the southwest. Often it seemed to them both that these partings were final, yet by fall each would miss the other. And every other year the cycle would start again.

After forty-eight years of alternate hope and grief the bull began to remember his juvenile days with his mother as times of happiness. His dejection and disappointment made him forget how lonely he'd been. Having sought her in vain for so long in the Weddell Sea and down both sides of Palmer Peninsula, he had all but given up hope, and as he swam back to the Indian Ocean in late March, he missed his mate and felt certain he wouldn't leave her to seek his mother again. He imagined his mother dead and envisioned only more infant deaths to mark the years that remained.

295

CHAPTER

29

By early January, three weeks be-
fore the finless calf was born, the mother whale had stopped calling out
for the bull in the Indian Ocean and near the Kerguelens. She was
swimming west for Palmer Peninsula, having searched for him from
September to December. She kept south of the polar front most of the
time. Like the Fin Whale when she'd swum all the way to the edge of
the Indian Ocean and turned back, she moved automatically, never
changing her six-knot speed. She didn't know that to her north the bull
was following his mate toward the Mauritius Trench, discouraged by his
fruitless search for his mother.

The cow felt abandoned. After the emptiness of the Atlantic, her
search had worn her down and her consciousness was closed to the

world outside her. Only her calf's call could have broken her trance, and in his dejection he never called, though early in the month he passed less than six hundred miles to her north. She feared for his life, yet the occasional Orcas she'd seen had been as thin as the three she'd fled the previous year.

Her search had confused her. It seemed strange that her calls had evaded him so long in a sea without traffic, especially last year when he and his mate had been hardly a half day's journey ahead. Perhaps he remained deliberately silent. Last year she had lost herself in dreams after failing to find him. This year she swam in a daze, instinctively shielding herself from the hurt she felt rising inside.

In mid-February she reached the sea off Palmer Peninsula. She lingered there till May, when daylight dwindled to less than six hours. As the nights lengthened around her and cyclone winds roared over the sea, she swam past the peninsula's northern tip, then hovered and listened with the white floes rising and falling on all sides. Hearing nothing except the waves and the roar of the wind, she imagined the spouts of other Blues on the horizon and pursued them, just as her mate had done in his fjord. Facing her loneliness day after day was unbearable. After three nights she started west to seek other whales.

She passed the Shetlands and swam down the western side of Palmer Peninsula where the ice floes were wide apart from the summer melt. Her constant long-distance signalling brought no replies, and as she swam past the Amundsen Sea, her loneliness deepened till she despaired of finding companions. She edged for the south, strangely drawn toward the dark, and soon she was travelling in constant night near where the permanent pack ice began. After twenty days of numb, automatic flight she thought she heard Minke Whales in the distance, and remembering the pod that she and her calf had met in their last year together, she travelled northwest until the day was six hours long. The calls faded out for forty-eight hours, then came more loudly. She speeded up to fifteen knots. Just past the polar front four Minkes came into sight.

When she approached them, she saw that all four had white pectoral stripes, like the childhood friends she had failed to save when they'd been trapped on top of the ice. Her heart beat fast and her spirits rose. Perhaps these, too, would welcome her in.

At first they greeted her eagerly, but all four were immature—she saw none of the older whales she'd met with the calf two years before. As they stroked and nuzzled her she shivered with pleasure, but after an hour the two bulls and two cows went back to their mating games. She tried to join in, nudging them from below and approaching them from behind to run her pectoral fins down their sides, but they were absorbed with one another and her exclusion brought her loneliness back again. Still, with the whales close by, it was less intense than before. Over the following weeks she set out many times to seek other whales but her isolation always brought her back.

It took over a month for her to decide to leave them completely. In late August she swam west, hearing the calls of the old Fin Whale inside her head. She'd ignored the old whale just as the juvenile Minke Whales had ignored her, and in the fourteen-hour nights that screamed with wind she wished the Fin were with her now.

She kept well down, constantly signalling, hearing her voice bounce up from the floor. When she was thirteen hundred miles out from the Ross Sea's eastern cape the echoes from below told her the ocean floor was rising.

A new signal came up through the dark from nine thousand feet. She answered and waited, hovering still. Twenty minutes passed. It came again, a call so low it had to be either a Blue Whale or a Fin. Her heartbeat racing, she called back and pursued the sound, then suddenly stopped, fearing she dreamed and that this signal, like the phantom spouts she'd pursued before, would disappear as soon as she approached. An hour passed and three more calls came down from the north. The Blue called back but didn't move, aware by now she wasn't dreaming, yet hanging still to savor the pleasure of being sought after so many months of seeking, for it was clear that the other rorqual was swimming toward her at full speed. For a moment she remembered her mate's approach above Ascension with such vividness that it seemed to be happening all over again. Then, as the signals neared, the Blue imagined that her calf had followed her west and was racing toward her, seeking comfort as when he'd been small and they had waited out the long night under the dust. When the signals came only minutes apart she hurried north, unable to wait any longer.

She roared. It was the middle of the night and auroral lights flickered like faint lightning across the sky. The ocean heaved. Each time she slanted to one side she saw white undersides of ice floes recede upward

298

on swelling waves, then grow huge as the waves collapsed and the ice came down. Her echoes kept rising from nine thousand feet and she knew she was over some sort of ridge. The undersea darkness was very deep and the other whale didn't come into sight till a few yards off. Both immediately arched up to break the surface, but the other whale rose more quickly. As its abdomen passed before the Blue Whale's eyes, she could see it was white, not a gray and white mottle like her own. It wasn't the calf, but in her loneliness she imagined she had found her friend again; that, despite her roars of pain, the old Fin Whale had survived. She broke the ocean, touched her throat grooves to the other whale's and clasped its sides with her fins. Both were upright for a moment, snouts to the sky, then one of the black fifty-foot waves smashed them sideways and drove them down. Underwater the Blue kept clasping the other whale with her pectoral fins and calling out. The other whale answered loudly, rubbing its throat grooves back and forth against the Blue's. As they embraced the Blue saw herself swim-ming beside the old Fin Whale, who encouraged her to eat warmwater plankton and called with delight and surprise when she did. She felt for a moment as if she were living part of her life over again. This time she wouldn't fail her friend. She was bubbling with joy when after five minutes the two swam apart.

When the stranger started to circle, arching her rostrum up and down and blowing bubbles, the Blue could tell that this wasn't the Fin Whale she had known. The sea was dark, but when she swam close the Blue could see that this Fin was more slender than the old one. The Blue Whale moaned as she ran her fins down the slender sides. At seventy-six feet she was shorter than the old Fin, very young. When the stroking stopped and the Fin Whale called out like a calf, eager for more, she brightened a little and envisioned her own calf, while the Fin contrasted the stroking with the rigidity of her parents, both of whom had been so terrified by the catchers they had lived their entire lives in obsessive fear. This was the youngster the old Fin Whale had ap-proached off South Georgia at the beginning of her long flight to the east. Both her parents had been killed soon after the old Fin Whale had left, and her explorations had led her west to the Macquarie Ridge, then north toward New Zealand where she had lived the last six years in isolation except for occasional play with Antarctic Minke Whales. Sexually mature at seven years old, she had spent the austral winter calling out for a mate in the waters to the north. At first, when she'd heard the Blue Whale's call, she'd imagined it was the voice of a Fin Whale bull. As the Blue embraced her again the Fin Whale closed her eyes. Soon her parents faded from mind and she imagined that this was the touch of her mate.

Her dream was sweet, but when she awoke from it, she was still overjoyed at having found a friend. The disappointed Blue stayed close, swimming under and over the youngster, reminded both of the young bull and the old Fin. Unlike her own round snout, this whale's was sharply tapered, and, despite her comparative slenderness, the young Fin Whale was stockier than the Blue, just as the old Fin Whale had been. Each of these things made the Blue Whale ache. She gave out rumbles of pain the Fin couldn't understand, though she tried to console her, gently moving her fins along her face. After some minutes the stroking started to soothe the Blue, and, in gratitude, she caressed the Fin once more. This kept on for much of the night as a deep bond formed between them. At dawn the two friends swam east together.

In the absence of a mate, what the Fin wanted most was a loving companion to mother her, and over the following weeks she let the Blue take the lead, eating whatever she ate and swimming wherever she swam. January found them off Palmer Peninsula, gorging on krill. When they swam north with the southern autumn, the Blue could sense the Fin's excitement and envisioned a mate for her. At latitude forty they separated to search and call on either side of the Mid-Atlantic Ridge. No answers came. By the middle of August, when the Fin had given up, the two swam side by side again, consoled by their bond.

With the southern hemisphere spring, the Fin was reluctant to return to Palmer Peninsula, preferring smelt to krill. Smelt were not abundant in temperate seas, but the Falkland herring population had partly recovered over the Patagonian shelf. The pair swam down the coast of Argentina, and when the Fin Whale stopped two hundred miles from Cape Horn, the Blue remembered the old Fin Whale trying to entice her into feeding outside the Antarctic. As if to compensate for her youthful stubbornness, she feasted on herring until March. By April, when the pair moved north to temperate seas again, the Blue was as fat as if she'd been feasting on polar krill.

*   *   *

300

Over the next forty-seven years the Fin Whale never found a mate, although the pair went searching and calling every winter, in the Atlantic first, then up the coast of Chile, and at last in the open Pacific Ocean. The Blue had no need to summer in the Antarctic now that she fed twelve months of the year, but every spring her migratory instinct made her homesick for Palmer Peninsula.

The young Fin Whale grew increasingly independent as time passed. Often, when the Blue Whale started for home, she stayed behind. With both mate and calf gone, the Blue Whale found it easier to resist the homing urge and frequently turned back to stay with her friend. She might have foregone the migration altogether were it not for her lingering hope that the young bull lived and that eventually he would seek her out on her summer feeding grounds. When she persisted in her flight, the Fin would hang still in hesitation and uncertainty, then race to catch up, unable to face her isolation. The Blue swam home every other year, in the summers when the young bull's calves were born, so that for forty-seven years the two whales sought each other in vain.

It was the forty-ninth December since the Blue had lost touch with her calf, and though she turned back from her flight when the Fin Whale called, she felt discontent. Both had fed on fish all winter, and the Fin was feeling lazy but the Blue was restless and tense. They were resting southwest of the Juan Fernandez Islands more than three thousand miles from Antarctica's Ross Sea when she noticed ice floes drifting westward in the quiet, moonlit night. At first she ignored them, but the ice continued to pass well after sunrise, not stopping till noon and starting again just after dusk. The whales were over a thousand miles past the usual northern limit of drifting ice. When they rested that night on a calm, unruffled sea, the floes caught the moonlight, making the Blue Whale yearn for longer days and shoals of polar krill. She started south, and after four hours' hesitation, the Fin Whale followed. Moving ninety miles a day, the Blue led her friend past the polar front toward the permanent pack ice above the Antarctic Circle, but the Fin was unwilling to turn for Palmer Peninsula. By late January they were feeding off McMurdo Sound near the Ross Sea's eastern cape. In February the ice melted so far back that the Blue found a clear strait all the way to the outer limit of the Ross Ice Shelf at seventy-eight degrees.

Here the sun shone all the time on a sea without wind. The empty water was transparent. The Fin was eager to turn north, but instead the Blue swam up to the gleaming shelf that stretched from the eastern to western horizon. From a distance it showed a random arrangement of inlets and unbroken stretches of smooth, uniform cliff. The Blue Whale neared until she saw only unbroken cliff from sky to sky.

Here she paused. Every springtime since she'd matured she had felt the pull of lengthening daylight but never before had she come to a place of permanent light, not even when leading the bull and calf down Palmer Peninsula, since the Weddell Sea never melted this far back. Fin Whales had always kept away from the coastal ice, and the Fin had an instinctive sense of having come too far. As she turned on one side at the very edge and looked up at the glistening wall that seemed to stretch all the way to the sun, the Blue felt a calm as great as her terror underneath the cloud of dust. Long ago, trying to make her mate swim south, she'd envisioned them both beneath perpetual sun in an ocean without ships. This could have been the sea she'd envisioned, and after an hour, she half expected to hear her mate swimming down the shelf. She tilted sideways to watch the ice with either eye, then righted herself, rubbing her flukes against the throat of the uneasy Fin, who was hanging just behind her, anxiously rattling her baleen, eager to leave. There were no seals on the white ice floes. The ice was motionless, transfixed by the brilliant sun.

The Fin Whale called and started north while the Blue turned sideways to look at the shelf one final time. Her eyes moved up to take the sun in. It didn't glare as much as the sun she'd fled with her mate after the dust and she didn't worry that it would make her blind. She rocked back and forth to watch it with either eye, then hurried north after the Fin's impatient calls.

Just as she turned to go she felt a sharp pain in her eyes and the world went black. She clenched her lids and dove for twilight forty feet down, but when she opened her eyes again she was still blind. She gave a loud call, and the Fin Whale turned to find out what had happened. Uncertain what was wrong but eager to leave, she caressed the Blue Whale with her pectorals, then started once more for the north. The Blue Whale followed, completely bewildered. In her movement from perfect light to a darkness deeper even than that under the dust, she had a sense of having come to the end of things, and as she opened and closed her lids, the after-image of the sun expanded and shrank again and again, as if it were going out in a series of explosions.

She was swimming faster, moving up beside the Fin, when the ocean exploded. With a tremendous grating sound the entire thirty-two thousand square miles of the Ross Shelf shifted upward, the rising ocean lifting it momentarily free of undersea rock with a rasp so loud that even the ears of the whales, uninjured by noise that would have deafened a man, throbbed with pain. The Fin called out and dove for the dark, only to feel the irresistible northward thrust of undersea waves that seemed to descend all the way to the floor. For a moment they pushed her as if she were no more than a matchstick, and the loss of control terrified her. She surfaced. After a minute the ice shelf settled and went silent, but seconds later a peal of thunder ran down the length of the shelf from eastern to western horizon as vast bergs crashed into the sea, raising enormous waves and smokelike clouds of flying snow and spray, as if the scaffolding that held the sky were crumbling down and the sky itself, a mass of snow and ice, were caving in on the ocean. The whales fled north while bergs a thousand feet long came down on either side of them to narrow the width of their swimming space to barely two dozen yards. A second series of undersea waves ran out from the coast, more powerful than the first. For several minutes the whales were swept helplessly ahead and the roaring ocean seemed malicious and alive. They moaned in pain as it thrust them sideways against icebergs that threatened repeatedly to collide. When the waves had passed, the Fin Whale rose in the narrowing strait of open water and looked back, paralyzed with pain and shock. The white-spotted ocean she'd seen only minutes before had turned into a plain of white with crooked cracks of blue. Some cracks were closing. The whales fled. Racing north in terror of being crushed, the Blue and Fin started an arching, "panting" motion.

After a thousand feet, the space between the icebergs widened out. The whales slowed down, then speeded up when the grating rasp reached them again. As the Blue moved headlong through a pitch-black night, she kept calling out to the Fin Whale, not with loud, low-frequency signals but with the desperate, bleating sound her calf had made when frightened. When the grating ended, the Fin kept swimming at full speed. The Blue kept close, completely dependent on her as the pair veered through ice floes toward the gap in the permanent pack ice through which, four days ago, they had entered this empty sea.

When the danger was apparently behind, the cautious Fin calmed only slightly, but after an hour she began to feel a tenderness almost as great as her fear. As she led her passive friend to the north, it was as if she were guiding her own calf. After five days they found the strait, and as the Blue swam through it behind the Fin, the night in her eyes began to lighten. They entered blue sea dotted with floes, where after two days she could make out shapes. When she could see again on the fourth day, she breached and fell in thunder, roaring for joy. The Fin Whale turned to caress her, then from the south the grating sound of the shifting ice shelf came again and they hurried north for another fourteen days.

When the terror was far behind them and they were resting under a ceiling of waves and wind in temperate sea, bruised and sore, the Blue stayed passive and self-absorbed. When ice floes passed again, the Fin Whale fled for warmer waters and the Blue Whale, still submissive, swam in her wake. As they moved northeast toward the South American coast, the Fin Whale stopped repeatedly to nuzzle the Blue in encouragement, though the Blue Whale seldom stroked her in return. Instead of putting it behind her, she grew more and more preoccupied with her memory of the blinding polar sun. She felt tired, unable to face any further change in sea and sky, and the memory of the ice shelf scraping its base kept her afraid. Slightly lowered by melting ice, the ocean temperature barely reflected that of the air, as gaseous chlorine and other pollutants held in heat that would have normally escaped back into space. For hundreds of years the earth's climate had been warming, and now the rising ocean level was finally lifting the shelves off their bases, something that last occurred a hundred twenty-five thousand years ago when Antarctic rorquals retreated north.

Withdrawing from the world, the Blue Whale let the Fin Whale set her course, like a calf following its mother. At first the Fin took pleasure in her new maternal role. Then, in early June, five hundred miles south of the Juan Fernandez Islands, she picked up the sound of another rorqual to the east. Ablaze with excitement, she pursued it all the way to Chile, then north and south, searching day after day with the Blue Whale close behind. For the next four months she kept on searching, living in hope, but the signal didn't come again.

In October the homing urge came back to the Blue Whale, and she swam south down the coast of Chile, yearning once more for her calf. Though she feared the loud noises and blinding sun she might find off Palmer Peninsula, a new resignation tempered her fear. She had always been eager to have the Fin Whale follow her, but now it seemed better that her friend remain behind, searching and calling for a mate in temperate ocean under moons that changed and suns that rose and set. Hovering still in a ten-foot sea, the Fin didn't move, letting the Blue Whale fade from sight.

Both were more than six hundred miles southeast of the Juan Fernandez Islands when the Blue Whale started south, the Fin more hesitant to follow than ever before. Even now, after four months, she hoped to hear the rorqual again. She burned with worry for the Blue as she swam away, just as the Blue Whale worried over her calf, but if she followed the Blue she would lose what seemed her final chance of having a calf of her own. For over four hours after the Blue had left, the Fin swam back and forth, sending out signals of shattering volume in the hope the twenty-hertz call she'd heard in June would come again. Her hope of an answer had dwindled with every day of silence, but to turn and follow the Blue would be to kill the hope for good.

Five hours passed before her worry for the Blue Whale and her loneliness overcame her. She sent one final call to the west, then swam in pursuit of her old and strangely troubled calf.

Seventy miles south, the Blue had stopped calling. She saw ice floes in the cool Peru Current, an arm of the West Wind Drift that flowed up the coast all the way to the equator, and they heightened her fear of a change in the Weddell Sea. Thunderclouds loomed to the south with slanting lines of rain beneath them, and every time she heard the echoes of the storm she envisioned icebergs splitting free from the shelf. But her growing resignation kept her strong, despite her fear. She pushed her speed past thirteen knots.

She swam through the storm for half an hour, almost deaf to the calls of the Fin arching up from the ocean floor, then suddenly stopped as the thunder faded behind. She could see the ice floes, larger and closer together. She looked at the sky, half expecting a glaring sun, but she saw only its faint outline through gray cloud. It was midmorning, the dark sky clearing toward the coast. She had been swimming south-southeast and now the cones of the Andes were dim in the eastern sky.

The sky had been bare and the ocean empty of fish since she set out, but now, near the outer edge of the shelf, sooty shearwaters screamed and wheeled, and under the sea, shoals of chub mackerel turned together while croaker calls came from the east.

She slowed down. The sounds of life made her miss her feasts with the Fin Whale and she felt regret, suddenly noticing that the echoing calls had stopped. Her time with the Fin was not like the time with her mate and her calf, something that she'd lost decades ago, but now the silence to the north and the thickening floes made it seem she'd been swimming alone for years.

She stopped her flight, wavering slightly, recalling again the terrible scraping that had come from the Ross Ice Shelf. Surely the blinding sun and the noise would turn the calf and his mate back north. She called for the first time since seeing the ice and turned up the coast. During the silence that answered her call, grief stirred inside her. She dove to two hundred feet and signalled repeatedly until her sound waves crossed the Fin Whale's path.

The Fin had started back north as well. As soon as she heard the Blue she answered and turned south. They swam at full speed, constantly calling for three hours, then dove. As they came together, the Fin Whale rose above the Blue, lowing softly and caressing, and they hung still for half an hour. The lure of the light passed from the Blue Whale's mind as the Fin led her north to safety, and after an hour, both felt resigned, almost content. Then the rorqual call came again, this time from the south. The Fin Whale wheeled and raced for the ice with the frightened Blue hanging behind.

CHAPTER

30

Iɴ their forty-ninth year together,
the Blue Whale bull followed his mate to the Kerguelens instead of
seeking the mother whale, whom by now he imagined dead. In estrus
from November to February, the cow conceived in November and in
September of the following year gave birth once again off Rodrigues
Island. For years after the death of the finless calf they had avoided
Rodrigues, but by now the other deaths had dimmed their memory of
the men, and though he imagined his mother dead, the bull even now
kept listening for long-range calls channeled up by the peak. He stayed
close to the island.

By now the Blue Whale bull, at a hundred feet long, was an especially able guardian. Her labor went on for two and a half hours, and as

he circled, he was absorbed now by her moans and now by the ice floes that kept drifting up from the south. Seeing ice in the tropics troubled him. The floes were very small, almost melted, but they'd been passing him night and day for over a week.

He looked up at the sky. The water was cool for this time of year, yet the sun had a brilliant glare, and when he looked west toward the island, he could see that the ocean continued to rise as it had for many weeks. The lower mountains had disappeared while Mount Limon, twelve hundred feet high, was completely surrounded by water. Earlier, swimming inshore, he'd heard screaming from the slowly shrinking hills. He didn't connect it with the men.

He was hovering to watch the albatrosses and petrels that had flown up from the south when the cow, her seventy-seven feet upside-down in the sea, made an especially loud moan. As he dove apprehensively and hovered where the tail of the calf had emerged, he was almost frightened to look closely. The sun illuminated the upper sea. He had closed his eyes, but when he dared to open them he found no flaw in the small flukes. They were perfectly formed. He called in encouragement to the cow, who moaned again as the rest of the abdomen came out. She arched for breath, then hung almost straight up and down. The flippers appeared. The bull's heart thudded with excitement. The head came out and the birth cord burst. Immediately he lofted the calf to the top and the cow came up to see if the youngster were alive. In only seconds it took its first breath, the sun illuminating its twenty-four-foot length, all perfectly formed from snout to tail. Beside herself with joy, she nuzzled it. The bull submerged as the Pygmy hovered beside the calf. It dove and in only a minute was feeding from her breasts. Overcome, the bull whale lofted a third of his length out of the ocean, roared to the sun, and fell off to one side. Then, as quickly as it had come, the outburst ceased. He remembered the first calf. While the newborn fed, he made shallow dives beneath it and circled it at the top, peeling his ears, but all he heard was the swishing tumult of the squid who were swimming up from the Southern Ocean.

The calf fed steadily all day. That night, when the bull and cow hung side by side with each of its flippers touching one of their pectoral fins, both felt the end of a time of nightmare and frustration and that now, at last, their lives could truly begin. They arched their heads to nuzzle each other, caressing more tenderly than at any time since the first shy hours forty-nine years ago when they had met in the subpolar sea. The cow would close one eye and doze for an hour at a time, but the diligent bull remained on guard for his mate and calf. When morning came he felt larger than he had ever felt before. Glowing with pride, he continued to circle the suckling female and her mother.

By midafternoon Mount Limon was rapidly shrinking at its base, and the armada of floes from the south had grown even thicker than yesterday. All day cold-weather petrels and terns kept landing amid the ice, often pausing to preen and rest near the mother and calf. The bull was doubly attentive, for he picked up the sounds of sharks breaking the water not far off, along with low-frequency sounds where tuna turned together. He only relaxed when he paused to stroke and admire the calf. By late afternoon it seemed to the bull she was already visibly longer. That night, as the three rested, the bull felt warm where she touched her pectoral fin to his side, and he remembered himself swimming south with his flipper pressed against his father. The memory made him feel even larger.

By dawn there were not only ice floes on the water but a line of bergs against the southern sky. The bull whale spyhopped, blinking again and again and rumbling to his mate, as if to confirm that what he saw was no apparition. He looked to the west. The sea was still rising up the sides of Mount Limon. His mate was scanning the southern sky, turning her head to watch with each eye. From beyond the horizon the bull caught a trace of dolphinsound and he remembered the Right Whale Dolphins he and his mother had heard in their trips round Antarctica. He hovered dreamily for a moment, eyes closed, wistfully looking at the image of his mother that had risen in his mind. When he awoke he went back to his circling. The dolphinsound had died away. The bull whale dove, hearing a hissing sound from the south. When he came up again, he saw a line of fifteen Killer Whales swimming parallel to each other, well apart, north from the wall of distant icebergs. As soon as he saw them he turned to his mate and urged her northward with the calf. She obeyed. Remembering his father, he called defiantly and swam south to confront the whales.

These were the first Killer Whales he had seen in forty-nine years. Scarce in previous years outside the polar zones where the survivors were concentrated, they had increased in number, and now, as climatic change drifted the ice shelves north from Antarctica, the Killer Whales were forced north as well, ahead of the ice, into oceans foreign to them.

He swam at fifteen knots, on the surface constantly, calling as loudly as he could to turn the whales in his direction. At first he felt as much anger as fear, but the nearer the Orcas came the more fear he felt. He remembered his father slowly descending, tailfirst, sideways, upside-down, hollow gouges in his sides. The part of his father he'd never known until his death—the courage and rage that had enabled him to face the Killer Whales—surfaced inside him, keeping his speed at fifteen knots despite the growing strength of his fear. He closed his eyes, hearing the angry call of his father inside his head and seeing the resolute stroke of his flukes as he'd turned for the Orcas. He'd always felt awe and dread at the memory. He started to tremble. When the Orcas were near enough that he could see spray rise from their heads as they arched from the sea, he chose the one who was approaching him head on, sent roaring blasts in its direction, then dropped ten feet under and accelerated his stroke until the pain of maintaining a speed of nineteen knots blacked out his memories.

He surfaced again to hear the desperate, fearful call of the Pygmy Blue well to the north and he answered loudly with the same low-frequency signal he had made when he'd turned her away. When her call came again she was farther off, and he answered more softly, trying to signal his approval. The Orcas were only a half mile south and the ice was rearing higher behind them. He trembled harder. The Killer Whales arched over the sea, looming larger with every second, the pointed snouts and towering dorsals growing clear. He closed his eyes, his bellow of rage rising in volume as he tried to compensate for the fear that shook him from snout to tail.

The next time he rose they were only a quarter mile away. They were still well apart, but as he dove, he expected they'd close their ranks and surround him in seconds. He heard the cow for what he guessed was the final time, and with her call, a succession of visions flooded his mind, making him ache for their first meeting near the Kerguelens, when the silvery, top-heavy shape so dear to him now had seemed so odd. Vividly he recalled the times he had let her travel alone and the estrangements that had followed the deaths of their calves. Then the voice of his father

310

came to him again. He was twelve feet down. His flukes had slowed but he managed to keep on pushing south.

Suddenly bold, he opened his eyes. Just a little way south the head of an Orca arched down, then rose for breath. He drove himself upward at full speed to ram it, but it veered to one side so that his snout, breaking the surface at eighteen knots, hit only air. His momentum lifted him fifteen feet from the sea and he saw the line of Orcas on either side, their arches whitening the surface again and again as they drove on past. His fear completely disappeared as he realized they were swimming for his family. He wheeled and dove, chasing the flash of their shrinking flukes, black above and white below, at first only yards away, then smaller and farther off. The screams of the Orcas rang through the sea like a terrible laughter, but instead of terrifying, it ended his fear and fueled his rage. He drove himself past eighteen knots to catch them and make them turn, but now they were swimming well down, at thirty knots. He roared to the cow and calf, urging them to flee faster. At first the cow answered in terror, so that he could trace the speed of her flight in the gradual fading of her voice.

Five minutes went by. The water was roaring in his ears as he raced to catch up. Then, well ahead, he heard the Orcas scream again. When his eyes rose clear, he saw a patch of white-water spray moving slowly across the surface to his north and heard the loud, low-frequency moans that came every second or two from the cow as they ripped her apart. By the time he had reached her the calf was gone and she was as bloody as his father had been before his descent to the floor, although the Orcas had left only seven wounds in her flesh. She hovered beside him, panting with shock and trembling like a sickly, newborn calf. He tried to help her, bearing her up just as he and his mother had borne up his father. Blood covered his skin, making him shake with rage and shame.

It took the Pygmy two hours to die. By that time the Orcas were far away, confused, displaced. He followed her down into the dark, watching her spin haphazardly as his father had spun. He roared in anguish— loud, hysterical blasts—then rose to the top where he sent air out of his blowholes in short rapid-fire puffs, feeling constriction in his chest, his grief a physical sensation inside his ribs. Several times he inverted himself, waved his flukes in the air and slapped them down on the sea as he had when he'd killed the men by the boat. He rose and fell backward, slapping the back of his head on the water, roaring with rage. Two wheeling gulls investigated. He dove and stayed under for an hour, bursting up into the light at the last second before suffocation with great loud gasps, then smacking his head on the water again, unable to find oblivion.

At last he went still. After hanging silent for three hours he started south toward the ice.

When the bull drew up on the icebergs, they were not as large as they'd seemed to him when the Orcas had approached, the largest twenty feet wide and ten feet high, all with hundreds of yards between them. He swam close to one and heard it hiss as its keel dissolved. It had a tabular shape, but the sun had hollowed it out and water was streaming down its sides. After he'd passed it he entered a world of continuous blue dotted with ice. He didn't know what he was seeking, but he wanted to leave Rodrigues well behind.

Motion dulled his pain slightly, and once he'd started, he kept to the same monotonous stroke, moving south at eight to ten knots for twenty-four hours a day, largely oblivious to what he saw, although he noticed the ever more frequent appearance of floes and bergs, some with polar birds perched on strange chimney formations the sun had made with its melting. After eight days the floes became so thick that it was almost like swimming through pack ice, even though he was more than three hundred miles above the Kerguelen Islands and nearly eight hundred from the shifting line that once had marked the polar front. He was too hurt to be deeply disturbed by the changing climate, but it still made him uneasy. He started veering among the floes, his general direction west by south. Cormorants and petrels hunted constantly over the ice, and once, when he veered, he could see shoals of Antarctic krill in the surface water.

The time of high solar activity had ended decades ago, and though the dust of the nuclear night had long since gone, the chlorine gases in the Antarctic stratosphere were still very thick. Over the last thirty years the frigid winters had seen the ozone in the sky over Antarctica reduced until by now the entire continental stratosphere was empty of it and radiation beat down on the ice cap as never before. Much of this light was reflected back by the snow, but still there was melting. More melting went on farther north where the atmospheric carbon had been warming the earth by about a degree a year for the last twenty years. By now the glaciers in the polar and temperate latitudes were dissolving and swelling the sea, and the water itself expanded with increased heat.

Flooding and expansion accounted for the ice the bull whale saw. The outer areas of the great Antarctic ice shelves such as the Filchner Shelf all floated on the sea, and the shelves were constantly being pushed farther to sea by advancing inland glaciers. In the past this had led to calving, where part of the shelf broke free to drift north in tabular bergs. Now, with the ocean water rising, the inner areas of the shelves were being lifted free of the bases where for millennia they had been anchored to undersea rock. Once free, the ice sheets drifted north and east in the West Wind Drift. Simultaneously the spreading of the ozone hole which made the winters colder had sent the great cyclonic winds whirling farther north every year, expanding the West Wind Drift. Soon, as the bull steered his way through the dense floes near latitude fifty, he could feel it against his skin.

He steered more for the south, less for the west, in anguish seeking his mother at Palmer Peninsula again. Two hundred miles from the Kerguelens, the ice made him pause. Intact, the ice shelves had occupied over eighty-four thousand square miles. Now, breaking up and drifting free, they approached him as snow-covered slabs sometimes thousands of feet in diameter. The farther south he went the larger they were. The West Wind Drift had speeded up from earlier years, and as bergs appeared to the west, passed the bull, and faded out toward his east, he saw crowds of birds and animals on them, some of them watching him in interest as the current pulled them by: crabeater seals, black-backed gulls, Adélie penguins, Weddell seals, diving or flying off occasionally to feed but always returning to the same berg as if they meant to keep to their old homes even while drifting thousands of miles in the polar sea.

The bull kept swimming southward, then looked up at a change in the light. Just a few miles north the light had been benign. Now, as he slanted his head to look at the sun with one eye, it was as if his eye were being stabbed with pins. Immediately he remembered the glaring light he had seen with his mother and father in the spring after the dust. After a minute he noticed an albatross approach on a smaller floe. The eyes were white; they looked as blind as his father's eyes. He paused to watch the snowy bird, then, turning west, he saw an iceberg that protruded thirty feet out of the sea and seemed to stretch to fill both

313

northern and southern skies. It was coming toward him at three knots. Suddenly frightened of getting caught beneath the ice, the bull turned north and swam below the bobbing keels of the smaller bergs. He continued north for half a week, then started west again.

The change in the ocean and his flight from the giant berg had distracted the whale, but still the memory of his father drove home to him his failure to save his family. Grief slowed him down again and again, but always the ice speeded him up, even though he was in normally ice-free water northwest of the Crozet Islands. It was as if the vast bergs had followed him north. For minutes at a time the drifting icebergs would stay far enough apart to allow the mindless, automatic flight that partially numbed his pain, but just as he was becoming oblivious of everything, another enormous berg would loom from the distance and he would be forced to regather his wits and swim out of its way. Often the berg would go over him and he would swim for its northern or southern edge for several minutes before getting clear. Beneath the center of the bergs it was totally dark, but near the edges the flickering light streaked in from the side, illuminating the glassy roof of blue freshwater ice. He would rise out into dazzling light, as often as not to see more seals resting and panting by the ice to his east and west. Every descent beneath the bergs revived his memory of his father calling him down into the dark. He grew to dread them. When, after ten days of zigzag flight, he saw another one draw near below Africa, he resolved to swim north until he'd left the ice behind.

He dove just moments before the berg went over him, then rose till his head was brushing its bottom. A few yards east he could see the purple of twilight water forty feet down and far to the north an almost indiscernible lightening of the dark. He sculled for the north, feeling defeated, turning due east into the light from time to time to rise and breathe. Every time he descended again he heard the voice of his father calling him more loudly. The berg was huge. His anguish swelled. A quarter hour passed and the distant lightening of the sea seemed still far off. Retreating from the dim light, he started edging in toward the iceberg's center, moving away from his air supply. The water went black as the keel deepened: a hundred feet, two hundred feet. The bull remembered the sight of his father sinking dead into the sea. He began a dive.

He was more than fifty feet beneath the keel when he heard the clicks

314

of Killer Whales overhead. He paused to listen, then, in silence, gradually rose, angling east toward the nearest ice edge. Just thirty feet from the keel, he picked up a series of high-pitched signals at the very upper limit of his hearing, the sound of Right Whale Dolphins. As he rose higher and the light seeped in from the east, he saw their stream-lined, eellike shapes and the white of their bellies. Their voices were higher than the Minkes' but still reminded him of the whales his mother and father had tried to free. Whatever else the voices might mean, their desperate shriek expressed great fear. The bull hung still about twenty feet down and looked to the east. In groups of two or three the nearest Right Whale Dolphins were racing out from beneath the berg and into the light. Yet, farther off, where the clicking came from, there were thuds against the ice and he could hear two kinds of screaming. One— the death cries of dolphins—was completely new to him, but the other was all too familiar.

Since the attack on his mate and calf, his rage at the Killer Whales who had fled from him had been bottled up. It was like some hard thing growing inside his chest. Now, with the screams of both the Orcas and their victims echoing down from the thick ice, his memory of the attack was mixed with his memory of his mother and father butting the ice to free the Minke Whales. He remembered especially the blood on his mother's head and his father's frustrated cries as he soared to smash the ice floe's keel, and failed. He envisioned the man he'd crushed against the boat.

Quickly he dove and started in silence toward the screaming. The high-pitched calls of the Right Whale Dolphins kept on passing over his head as more and more rushed east to the light, but the Killer Whales were farther off. After their first volley of screams, he heard nothing from them. Then, well in from the eastern edge of the berg, he caught faint moans from seventy feet over his head and heard hard thuds against the ice, too powerful to be made by the Right Whale Dolphins. The bull hung silently as they continued, moving now to-ward the east. He let himself sink a little way as the thuds came again. This time they were followed immediately by clicking sounds that descended toward him. He stayed where he was, ready to strike when the Orcas neared, but then he heard a lifeless, rushing sound. Just as it peaked, the bull felt a fin brush at his side in the pitch-black sea. He wheeled to nose a sinking Orca. With its herd it had followed the

315

dolphins under the western edge of the ice, stopping to feed after each kill, in its greed oblivious of time. Now, near the end of its swim, it had been without air for so long that it had drowned.

The bull didn't reflect on the sinking Orca, but the thudding made it clear that its herd was eager to break through the ice. Twenty-five minutes was an Orca's maximum time between taking breaths. The bull, with his many dives for squid, had extended his time to an hour. As the thudding sound came down to him again, he inverted himself, dove fifty feet, arched in a wide, swift curve, then accelerated upward, the clicks of the Orcas guiding him in.

He made little sound but the Orcas heard him before he struck. In their desperation, confused and foggy from lack of breath, they kept on swimming toward the east almost till the moment he hit the ice. As he neared the top he levelled out, arching his back to crush the whales with a deafening thump and drag their bodies against the ice for several feet with a loud scraping, cracking sound. When he arched down, four had been crushed, four others injured and unable to swim on. The bull began to feel large again. He went deep until he'd left the echoing clicks behind.

He hung still at a thousand feet, then slowly rose, constantly listening for the clicks. But they had died. After two minutes, facing east, he saw the outer edge of the ice. There was thudding about three hundred yards from the edge. He glided in silence until the thudding was to his west. Slowly he started his rise for the ice edge. The clicking reached him again when he was less than a hundred feet from the Killer Whales. Picking up speed, he pushed himself to seventeen knots. The sea grew purple as he neared the edge of the ice, then black again as he arched in.

He felt their teeth behind his blowholes and along the length of both sides as he hit the ice with his back, crushing three more. The remaining six, almost in the light, broke for escape as he curved down and rose again. Just before he reached the ice he saw three survivors arch up from under the berg. He brought his back up hard on the others, killing all three, then, moving out from the edge of the ice, thrust up with his tail and brought it down again and again in the general area where the Orcas had come out. He smashed at both sea and ice in a frenzy, chipping large pieces out of the berg and crushing the bodies of all three whales in a matter of seconds. As he struck he roared his rage, so

316

overcome that for nearly a quarter hour after the whales had died he continued to smash at the sea. When at last he stopped and arched backward, all the whales had sunk from sight, and there was blood on the edge of the ice. He nosed the blood and thought of his mate's. He had been down for nearly an hour, and his blowholes sucked the air in with a desperate sound like the sound of the Fin when she'd found the harpooned Minke. The sense of expansiveness that had come with the deaths of the Orcas quickly gave place to the old contraction, as if again they had come to trick him, to offer escape from his pain and at last only prolong it.

He spouted and breathed for a quarter hour. When he stopped the Right Whale Dolphins had long since crossed the northern horizon, and at the edge of the ice the chop of the sea had already washed the Orcas' blood away. They faded immediately out of his mind and he felt like diving forever. Twice he inverted himself and went down for several hundred yards before turning. Confused and uncertain, he swam east for about an hour at five knots, just ahead of the berg. Then he remembered his mother. Very likely she was dead, but the loss of his mate and calf and the strange changes in the sea left him desperate for any hope. He turned back and dove beneath the berg to rise out at its northern edge, then swam west to seek his mother again.

CHAPTER

31

THE Blue and the Fin had swum for
an hour up the coast of Chile when a rorqual call like the one in June
came up from the south. The Fin answered and wheeled to pursue it,
even more eager for southward flight than the Blue had been a few hours
before. The Blue hung back at first, but when her friend continued on,
her choice was either the ice or loneliness. She hesitated another
minute, then when the call came again, she envisioned the calf swimming north, having failed to find her off Palmer Peninsula, and she
raced to join the Fin.

The calls continued to come at irregular intervals and the pair
pursued the sounds for fourteen days. They passed Puerto Montt below
the fortieth parallel, then swam east of Chiloé Island with the Andes

looming larger on the land. The ice floes grew larger and closer together until, by the time they were passing the islands of the Los Chonos Archipelago seven hundred miles north of Cape Horn, it seemed they were already in the Antarctic, approaching the permanent ice of the shelf.

When the last of the islands had faded in the distance and they had rounded the jutting coast of Taitao Peninsula, the rorqual voice went dead. It was night. For several hours they'd seen occasional tabular icebergs among the floes, but now icebergs hundreds of feet in length and breadth filled the sea to their south from horizon to horizon. The sky was clear and the moon full, but the ocean surface roared with waves forty feet high. The enormous slabs of ice ascended and descended, shining a deathly white under the moon. The Blue and Fin had only a moment before the nearest berg approached and passed over their heads. They swam west for a dozen minutes before re-entering open water. As they rose to spout and breathe in the tossing waves, both saw only white where another enormous berg was drifting a couple of yards to their west. When they looked south they saw a dazzling, moon-white berg with a crooked **W** shape to its bow bear down on them. They dove again and swam back to the east until they were clear, then rose to see a line of parallel icebergs drifting north. It took them nearly a dozen minutes to swim the length of the nearest berg as it passed over.

The farther they went the less they were able to swim straight south. The Blue had swum under icebergs during every spring migration, but there had always been time to breathe and rest between them. Normally whales could avoid rough sea by swimming below the waves, but as the spaces between the icebergs became smaller and farther apart, they found it necessary to stay near the top all the time, constantly looking for breathing spaces. All that night, as the slabs loomed larger and closer together, the pair were either swimming beneath one or watching the south while they spouted and breathed in preparation for the next. By dawn, with the black and white pattern of ice and ocean dancing in their minds, they'd both stopped calling, yearning to rest in open water as much as to hear the rorqual again.

The voice had gone dead for two hours. A west-wind gale screamed over their heads, and the Blue Whale knew the farther they swam the rougher the sea would get. She had thought she'd bear anything to see the calf once more but now she saw only ranks of rectangular icebergs

319

bearing down on her day after day. She called in fright between two rocking slabs that towered forty feet out of the water, then started north with the Fin behind her.

They were sixty feet under the surface, stroking their way up an endless keel, when the sound of the rorqual, louder now, came twice from the south. The Fin Whale barely resisted the first call, and at the second her vision of mating blazed as brightly as in June. She turned back, wheeling so fast that for a moment she was head to head with the Blue whom she swam under without a sound, ignoring her completely. Hurt and angry, the Blue Whale chased her but the Fin swam at full speed, constantly calling, her fifteen-foot flukes ticking the underside of the ice. The Blue remembered pursuing the bull whale's call with the old Fin racing behind her more than fifty years ago, then envisioned herself swimming south while the old Fin tried to turn her back. She pushed herself past sixteen knots, eager to catch her friend and turn her, as she knew the chances of overtaking another whale were slim with the dazzling bergs dictating the course of their flight.

Her resolution was strong at first, but when the call came again and the Fin Whale answered even more loudly, she thought once more of her calf. Her resolution began to weaken. Why would a rorqual be sending out long-distance signals in this sea? She imagined again that her calf was seeking her off the coast. Likely the bergs had put him in danger. The maze of ice that could stop the Fin could stop her as well, but after a minute's vacillation, she followed the sound.

With their change of direction the pair had been under the berg for half an hour when they rose out at its southern edge. They huffed explosively and sucked air into their heads with desperate breaths, then continued on. At first they swam fast, then, when the calls went dead for nearly three hours and the traffic of ice from the south grew denser than ever, they slowed to a stop. For twenty minutes they barely moved, letting the current push them north at the speed of the ice, wanting to hear the rorqual call before they pressed for the south again. When after twenty minutes the call still hadn't come they started back north under the ice.

They swam under an iceberg six hundred feet long. When they had travelled a hundred feet the sound of the rorqual reached them once more and they hovered still, brushing the keel with their backs. As they dreamed, each with her vision of the rorqual to the south, the Fin made calflike sounds, leaving it to the Blue to choose their direction. The thickening ice had made the Blue even more certain that the world to the south was dangerous and she still feared that following the voice would imperil their lives. She had two visions, one of herself and the calf together in blinding light and the other of herself and the Fin feeding placidly on smelt in warmwater seas. She made a weary sound, as tired as the Fin of making choices, wishing the old Fin Whale were there to show the way. It seemed that for most of her life she'd been pulled in opposing directions: north to the bull or south to the krill, north to warm temperatures for the calf or south to refuge from the dust, north to the tropical mating grounds or south to safety from the blinding glare of the sun. She dove submissively under the Fin, who followed the pull of her passion southward. The Blue made querulous, clicking sounds as she followed her friend, just as she would have if the Fin had started north, but when the Fin gave an angry, impatient moan, the Blue went silent, retreating once more into dreams.

With constant shifts of direction it was almost the end of October when they approached latitude fifty. They saw occasional seals and penguins on the icebergs, most of them blind. Cloud and storm shut the sun from view most of the time, but once a shaft of glaring light broke through at noon. The Blue could see that it was dangerously bright, like the light off the shelf. She called the Fin Whale to turn back, but she ignored her.

The rorqual call kept dying out, then resurfacing out of the constant background roar of storming water, always closer, always louder. Each time she heard it the Blue woke up and answered loudly, and for the last three hundred miles before Cape Horn she was always awake, the call coming every few minutes to tantalize them both. The icebergs were so enormous and so thick that they had less control than ever over their swimming, again and again turning west or east to get out from under a berg that passed interminably north over their heads.

When they neared the tip of the continent in November, the spires and cones and chimneys of the icebergs made it look as though a desolate, ruined city were drifting north, so vast it covered the whole sea. Once, as they swam east past the edge of a glimmering slab, the berg beside it shifted sideways, closing the open water off with an explosive smack and almost crushing the Fin. The whales hung stunned, hearing the echo of the collision bounce up from below as the

321

bergs parted, allowing gray light to outline the upper twenty feet of the two vast walls, each over a hundred feet high and nearly eight hundred feet long. The rorqual call came north again, bouncing between the shelf and the ice. The two whales answered, swimming four hundred and fifty feet toward the east to rise and breathe, then turning south down a narrowing strait between a pair of thousand-foot bergs that, on the surface, looked like squat ships, low on the water, almost perfectly rectangular and grooved with crooked lines where they had scraped each other's sides. Rain pelted the ocean, and sheets of fog began drifting between the bergs as the whales raced south, constantly calling and listening.

The voice stopped but they swam on, passed Waterman and Hoste islands. There were low mountains to their east, and to their northeast was the sixty-five-hundred-foot cone of Sarmiento Mountain. The voice stayed silent for several hours; then, ninety miles from Cape Horn, it came to them from the north. It seemed less than five miles off. In the obstacle course of ice, the other whale had probably overshot the Blue and Fin as it tried to follow their calls.

Both reversed direction and followed the voice, but after a moment the Blue slowed down. Out of her westward eye she could see an enormous wall. Three hundred feet high, it was moving east and closing in on the land. In calmer, quieter sea both whales would have seen it long ago and, before seeing it, heard the sound of the water against it. But they'd been preoccupied with the rorqual call and the bergs. The Blue only paused to watch for a few moments, but when she looked toward the north the Fin was gone. She called out, then discerned a trace of spray where her friend had spouted in the waves. She looked beyond to scan the horizon. It was foggy but she could make out a gap of gray between the northern tip of the wall and the distant mountains on the coast. She started racing at full speed, for the calls of the Fin were fading and she feared she would swim through the gap and leave her behind. When the rorqual sound came down from the north again, her heartbeat raced. Forgetting the Fin, she answered back and pursued the sound at sixteen knots, the bull calf's image bright in her mind.

With a desperate panting motion the Blue arched in and out of the sea between the bergs. The light was gray, the clouds so low that half the time she moved through fog. The rorqual calls grew steadily louder;

322

they seemed to come from only a mile or so away, yet the other whale failed to appear. Every time the fog rolled back the Blue Whale's westward eye could see that the ice-covered water between her and the wall was narrowing while her eastward eye saw the icebergs spreading west in steadily wider ranks as they drifted up the coast. If she were to thread the gap between the wall of ice and the coast it would have to be soon. Both she and the Fin started calling at higher frequencies to encourage the other whale. Ten minutes after she started swimming north the wall of ice was only a quarter mile to her west. The sight of the Fin rising in and out of the waves kept clearing, then fading in fog. Slightly beyond the spouts of the Fin, the northeastern tip of the wall was nearing the dark gray coastline.

Just before the ice closed off the ocean to her north, the rorqual call came south more loudly than ever. Ablaze, the Fin drove straight north at eighteen knots and sent out several signals at once: the twenty-hertz call, the more expressive, higher frequency call with which she'd tried to encourage the other whale, and a series of sequences like the bugling calls the Blue had exchanged with her mate above Ascension Island. The sounds made the Blue feel such compassion for the Fin that for several seconds her memory of the bull calf was replaced by a Fin Whale bull racing south to join her friend. The image shone, then faded out as the lifting fog showed the northeastern tip of the wall drawing up on the coast.

While the Fin raced for the north she heard the rorqual call one moment and the next only the scraping, crackling sound of the wall as it rammed and split the ice. It was only a few feet ahead. She tried to swim underneath it as the Blue drew near, but after ten minutes she spouted in frustration, having gone down for six hundred feet and failed to find the bottom. Now it had met the land. Both whales dove for nine hundred feet and swam below it. As they moved north they kept scraping their heads on the bottom, expecting at first that at any second they would be able to rise out on the other side. Fifteen minutes passed and the ice stayed solid above them. The Blue Whale butted the Fin to turn her, then followed her back. When they were clear again they hurried for the top, aching for breath, but the wall had jammed the bergs so tightly against each other that there was little breathing room. Almost fifteen minutes passed before they found a narrow opening, filled their lungs, and started south again.

It seemed that the other whale was lost to them. Both ached with grief. Racing southeast, they eyed the undersides of the icebergs, looking for openings, but saw only a crooked ceiling of jammed keels. As the bergs pressed one another the ceiling crackled, constantly shifting as if alive, and as the rest of the wall closed in, they heard the ceiling buckle behind them. Unable to breathe, the whales drove on to the southeast for another eight miles. Grief made them rumble and their high-speed flight was exhausting. Desperate for breath, they started swimming with their heads against the undersides of the bergs. The faint gray light began to alternate with blackness in their eyes. In their agony they'd started to bang their heads against the ice when a gleam of light to the southeast showed they were nearing open water.

In another minute they broke the surface. The sky was still gray, but the light seemed dazzling after their long swim under the ice. Behind them and to their north the wall was making an even louder din where it scraped against the islands south of Tierra del Fuego. As they passed Cape Horn, moving east, they breathed while racing, pushing themselves past fifteen knots.

Now that they were clear of the closing vice between the ice and land, a sorrowful, rhythmic grunt accompanied the Fin Whale's exhalations. The rorqual was gone; she had missed her only chance at mating. Initially sharing her frantic grief, by now the Blue was calmly sad. Still doubting that the whale had been a Fin, the Blue Whale wanted to comfort her companion but the ice kept pushing them both east. Perhaps the call had *been* a Fin's; perhaps the Blue Whale hadn't missed her final chance to rejoin her calf. Yet it seemed unlikely. The Blue remembered her failure to save the Minkes trapped on the ice. She doubted that the rorqual, whether Blue or Fin, had survived. She had failed again. And the voice had been low, surely a Blue's. She began to resign herself to her youngster's death.

The ice sheet behind the wall had an area of thousands of square miles, but here, off southern Tierra del Fuego, the icebergs ahead of it had open water between them. The whales swam past the Wollaston Islands. When they veered northeast toward Staten Island and the eastern coast of Tierra del Fuego, they were able to swim at a comfortable speed, between nine and twelve knots. They moved northeast for a day and a night and on the morning of the second day approached the northeast tip of Staten Island, icebergs obscuring the dark gray line of the barren shore. Off the island the sea was loud with the sound of the icebergs scraping together, some going north in the Falkland Current and some continuing east or northeast in the West Wind Drift. Both whales wanted to leave the ice completely behind. They turned northwest toward Argentina and followed the Falkland Current up the coast.

They could swim on the top for ten to twelve minutes at a time, though the pitching sea usually kept them below. After two hours the Fin Whale started holding back, at last hanging listlessly in the dark five fathoms down. The Blue urged her forward, nudging her flukes, but the Fin ignored her now that waves and Falkland herring made the loudest sounds in the sea. With the gnawing ache in her muscles and the long wait between breaths taken away, grief overwhelmed her. She was certain that, without the wall of ice, she and her bull would have formed a permanent bond, swimming north to mate in the tropics. She moaned. What was the point of swimming into the vacant Atlantic which she and the Blue had searched in vain year after year? It seemed her entire life since the deaths of her mother and father had been only a wait for the rorqual call. As the Blue kept swimming north and returning, she moved away from her, facing west. After two hours the Blue gave up and hovered beside her, subdued as well, remembering the Minkes again, and her early years with the calf.

They hung side by side for a quarter hour, each lost in her own grief, but then the Blue Whale swam away from the Fin, at only one knot. A strange abstraction overcame her. Her mate was gone, her calf was gone, and the sea and sky, their life-giving cycles once almost completely predictable, had changed for the worse again and again over the decades, the sky growing dark, the populations only partially recovering, and now the ice drifting north from the polar sea. For some minutes she saw all these things in a single vision. She had a sense that the more predictable world she had known in her youth would never come again. Though the sense was connected with her fear she had lost the calf, it brought a detachment, a resignation, deeper than any she'd known before. Her entire universe seemed to be narrowing, closing in. This brought a sorrow deeper than grief, but she felt no impulse to mourn or cry out because she knew that protest was useless. She felt a fatalistic calm. Her trance of abstraction made her go still until she awakened once more to her worry over the Fin.

She swam back to rejoin her. They were hovering at a hundred feet when Orca clicks rang out almost straight overhead. Drifting east, the enormous ice sheet had pushed Orcas, dolphins, seals, fish, and even krill ahead of it, while birds had followed to feed along its edge. Tired of swimming through close-packed bergs, Orcas and dolphins had turned north for open water. Two schools of sixteen Killer Whales went over the Fin and Blue in only seconds.

The Fin had felt beyond both hope and fear, but she was frightened now that two schools of Killer Whales had passed overhead, and she followed the Blue northeast. Thirty-five hours of flight took them north of the Falkland Islands where the surface calmed a little and bright sun broke through the clouds. The Blue looked up, relaxing. Then the dangerous glare made them both dive and swim on.

The Falkland Current flowed straight north, close to the coast, while farther east the West Wind Drift curved farther and farther north as it left Cape Horn behind. Icebergs were thicker in the West Wind Drift than in the Falkland Current. The pair re-entered the drift, not wanting to swim straight north as the Killer Whales had done, but, when clicks came from the east, they moved back west until the bergs spread out again. Cloud covered the sky at dusk, but with morning the Blue once more saw the dazzling glare. They swam well down, eighty miles out from Bahía Grande. Twenty-four hours put them north of latitude fifty and a day after that they passed Cape Tres Puntas, the southern cape of the Gulf of St. George.

Here the light was gentle again. The Fin moved forward until one eye looked into the Blue's, then lowed very mournfully and softly. The Blue slowed down and they swam abreast with synchronized strokes. The Blue called gently and kept to a speed of seven knots. As the Fin Whale answered with calflike sounds the Blue felt the same compassion she'd felt when her calf had grieved at his certainty he'd never find a mate. She didn't pause to caress her friend, but where the pectoral touched her side she felt a warm, throbbing sensation she'd all but forgotten since weaning the calf. Perhaps he still lived. She felt torn between her fear that the call had been his and the hope that she'd find him in the Atlantic. Soon the Fin was sending low-frequency roars of grief in all directions. The Blue tensed slightly, fearing that Orcas might hear the sounds, but she answered each outburst with soft calls. With every exchange she felt warmer where the Fin Whale touched her side. As they arched sideways she could see icebergs drifting on to the northern

326

limit of her vision, but there was no need to keep moving now. Swarms of euphausia vallentini clouded the sea.

She stopped travelling and made slow runs through the krill, grunting with pleasure, turning upright after each run to look at the Fin, then tightening her throat-pouch and swallowing noisily, hoping to tantalize her friend into doing the same, since she remembered how after the old Fin Whale had died she had consoled herself by gorging on euphausiids. At first the Fin watched indifferently. After three runs the Blue swam beneath her, clicking encouragement and running the top of her head along her quivering underside. When she went back to her feast and the Fin still hesitated, the sight of the old Fin Whale encouraging her to eat warmwater plankton grew as clear inside her head as when she'd mistaken the Fin for the old one, fifty years ago on the night of their first meeting.

She paused at her runs, remembering the old one, looking around her. Now she was eating coolwater plankton in temperate water amid icebergs while another Fin looked on, as filled with grief as she herself had been in that first tropical spring after leaving her mate. She hung still for several minutes, losing awareness of even the Fin as she felt the bitterness and sweetness of the memory. Then the Fin once more touched her pectoral to her side and the warm sensation came again. Her friend made feeding runs through the krill, pausing to look at her after each run. The Blue stayed still to watch, then caressed her for twenty minutes with her pectorals—long, slow strokes of consolation. When she stopped, the Fin Whale fed more eagerly, momentarily calmed. The Blue joined in, both of them bolting the krill with loud, satisfied gulps, one eye on the sky and one on the depths. Under the morning sun their sounds drowned out everything else for half a mile. After five minutes the Blue Whale paused a second time as her vision of the old Fin Whale returned. She thought of the calf. So much had gone. Yet what could be done to stop the losses? The Blue Whale started stroking east, once more feeling resigned. Then the younger Fin called out to turn her back, and again they bolted krill together.

CHAPTER

32

THE Blue was hanging a few feet under the surface, facing northeast, watching the Fin eat her way northward, when the largest Orca she'd ever seen appeared out of the shadows. Thirty feet long, he wasn't swimming—rather, he seemed to hang suspended just a few feet from the top toward her west. His eastward eye watched her with interest, and even though he was near the edge of her field of vision, she saw clearly the sharp contrast between the black that covered most of his well-fed side and the white that ran downward behind his eye and upward again between his flukes and chest. She tensed with fear. As soon as she did, he faded soundlessly back into shadow without any apparent movement of his fins. She peeled her ears for the sounds of the others who would be with him—

she had never seen one alone—but heard nothing. Wondering how long he'd been watching her and why he hadn't attacked, she approached the Fin and ran her dorsal very lightly down her belly. The Fin picked up her fear and the two started northeast without a sound. They swam nearly constantly, leaving shelf and slope behind, then after a day kept on in fits and starts, ever watchful, their course veering farther toward the east.

Both were bewildered. Before the dust they had seen Orcas on the average perhaps three or four times a year and after the dust they had been rare, though they had partially recovered over the decades. Now there seemed to be many. The two whales couldn't know that since the ice shelves had come free and drifted north, Orca and dolphin populations from the Antarctic and subantarctic Pacific, swept east by the ice, had entered the western Atlantic Ocean. Others in the Atlantic had already been pushed north from the Weddell Sea when the Filchner Ice Shelf had drifted off its base. Though found in all oceans, the world population of Killer Whales had never been more than a hundred thousand. Populations were thickest toward the poles, and this had facilitated matings in the Antarctic after the dust. Over the fifty-five years since the cloud, the population in the Antarctic and southern Atlantic and Pacific had grown to almost fifteen thousand from little more than fifteen hundred survivors, a sharp contrast to the Blue Whale population: before the dust two thousand worldwide, after the dust all but extinct. Now the better part of the Orca population was fanning out from below Cape Horn and the waters above the Weddell Sea.

The Blue and Fin stopped two thousand miles from Argentina and hung still under the roaring westerly swell, far enough down that even the thickest of the eastward-drifting icebergs passed over their heads. As much as a hundred yards apart, the icebergs left ample breathing room, and after four days of hearing nothing but waves and wind, the Blue felt more secure, though when she looked into the distance she partly expected to see Orcas watching and waiting, and every few hours, between their rests, they both scanned the horizons. When no Orcas appeared for three days they scanned less often, and after two more, in the last third of November, they sometimes dropped their guard for whole days at a time. When toward December their sense of security stretched past a week, the Blue Whale felt as if a weight had been lifted away.

329

But the weight that remained—hope and grief over the calf—made her reflect on her narrowing circle of losses. More and more she took to swimming off by herself, her resignation strengthening. Though painful, it made her remember the calm that preceded the birth of the calf and she had a sense that now, as then, she was changing inside. Despite their physical intimacy, she felt distant from the simple alternation of grief and forgetfulness she'd once shared with the Fin. More and more she started to feel alone.

In the second half of December a rorqual call came from the east. The whales were hanging two hundred feet down when they picked up the refracted signal of fifteen hertz. The Blue answered loudly in the hope she had heard her calf, and the Fin started swimming east, giving out prodigious twenty-hertz calls.

At first they swam at two hundred feet, breathing separately so one was always listening. Then, when she spouted, the Blue heard the long-range call echo up from the ocean floor and she summoned the Fin Whale to the top. She was almost certain her calf was approaching, but the Fin's excitement showed she envisioned a mate. The Blue Whale knew that so deep a call was not likely a Fin's.

As the Fin Whale raced ahead, her trials in the Pacific, even her failure to unite with the other whale, seemed parts of a journey toward this rorqual whose image grew clearer with every call, a Fin Whale bull, his passion deepened by his barren years alone. While she imagined his touch on her ventral pleats, the Fin Whale arched across the top. In late December there could be no consummation—their caresses would go on for days on end. She saw her life from now until winter as constant love play, her years of loneliness, like the cold years with her parents, over forever, part of a dim and distant time that might never have been.

When the other whale came fully into sight, the Blue immediately knew him, her recognition all the more certain for his length of a hundred feet. She called in greeting, but the Fin Whale raced ahead to rise from the water and press her throat grooves against his, wagging her head backward and forward until they both fell to one side and plunged below. She pressed her whole body against him, her snout a foot below his snout and her pectorals tight against his chest, although too short to reach to his sides. She held herself close as long as she could, delaying the time when she'd have to move away and see him as he was. Already his size had disturbed her, and when she stretched to nuzzle, her fear

330

increased. Her excitement had blinded her at first, but she could feel that his upper jaw was differently shaped from her own.

Hanging above to watch with one eye and hear the Fin Whale's passionate calls, the mother saw her calf's eye and her friend's eye turn toward her as they both rolled on one side. The Fin still moved her throat against the bull's and her eye was closed. She wanted to hang with him forever, but, seeing his mother, he fell away. For several minutes he ran his snout along his mother's belly and nudged the region of her breasts, making it seem like only hours since she had suckled him and worried about his breathing. Emotions from long ago overwhelmed them, and she started making the low calls that used to accompany her suckling.

At first her fatalistic resignation was all but forgotten. Her fifty years of fruitless search had not been in vain. In joy they stroked and caressed. Yet even now, once her initial joy was spent, she felt a faint trace of resignation.

She moved a few yards off to take him in. His mate's absence troubled her, but seemed the inevitable consequence of their new world. He knew from the way she called and swam back and forth that she missed his mate. When she stopped swimming and touched her snout to his, still clicking, he lowered his head. The Fin was underneath the vast gray width of his chest, hurt by its contrast with her own white underside, when he gave out calflike calls and bowed beneath his mother. The Fin drew back. As the mother lowered her head to stroke his jaw and the light wounds on his sides, the Fin Whale faintly touched his chest.

Though the mother whale felt sorrow for his mate, she had not known her, and it was mixed with happiness, for he had come to her as she'd dreamed her mate would come while she had waited out his fight with the Killer Whales: whole, his wounds shallow enough that she could nurse him. As she continued to run her pectorals over the tooth marks and light gashes, his resemblance to his father seemed so clear that for a moment it was as if her mate had survived. After a minute she turned away, feeling both sorrow and joy, grief and consolation. The bull whale stopped his calflike bubbling, swam over his mother from behind, then turned to watch her. She pressed against him, closing her lids, trembling and lowing against his side till he forgot his own despair.

The Fin Whale watched from below. She'd already surmised from their passion that the pair were mother and calf, but she couldn't know

331

why the Blue Whale trembled against him. She rose to the surface, spouted ten times, then dove to embrace the mother whale. When the Blue had calmed, the three surfaced together.

They looked around, feeling better. It was late spring, the time for gorging on polar krill. There was only moderate swell, and in the fifty-to hundred-yard widths between the bergs, more shoals of euphausia vallentini spotted the ocean, sparse compared to Antarctic krill—still, the three spread out and fed. From time to time one whale would pause to watch the two others, and with late afternoon they played among the waves. At dusk the mother whale rested between the bull and the Fin. Despite their lingering grief, all three could feel a faint glow of well-being.

Over the following days the bull often awakened from his rest with groans and roars. Each time she heard them the cow would remember the roar of her mate as he faced the Orcas and would stroke the bull's sides till he rested again. He could sense himself slowly returning to the passivity and dependence of his first year, but the shallow bites still healing on his sides aroused awe in the Fin, who imagined he'd faced down Killer Whales. Swimming below him during the day, she sometimes thought she could hear Orcas not far off, but now the sounds made her tremble a little less. Eventually his differences in marking and conformation seemed less significant, and when he and his mother slept, she would slip below the surface, roll on her back, and swim up and down, moving her underside within inches of his but brushing him only lightly, afraid to do more now that she'd seen he was a Blue. Sexual play between species might go on for hours with juveniles, and non-reproductive sex occurred among adults, but instinct normally made the adult whales draw back from interbreeding. Neither the bull nor Fin felt drawn to casual play.

They moved from place to place in pursuit of fish but kept to the same general area, twenty-one hundred miles east of the South American coast in the Argentine Basin. Birds who had followed the drifting icebergs from the south—pintado petrels and dove prions—came down beside them as they rested in the waves. After swimming among icebergs for five thousand miles, the bull had grown used to seeing Antarctic birds, but now, with the mother whale floating among them, they made his first Antarctic summer by Palmer Peninsula blaze in his mind, and when he fell into semi-sleep, he half expected to hear her slap her tail on the sea to drive them away or see his father making feeding runs by the shelf. The illusion was sweet, and after the first few days, he dreamed as much as he could, just as his father had after fleeing the southern stars. He dimly sensed that wounds were closing inside him. Except when he fed, he started to live in a semi-sleep most of the time.

With his mother beside him, the bull whale's dreams were all of his childhood to begin with. Then, on one of the few nights when the ocean calmed enough to let him dream on the top, he started awake at the sight of his mate and his last calf swimming toward him. The moonlight gleamed against the icebergs, and as he awoke, the bull could feel faint caresses against his chest. Thinking his mother was stroking him, he let out slow, regretful sighs, then closed his lids, noticing dimly that the strokes were gentler than usual, barely palpable at times.

Just before he returned to his sleep, one eye open, one eye closed, he saw his mother swimming toward him from the west. He was so drowsy that she seemed at first to be only part of a dream. Sighing again, he tilted slightly to one side and submerged one eye. The moon was so bright that it partly illuminated the back of the Fin Whale where she swam silently up and down, raising her snout from time to time to touch his skin. Awakening again but remaining still, he studied her. The lines of her body were stouter than his own but they seemed streamlined where the moon only partly revealed them. His interest grew until he glowed at her tentative touch. It called to mind the hesitant passion of his first shy embraces with his mate. As the memory brightened, he found himself gazing at the Fin in fascination. Over the seven days he had known her he had never felt even a trace of sexual attraction, but soon, in the moonlight, he closed his eyes to shut the differences from sight and concentrate on her gentle strokes. When he was partly asleep again, he glimpsed his mate and, fearing to dream, arched down to the Fin. She moved away but he glided beneath her, moaning softly and caressing her with the same hesitant passion he'd felt in her touch. At first she retreated upward, then after a second hung suspended in the moonlight, her undersides shivering at his caresses.

The bull was still only partly awake, and by now the mother whale was above him, looking down. She had been swimming alone again, lost in reflection. As one of his eyes met one of hers he came fully awake and suddenly stopped caressing the Fin. Both bull and Fin had neared the top, and for a minute they stared at each other, their different shapes now vividly outlined under the moon. Though the differences were slighter than those between him and the Pygmy, he drew back. After a minute, they surfaced on either side of the mother and half slept, the bull escaping to visions of childhood and the Fin to a dreamless rest, while the mother whale remained awake to watch them.

After a while dreams reawakened the bull and he sent out long-range signals for his mate. The mother attempted to comfort him, but he wheeled and swam away. The longer the mother watched him the more the thwarted desire of her first tropical winter and her first southward migration burned in her memory. When he swam east, she envisioned her mate swimming east in the tropical sea and signalling for his cow and calf.

After ten minutes the bull returned and the mother slept. She dreamed of the first tumultuous days after the meeting above Ascension, calling out loudly several times until toward morning the bull and the Fin caressed her together. Each time the Fin Whale brushed the bull she trembled slightly. Dawn found them asleep on either side of the mother whale.

The bull's attraction to the Fin was a passing thing, forgotten by morning in his grief for his mate and calves. He encouraged both cows to stroke him, but the Fin swam off by herself for hours on end. Though the mother whale still caressed him, his sleepy happiness never returned, and soon, like the Fin, he was swimming alone for hours at a time, showing no interest in fish or krill.

This troubled his mother. Sometimes, when the Fin and her calf had swum off in opposite ways, she would dwell on his long-range calls and she could tell that, like her mate at the beginning, he'd become obsessed with his family, calling compulsively as if he meant to raise them from the depths. His calls made her fear he'd attract Killer Whales, but his moody silence was just as disturbing.

Although the Fin paid little attention to the bull, the Blue Whale cow could sense her attraction, in normal times as strange as the union of whales from opposite ends of the earth but hardly strange to the mother whale after the dust and the disappearance of her kind. Now, in January, mating time had passed, but her awareness of the Fin's unseasonal yearning stirred her own. Soon she grew angry at the sight of her grief-stricken calf swimming alone and calling as stubbornly as his father. Often, when the two whales hung on either side of her, she would dive out from between them and push them together.

It was a week before the Fin began to follow the bull on his solitary swims. From her own grief over the rorqual in the Pacific she dimly surmised what he felt. He ignored her at first, but, encouraged by his mother, she persisted. After ten days they swam abreast and by the end of the month were together most of the time. There was no love play, but it gratified the mother whale to see them side by side. Though she had worried about the calf since the day of his birth, she hadn't realized the depth of her worry for the Fin Whale until now, as it lifted away. It made her calm to watch the pair together.

The days were shortening. More and more often she moved away from them as they slept. Looking back at them as she swam off in the dark, she would feel the glow of well-being she'd felt at her reunion grow brighter and warmer than ever before, but when the *huffs* of their exhalations faded out among the icebergs, she would forget them, swimming for hours among the slabs, her recollections of her mate and the old Fin flooding over her so strongly that she could see them coming toward her in the dark, first her mate, his spout of spray distant and faint as he swam in from the horizon but his underwater signals close and clear. She would go down as she'd first dived to overtake him and his signals would die out. She would rise out from under the ice to spout and breathe, and the old Fin's calls might come to her from any direction, sometimes from the south, her twenty-hertz signal as she fled the navy cruiser shaking the two-mile Trinidad Rise; sometimes from the north, her calls ringing clear after days of confusion off Argentina; sometimes from the east as she died on the harpoon.

Mixed with all these memories was the new sense of resignation, unknown to either the bull or the living Fin. Sometimes the Blue swam by herself for half the night, and when she returned, they'd hardly have noticed she'd been gone. Sleeping beside them under the stars, still surrounded by visions and sounds from long ago, she'd dream that the old Fin Whale was watching over the pair. More and more she felt as at home with the old Fin Whale as with the younger Fin and the bull.

In early February Orcas appeared again. They made no sound. Just before nightfall the Blue looked west to see a dozen of them together. The weather was calm. Rough sea could have shut them out of sight, and the Blue Whale wondered if they'd been there on previous eve-

nings, under the waves. The largest bull blew ten-foot spouts, sometimes moving ahead so his five-foot dorsal cut through his puff of spray.
An Orca calf was between its parents, and the others hung a few yards
east of the family.

The bull whale and the Fin slept east of the mother, who expected
she'd be able to flee in the night. There was no point in rousing them
yet. She waited for darkness, watching the Orcas out of one eye and the
Fin and bull out of the other.

With night she nudged them awake and turned for the east, diving
under a tabular berg. They were nearing the eastern edge of the berg
when Orca clicks and the sounds of shoaling fish told all three that the
Killer Whales were hunting by night. The Fin attempted to swim faster
but the bull whale suddenly turned around and stopped, wheeling so
swiftly that his mother almost hit him. He paused for only a second,
then dove and started west. The Fin Whale shivered, hanging still just
east of the iceberg while the mother whale pursued him at full speed.

Killing the Orcas under the ice had been very easy, and in his rage, it
hadn't occurred to him that his victims had been exhausted from their
long time without breath. They had assisted in their deaths by lingering
needlessly under the keel to gorge on Right Whale Dolphins. Now,
having killed them with such ease, he felt no fear of these new Orcas—
only rage flaring up again.

Most of the Orcas were hunting beyond the iceberg, but four were
hanging just under its western edge. Hearing their clicks, he started to
rise, meaning to hit them from below, but their echo-location picked
him out in only seconds and they dove and rose beside him, two on each
side. The mother whale followed him, trembling with fear. He attempted to smash one with his jaw, suddenly jerking his head to one
side and bringing it down, but the Orca veered out of his way. He
inverted himself to smash them with his flukes, but they swam close to
each side of his head, and after a minute of useless maneuvering he
knew he was powerless against them. Vaguely he marvelled that he'd
been able to kill the others so easily. His mother called him to follow.
As he started east below and behind her the Orcas circled, from time to
time nudging the light wounds on his sides. Their snouts were sharp,
and as they poked, their clicks speeded up with excitement, for this was
only the third large rorqual they had encountered. The rest of their

336

school clicked loudly from below where they fed on horse-eye jacks and frigate mackerel as the bull and his mother continued toward the Fin.

He shook as he followed. His rage and courage were not as great as they had seemed when he'd had Orcas at his mercy under the ice. He followed his mother and the Fin for the rest of the night, constantly listening, but never heard the Orcas again. Once he felt sure he'd left them behind, fear no longer tempered his rage and by dawn he was brave again.

Yet the anger gradually waned. The Fin Whale hung above him but he ignored her now, beginning to reflect. He saw his father in his mind, killed by Orcas. All his life that sacrifice had haunted him, and, with his grief for his mate, it had made him turn to face the Killer Whales. Fear had turned him back, but now that rage and fear were fading, he sensed instinctively that facing the Killer Whales as his father had brought no release. His instinct for the survival of the race was even deeper than that for self-preservation. He had not mated with the Fin, but their bond was strong, and the appearance of the Orcas strengthened their sense they would reproduce eventually. His heroic father had sacrificed himself for a living family, but in this new and lesser world, even stranger than the one his father had known, instinct demanded retreat for the sake of generations that perhaps might be born dead or horribly changed by radiation.

All this was too complex for the bull to reason out in detail, but it underlay his instinctive sense that facing the Orcas was wrong. He was hanging still, dimly reflecting, when the sound of the Orcas still following from the west and the urgent nudge of his fearful mother made all three swim east at full speed.

The Orcas had been carrying on a leisurely pursuit, and at one point during the day they actually passed the three rorquals to hunt for fish farther east. Seeing them pass, the mother's awareness she'd never outswim them heightened her resignation, stronger than ever since they'd appeared. When they came into sight again that afternoon they were swimming west in a straggling file, so close to the underside of an iceberg that, as they approached, the bull heard the intermittent swish of their dorsal fins against the ice. Now all three whales were racing west, keeping well down. They dove under an especially long iceberg, staying silent, hoping to hide.

337

The westerly wind had strengthened and the surface rumbled loudly, but as they descended toward the iceberg's maximum thickness, the surface noise faded out along with the light. Soon they were swimming in total blackness under ice a hundred feet thick where sounds unheard or unnoticed farther up seemed amplified.

Bubbles echoed against the keel. The mother tensed as soon as she heard them. After a silence, all three could hear swimming sounds and dorsals brushing the ice with a sharp hiss. As the whales re-entered the light, three twenty-five-foot Orcas pushed their snouts into the mother whale's left side, clicking back and forth to each other. The bull trembled. Certain they'd kill her, he looked at her terrified right eye, then saw six Orcas rise beside him, three about twenty feet away and, beyond them, the mother, father, and calf. Dread made him shake, yet both he and his mother craned to see what had happened to the Fin. Almost lost to sight in the east, she was fleeing the Orcas at full speed. Realizing that the entire pack had concentrated on them, leaving the Fin free to escape, both mother and bull continued west. Though his fear was great, even now intermittent rage threatened to overcome the bull and make him fight the Killer Whales. Once he veered sideways to butt them, but his fear, reinforced by instinct, made him resume his passive swim. The mother whale remained resigned as they stroked on. Despite her fear, she urged him to flee, but he couldn't bring himself to leave her. He closed the eye that faced the Orcas and focussed on her as she looked at him with terror and compassion. She lowed. Bubbles burst out of her head and he felt like a shivering calf. When they surfaced to breathe with the Orcas still beside them, sooty shearwaters tilted and wheeled across the waves, one almost brushing the flashing dorsal of an Orca who swam about fifteen feet ahead. The shearwater soared, then glided back toward the Orca, searching for food. The bull felt strangely fascinated by the bird that danced over the water as if the terrible fin were only bobbing wood. They neared more ice. His mother lowed to him again and they arched below.

They dove back into the night, the surface thunder fading out and the silence amplifying the swish of the Orca fins. Content to wait things out before, the mother panicked in the dark. She led the bull five hundred feet down and reversed direction, but the Orcas easily followed. When she spouted and breathed, the pack surrounded them both.

338

There were twelve Orcas but only ten attackers; the mother Orca stayed with her calf. They could have divided to chase both whales, but with only five attackers it would be hard to control the victim while they fed. They screamed, watching to see if either whale would freeze with fright like the Minke Whales and dolphins in the Antarctic.

When the screams began the whales were a few yards apart, but with every scream they swam closer together. They started to dive but the Orcas sliced them from below, and when they came up, both bled from the chest. When the Orcas screamed again the mother whale went stiff. Six dove beneath her, slicing and pushing at the part of her underside nearest the bull. As the pair parted, the Orcas entered the strait between them, seven biting at the mother while three others sliced off the bull's left pectoral fin. Roaring with pain, he fled for fifty yards, then surfaced and looked back. His mother had stopped. Four Orcas lined up on either side of her while two dove underneath. Out of one eye he glimpsed a black head rising out at her side, then waves, then, just for an instant, the reddening white of the oval wound, then waves again, then another Orca and another oval of red. She was in such agony from the slashes in her side that she hardly heard them when they screamed, and to the bull, her rhythmic groans sounded more frightening. They prodded and poked her from either side till she started to swim.

As he followed, the bull trailed blood from his chest and the place where his fin had been. At first he swam on the surface a hundred yards behind, where all he could see were glimpses of dorsals and his mother's arching back. Waves kept shutting her out of sight and muffling her exhalations. Then the gauntlet went under an iceberg. As he followed, diving far into the dark and moving closer, her groans were loud, coming once every two or three seconds, interspersed by roars of pain when the Orcas opened a new wound. He followed two hundred feet down with his mother and the Orcas just under the ice. Each time she roared he rose in rage, only to turn back down in fear, sometimes envisioning the Fin. By the time the gauntlet approached the eastern edge of the berg he had stopped rising.

Light poured in under the ice edge. Looking up through the towering dark he could discern his mother's mottled underside with four Orcas beneath it and the family of three a little behind. There was an enormous wound behind her umbilicus. The whales shifted places, three of them butting to keep her above and one slicing meat out of the wound. As the barely weaned calf began to feed, the bull saw the water go dark by its head and heard the maddening roar of pain come again and again. He seethed with rage. When the water cleared he saw the calf lower its head, then lift it up to the open wound as if it were suckling. The water reddened. His mother dove and he plunged farther into the dark. From her loud cries he knew they were slicing her again.

When she came up beyond the ice and he surfaced a quarter mile behind her, she'd slowed to two knots and he could see no Killer Whales. Two hours went by. Her roars let up and there was only the rhythmic groaning. He edged ahead, stopping repeatedly to listen. After half an hour he was thirty yards behind her. Still seeing no Orcas, he gave a low call, remembering how they'd swum away from his father. He edged forward a few yards more, called again and peeled his ears. It took him nearly an hour to draw up on his mother.

He swam up and down her body. The largest wound could have held ten men, under her dorsal, and the others, none of them less than three feet square, were widely spaced from just back of her head to fourteen feet ahead of her flukes. The flukes were ragged, but the Orcas hadn't broken the caudal vertebral connection—her slowness came from exhaustion. Aching with shame and compassion, he looked into one of her eyes, but she seemed blind and didn't respond when he touched her cheek with his pectoral fin. Her groans kept up. He groaned as well. Soon, in his shock, he had the illusion that they answered one another, and he began to make other sounds—clicks and lows and very soft calls—but his mother only continued the rhythmic groaning. After two minutes he went silent, hearing Orca sounds to the north. Three approached, but long before they drew up on his mother he had fled. Once he was sure they hadn't followed he stopped five hundred yards to the west.

The pod was resting just to the north. Nine others had joined it now, drawn by the feeding din during the day, and the Orcas who'd left it were the family of three. They swam up and down the mother's sides for several minutes, poking occasionally, then rested again, half sleeping as they swam. Sated, they had no interest in the bull. With dark the rest of the pod approached, and for the better part of the night they idled east, resting quietly beside her, once in a while poking her forcefully from one side or the other to make her turn as they neared an iceberg. The calf was confused that they stayed with her but didn't attack.

She was barely conscious. Her eyes were closed most of the time and she heard nothing except the occasional clicks of the Orcas when they drew near. The pain from her wounds was great, but equally strong was the piercing cold where her blubber was gone. All her life her fear that the cold might pierce her blubber and chill her blood had remained with her like a child's first terror of falling. Now that it was happening her semi-consciousness didn't dim the pain and she shivered uncontrollably. Only when she blacked out did it cease. She started to sink, but the Orcas awakened her with their teeth. She roared and arched back to the top. The calf felt an impotent fury where he hung in the dark and listened.

At dawn the Orcas fed again. The well-spaced wounds were almost exhausted of their meat, so they opened new ones. The mother uttered a terrible high-pitched call that the bull had never heard from a Blue Whale before. The sky was clear and the sea had calmed. The bull saw the dark heads twist and jerk where they dug at her sides. His fury gave way to a desperate hope she would die, but the Orcas kept feeding well past dawn. By early morning her sides were little more than wounds between thin borders of blue-gray skin.

He didn't see her sink to the bottom, her wounds even more numerous than his father's. Like him, she descended snout first to begin with, but after the first minute fell sideways, then continued haphazardly with now her head and now her tail facing the top. Once she was gone the Orcas rested, hanging still for half the day before they started east again, all feeling restless and displaced. By then the bull had long since fled to their south and travelled east by a hundred miles. He would have gone west but he hoped to rejoin the Fin. His handful of gouges were shallower than his mother's, but the pain was very bad and it steadily worsened, since the farther he swam the less he was shielded by shock.

He travelled east for a month. When the pain began to subside, his isolation became unbearable, and he started to send out loud long-distance signals once again, despite his fear. When there was no answer he persisted, grieving bitterly both for his mother and for his family, but remembering the lines of the Fin Whale as she swam beneath the moon. The memory was dim at first, a faint light in his inner night. After another month, when the pain had grown sporadic and the hollow ovals of white flesh on his chest and sides had grayed, the memory brightened, heightening both his loneliness and his hope.

341

He swam east all the way to Tristan da Cunha. He thought of the Right Whales and the sooty albatrosses soaring over the cliffs. He remembered his father calling from well offshore and doubled back toward the west in his dejection, still signalling without answer, almost ready to give up. The bull wished he were still with his parents under the dust, wished that the dust had never cleared. By the end of April he didn't bother to send out signals. It seemed that the sacrifice of his mother had been in vain and his fearful restraint no more than betrayal. He imagined himself descending to the floor and more than once let himself fall for thousands of feet into the dark. Only the reflexive urge to breathe kept him from going down all the way, with the deeper instinct for the survival of the race. Yet the Fin had gone. He lived for sleep. Hanging still for days on end, partly unconscious, he didn't awaken even when storms made the water roar around his head, yet one morning in early May his sleep was broken by a faint twenty-hertz call.

CHAPTER

33

THE bull was over the Mid-Atlantic Ridge west of Tristan da Cunha when he picked up the Fin Whale's voice. It had been faint from fear, not distance, and once he answered they joined within minutes. In their first moments together his depression partly lifted, but, for the Fin, the joy of meeting dimmed when she saw that he was alone. She missed his mother but hadn't seen him leave her, and it seemed from his wounds he had tried to make a stand. Lowing with sympathy, she pressed one pectoral fin against his side. He led her north, slightly stronger despite his pain.

They swam up the Mid-Atlantic Ridge all the way to Ascension Island. She shared his grief. All winter they hung off Ascension, as if some part of his mother lingered in the place where she'd given birth and where he'd first heard his father's voice. Rage at his failure to save her outweighed his relief at finding the Fin. When he had restrained himself from fighting, his instinct for racial survival had strengthened his fear, but the sight of his mother's death had broken him, and by now the instinct that had saved him from self-destruction was an inaudible voice buried deeply beneath his pain. The sea and light north of Ascension, which had aroused his mother and father to conceive him, failed to stir his mating drive. Throughout the winter he hardly moved. In spring the Fin led him south, but he turned back when he saw icebergs still drifting past the usual limit of ice.

Years passed. There were no calves, but as the ice receded, the pair travelled farther south in the springs. In the fourth year after the ice surge they passed Cape Horn before being turned back north by the labyrinth of ice in the West Wind Drift. For the first five years she always led when they travelled, but in the sixth year he began to put his rage and grief behind, and she followed him all the way to Palmer Peninsula.

They kept looking up as they swam, watching for glare. Though they never saw the blinding light they dreaded, they found the sea above the peninsula poor in krill. The bull pushed on, remembering the late-blooming krill in the lean spring after the dust, but the farther they swam the sparser the krill became, and without fish, dolphins, or seals, the polar sea seemed a vast waste. Where the Filchner Ice Shelf had been there was open water studded with ice floes, and they were able to approach the southern shore of the Weddell Sea. Here the glare un-nerved the Fin, who, after her escape from the sea of perpetual light by the Ross Ice Shelf, half expected some new disaster. The bull led her north, and for the next six years they shunned the Antarctic, feeding on plankton and fish in temperate and tropical seas.

For their first six years together the Fin Whale bore no calves. As before, the pair were shy after they met, and when his sense of loss overpowered him off Ascension, the bull spent most of his time alone. They didn't mate until the height of their fifth winter, in mid-July, and then the Fin failed to conceive. Two years later a premature calf died soon after birth.

At last, in their eighth year, the Fin bore a calf that survived, but like

344

her mate and the Pygmy Blue, she had been altered by the dust. She conceived irregularly, giving birth every three to four years. By now the bull whale's grief was fainter, and the survival drive, first firing his desire for the Fin, moved him to swim and call through most of the South Atlantic and part of the North in search of mates when his calves matured.

In their thirteenth year, with their oldest calf, they made another exploratory swim to Palmer Peninsula. As they moved south they found no ice in temperate waters, and off Antarctica the number of bergs had sharply declined. Antarctic light was gentle all the way to the southern shore of the Weddell Sea, but krill remained scarce and they only lingered for a month. There was no Antarctic mate for their lonely youngster.

They swam south several more times in subsequent springs, but the polar krill never recovered and they never found mates for their surviving calves. While it saddened them with its emptiness, the Antarctic Ocean also puzzled them. Dimly they wondered what had made the ice surge north in the year they'd met and why the blinding glare had come and gone. Despite the dearth of life, they sensed a return to normal in the temperatures of the ocean and the air.

This change was worldwide. The sun had entered a cycle of strong activity, boosting winter temperatures over Antarctica till stratospheric ice clouds ceased to form. Atmospheric pollutants were steadily decreasing now that man-made gases no longer entered the sky. Ten years after the ice shelves had come loose, ozone once more protected the earth. In the Antarctic the light first softened over the coastal sea, then inland to the pole. Many plant species had died under the dust, but the longer the sky stayed clear the farther the surviving species spread. To the north, new vegetation covered millions of square miles men had left bare, and as it spread, photosynthesis absorbed more and more carbon dioxide, while an end to the burning of fossil fuels cut down the amount of carbon entering the sky. As man-made gas decreased, the atmosphere held in less radiation, and with more sunlight reflected back into space, the planet cooled. By the time the whales swam south in their thirteenth year together, the ice caps had stopped melting and the ocean level was slowly going down.

* * *

345

At first, the more he searched for mates for his calves, the more strongly the bull whale hoped to see his offspring start new generations, but, after twenty years of failure, his hope dimmed. The loneliness of his youngsters began to weigh on him. It seemed that, despite his calves' survival, they would bear no young of their own.

The bull returned to despondency and finally despaired, but the Fin's great love for her calves kept her hope alive. When the bull began holding back from the annual search for mates, she went without him, sometimes accompanying one youngster and keeping in touch with others by sound. She felt an impulse to leave the Atlantic and go searching in the Pacific where she had heard the rorqual voice. It began to haunt her. Had the rorqual died when the ice closed on the South American coast? At the time she had thought so, but why need it have been? She worried. Might there be mates for her young in the west? She wore herself out trying to rouse the despondent bull and make him travel.

She loved him too much to leave him completely behind by swimming into the Pacific, though she would search the Atlantic Ocean on her own. When, thirty years after their reunion, he grew ill, she remained with him out of loyalty, and their young searched by themselves. Births became less frequent over the decades, but even so she remained fertile; her ovulations had been irregular and the follicles of her ovaries were not being used up at the usual rate. Despite her joy at each new birth, the emptiness of the Atlantic made her sad when mature offspring swam away. Five of the first seven calves returned from time to time, always as lonely as when they had departed.

In their thirty-first year together, after six years of constant urging, the cow persuaded her mate to travel west, seeking a mate for one of the bulls, but he found only the old emptiness and quickly despaired again. Radiation damage sustained years ago began to affect him. There were growths inside his chest. With the passage of the years they increasingly troubled him and pain attacks kept him permanently on edge. The older he grew, the less interest he showed in his children. The aging Fin found it more and more painful to let them go. When a calf started off by itself she would fight it, trying to make it remain behind with her and her mate. She never stopped hoping for his recovery, for a time when the family would search together again. When the last of their calves matured in their thirty-fourth year together she was unwilling to let it

346

leave for even an hour, cajoling and coaxing to keep it from swimming away. When it ignored her she would pursue it for days on end if necessary, butting and fighting until it turned back.

Thirty-five years after the ice surge and ninety years after the cloud of dust, the pair led their five-year-old calf to Palmer Peninsula. It was a dark, overcast January day when they entered the strait of open water between the pack ice and the peninsula's northeast tip. It drizzled steadily on a calm sea. The round concentric ripples concealed the near transparency of the water when the whales swam on the top, though when they dove they saw it clearly. It sustained nothing. The bull still remembered the recovery of plants and krill after the dust and hoped even now that aquatic life would recover again. But under the dust the dormant plankton had waited less than two months before rising, while the lethal ultraviolet radiation had lasted two years.

The pair lifted their heads to see pale fog all down the coast. There were no calls of crabeater seals, no cries of birds. Depressed and anxious from his sporadic attacks of pain, the bull whale spouted seven times and hovered still, the Fin beside him, half her attention on him and half on the calf who moved a few yards off.

Alone, the five-year-old male might have seemed a new species, but not with his parents nearby. He combined the features of both, and the Fin Whale delighted in comparing his shape and color with hers and her mate's. She knew he was eager to be on his own, but she had a sense that he was the last calf she would bear. He seemed more beautiful to her than the seven others, and now, with the bull withdrawn, she watched him very closely, dwelling for minutes at a time on each of his markings.

He swam a little farther away from her, sad and aloof. For the first five years of his life the Fin had found only happiness in her love for him, but now he was mature, and like her mate at the same age, he took less pleasure in play with his mother. She knew he was lonely and would almost certainly never find a mate in the Atlantic. At the same time as his beauty lifted her up, over the past four months she had felt a growing undercurrent of pain.

While the Fin had only begun to ache with sympathy, her mate had anticipated the loneliness of the calf since he'd entered his sixth year in early May. His indifference to his children disappeared when he looked at this male. Like the finless calf of his first year with the Pygmy or the healthy calf of his last, the youngster brought his childhood back. Each time he stroked him he remembered his father's gentleness, and whenever he saw him hover alone he remembered the years of loneliness that had followed his father's death. Still, he discouraged the calf when he tried to swim off by himself, thinking it futile to search for a mate. The bull and cow were nearly a hundred, and while both had glowed with pride at the youngster's birth, only the Fin found him sufficient consolation for the loss of the mother whale. The bull had never been able to regain his former strength.

With his parents still, the calf stayed silent, watching and waiting. Five Atlantic years had made him despair of finding a mate in that empty sea. Even though his mother had followed when he'd swum off, eventually turning him back to keep the family together, his brothers and sisters had made long flights down the Mid-Atlantic Ridge, calling out for months on end without reply, and he'd seen the desolation of those who'd returned. His parents had accompanied one of his brothers on his search toward the west, but his father refused to accompany him. He had hoped that in the Antarctic his father would shake off his depression and the two old whales would let him take the lead, staying with him on his travels till he finally found a mate or, failing that, at least letting him go without a struggle. But, with his father hanging immobile and his mother desperately calling him each time he tried to escape, that hope had died. More eager than ever to leave, he was also more hopeful than either parent, and at the back of his mind he envisioned the family together again the following spring. In his vision a Blue or Fin Whale mate, or a mate marked like himself, was at his side.

The lonely male reminded his father of himself after his own father had died, but in fact there was little resemblance. The parents of the father whale had been hopeful up to the time of the old bull's death, and the death itself had been a heroic sacrifice that haunted the son for the rest of his life. The old bull had been an example of love, courage, endurance, and sacrifice, but the five-year-old male had never witnessed his father's attacks on the Killer Whales, nor even the love and enthusiasm with which he'd accompanied the oldest calves on their quests. His relationship to his father was less like his father's to the old, heroic bull

348

than like the old bull's to his parents off Newfoundland. Like his grandfather, the male was hurt and puzzled by his parents' passivity. He was a strong whale, healthy, defiant, and, like his grandfather after the death of his mother and father, eager to seek a new life.

He attempted to leave a number of times before nightfall. All afternoon the Fin kept setting out with him and calling her mate, dimly hopeful of finding life beyond the horizon, but the bull stayed where he was, and eventually she always managed to turn the youngster back. As dusk came on she was hanging beside her mate. Again one eye watched the calf and one looked into the bull's, who clicked to himself, envisioning icebergs and Killer Whales. She nudged his side, sensing his tension, but his only response was to close his lids.

The calf moved away from his mother by twenty yards and called out in frustration. The bull whale opened his eyes, moved toward him, then, feeling suddenly very weak, closed his eyes again. Intermittently for days he'd felt a constriction in his chest, something he'd only known before when the fifteen Orcas had attacked. As it returned, he went down for a couple of yards and moaned in the dark, his tailfins stiff and his one pectoral stretched out straight. His lids sprang open as the Fin went down beside him, still watching one eye. His fins stayed stiff for a full three minutes. Then his whole body relaxed.

Moving faster the farther he sank, he saw once more the fifteen Orcas, then his first days with his mother, then his dead father descending for the floor. The sights were vivid and familiar, but the emotions they used to bring with them—love, rage, terror, and joy—no longer came, and when they faded he half realized that the blackness that replaced them would never break. His muscles went limp with relief and he plummeted like a stone, exhaling slowly so that, for minutes after the Fin had ceased to follow, his spiralling bubble train continued to rise.

When the Fin came up to the top, the calf was gone. The fog had spread well out from the land. She called him repeatedly, searching vainly in all directions. It seemed for a moment that she dreamed. All that mattered in her life had been stripped away in a matter of minutes, and as night closed from the east, she circled the place where her mate had gone down, swimming in narrow desperate rings and puffing loudly.

For weeks she swam haphazardly, constantly calling for the calf, until

349

with early February she turned northeast. Autumn darkness found her idling in South Georgia's Cumberland Bay, where her fearful parents had been killed and where the old Fin Whale's caresses had awakened her to the prospect of a brave, full-blooded life. Now that the life was past and she was back where she had begun, it seemed to have been little more than a dream. She swam in circles, as cold and subdued as her parents had been.

With March a wave at the outer edge of the bay, flickering and white and moving east instead of shoreward, caught her attention and snapped her to life. Dove prions swept low where it passed. Remembering the old Fin travelling east, she raced in pursuit, calling loudly, but there was no answer and after a minute the wave had gone.

Once she had stopped she dwelt on the old Fin Whale. Surely her spirit and warmth had shown the way to live. Despite the dangers, she felt her passive, fearful parents had been wrong to hide from life. She remembered the rorqual in the ice off the Chilean coast and exhaled with a sound of explosive frustration. Perhaps he lived, more likely not. She spouted a second time, starting west. Either way, she would not stay here. She called defiantly, seeing the young male in her mind. In twelve days she entered the Pacific.

In March the day was fourteen hours long at the northern rim of the Ross Sea where the calf swam west between the ice floes. He had grown tired, seeking a mate since January, yet when Minkes approached from the north, he didn't pause for rest or play. Except for his mother, these were the only whales he'd heard since setting out, and food was sparse, but his hope was strong. The growing intensity of his desire made him unable to accept his isolation, but besides desire, the young male felt a strong, intuitive calm. As he neared the Macquarie Ridge and the waters below New Zealand, he signalled constantly, alert for the call he knew would come.

Blue Whales over the Mid-Atlantic Ridge

Down his Atlan-
tic floor in
vertebrae
of stone
God trails
his spine.
Blue whales
pass there.
Though they
are bone
they climb from ocean
into air
and, though they
track God's
sunken spine
on their migration,
their blue heads
retain
his rivulets
of blood,
his running threads,
each whale an arc
of night and skin
with light inside
with light inside—
so sings the Blue Whale
to his bride.

GLOSSARY

alcyonarian: small corallike animal, with a cavity occupying entire interior of body and functioning as both vascular and digestive system. Unlike true corals, which have a free-swimming medusa stage and an anchored polyp stage, these exist only as polyps. Eight tentacles grow out from mouth. Sea pen, sea fan, and gorgonian are alcyonarians.

arrowworm: small transparent planktonic worm common in scattering layer.

benthic: found only on bottom of sea (including shallow-water areas).

blue whiting: the whiting is a codlike fish, resembling the hake but found at shallower depths. To the best of my knowledge, the blue whiting is a northern fish, but whalemen and fishermen have applied the term "blue whiting" to a Patagonian marine species. I believe this fish is actually the Couch's whiting (*Micromestius australis*), but I have retained the more widely used "blue whiting" in the book.

bryozoan: moss animalcule. Stalked, with limey covering that remains after death. Tentacles circulate water and food into mouth. Individuals less than a quarter inch, but colonies can cover many square feet.

***Calanus* copepods:** copepods of great importance as food for fish and cetaceans. *Calanus finmarchicus,* or "herring feed," an important species, though probably too small for Blue Whale. Other larger species are found with *finmarchicus.*

cape pigeon: pintado petrel. Petrels are mostly small, wave-skimming birds of the open sea. The pintado petrel is about fifteen inches long with checkered black and white plumage.

cavitation: literally the creation of cavities. A propeller turning at high speed in the water creates a low-pressure area where vaporization produces bubbles. When the bubbles collapse, the water closes in on the partial vacuum and noisily pounds the propeller blades.

copepod: common crustacean of fresh and salt water: "water flea."

ctenophore: planktonic animal with comb plates on gelatinous body. Many species. Generally small. Predatory and often beautiful.

decibel: unit for measuring loudness. The faintest sound the human ear can hear is one decibel, the loudest about a hundred and thirty decibels.

denticle: on sharks, the rough body covering, a platelike scale.

diatom: one-celled plant encapsulated in silica. Important both directly as food and indirectly for mineral nutrients.

dinoflagellate: tiny floating plant, sometimes luminescent.

euphausiid: "krill," shrimplike crustacean. Many species. *Euphausia superba* the sole food of southern Blue Whale. *Euphausia vallentini* another important whale food. The closely related *Thysanoessa*, though not strictly an euphausiid, is also important.

flense: to peel blubber off with a knife.

foraminifera: minute planktonic animals whose shells cover vast areas of the ocean floor. Important source of mineral nutrients.

fulmar: seabird. Antarctic or silver-gray fulmar the only southern hemisphere species. More pelagic than gull, which it resembles. Breeds from South Georgia to Palmer Peninsula.

gastropod: snail, slug, whelk, etc. There are innumerable small planktonic forms.

gorgonian: a form of alcyonarian.

grimothea: *see Munida* crustacean.

heavy metal: metal with a density at least five times greater than that of water. Mercury and lead are heavy metals. The ingestion of heavy metals may damage an animal's system and even cause death. Dead cetaceans have been found with high levels of mercury concentration.

hertz: in measuring the frequency of sound or electromagnetic waves, one hertz equals one cycle per second.

hydroid: animal similar to coral. Corals secrete a cuplike extension into which they can withdraw and which survives the animals themselves: hence coral reefs. Hydroids are "naked," lacking the protective extension, but do have medusa and polyp phases. Essentially "naked corals."

Isistius shark: in undersea shadow this shark attracts would-be predators with its faint light and its stillness. From a distance its luminescence suggests that of a squid. When predator nears to investigate, the shark attaches itself with its circular mouth, and as predator swims, the sharp-toothed mouth digs in with a cookie-cutter rotation.

jaeger: this seabird (many species) lives largely by chasing smaller birds and forcing them to disgorge. Long central tail feathers. With frigatebird, the most agile seabird in flight. Roughly the size of a skua, but, unlike skua, all species breed in northern hemisphere.

krill: euphausiids, or any planktonic crustaceans eaten by whales.

macrocystis: sea plant growing from depths down to a hundred feet. Many varieties.

man-o'-war or **Portuguese man-of-war:** predator with bladderlike float and long stinging tentacles. Looks like a jellyfish, but is a colony of specialized organisms rather than a single animal. Such swimming or floating colonies of cells are called siphonophores. Most are planktonic, inconspicuous, and tiny compared to the man-o'-war.

medusa: free-swimming form of corals and hydroids, resembling minute jellyfish. The term also denotes the jellyfish.

melon: in toothed whales, head area between blowhole and snout.

Munida crustacean: most important species is *Munida gregaria*. Adults, over half an inch, leave plankton and descend to bottom. Occasionally surface in large swarms. Planktonic larvae grow by successive molts. Subadults or "grimothea" form enormous planktonic swarms from the surface to depths of over three hundred feet. Vivid red. Called "lobster krill." Patagonia, New Zealand, southern waters.

murre: cliff-nesting northern seabird. Black and white. About a foot and a half long. Nests in colonies. Extent of winter dispersal depends on ice.

myctophid: most widespread fish at intermediate depths, often rising at night. Many species. Myctophidae are the lanternfish family. Myctophiformes are a suborder of teleosts (bony fishes) with soft fins, abdominal pelvic fins, and cycloid scales.

mysid: small shrimp found in the scattering layer and elsewhere.

nematode: roundworm.

nekton: all marine organisms whose swimming determines their movements.

neritic: inshore.

Noctiluca: floating plant that shines when touched.

nototheniid: any member of the large family of fishes confined to the Antarctic, including the dragonfish and the Antarctic cod.

Patagonian hake: hake resemble cod but are smaller. It is difficult to know exactly what species the popular names denote. Some writers seem to identify the poutassou with the Patagonian hake, although the poutassou is really a species of whiting. In this book I use the term "Patagonian hake" to denote *Merluccius hubs*, a hake species found off Argentina. Mature hake are deepwater fish, with younger individuals occurring higher up.

pelagic: open sea (excluding bottom).

penella: parasitic copepod. Eggs hatch in sea. Females burrow into whale's blubber to metamorphose into wormlike form. Head end draws nourishment from tissues under blubber. Hind end with egg sacs projects into the sea as a pink tassel. Dies when eggs released.

pheromones: secretions signalling sexual readiness by scent and possibly by taste (*note:* baleen whales appear to possess sense of smell; toothed whales appear to lack it).

photophore: a light-emitting organ. On fishes most often a luminous spot.

phytoplankton: vegetable plankton.

plankton: small aquatic organisms whose travel is controlled by currents, tides, etc.

pod: whale family group or school.

polar front: boundary between the cold water and air of the polar region and the warmer water and air of subpolar latitudes.

porpoise: to swim by arching in and out of the water.

prion: blue-gray seabird of Antarctic and Southern oceans. A little less than a foot long. Plankton-feeder. Many nest in burrows. Some species follow whales.

radiolarian: unicellular animal, some encapsulated, some only with spines. In decay, a source of mineral nutrients.

Right Whale Dolphin (Southern): dolphin of the temperate and far south, circumpolar in the West Wind Drift, and sometimes found below the polar front.

rorqual: the term is Norwegian. Its meaning has been disputed but it likely refers to the longitudinal pleats on certain baleen whales. The species and subspecies of the genus *Balaenoptera*—Blue, Pygmy Blue,

Fin, Sei, Bryde's, and Minke—are rorquals. Most writers include the Humpback, a whale of a different genus, in the rorqual group. The term "rorqual" has also been used as a synonym for "baleen whale," and in some older sources the term denotes only the Fin. In this book I use the term to denote the *Balaenoptera* species and subspecies. All of these are much faster than the Humpback and were therefore the last whales to be hunted.

rostrum: strictly the upper jaw. More generally, the frontal extremity of the skull.

scad: family of medium-to-large predatory fish, including the *Caranx* genus and the horse mackerel.

scattering layer or **deep scattering layer:** an aggregation of aquatic animals found at various depths during the day. It reflects sound sufficiently well to create "false bottom" effect. Rises and spreads out in late afternoon and at dusk; descends before dawn. Many of these creatures live in continuous vertical migration.

scree: a heap of stones or rocky debris at the base of a cliff.

sergestid shrimp: the Sergestidae shrimp form a large family, closely related to the commercially important Penaeus shrimp. Found in scattering layer. Some luminescent. The taxonomic definition is based on minute, fairly technical distinctions such as the number of gills.

shad: silvery, herringlike fish. Deep-bodied and compressed from side to side. Many species. The term is used in this book to denote small, flat-sided *Sardinella* (*Sardinella aurita* has round sides).

siphonophore: *see* man-o'-war.

skimmer: bird of coastal regions. African skimmer fifteen inches long. Long bill, long pointed wings. Adults black above and white below. Feeds by shallow plowing of water with lower mandible.

skua: brown seabird roughly two feet long. Wingspan four feet or more, depending on species (wingspan of McCormick's skua is over four feet). Predator and scavenger. Also piratical (robs other birds of their food).

spyhop: said of whales, dolphins. To stand up at ninety degrees in the water, often to "look around."

thermocline: a layer of rapidly decreasing temperature in a thermally stratified body of water, separating an upper, warmer, oxygen-rich zone from a lower, colder, oxygen-poor zone.

thoracic system: lymphatic vessels lying along the spinal column (the thoracic duct) and the organs connected to them. Includes circulatory and digestive systems.

tunicate: sea squirt. Many species, microscopic to one foot in diameter. All have thin, transparent tunic and begin as free-swimming larvae. Later many attach themselves to objects or bottom. Some form colonies with common shell. Resemble small sponges.

tussock grass: very high grass that grows in clumps, and in the subantarctic, provides shelter for nesting seabirds.

whalebird: prion.

whale louse: crustacean of roughly an inch with strong claws that allow it to cling to host. It lives on skin of large whales, usually sheltering under flipper or in genital groove. The excrescences on the heads of Right Whales shelter large numbers.

zooplankton: animal plankton.

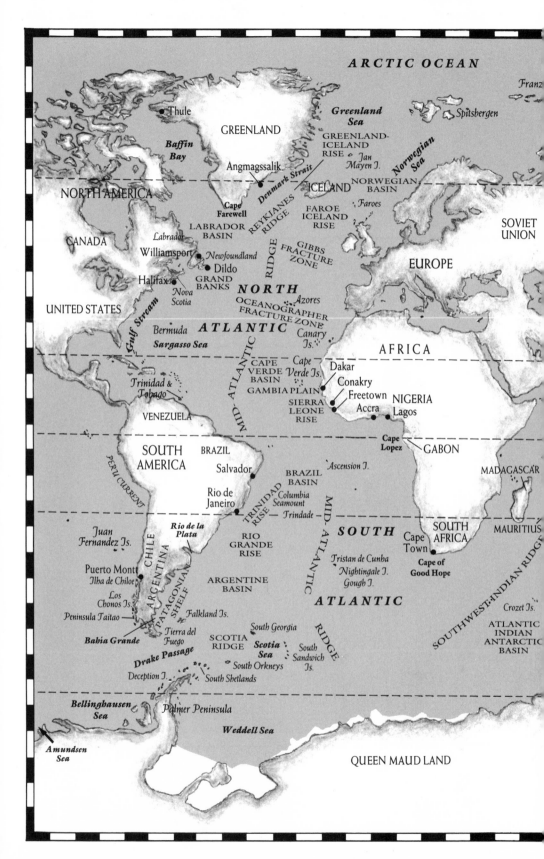